S.00

VERSES
from
1929 On

OGDEN NASH

VERSES
from
1929 On

LITTLE, BROWN AND COMPANY
Boston   Toronto

MV

Published simultaneously in Canada
by Little, Brown & Company (Canada) Limited

PRINTED IN THE UNITED STATES OF AMERICA

10   9   8

For Frances —
then, now, and always.

How these curiosities
would be quite forgott,
did not such idle fellowes
as I am putt them downe.

JOHN AUBREY

CONTENTS

Many Long Years Ago

[xiii]

[xv]

[xvi]

I'm a Stranger Here Myself

[xviii]

Good Intentions

[xxii]

The Private Dining Room

You Can't Get There from Here

[xxx]

Many Long Years Ago

THAT REMINDS ME

Just imagine yourself seated on a shadowy terrace,
And beside you is a girl who stirs you more strangely than an
heiress.
It is a summer evening at its most superb,
And the moonlight reminds you that To Love is an active verb,
And your hand clasps hers, which rests there without shrinking,
And after a silence fraught with romance you ask her what she is
thinking,
And she starts and returns from the moon-washed distances to the
shadowy veranda,
And says, Oh I was wondering how many bamboo shoots a day it
takes to feed a baby Giant Panda.
Or you stand with her on a hilltop and gaze on a winter sunset,
And everything is as starkly beautiful as a page from Sigrid Undset,
And your arm goes round her waist and you make an avowal which
for masterfully marshaled emotional content might have been
a page of Ouida's or Thackeray's,
And after a silence fraught with romance she says, I forgot to order
the limes for the Daiquiris.
Or in a twilight drawing room you have just asked the most mo-
mentous of questions,
And after a silence fraught with romance she says, I think this
little table would look better where that little table is, but
then where would that little table go, have you any suggestions?
And that's the way they go around hitting below our belts;
It isn't that nothing is sacred to them, it's just that at the Sacred
Moment they are always thinking of something else.

A BAS BEN ADHEM

My fellow man I do not care for.
I often ask me, What's he there for?
The only answer I can find

Is, Reproduction of his kind.
If I'm supposed to swallow that,
Winnetka is my habitat.
Isn't it time to carve Hic Jacet
Above that Reproduction racket?

To make the matter more succinct:
Suppose my fellow man extinct.
Why, who would not approve the plan
Save possibly my fellow man?
Yet with a politician's voice
He names himself as Nature's choice.

The finest of the human race
Are bad in figure, worse in face.
Yet just because they have two legs
And come from storks instead of eggs
They count the spacious firmament
As something to be charged and sent.

Though man created smocks and snoods
And one-way streets and breakfast foods,
And double features and mustard plasters,
And Huey Longs and Lady Astors,
He hails himself with drum and fife
And bullies lower forms of life.

Not that I think that much depends
On how we treat our feathered friends,
Or claim the wart hog in the zoo
Is nearer God than me or you;
Just that I wonder, as I scan,
The wherefore of my fellow man.

SEASIDE SERENADE

It begins when you smell a funny smell,
And it isn't vanilla or caramel,
And it isn't forget-me-nots or lilies,
Or new-mown hay, or daffy-down-dillies,
And it's not what the barber rubs on Father,
And it's awful, and yet you like it rather.
No, it's not what the barber rubs on Daddy,
It's more like an elderly finnan haddie,
Or, shall we say, an electric fan
Blowing over a sardine can.
It smells of seaweed, it smells of clams,
It's as fishy as ready-made telegrams,
It's as fishy as millions of fishy fishes,
In spite of which you find it delishes,
You could do with a second helping, please,
And that, my dears, is the ocean breeze.
And pretty soon you observe a pack
Of people reclining upon their back,
And another sight that is very common
Is people reclining upon their abdomen.
And now you lose the smell of the ocean
In the sweetish vapor of sunburn lotion,
And the sun itself seems paler and colder,
Compared to vermilion face and shoulder.
The beach is peppered with ladies who look
Like pictures out of a medical book.
Last, not least, consider the kiddies,
Chirping like crickets and Katydiddies,
Splashing, squealing, slithering, crawling,
Cheerful, tearful, boisterous, bawling,
Kiddies in clamorous crowds that swarm
Heavily over your prostrate form,
Callous kiddies who gallop in myriads
'Twixt ardent Apollos and eager Nereids,

Kiddies who bring, as a priceless cup,
Something dead that a wave washed up.
Oh, I must go down to beach, my lass,
And step on a piece of broken glass.

SEDATIVE REFLECTION

Let the love-lorn lover cure insomnia
By murmuring AMOR VINCIT OMNIA.

PEOPLE

Some people are popular with other people because their wit is
    pointed
And they can sing tenor and are double-jointed
And have had experiences in the Shetlands and the Hebrides
And have private anecdotes about public celebrides,
And are bright and amusing in the entr'acte
And always do the right thing in backgammon and contr'acte.

Other people are unpopular with other people because they discuss
    Bertrand Russell
And keep wanting you to feel their muscle
And point out that your furniture is oak, not mahogany,
And tell you all about their ancestors and progeny
And advise you to move to a suburb
And get away from all this tumult and huburb.

Both kinds of people, however, will eventually succumb to acidity;
Or perhaps they will be victims of the humidity
Or even approach metempsychosis
Through the various stages of cirrhosis.
But whatever the manner of their passing may be
It's all all right with me.

NEVERTHELESS

I am not fond of Oliver Montrose.
Oliver is a person I despise;
The purple veins that bulbify his nose,
The crimson veins that irrigate his eyes.
His wheezy breath his vinous weakness shows;
He is the slave of whisky, beer and gin.
I am not fond of Oliver Montrose;
I hate the sinner. But what a warming sin!

Bibesco Poolidge is a man of jowl;
I've never seen a dewlap, but on him;
He shines with the grease of many a basted fowl;
Ten thousand sauces round his innards swim.
The ghosts of hosts of kine about him prowl,
Lamb, pig, and game blood trickles from his chin;
I cannot look on him without a scowl;
I hate the sinner. But what a luscious sin!

I do not dote on Murgatroyd Van Rust,
So tasty to the tenderest of genders.
Practically everything that has a bust
Surveys his suave ensemble and surrenders.
The way he parts his hair I do not trust;
Let the phone ring, I loathe his knowing grin.
You cannot see his diary for the dust,
I hate the sinner. Still, if one had to sin . . .

O Mammonites and spendthrifts, draw ye nigh,
Fingernail-biters and sluggards, come on in,
Consider now how tolerant am I
Who hate the sinner, yet who love the sin.

WHEN THE DEVIL WAS SICK COULD
HE PROVE IT?

Few things are duller
Than feeling unspecifically off-color,
Yes, you feel like the fulfilment of a dismal prophecy,
And you don't feel either exercisey or officey,
But still you can't produce a red throat or a white tongue or uneasy
respiration or any kind of a symptom,
And it is very embarrassing that whoever was supposed to be pass-
ing out the symptoms skymptom,
Because whatever is the matter with you, you can't spot it
But whatever it is, you've got it,
But the question is how to prove it,
And you suck for hours on the mercury of the thermometer you
finally sent out for and you can't move it,
And your entire system may be pneumococci'd or streptococci'd,
But the looks you get from your loved ones are simply skepticocci'd,
And Conscience glares at you in her Here comes that bad penny
way,
Crying There's nothing the matter with you, you're just trying to
get out of doing something you never wanted to do anyway,
So you unfinger your pulse before Conscience can jeer at you for a
fingerer,
And you begin to believe that perhaps she is right, perhaps you are
nothing but a hypochondriacal old malingerer,
And you take a farewell look at the thermometer,
And that's when you hurl the bometer.
Yes sir, it's as good as a tonic,
Because you've got as pretty a ninety-nine point one as you'd wish
to see in a month of bubonic.
Some people hold out for a hundred or more before they collapse,
But that leaves too many gaps;
As for me,
I can get a very smug Monday, Tuesday, Wednesday, Thursday,
or Friday in bed out of a tenth of a degree.

It is to this trait that I am debtor
For the happy fact that on week ends I generally feel better.

OH, STOP BEING THANKFUL ALL OVER
THE PLACE

In the glittering collection of paste diamonds one in particular
　　ranks very high,
And that is the often-quoted remark of the prominent and respect-
　　able dignitary who on seeing a condemned man on his way to
　　the scaffold crashed into a thousand anthologies by remark-
　　ing, There but for the grace of God go I.
Here is a deplorable illustration
Of sloppy ratiocination;
Here is a notable feat
Of one-way thinking on a two-way street.
It must certainly have been the speaker's lucky day,
Or otherwise he would have been run over by his speech turning
　　around and coming back the other way,
Because did he stop to work out his premise to its logical conclu-
　　sion? Ah no,
He just got it off and let it go,
And now whenever people are with people they want to impress
　　with their combined greatheartedness and book-learning they
　　cry
Oh look at that condemned man on his way to the scaffold, there
　　but for the grace of God go I.
Which is so far so good, but they neglect to continue with the
　　heretofore unspoken balance of the theme, which is equally
　　true,
That there but for the grace of God goes Jimmie Durante or the
　　Prince of Wales or Aimee Semple McPherson or Dr. Welling-
　　ton Koo,
Or Moses or Napoleon or Cleopatra or P. T. Barnum,
Or even William or Dustin Farnum.

So away with you, all you parrot-like repeaters of high-sounding
    phrases that you never stop to consider what they actually
    mean,
I wouldn't allow you to stay in any college of which I was the
    Dean.
I can never listen to you without thinking Oh my,
There but for the grace of God speak I.

"MY CHILD IS PHLEGMATIC . . ."
— ANXIOUS PARENT

Anxious Parent, I guess you have just never been around;
I guess you just don't know who are the happiest people anywhere
    to be found;
So you are worried, are you, because your child is turning out to
    be phlegmatic?
Forgive me if I seem a trifle unsympathetic.
Why do you want your child to be a flashing, coruscating gem?
Don't you know the only peace the world can give lies not in flame
    but in phlegm?
Don't you know that the people with souls of putty
Are the only people who are sitting prutty?
They never get all worked up at the drop of a pin or a feather or
    a hat,
They never go around saying bitterly to themselves: "Oh God, did
    I really do, did I really say that?"
They never boil over when they read about stool pigeons getting
    girls into reformatories by making treacherous advances;
They never get perfectly futilely harrowed about Sacco and Van-
    zetti, or Alice Adamses who don't have good times at dances;
They never blink an eyelash about colleges that are going to the
    dogs because of football overemphasis;
They never almost die with indignation over a lynching near
    Natchez or Memphasis.
No, when they eat they digest their food, and when they go to bed
    they get right to sleep,

And four phlegmatic angels a stolid watch over them keep.
Oh to be phlegmatic, Oh to be stolid, Oh to be torpid, Oh to be
    calm!
For it is only thus, Anxious Parent, that we can get through life
    without a qualm.

HA! ORIGINAL SIN!

Vanity, vanity, all is vanity
That's any fun at all for humanity.
Food is vanity, so is drink,
And undergarments of gossamer pink,
P. G. Wodehouse and long vacations,
Going abroad, and rich relations,
The kind of engagements you want to keep,
A hundred honors, and twelve hours' sleep.
Vanities all — Oh Worra, worra!
Rooted in Sodom and Gomorrah.

Vanity, vanity, all is vanity
That's any fun at all for humanity.
That is the gist of the prophet's case,
From Bishop Cannon to Canon Chase.
The prophets chant and the prophets chatter,
But somehow it never seems to matter,
For the world hangs on to its ancient sanity
And orders another round of vanity.
Then Hey! for Gomorrah! and Nonny! for Sodom!
Marie! the Chanel model for Modom!

THE PARTY

Come Arabella, fetch the cake,
On a dish with silver handles.
Oh mercy! Feel the table shake!
Lucinda, light the candles.

For Mr. Migg is thir–ty,
Is thir—ty,
Is thir——ty.
The years are crawling over him
Like wee red ants.
Oh, three times ten is thir–ty,
Is for—ty,
Is fif——ty.
The further off from England
The nearer is to France.

The little flames they bob and jig,
The dining hall is breezy.
Quick! puff your candles, Mr. Migg,
The little flames die easy.
For Mr. Migg is for–ty,
Is for—ty,
Is for——ty.
The years are crawling over him
Like wee red ants.
Oh four times ten is for–ty,
Is fif—ty,
Is six——ty,
And creeping through the icing,
The other years advance.

Why, Arabella, here's a ring!
Lucinda, here a thimble!
For Mr. Migg there's not a thing —
'Tis not, I trust, a symbol!

For Mr. Migg is fif–ty,
Is fif—ty,
Is fif——ty.
The years are crawling over him
Like wee red ants.

Oh, five times ten is fif–ty,
Is six—ty,
Is seven——ty.
Lucinda, put the cake away.
We're going to the dance.

KINDLY UNHITCH THAT STAR, BUDDY

I hardly suppose I know anybody who wouldn't rather be a success
   than a failure,
Just as I suppose every piece of crabgrass in the garden would much
   rather be an azalea,
And in celestial circles all the run-of-the-mill angels would rather
   be archangels or at least cherubim and seraphim,
And in the legal world all the little process-servers hope to grow up
   into great big bailiffim and sheriffim.
Indeed, everybody wants to be a wow,
But not everybody knows exactly how.
Some people think they will eventually wear diamonds instead of
   rhinestones
Only by everlastingly keeping their noses to their ghrinestones,
And other people think they will be able to put in more time at
   Palm Beach and the Ritz
By not paying too much attention to attendance at the office but
   rather in being brilliant by starts and fits.
Some people after a full day's work sit up all night getting a college
   education by correspondence,
While others seem to think they'll get just as far by devoting their
   evenings to the study of the difference in temperament be-
   tween brunettance and blondance.
In short, the world is filled with people trying to achieve success,
And half of them think they'll get it by saying No and half of them
   by saying Yes,
And if all the ones who say No said Yes, and vice versa, such is
   the fate of humanity that ninety-nine per cent of them still
   wouldn't be any better off than they were before,

Which perhaps is just as well because if everybody was a success
   nobody could be contemptuous of anybody else and everybody would start in all over again trying to be a bigger success than everybody else so they would have somebody to be
   contemptuous of and so on forevermore,
Because when people start hitching their wagons to a star,
That's the way they are.

THE PASSIONATE PAGAN AND THE
DISPASSIONATE PUBLIC

A TRAGEDY OF THE MACHINE AGE

Boys and girls,
Come out to play,
The moon is shining
Bright as day.

If the moon is shining
Bright as day,
We think that we'll
Stay in and play.

Hey nonny nonny!
Come, Jennie! Come, Johnnie!
The year's adolescent!
The air's effervescent!
It bubbles like Schweppes!
Aren't you going to take steppes?

It's one of the commoner
Vernal phenomena.
You may go wild
Over air that is mild,
But Johnnie and Jennie
Are not having any.

It is Spring! It is Spring!
Let us leap! Let us sing!
Let us claim we have hives
And abandon our wives!
Let us hire violins
To encourage our sins!
Let us loll in a grotto!
Let this be our motto:
Not sackcloth, but satin!
Not Nordic, but Latin!

An epicene voice
Is our amorous choice!
Tell us that Luna
Compares with that cruna.
Away with your capers!
Go peddle your papers!

It is Spring! It is Spring!
On the lea, on the ling!
The frost is dispersed!
Like the buds let us burst!
Let the sap in our veins
Rush like limited trains!
Let our primitive urges
Disgruntle our clergies,
While Bacchus and Pan
Cavort in the van!

Spring is what winter
Always goes inter.
Science finds reasons
For mutable seasons.
Can't you control
That faun in your soul?
Please go and focus
Your whims on a crocus.

It is Spring! Is it Spring?
Let us sing! Shall we sing?
On the lea, on the ling
Shall we sing it is Spring?
Will nobody fling
A garland to Spring?
Oh, hey nonny nonny!
Oh, Jennie! Oh, Johnnie!
Doesn't dove rhyme with love
While the moon shines above?
Isn't May for the wooer
And June for *l'amour?*
No, it couldn't be Spring!
Do not dance! Do not sing!
These birds and these flowers,
These breezes and bowers,
These gay tirra-lirras
Are all done with mirrors!
Hey nonny! Hey nonny!
Hey nonny! Hey nonny!
Hey nonny! Hey nonny!
Hey nonny . . .

THEATRICAL REFLECTION

In the Vanities
No one wears panities.

PORTRAIT OF THE ARTIST AS A
PREMATURELY OLD MAN

It is common knowledge to every schoolboy and even every Bachelor of Arts,
That all sin is divided into two parts.

One kind of sin is called a sin of commission, and that is very important,

And it is what you are doing when you are doing something you ortant,

And the other kind of sin is just the opposite and is called a sin of omission and is equally bad in the eyes of all right-thinking people, from Billy Sunday to Buddha,

And it consists of not having done something you shuddha.

I might as well give you my opinion of these two kinds of sin as long as, in a way, against each other we are pitting them,

And that is, don't bother your head about sins of commission because however sinful, they must at least be fun or else you wouldn't be committing them.

It is the sin of omission, the second kind of sin,

That lays eggs under your skin.

The way you get really painfully bitten

Is by the insurance you haven't taken out and the checks you haven't added up the stubs of and the appointments you haven't kept and the bills you haven't paid and the letters you haven't written.

Also, about sins of omission there is one particularly painful lack of beauty,

Namely, it isn't as though it had been a riotous red-letter day or night every time you neglected to do your duty;

You didn't get a wicked forbidden thrill

Every time you let a policy lapse or forgot to pay a bill;

You didn't slap the lads in the tavern on the back and loudly cry Whee,

Let's all fail to write just one more letter before we go home, and this round of unwritten letters is on me.

No, you never get any fun

Out of the things you haven't done,

But they are the things that I do not like to be amid,

Because the suitable things you didn't do give you a lot more trouble than the unsuitable things you did.

The moral is that it is probably better not to sin at all, but if some
    kind of sin you must be pursuing,
Well, remember to do it by doing rather than by not doing.

SCRAM, LION!

Gentlemen, I give you the British Empire,
And the late Queen Victoria, by no means a vampire.
Britain and Britons I far from excoriate,
I deeply admire their Poet Laureate,
I prefer an evening with A. P. Herbert
To a sail in the moonlight sipping sherbert,
And I'd rather hear a Savoy opera
Than loll in the tropics cornering copra,
And I think Miss Lillie is quite a card
And I'm all agog over Scotland Yard.
I'm impressed by squires who run for Parliament
And serve their country for a modest emolument.
Yes, I praise their peers and I praise their commoners,
Their fogs and faces and other phenomenas;
I'm even sufficiently flibberty-gibberty
To praise their premise of personal liberty.
But bo, I'll hand you the whole shebang
When they start to sling Amurrican slang,
And calculate you will lose your lunch
When you glim an Amurrican joke in *Punch*,
For Piccadilly is less spectacular
Than its torture of Transatlantic vernacular.
Then, Bravo, Britain! and Long Live George!
Away with Yorktown and Valley Forge;
I've a spilth of open-mouthed admiration
For a top-hole pukka sahib nation
But nix on our chatter — it can't be did.
Twenty-three, skiddoo! — Yours,
                              The Candy Kid.

A BRIEF GUIDE TO NEW YORK

In New York beautiful girls can become more beautiful by going
    to Elizabeth Arden
And getting stuff put on their faces and waiting for it to harden,
And poor girls with nothing to their names but a letter or two can
    get rich and joyous
From a brief trip to their loyous.
So I can say with impunity
That New York is a city of opportunity.
It also has many fine theaters and hotels,
And a lot of taxis, buses, subways and els,
Best of all, if you don't show up at the office or at a tea nobody
    will bother their head,
They will just think you are dead.
That's why I really think New York is exquisite,
And even nicer to live in than to visit.

BIRDIES, DON'T MAKE ME LAUGH

Once there was a poem, and it was serious and not in jest,
And it said children ought to agree like little birdies in their nest.
Oh forsooth forsooth!
That poem was certainly more poetry than truth,
Because do you believe that little birdies in their nest agree?
It doesn't sound very probable to me.
Ah no, but I can tell you what does sound probable,
And that is that life in a nest is just one long quarrel and squab-
    bable.
Look at that young mother robin over in that elm, or is it a beech,
She has two little robins and she thinks she has solved her prob-
    lem because she has learned not to bring home just one worm
    but a worm for each.
She is very pleased with her understanding of fledgling psychol-
    ogy, but in just about two minutes she is going to lose a year's
    growth,

Because she's going to find that one little robin gets no worms and
    the other little robin gets both,

And if one little robin gets out of the nest on the wrong side and
    nothing can please it,

Why the other little robin will choose that moment to tease it,

And if one little robin starts a game the other little robin will
    stop it,

And if one little robin builds a castle the other little robin will
    knock it down and if one little robin blows a bubble the other
    little robin will pop it.

Yes, I bet that if you walked up to any nest and got a good reveal-
    ing glimpse,

Why, you would find that our little feathered friendlets disagree
    just like human imps,

And I also bet that their distracted feathered parents quote feath-
    ered poetry to them by whoever the most popular feathered
    poet may be,

All about why don't they like little children in their nurseries agree.

Well, to put the truth about youth in a very few words,

Why the truth is that little birds do agree like children and chil-
    dren do agree like little birds,

Because you take offsprings, and I don't care whether a house or
    a tree is their abode,

They may love each other but they aren't going to agree with each
    other anywhere except in an ode.

It doesn't seem to have occurred to the poet,

That nobody agrees with anybody else anyhow, but adults conceal
    it and infants show it.

THE PIG

The pig, if I am not mistaken,
Supplies us sausage, ham, and bacon.
Let others say his heart is big —
I call it stupid of the pig.

LINES TO A WORLD–FAMOUS POET WHO FAILED TO COMPLETE A WORLD–FAMOUS POEM

or

COME CLEAN, MR. GUEST!

Oft when I'm sitting without anything to read waiting for a train
in a depot,

I torment myself with the poet's dictum that to make a house a
home, livin' is what it takes a heap o'.

Now, I myself should very much enjoy makin' my house a home,
but my brain keeps on a-goin' clickety-click, clickety-click,
clickety-click,

If Peter Piper picked a peck o' heap o' livin', what kind of a peck
o' heap o' livin' would Peter Piper pick?

Certainly a person doesn't need the brains of a Lincoln

To know that there are many kinds o' livin', just as there are many
kinds o' dancin' or huntin' or fishin' or eatin' or drinkin'.

A philosophical poet should be specific

As well as prolific,

And I trust I am not being offensive

If I suggest that he should also be comprehensive.

You may if you like verify my next statement by sending a stamped,
self-addressed envelope to either Dean Inge or Dean Gauss,

But meanwhile I ask you to believe that it takes a heap of other
things besides a heap o' livin' to make a home out of a house.

To begin with, it takes a heap o' payin',

And you don't pay just the oncet, but agayin and agayin and
agayin.

Buyin' a stock is called speculatin' and buyin' a house is called
investin',

But the value of the stock or of the house fluctuates up and down,
generally down, just as an irresponsible Destiny may destine.

Something else that your house takes a heap o', whether the
builder come from Sicily or Erin,

Is repairin',

In addition to which, gentle reader, I am sorry to say you are
    little more than an imbecile or a cretin
If you think it doesn't take a heap o' heatin',
And unless you're spiritually allied to the little Dutch boy who
    went around inspectin' dikes lookin' for leaks to put his
    thumb in,
It takes a heap o' plumbin',
And if it's a house that you're hopin' to spend not just today but
    tomorrow in,
It takes a heap o' borrowin'.
In a word, Macushla,
There's a scad o' things that to make a house a home it takes not
    only a heap, or a peck, but at least a bushela.

TABOO TO BOOT

One bliss for which
There is no match
Is when you itch
To up and scratch.

Yet doctors and dowagers deprecate scratching,
Society ranks it with spitting and snatching,
And medical circles consistently hold
That scratching's as wicked as feeding a cold.
Hell's flame burns unquenched 'neath how many a stocking
On account of to scratch in a salon is shocking!

'Neath tile or thatch
That man is rich
Who has a scratch
For every itch.

Ho, squirmers and writhers, how long will ye suffer
The medical tyrant, the social rebuffer!

On the edge of the door let our shoulder blades rub,
Let the drawing room now be as free as the tub!

I'm greatly attached
To Barbara Frietchie.
I bet she scratched
When she was itchy.

THE COBRA

This creature fills its mouth with venum
And walks upon its duodenum.
He who attempts to tease the cobra
Is soon a sadder he, and sobra.

VERY LIKE A WHALE

One thing that literature would be greatly the better for
Would be a more restricted employment by authors of simile and
metaphor.
Authors of all races, be they Greeks, Romans, Teutons or Celts,
Can't seem just to say that anything is the thing it is but have to
go out of their way to say that it is like something else.
What does it mean when we are told
That the Assyrian came down like a wolf on the fold?
In the first place, George Gordon Byron had had enough experi-
ence
To know that it probably wasn't just one Assyrian, it was a lot of
Assyrians.
However, as too many arguments are apt to induce apoplexy and
thus hinder longevity,
We'll let it pass as one Assyrian for the sake of brevity.
Now then, this particular Assyrian, the one whose cohorts were
gleaming in purple and gold,

Just what does the poet mean when he says he came down like a
    wolf on the fold?
In heaven and earth more than is dreamed of in our philosophy
    there are a great many things,
But I don't imagine that among them there is a wolf with purple
    and gold cohorts or purple and gold anythings.
No, no, Lord Byron, before I'll believe that this Assyrian was actu-
    ally like a wolf I must have some kind of proof;
Did he run on all fours and did he have a hairy tail and a big red
    mouth and big white teeth and did he say Woof woof?
Frankly I think it very unlikely, and all you were entitled to say,
    at the very most,
Was that the Assyrian cohorts came down like a lot of Assyrian
    cohorts about to destroy the Hebrew host.
But that wasn't fancy enough for Lord Byron, oh dear me no, he
    had to invent a lot of figures of speech and then interpolate
    them,
With the result that whenever you mention Old Testament sol-
    diers to people they say Oh yes, they're the ones that a lot of
    wolves dressed up in gold and purple ate them.
That's the kind of thing that's being done all the time by poets,
    from Homer to Tennyson;
They're always comparing ladies to lilies and veal to venison,
And they always say things like that the snow is a white blanket
    after a winter storm.
Oh it is, is it, all right then, you sleep under a six-inch blanket of
    snow and I'll sleep under a half-inch blanket of unpoetical
    blanket material and we'll see which one keeps warm,
And after that maybe you'll begin to comprehend dimly
What I mean by too much metaphor and simile.

ADVICE OUTSIDE A CHURCH

Dear George, behold the portentous day
When bachelorhood is put away.
Bring camphor balls and cedarwood

For George's discarded bachelorhood;
You, as the happiest of men,
Wish not to wear it ever again.
Well, if you wish to get your wish,
Mark well my words, nor reply Tush-pish.
Today we fly, tomorrow we fall,
And lawyers make bachelors of us all.
If you desire a noisy nursery
And a golden wedding anniversary,
Scan first the bog where thousands falter:
They think the wooing ends at the altar,
And boast that one triumphant procession
Has given them permanent possession.
They simply desist from further endeavor,
And assume that their brides are theirs forever.
They do not beat them, they do no wrong to them,
But they take it for granted their brides belong to them.
Oh, every trade develops its tricks,
Marriage as well as politics,
Suspense is silk and complacence is shoddy,
And no one belongs to anybody.
It is pleasant, George, and necessary
To pretend the arrangement is temporary.
Thank her kindly for favors shown;
She is the lender, and she the loan;
Nor appear to notice the gradual shift
By which the loan becomes a gift.
Strong are the couples who resort
More to courtship and less to court.
And I warn you, George, for your future good,
That ladies don't want to be understood.
Women are sphinxes, Woman has writ it;
If you understand her, never admit it.
Tell her that Helen was probably beautifuller,
Call, if you will, Penelope dutifuller,
Sheba charminger, Guinevere grander

But never admit that you understand her.
Hark to the strains of Lohengrin!
Heads up, George! Go in and win!

PLATITUDINOUS REFLECTION

A good deal of superciliousness
Is based on biliousness.
People seem to be proud as peacocks
Of any infirmity, be it hives or dementia praecox.

FRAGONARD

There was an old miser named Clarence,
Who simonized both of his parents.
"The initial expense,"
He remarked, "is immense,
But I'll save it on wearance and tearance."

ELECTRA BECOMES MORBID

I

Abandon for a moment, friends,
Your frivolous means, your futile ends;
Life is not wholly beer and skittles,
A treasure hunt for love and victuals;
And so at times I think we ought
To pause and think a sobering thought.
Myself, I feel a dark despair
When I consider human hair.
I'm chicken-hearted, beetle-browed,
As I behold the heedless crowd,
Knowing each carefree individual
The slave of hair that runs on schedule.

On every human head or chin
It's falling out or growing in.
Your whistling adolescent scholar,
Released from Ye Olde Tonsorial Parlor,
Runs up his neck with fingers tense
Like sticks along a picket fence.
His scalp is all Bay Rum and bristles,
Therefore he's pleased and therefore whistles.
Yea, he rejoices, quite unknowing
That all the time his hair is growing.
O woe is you, unhappy scholar,
Next month you'll be back in the tonsorial parlor.

II

Myself I feel a dark despair,
When I consider human hair,
(Fine filaments sprouting from the skin),
Reflecting, as I stroke my chin,
That men and women everywhere
Unconsciously are growing hair,
Or, if the other hand you choose,
With every breath a hair they lose.
Unbid it cometh, likewise goeth,
And oftentimes it's doing boeth.
This habit is the chief determinant
Why permanent waves are less than permanent.
You rise, Madame, you face your mirror,
You utter cries of shame and terror.
What though to males you look all right?
For heaven's sake, your hair's a sight.
You hasten to the Gallic lair
Where lurks Maurice, or Jean or Pierre.
Between arrival and departure
You suffer hours of vicious torture,
At last emerging, white and weak,
But sure at least your mane is chic.

[27]

Thus you rejoice, my dear, unknowing
That all the time your hair is growing.
The waves so dearly purchasèd
Next month will have grown a foot or so away from your head.

III

I've said, I think, I think we ought
To think at times a sobering thought.
Man's lot it is to be a field
For crops that no nutrition yield,
That filter through his tender skin
And ripen on his head or chin.
I face mankind and shudder, knowing
That everybody's hair is growing;
That lovers, linked in darkened hallways,
Are capped with hair that groweth always;
That millions, shaven in the morning,
At eve find beards their jowls adorning;
That hair is creeping through the scalps
Of yodelers yodeling in the Alps,
And pushing through the epidermises
Of peasants frolicking at kermises;
And poking bravely through the pores
Of cannibals on tropic shores;
That freezing, scorching, raining, snowing,
People's hair is always growing.
I contemplate with dark despair
The awful force of growing hair,
Although admitting, to be quite honest,
That it will be worth a million Niagaras to humanity if Science
can ever get it harnessed.

REFLECTION ON A WICKED WORLD

Purity
Is obscurity.

OUR CHILD DOESN'T KNOW ANYTHING
or
THANK GOD!

I am now about to make a remark that I suppose most parents will
    think me hateful for,
Though as a matter of fact I am only commenting on a condition
    that they should be more than grateful for.
What I want to say is, that of luckiness it seems to me to be the
    height
That babies aren't very bright.
Now listen to me for a minute, all you proud progenitors who
    boast that your bedridden infant offspring of two months or
    so are already bright enough to get into Harvard or Stanford
    or Notre Dame or Fordham;
Don't you realize that the only thing that makes life at all bearable
    to those selfsame offspring is being rather backward, and that
    if they had any sense at all they would lose no time in perish-
    ing of boredom?
Good heavens, I can think of no catastrophe more immense
Than a baby with sense,
Because one thing at least, willy-nilly, you must believe,
And that is, that a baby has twenty-four hours a day to get through
    with just the same as we've.
Some people choose to wonder about virtue and others about crime,
But I choose to wonder how babies manage to pass the time.
They can't pass it in tennis or badminton or golf,
Or in going around rescuing people from Indians and then mar-
    rying somebody else the way Pocahontas did with the Messrs.
    Smith and Rolfe;
They can't pass it in bridge or parchesi or backgammon,
Or in taking the subway to Wall Street and worshipping Mam-
    mon;
How then do they manage to enthuse themselves,
And amuse themselves?
Well, partly they sleep,

And mostly they weep,
And the rest of the time they relax
On their backs,
And eat, by régime specifically, but by nature omnivorously,
And vocalize vocivorously.
That, to make it short,
Is about all they can do in the way of sport;
So whatever may come,
I am glad that babies are dumb.
I shudder to think what for entertainment they would do
Were they as bright as me or you.

LISTEN . . .

There is a knocking in the skull,
An endless silent shout
Of something beating on a wall,
And crying, Let me out.

That solitary prisoner
Will never hear reply,
No comrade in eternity
Can hear the frantic cry.

No heart can share the terror
That haunts his monstrous dark;
The light that filters through the chinks
No other eye can mark.

When flesh is linked with eager flesh,
And words run warm and full,
I think that he is loneliest then,
The captive in the skull.

Caught in a mesh of living veins,
In cell of padded bone,

He loneliest is when he pretends
That he is not alone.

We'd free the incarcerate race of man
That such a doom endures
Could only you unlock my skull,
Or I creep into yours.

THE RABBITS

Here's a verse about rabbits
That doesn't mention their habits.

YOU HAVE MORE FREEDOM IN A HOUSE

The Murrays have moved to a house,
They are finished forever with flats;
They longed for a personal mouse,
And room to swing dozens of cats.
They longed for a hearth and a doorway,
In Arden, or maybe in Eden,
But the Eden is rather like Norway,
And the Arden like winter in Sweden.
How baffled the Murrays have grown
Since they live in a house of their own!

Oh hurry hurry!
Says Mrs. Murray.
But listen, my dear, says he,
If you want the house
A temperate house,
You'd better not leave it to me.
I've learned the knack of swinging a cat,
But I can't coerce the thermostat.
The furnace has given a gruesome cough,

And something has cut the fuel off,
And the heart of the nursery radiator
Is cold as the nose of an alligator,
And I've telephoned for the service men
But they can't get here until after ten,
So swaddle the children,
And hurry, hurry —
I'm a practical man,
Says Mr. Murray.

The Murrays are vague about fuses,
And mechanical matters like that,
And each of them frequently muses
On the days when they lived in a flat.
Was the plumbing reluctant to plumb?
Was the climate suggestive of Canada?
Did the radio crackle and hum?
You simply called down to the janitor!
The Murrays have found no replacement
For the genius who lived in the basement.

Oh, hurry, hurry!
Says Mr. Murray.
I'm doing my best, says she,
But it's hard to scrub
In a tepid tub,
So the guests must wait for me;
And tell them they'll get their cocktails later
When you've managed to fix the refrigerator.
And explain if the coffee looks like water,
That the stove is as queer as a seventh daughter,
And I will be down as soon as able
To unstick the drawers of my dressing table.

There's a car at the door, says Mrs. Murray,
The doorbell's broken, so hurry, hurry!

Oh, I don't regret
Being wed to you,
But I wish I could wed
A janitor too.

LOVE UNDER THE REPUBLICANS
(OR DEMOCRATS)

Come live with me and be my love
And we will all the pleasures prove
Of a marriage conducted with economy
In the Twentieth Century Anno Donomy.
We'll live in a dear little walk-up flat
With practically room to swing a cat
And a potted cactus to give it hauteur
And a bathtub equipped with dark brown water.
We'll eat, without undue discouragement
Foods low in cost but high in nouragement
And quaff with pleasure, while chatting wittily,
The peculiar wine of Little Italy.
We'll remind each other it's smart to be thrifty
And buy our clothes for something-fifty.
We'll stand in line on holidays
For seats at unpopular matinees,
And every Sunday we'll have a lark
And take a walk in Central Park.
And one of these days not too remote
I'll probably up and cut your throat.

DON'T LOOK NOW

There is something to be said for the Victorians
Even though they refused to believe they were descended from
    apes and saurians;

Because take their low opinion of exposure anatomical,
Why I have a feeling that they felt it was not so much immoral
as just plain comical.
They realized that most people are big where they should be littler
and little where they should be bigger,
And they would rather have had their bathing suit laughed at
than their figure.
Yes they wore the costumes they did because they knew that they
were not ancient Greeks,
And it is a moot question which is more ludicrous on the beach,
the cloistered rompers of the Nineties, or today's unescapable
physiques.
The belle of the Nineties tiptoeing down the steps of the bathing
machine may have had the natural lines of a Langtry or again
of a prize-winning pumpkin or of a homeless heifer after an
extended drought,
But thanks to the marquee enswathing her she got the benefit of
the doubt.
Whereas today at Miami or Coney or Catalina,
Why practically everyone is forced to face the fact that their beloved is built like either a flute or a concertina.
I have a theory about physiological disclosures along the strand;
I believe they account for Sally Rand;
I believe that when people have seen a certain number of un-
draped figures like a concertina or a flute,
Well, finally they are willing to pay any amount just to see a beaut,
So now it's a hot sultry day and you may all run down to the beach
for a swim and a look.
I'm going to put on Uncle Elmer's bathing suit and sit in the tub
and read a Victorian book.

REMINISCENT REFLECTION

When I consider how my life is spent,
I hardly ever repent.

LINES TO BE MUMBLED AT OVINGTON'S

Mr. and Mrs. F. X. Pleasants
Request the honor of my presence,
On Saturday the twenty-fourth,
To watch their daughter, Barbara North,
Succumb in holy matrimony
To Mr. Maximilian Coney.
A murrain on you, Mr. and Mrs. Pleasants!
I hope you turn into friends of Annie Besant's!

Bishop Apse will do the trick;
He's just the kind that mothers pick.
He has a noble velvet voice
That makes a mother's heart rejoice
And fills a mother's handkerchief
With briny evidence of grief.
A murrain on you too, old Bishop Apse!
I hope you get caught in some vicious moral lapse!

The ushers in their coats of black
Will lead old ladies forth and back,
While bridesmaids in their flowery frocks
Bloom round the bride like hollyhocks.
Who knows but what some sidelong glance
Will propagate a new romance?
A murrain on every bridesmaid and every usher!
I hope they all get spattered with oil from a gusher!

I'll wish some wishes for Mr. Coney
In honor of his matrimony.
I wish him moths, I wish him mice,
I wish him cocktails lacking ice.
I wish him a life abrupt and lonely,
I wish him a wife in title only.

A murrain, a murrain upon you, Maximilian!
If I wish you one death before evening I wish you a billion!

What have I left for Barbara North
Who changes her name on the twenty-fourth?
A hundred theater-ticket stubs,
Matches and corks from supper clubs,
A dozen notes whose theme is If,
Some lipstick on a handkerchief —
A lesser soul of spite would be a harborer;
Not I. No murrain at all upon you, Barbara!

DON'T CRY, DARLING, IT'S BLOOD ALL RIGHT

Whenever poets want to give you the idea that something is par-
ticularly meek and mild,
They compare it to a child,
Thereby proving that though poets with poetry may be rife
They don't know the facts of life.
If of compassion you desire either a tittle or a jot,
Don't try to get it from a tot.
Hard-boiled, sophisticated adults like me and you
May enjoy ourselves thoroughly with *Little Women* and *Winnie-
the-Pooh,*
But innocent infants these titles from their reading course elim-
inate
As soon as they discover that it was honey and nuts and mashed
potatoes instead of human flesh that Winnie-the-Pooh and
Little Women ate.
Innocent infants have no use for fables about rabbits or donkeys
or tortoises or porpoises,
What they want is something with plenty of well-mutilated
corpoises.
Not on legends of how the rose came to be a rose instead of a
petunia is their fancy fed,

But on the inside story of how somebody's bones got ground up
   to make somebody else's bread.
They'll go to sleep listening to the story of the little beggarmaid
   who got to be queen by being kind to the bees and the birds,
But they're all eyes and ears the minute they suspect a wolf or a
   giant is going to tear some poor woodcutter into quarters or
   thirds.
It really doesn't take much to fill their cup;
All they want is for somebody to be eaten up.
Therefore I say unto you, all you poets who are so crazy about
   meek and mild little children and their angelic air,
If you are sincere and really want to please them, why just go out
   and get yourselves devoured by a bear.

REFLECTIONS ON ICE–BREAKING

Candy
Is dandy
But liquor
Is quicker.

INVOCATION

("Smoot Plans Tariff Ban on Improper Books" — NEWS ITEM)

Senator Smoot (Republican, Ut.)
Is planning a ban on smut.
Oh root-ti-toot for Smoot of Ut.
And his reverent occiput.
Smite, Smoot, smite for Ut.,
Grit your molars and do your dut.,
Gird up your l—ns,
Smite h—p and th—gh,
We'll all be Utah
By and by.

[37   ]

Smite, Smoot, for the Watch and Ward,
For Hiram Johnson and Henry Ford,
For Bishop Cannon and John D., Junior,
For Governor Pinchot of Pennsylvunia,
For John S. Sumner and Elder Hays
And possibly Edward L. Bernays,
For Orville Poland and Ella Boole,
For Mother Machree and the Shelton pool.
When smut's to be smitten
Smoot will smite
For G—d, for country,
And Fahrenheit.

Senator Smoot is an institute
Not to be bribed with pelf;
He guards our homes from erotic tomes
By reading them all himself.
Smite, Smoot, smite for Ut.,
They're smuggling smut from Balt. to Butte!
Strongest and sternest
Of your s—x
Scatter the scoundrels
From Can. to Mex.!

Smite, Smoot, for Smedley Butler,
For any good man by the name of Cutler,
Smite for the W.C.T.U.,
For Rockne's team and for Leader's crew,
For Florence Coolidge and Admiral Byrd,
For Billy Sunday and John D., Third,
For Grantland Rice and for Albie Booth,
For the Woman's Auxiliary of Duluth,
Smite, Smoot,
Be rugged and rough,
Smut if smitten
Is front-page stuff.

KING LEER

One human hellgrammite that I think we could all dispense with
Is he who in every pleasant mixed gathering insists on dragging
    in the kind of anecdote that should, if employed, be em-
    ployed only to entertain gents with.
His persiflage would embarrass
The late Frank Harris,
And as you watch him scintillating
You have an overwhelming conviction that the room needs vin-
    tilating.
It isn't that you yourself have never guffawed
At humor that is, to put it mildly, broad,
Or consider yourself too nice
To indulge once in a while in a bit of risquéting on thin ice;
It's just that under the circumstances the mildew that passes for
    wit with this weevil
Happens to throw your digestive system into a revulsive up-
    heaval.
But if you chance to grow restive
As his quips and cranks and wanton wiles get continually more
    suggestive,
And venture the opinion that a trip to the laundry
Could hardly fail to benefit some of the double entendry,
He will retort that his intentions and his remarks are all irreproach-
    ably refined,
And that if you see something wrong about them it only proves
    conclusively that you have a vulgar mind.
So after that, everybody is on the spot
And nobody knows whether to laugh or not,
And the evening gets more and more uncomfortable and at the
    same time duller and duller
As every few minutes he trots out a horse of another off-color.
This I believe is his way of demonstrating that he is Sophisticated
    and not Provincial,
And if every good old sophisticated night-club proprietor and

gangster on Broadway took him for a good old sophisticated
ride I should consider it nothing less than Providintial.

MY DADDY

I have a funny daddy
Who goes in and out with me,
And everything that baby does
My daddy's sure to see,
And everything that baby says
My daddy's sure to tell.
You *must* have read my daddy's verse.
I hope he fries in hell.

WHEN YOU SAY THAT, SMILE!
or
ALL RIGHT THEN, DON'T SMILE

When the odds are long,
And the game goes wrong,
Does your joie de vivre diminish?
Have you little delight
In an uphill fight?
Do you wince at a Garrison finish?
Then here's my hand, my trusty partner!
I've always wanted a good disheartener.

Oh, things are frequently what they seem,
And this is wisdom's crown:
Only the game fish swims upstream,
But the sensible fish swims down.

Well, how is your pulse
When a cad insults
The lady you're cavaliering?

[40]

Are you willing to wait
To retaliate
Till the cad is out of hearing?
Then here's my hand, my trusty companion,
And may neither one of us fall in a canyon.

For things are frequently what they seem,
And this is wisdom's crown:
Only the game fish swims upstream,
But the sensible fish swims down.

IT MUST BE THE MILK

There is a thought that I have tried not to but cannot help but
    think,
Which is, My goodness how much infants resemble people who
    have had too much to drink.
Tots and sots, so different and yet so identical!
What a humiliating coincidence for pride parentical!
Yet when you see your little dumpling set sail across the nursery
    floor,
Can you conscientiously deny the resemblance to somebody who
    is leaving a tavern after having tried to leave it a dozen times
    and each time turned back for just once more?
Each step achieved
Is simply too good to be believed;
Foot somehow follows foot
And somehow manages to stay put;
Arms wildly semaphore,
Wild eyes seem to ask, Whatever did we get in such a dilemma for?
And their gait is more that of a duckling than a Greek goddessling
    or godling,
And in inebriates it's called staggering but in infants it's called
    toddling.
Another kinship with topers is also by infants exhibited,

Which is that they are completely uninhibited,
And they can't talk straight
Any more than they can walk straight;
Their pronunciation is awful
And their grammar is flawful,
And in adults it's drunken and maudlin and deplorable,
But in infants it's tunnin' and adorable.
So I hope you will agree that it is very hard to tell an infant from
     somebody who has gazed too long into the cup,
And really the only way you can tell them apart is to wait till next
     day, and the infant is the one that feels all right when it
     wakes up.

A LADY THINKS SHE IS THIRTY

Unwillingly Miranda wakes,
Feels the sun with terror,
One unwilling step she takes,
Shuddering to the mirror.

Miranda in Miranda's sight
Is old and gray and dirty;
Twenty-nine she was last night;
This morning she is thirty.

Shining like the morning star,
Like the twilight shining,
Haunted by a calendar,
Miranda sits a-pining.

Silly girl, silver girl,
Draw the mirror toward you;
Time who makes the years to whirl
Adorned as he adored you.

Time is timelessness for you;
Calendars for the human;
What's a year, or thirty, to
Loveliness made woman?

Oh, Night will not see thirty again,
Yet soft her wing, Miranda;
Pick up your glass and tell me, then —
How old is Spring, Miranda?

PROCRASTINATION IS ALL OF THE TIME

Torpor and sloth, torpor and sloth,
These are the cooks that unseason the broth.
Slothor and torp, slothor and torp
The directest of bee-line ambitions can warp.
He who is slothic, he who is torporal,
Will not be promoted to sergeant or corporal.
No torporer drowsy, no comatose slother
Will make a good banker, not even an author.
Torpor I deprecate, sloth I deplore,
Torpor is tedious, sloth is a bore.
Sloth is a bore, and torpor is tedious,
Fifty parts comatose, fifty tragedious.
How drear, on a planet redundant with woes,
That sloth is not slumber, nor torpor repose.
That the innocent joy of not getting things done
Simmers sulkily down to plain not having fun.
You smile in the morn like a bride in her bridalness
At the thought of a day of nothing but idleness.
By midday you're slipping, by evening a lunatic,
A perusing-the-newspapers-all-afternoonatic,
Worn to a wraith from the half-hourly jaunt
After glasses of water you didn't want,
And at last when onto your pallet you creep,

You discover yourself too tired to sleep.
O torpor and sloth, torpor and sloth,
These are the cooks that unseason the broth.
Torpor is harrowing, sloth it is irksome —
Everyone ready? Let's go out and worksome.

EDOUARD

A bugler named Dougal MacDougal
Found ingenious ways to be frugal.
He learned how to sneeze
In various keys,
Thus saving the price of a bugle.

THE INDIVIDUALIST

Once there was a man named Jarvis Gravel who was just a man
    named Jarvis Gravel except for one thing:
He hated spring.
Anything at all vernal
Was to him strictly infernal.
When he saw the first crocus poke its head up
He'd get a shovel and dig the entire bed up,
And he bought a horse and galloped back and forth
Tipping off the worms when the first robin started North.
To love the way of a man with a maid in the moonlight was some-
    thing he never learnt,
And he spent a lot of beautiful balmy evenings moving FRESH
    PAINT signs from park benches that were freshly painted
    to ones that weren't,
And when he finally did marry a girl who made his pulses quicken
It was merely because her name was Gale Winterbottom and she
    was no spring chicken,
And one day during the worm-warning season he came home
    hungry after a hard day in the stirrup,

[44]

And she served him waffles and he objected to the May-pole syrup,
So she shot him through the heart, but his last words were ecstatic.
He said Thank you honey, it was thoughtful of you to use the
    autumnatic.

IN WHICH THE POET IS ASHAMED BUT PLEASED

Of all the things that I would rather,
It is to be my daughter's father,
While she, with innocence divine,
Is quite contented to be mine.

I am distressingly aware
That this arrangement is unfair,
For I, when in my celibate garrison,
Acquired some standard of comparison.

I visited nurseries galore,
Compiled statistics by the score,
And gained experience from a crew
Of children passing in review.

I saw the best that parents vaunted;
They weren't exactly what I wanted;
Yet, all the offspring that I faced,
They served to cultivate my taste.

Thus, let the miser praise the mintage,
And let the vintner praise the vintage;
I'm conscious that in praising her,
I'm speaking as a connoisseur.

While she, poor dear, has never known
A father other than her own.
She wots of other girls' papas
No more than of the Persian Shah's.

Within her head no notion stirs
That some are better men than hers;
That some are richer, some are kinder,
Some are solider, some are refineder,

That some are vastly more amusing,
Some fitter subjects for enthusing,
That some are cleverer, some are braver,
Than the one that fortune gave her.

What fortune set us side by side,
Her scope so narrow, mine so wide?
We owe to this sweet dispensation
Our mutual appreciation.

FUNEBRIAL REFLECTION

Among the anthropophagi
One's friends are one's sarcophagi.

I KNOW YOU'LL LIKE THEM

You don't need to study any ponderous tome
To find out how to make your out-of-town guests feel not at home,
Because there is one way which couldn't be exquisiter
For enthralling the visitor.
You plan a little gathering informal and sociable
And you ask a few friends whose manners are irreproaciable,
And you speak up with all the pride of Mr. Dewey announcing
    a couple of important impending arrests,
And you say Friends, this is Mr. and Mrs. Comfitmonger, my
    out-of-town guests,
And you even amplify your introduction so as to break the ice
    with more velocity,
And you tell them that Mrs. Comfitmonger used to be a police-

woman and Mr. Comfitmonger is a piano tuner of no mean
virtuosity,

And you hint that Mr. Comfitmonger has had some pretty intri-
guing experiences in his years as a virtuoso,

And that Mrs. Comfitmonger while pounding her beat has dealt
with personalities who would scare the pants off Lombroso,

And that everything is all set for a dandy evening of general chitchat is what you think,

And you retire to the pantry to prepare everybody a drink,

And you hear the brouhaha of vivacious voices,

And your heart rejoices,

Because it seems that your friends find Mr. Comfitmonger's anecdotes of life inside the Steinways fascinating,

And are spellbound by Mrs. Comfitmonger's articulate opposition
to arson and assassinating,

And you say This party is indeed de luxe,

And you emerge to find all your friends excitedly discussing putts
that wouldn't go down and stocks that wouldn't go up, and
Mr. and Mrs. Comfitmonger over in a corner leafing through
your books,

And if you think you can turn the conversation to Palestrina or
police work,

You've taken on a mighty pretty job of piecework,

Because if there is one thing in which everybody's home-team
friends are unerring,

It is to confine their conversation to mutual acquaintances and
episodes as to which your visiting friends have no idea of to
what they are referring.

Most people are only vocal
When talking local.

JUDGMENT DAY

This is the day, this is the day!
I knew as soon as the sun's first ray
Crept through the slats of the cot,

And opened the eyes of a tot,
And the tot would rather have slept,
And, therefore, wept.
This is the day that is wrong,
The day when the only song
Is a skirling lamentation
Of continuous indignation,
When the visage is ireful,
The voice, direful,
And the early, pearly teeth
Snick like a sword in the sheath,
When the fists are clenched,
And the cheeks are drenched
In full-fed freshets and tumbling, tumultuous torrents
Of virtuous abhorrence,
When loud as the challenging trumpets of John at Lepanto
Rings the clarion, "I don't want to."
This is the day, the season,
Of wrongs without reason,
The day when the prunes and the cereal
Taste like building material,
When the spinach tastes only like spinach, and honey and sugar
Raise howls like the yowls of a quarrelsome puma or cougar,
When the wail is not to be hushed
Nor the hair to be brushed,
When life is frustration, and either
A person must be all alone or have somebody with her, and toler-
    ates neither,
When outdoors is worse than in, and indoors than out, and both
    too dull to be borne,
And dolls are flung under the bed and books are torn,
When people humiliate a person
With their clumsily tactful attempts to conciliate a person,
When music no charm possesses,
Nor hats, nor mittens, nor dresses,
When the frowning fortress is woe

And the watchword is No.
You owners of children who pass this day with forbearance,
You indeed are parents!

THE CANARY

The song of canaries
Never varies,
And when they're moulting
They're pretty revolting.

THE TERRIBLE PEOPLE

People who have what they want are very fond of telling people
    who haven't what they want that they really don't want it,
And I wish I could afford to gather all such people into a gloomy
    castle on the Danube and hire half a dozen capable Draculas
    to haunt it.
I don't mind their having a lot of money, and I don't care how
    they employ it,
But I do think that they damn well ought to admit they enjoy it.
But no, they insist on being stealthy
About the pleasures of being wealthy,
And the possession of a handsome annuity
Makes them think that to say how hard it is to make both ends
    meet is their bounden duity.
You cannot conceive of an occasion
Which will find them without some suitable evasion.
Yes indeed, with arguments they are very fecund;
Their first point is that money isn't everything, and that they have
    no money anyhow is their second.
Some people's money is merited,
And other people's is inherited,
But wherever it comes from,
They talk about it as if it were something you got pink gums from.
Perhaps indeed the possession of wealth is constantly distressing,

But I should be quite willing to assume every curse of wealth if I
    could at the same time assume every blessing.
The only incurable troubles of the rich are the troubles that money
    can't cure,
Which is a kind of trouble that is even more troublesome if you
    are poor.
Certainly there are lots of things in life that money won't buy, but
    it's very funny —
Have you ever tried to buy them without money?

THE TALE OF CUSTARD THE DRAGON

Belinda lived in a little white house,
With a little black kitten and a little gray mouse,
And a little yellow dog and a little red wagon,
And a realio, trulio, little pet dragon.

Now the name of the little black kitten was Ink,
And the little gray mouse, she called her Blink,
And the little yellow dog was sharp as Mustard,
But the dragon was a coward, and she called him Custard.

Custard the dragon had big sharp teeth,
And spikes on top of him and scales underneath,
Mouth like a fireplace, chimney for a nose,
And realio, trulio daggers on his toes.

Belinda was as brave as a barrel full of bears,
And Ink and Blink chased lions down the stairs,
Mustard was as brave as a tiger in a rage,
But Custard cried for a nice safe cage.

Belinda tickled him, she tickled him unmerciful,
Ink, Blink and Mustard, they rudely called him **Percival,**
They all sat laughing in the little red wagon
At the realio, trulio, cowardly dragon.

Belinda giggled till she shook the house,
And Blink said Weeck! which is giggling for a mouse,
Ink and Mustard rudely asked his age,
When Custard cried for a nice safe cage.

Suddenly, suddenly they heard a nasty sound,
And Mustard growled, and they all looked around.
Meowch! cried Ink, and Ooh! cried Belinda,
For there was a pirate, climbing in the winda.

Pistol in his left hand, pistol in his right,
And he held in his teeth a cutlass bright,
His beard was black, one leg was wood;
It was clear that the pirate meant no good.

Belinda paled, and she cried Help! Help!
But Mustard fled with a terrified yelp,
Ink trickled down to the bottom of the household,
And little mouse Blink strategically mouseholed.

But up jumped Custard, snorting like an engine,
Clashed his tail like irons in a dungeon,
With a clatter and a clank and a jangling squirm
He went at the pirate like a robin at a worm.

The pirate gaped at Belinda's dragon,
And gulped some grog from his pocket flagon,
He fired two bullets, but they didn't hit,
And Custard gobbled him, every bit.

Belinda embraced him, Mustard licked him,
No one mourned for his pirate victim.
Ink and Blink in glee did gyrate
Around the dragon that ate the pyrate.

But presently up spoke little dog Mustard,
I'd have been twice as brave if I hadn't been flustered.
And up spoke Ink and up spoke Blink,
We'd have been three times as brave, we think,
And Custard said, I quite agree
That everybody is braver than me.

Belinda still lives in her little white house,
With her little black kitten and her little gray mouse,
And her little yellow dog and her little red wagon,
And her realio, trulio, little pet dragon.

Belinda is as brave as a barrel full of bears,
And Ink and Blink chase lions down the stairs,
Mustard is as brave as a tiger in a rage,
But Custard keeps crying for a nice safe cage.

POLITICAL REFLECTION

Like an art-lover looking at the Mona Lisa in the Louvre
Is the *New York Herald Tribune* looking at Mr. Herbert Houvre.

IT'S NEVER FAIR WEATHER

I do not like the winter wind
That whistles from the North.
My upper teeth and those beneath,
They jitter back and forth.
Oh, some are hanged, and some are skinned,
And others face the winter wind.

I do not like the summer sun
That scorches the horizon.
Though some delight in Fahrenheit,

To me it's deadly pizen.
I think that life would be more fun
Without the simmering summer sun.

I do not like the signs of spring,
The fever and the chills,
The icy mud, the puny bud,
The frozen daffodils.
Let other poets gayly sing;
I do not like the signs of spring.

I do not like the foggy fall
That strips the maples bare;
The radiator's mating call,
The dank, rheumatic air.
I fear that taken all in all,
I do not like the foggy fall.

The winter sun, of course, is kind,
And summer wind's a savior,
And I'll merrily sing of fall and spring
When they're on their good behavior.
But otherwise I see no reason
To speak in praise of any season.

ARTHUR

There was an old man of Calcutta,
Who coated his tonsils with butta,
Thus converting his snore
From a thunderous roar
To a soft, oleaginous mutta.

MA, WHAT'S A BANKER?
or
HUSH, MY CHILD

The North wind doth blow,
And we shall have snow,
And what will the banker do then, poor thing?
Will he go to the barn
To keep himself warm,
And hide his head under his wing?
Is he on the spot, poor thing, poor thing?
Probably not, poor thing.

For when he is good,
He is not very good,
And when he is bad he is horrider,
And the chances are fair
He is taking the air
Beside a cabaña in Florida.
But the wailing investor, mean thing, mean thing,
Disturbs his siesta, poor thing.

He will plunge in the pool,
But he makes it a rule
To plunge with his kith and his kin,
And whisper about
That it's time to get out
When the widows and orphans get in.
He only got out, poor thing, poor thing,
Yet they call him a tout, poor thing.

His heart simply melts
For everyone else;
By love and compassion he's ridden;
The pay of his clerks
To reduce, how it irks!

But he couldn't go South if he didden.
I'm glad there's a drink within reach, poor thing,
As he weeps on the beach, poor thing.

May he someday find peace
In a temple in Greece,
Where the Government harbors no rancor;
May Athens and Sparta
Play host to the martyr,
And purchase a bond from the banker.
With the banker in Greece, poor thing, poor thing,
We can cling to our fleece, Hot Cha!

GOLLY, HOW TRUTH WILL OUT!

How does a person get to be a capable liar?
That is something that I respectfully inquiar,
Because I don't believe a person will ever set the world on fire
Unless they are a capable lire.
Some wise man said that words were given to us to conceal our
    thoughts,
But if a person has nothing but truthful words why their thoughts
    haven't even the protection of a pair of panties or shorts,
And a naked thought is ineffectual as well as improper,
And hasn't a chance in the presence of a glib chinchilla-clad whop-
    per.
One of the greatest abilities a person can have, I guess,
Is the ability to say Yes when they mean No and No when they
    mean Yes.
Oh to be Machiavellian, Oh to be unscrupulous, Oh to be glib!
Oh to be ever prepared with a plausible fib!
Because then a dinner engagement or a contract or a treaty is no
    longer a fetter,
Because liars can just logically lie their way out of it if they don't
    like it or if one comes along that they like better;

And do you think their conscience prickles?
No, it tickles.
And that is why I admire a suave prevarication because I myself prevaricate so awkwardly and gauchely,
And that is why I can never amount to anything politically or socially.

THE CAMEL

The camel has a single hump;
The dromedary, two;
Or else the other way around.
I'm never sure. Are you?

WILL CONSIDER SITUATION

These here are words of radical advice for a young man looking for a job;
Young man, be a snob.
Yes, if you are in search of arguments against starting at the bottom,
Why I've gottom.
Let the personnel managers differ;
It's obvious that you will get on faster at the top than at the bottom because there are more people at the bottom than at the top so naturally the competition at the bottom is stiffer.
If you need any further proof that my theory works,
Well, nobody can deny that presidents get paid more than vice-presidents and vice-presidents get paid more than clerks.
Stop looking at me quizzically;
I want to add that you will never achieve fortune in a job that makes you uncomfortable physically.
When anybody tells you that hard jobs are better for you than soft jobs be sure to repeat this text to them,
Postmen tramp around all day through rain and snow just to deliver people's in cozy air-conditioned offices checks to them.

You don't need to interpret tea leaves stuck in a cup
To understand that people who work sitting down get paid more
than people who work standing up.
Another thing about having a comfortable job is you not only ac-
cumulate more treasure;
You get more leisure.
So that when you find you have worked so comfortably that your
waistline is a menace,
You correct it with golf or tennis.
Whereas if in an uncomfortable job like piano-moving or stevedor-
ing you indulge,
You have no time to exercise, you just continue to bulge.
To sum it up, young man, there is every reason to refuse a job that
will make heavy demands on you corporally or manually,
And the only intelligent way to start your career is to accept a
sitting position paying at least twenty-five thousand dollars
annually.

THE ROOSTER

The rooster has a soul more bellicose
Than all your Ludendorffs and Jellicoes.
His step is prouder than Davy Crockett's,
As he swaggers by with his hands in his pockets.

PRETTY HALCYON DAYS

How pleasant to sit on the beach,
On the beach, on the sand, in the sun,
With ocean galore within reach,
And nothing at all to be done!
No letters to answer,
No bills to be burned,
No work to be shirked,

No cash to be earned.
It is pleasant to sit on the beach
With nothing at all to be done.

How pleasant to look at the ocean,
Democratic and damp; indiscriminate;
It fills me with noble emotion
To think I am able to swim in it.
To lave in the wave,
Majestic and chilly,
Tomorrow I crave;
But today it is silly.
It is pleasant to look at the ocean;
Tomorrow, perhaps, I shall swim in it.

How pleasant to gaze at the sailors,
As their sailboats they manfully sail
With the vigor of vikings and whalers
In the days of the viking and whale.
They sport on the brink
Of the shad and the shark;
If it's windy they sink;
If it isn't, they park.
It is pleasant to gaze at the sailors,
To gaze without having to sail.

How pleasant the salt anaesthetic
Of the air and the sand and the sun;
Leave the earth to the strong and athletic,
And the sea to adventure upon.
But the sun and the sand
No contractor can copy;
We lie in the land
Of the lotus and poppy;
We vegetate, calm and aesthetic,
On the beach, on the sand, in the sun.

MR. PEACHEY'S PREDICAMENT
or
NO MOT PARADES

Once there was a man named Mr. Peachey and he lived on Park
    Avenue and played the harp and was an eligible bachelor but
    his social life was hapless,
And he thought at first it was because his parents came from In-
    dianapless,
But one day he awoke from a troubled nap,
And said I am tired of this hapless social life, what I want is a
    social life simply teeming with hap.
It can't be, he said, that I don't play the harp enough,
I wonder if just possibly my wits are not sharp enough.
I know that I'm pretty noted
But I've never been quoted;
Perhaps the solution for me
Is some iridescent repartee;
Suppose before I next dine out I compose a series of epigrams of
    searing astringency
And then I shall be ready with a quip for any conversational con-
    tingency.
So he composed a series of epigrams of indubitable variety,
And went to dine with some people way up in society.
And in the taxi he memorized his lines and held a solo rehearsal,
And he was delighted, because he said some people's humor is spe-
    cialized but mine is universal.
There may well be a Mr. Shoemaker there who has divorced a
    beautiful rich virtuous wife for a debt-ridden hideous wife
    with a past,
And I'll say Shoemaker you should have stuck to your last;
And suppose somebody remarks that the hostess looks like a Titian
    I bring them up short,
I can answer, Looks like a Titian, eh? Do you mean beaut- or
    mort-?
And I'll go right on and say While we're on the subject of waltzes

[59]

I'd like to play a little Haydn for you, and I'll go to the piano
and grope at the keys and then look up impishly and speak,
And say I really don't know whether I'm playing Haydn or Haydn
seek.
Then after the laughter has died down I shall approach some Yale
man who has just returned from abroad whom I wish to em-
barrass
And I'll ask him how he enjoyed the Boola-Boolavards of Paris.
Oh, said Mr. Peachey gleefully, the days of my hapless social life
are over, I cannot help but be a wow,
I wish I was at the party right now.
But when he got to the party his hostess, who didn't look like a
Titian at all, she looked like a Dali, was quite sharp,
And sent him right back to his Park Avenue apartment to get his
harp,
And today he is living in the old family mansion in Indianapless
Where I'm sorry to say his social life is just as hapless.

THE SEA–GULL

Hark to the whimper of the sea-gull;
He weeps because he's not an ea-gull.
Suppose you were, you silly sea-gull,
Could you explain it to your she-gull?

THE BIG TENT UNDER THE ROOF

Noises new to sea and land
Issue from the circus band.
Each musician looks like mumps
From blowing umpah umpah umps.

Lovely girls in spangled pants
Ride on gilded elephants.
Elephants are useful friends,
They have handles on both ends;

They hold each other's hindmost handles
And flee from mice and Roman candles.
Their hearts are gold, their hides are emery,
And they have a most tenacious memory.

Notice also, girls and boys,
The circus horses' avoirdupois.
Far and wide the wily scouts
Seek these snow-white stylish stouts.
Calmer steeds were never found
Unattached to a merry-go-round.
Equestriennes prefer to jump
Onto horses pillow-plump.

Equestriennes will never ride
As other people do, astride.
They like to balance on one foot,
And wherever they get, they won't stay put.
They utter frequent whoops and yips,
And have the most amazing hips.
Pink seems to be their favorite color,
And very few things are very much duller.

Yet I for one am more than willing
That everything should be less thrilling.
My heart and lungs both bound and balk
When high-wire walkers start to walk.
They ought to perish, yet they don't;
Some fear they will, some fear they won't.

I lack the adjectives, verbs and nouns
To do full justice to the clowns.
Their hearts are constantly breaking, I hear,
And who am I to interfere?
I'd rather shake hands with Mr. Ringling
And tell him his circus is a beautiful thingling.

[61   ]

DRUSILLA

There was an old man of Schoharie
Who settled himself in a quarry.
And those who asked why
Got the candid reply,
"Today is the day of the soirée."

A GOOD PARENT'S GARDEN OF VISION

PART I: THE DREAM

In my bachelor days, no parent I,
My spirits fell as the weeks ran by,
And, tossing on my pallet, I dolefully thought
Of Time, the tri-motored Juggernaut,
Or paused at whiles amid my gardening
To listen for the sound of my arteries hardening.
But now I eagerly listen for
Senility knocking at the door.
Come dotage, envelop me in your arms,
Old age, I ween, has its special charms.
I'll camp awhile by Jordan's water
And enjoy being a nuisance to my daughter.
The loving offspring of Mr. N.
Won't trouble her head with raw young men,
Young men who cry she is lissome and flowery,
Young men who inquire about her dowery.
She'll make young men all keep their distances,
She'll listen to her father's reministances,
She'll fondly lay out his favorite slippers,
And when he wears arctics she'll zip his zippers,
She'll nogg his eggs and she'll toast his kippers,
And disparage the quips of the current quippers.
She'll light his pipe and she'll mix his drinks
And tell her father every thought she thinks,

And he in his way and she in hern
Will be merry as a melody by Mr. Kern.

And he in his way and she in hern
Will be merry as ashes in a funeral urn.
She'll discourage his pipe and she'll hide his drinks,
And conceal from her father every thought she thinks.
She'll make audible comments on his taste in togs,
She'll put his eggs in custards and not in noggs,
She'll object to the odor of kippering kippers,
She will laugh Ha Ha! at the current quippers,
She will leave the room when he dons his slippers,
When his buttons unbutton she will advocate zippers.
She'll see that parents keep their proper distances,
And she'll give young men a lot of reminiscances,
She'll look at her father like a beetle from the Bowery,
And ask why she hasn't a decent dowery,
And the only moments she'll be really merry
Will be pricing plots at the cemetery.

O pleasing daughter of Mr. N.,
His forebodings are happily beyond your ken,
And I gravely doubt that his querulous words
Retard the digestion of your whey and curds,
For children all choose their own sweet way —
Say Disobey, and they Datobey.
It's not that they're all in the train of Belial,
It's only their way of being filial.
Some grow up hideous, others beautiful,
Some ungrateful and others dutiful;
Why try to prognosticate which yours will be?
There's nothing to do but wait and see.
Only nasty parents lose their nerve

At the prospect of getting what they deserve.
With a conscience as clear as mountain water
I await the best from my loving daughter.

LITERARY REFLECTION

Philo Vance
Needs a kick in the pance.

TWO AND ONE ARE A PROBLEM

Dear Miss Dix, I am a young man of half-past thirty-seven.

My friends say I am not unattractive, though to be kind and true
is what I have always striven.

I am open-minded about beverages so long as they are grape,
brandy or malt,

And I am generous to practically any fault.

Well Miss Dix not to beat around the bush, there is a certain
someone who thinks I am pretty nice,

And I turn to you for advice.

You see, it started when I was away on the road

And returned to find a pair of lovebirds had taken up their resi-
dence in my abode.

Well I am not crazy about lovebirds, but I must say they looked
very sweet in their gilded cage,

And their friendship had reached an advanced stage,

And I had just forgiven her who of the feathered fiancés was the
donor of

When the children caught a lost lovebird in the yard that we
couldn't locate the owner of.

So then we had three, and it was no time for flippancy,

Because everybody knows that a lovebird without its own lovebird
to love will pine way and die of the discrepancy,

So we bought a fourth lovebird for the third lovebird and they sat
around very cozily beak to beak

And then the third lovebird that we had provided the fourth lovebird for to keep it from dying died at the end of the week,
So we were left with an odd lovebird and it was no time for flippancy,
Because a lovebird without its own lovebird to love will pine away
   and die of the discrepancy,
So we had to buy a fifth lovebird to console the fourth lovebird that
   we had bought to keep the third lovebird contented,
And now the fourth lovebird has lost its appetite, and Miss Dix, I
   am going demented.
I don't want to break any hearts, but I got to know where I'm at;
Must I keep on buying lovebirds, Miss Dix, or do you think it
   would be all right to buy a cat?

SONG OF THE OPEN ROAD

I think that I shall never see
A billboard lovely as a tree.
Indeed, unless the billboards fall
I'll never see a tree at all.

THUNDER OVER THE NURSERY

Listen to me, angel tot,
Whom I love an awful lot,
It will save a barrel of bother
If we understand each other.

Every time that I'm your herder
You think you get away with murder.
All right, infant, so you do,
But only because I want you to.

Baby's muscles are prodigious,
Baby's beautiful, not higious,

[65]

She can talk and walk and **run**
Like a daughter of a gun.

Well, you may be a genius, child,
And I a parent dull and mild;
In spite of which, and nevertheless,
I could lick you yet, I guess.

Forgive me, pet, if I am frank,
But truth is money in the bank;
I wish you to admire and love yourself,
But not to get too far above yourself.

When we race, you always win;
Baby, think before you grin.
It may occur to you, perhaps,
That Daddy's running under wraps.

When you hide behind the chair
And Daddy seeks you everywhere,
Behind the door, beneath the bed —
That's Daddy's heart, not Baby's head.

When I praise your speech in glee
And claim you talk as well as me,
That's the spirit, not the letter.
I know more words, and say them better.

In future, then, when I'm your herder,
Continue getting away with murder;
But know from him who murder endures,
It's his idea much more than yours.

THE CLEAN PLATTER

Some singers sing of ladies' eyes,
And some of ladies' lips,
Refined ones praise their ladylike ways,
And coarse ones hymn their hips.
The *Oxford Book of English Verse*
Is lush with lyrics tender;
A poet, I guess, is more or less
Preoccupied with gender.
Yet I, though custom call me crude,
Prefer to sing in praise of food.

Food,
Yes, food,
Just any old kind of food.
Pheasant is pleasant, of course,
And terrapin, too, is tasty,
Lobster I freely endorse,
In pâté or patty or pasty.
But there's nothing the matter with butter,
And nothing the matter with jam,
And the warmest of greetings I utter
To the ham and the yam and the clam.
For they're food,
All food,
And I think very highly of food.
Though I'm broody at times
When bothered by rhymes,
I brood
On food.

Some painters paint the sapphire sea,
And some the gathering storm.
Others portray young lambs at play,
But most, the female form.
'Twas trite in that primeval dawn

When painting got its start,
That a lady with her garments on
Is Life, but is she Art?
By undraped nymphs
I am not wooed;
I'd rather painters painted food.

Food,
Just food,
Just any old kind of food.
Go purloin a sirloin, my pet,
If you'd win a devotion incredible;
And asparagus tips vinaigrette,
Or anything else that is edible.
Bring salad or sausage or scrapple,
A berry or even a beet.
Bring an oyster, an egg, or an apple,
As long as it's something to eat.
If it's food,
It's food;
Never mind what kind of food.
When I ponder my mind
I consistently find
It is glued
On food.

THE DUCK

Behold the duck.
It does not cluck.
A cluck it lacks.
It quacks.
It is specially fond
Of a puddle or pond.
When it dines or sups,
It bottoms ups.

MR. ARTESIAN'S CONSCIENTIOUSNESS

Once there was a man named Mr. Artesian and his activity was
tremendous,

And he grudged every minute away from his desk because the im-
portance of his work was so stupendous;

And he had one object all sublime,

Which was to save simply oodles of time.

He figured that sleeping eight hours a night meant that if he lived
to be seventy-five he would have spent twenty-five years not
at his desk but in bed,

So he cut his slumber to six hours which meant he only lost eight-
een years and nine months instead,

And he figured that taking ten minutes for breakfast and twenty
minutes for luncheon and half an hour for dinner meant that
he spent three years, two months and fifteen days at the
table,

So that by subsisting solely on bouillon cubes which he swallowed
at his desk to save this entire period he was able,

And he figured that at ten minutes a day he spent a little over six
months and ten days shaving,

So he grew a beard, which gave him a considerable saving,

And you might think that now he might have been satisfied, but
no, he wore a thoughtful frown,

Because he figured that at two minutes a day he would spend
thirty-eight days and a few minutes in elevators just traveling up and down,

So as a final timesaving device he stepped out the window of his
office, which happened to be on the fiftieth floor,

And one of his partners asked "Has he vertigo?" and the other
glanced out and down and said "Oh no, only about ten feet
more."

THE LAMA

The one-l lama,
He's a priest.
The two-l llama,
He's a beast.
And I will bet
A silk pajama
There isn't any
Three-l lllama.*

GOODY FOR OUR SIDE AND YOUR
SIDE TOO

Foreigners are people somewhere else,
Natives are people at home;
If the place you're at is your habitat,
You're a foreigner, say in Rome.
But the scales of Justice balance true,
And tit leads into tat,
So the man who's at home when he stays in Rome
Is abroad when he's where you're at.

When we leave the limits of the land in which
Our birth certificates sat us,
It does not mean just a change of scene,
But also a change of status.
The Frenchman with his fetching beard,
The Scot with his kilt and sporran,
One moment he may a native be,
And the next may find him foreign.

There's many a difference quickly found
Between the different races,

* The author's attention has been called to a type of conflagration
known as the three-alarmer. Pooh.

[70]

But the only essential differential
Is living different places.
Yet such is the pride of prideful man,
From Austrians to Australians,
That wherever he is, he regards as his,
And the natives there, as aliens.

Oh, I'll be friends if you'll be friends,
The foreigner tells the native,
And we'll work together for our common ends
Like a preposition and a dative.
If our common ends seem mostly mine,
Why not, you ignorant foreigner?
And the native replies contrariwise;
And hence, my dears, the coroner.

So mind your manners when a native, please,
And doubly when you visit
And between us all a rapport may fall
Ecstatically exquisite.
One simple thought, if you have it pat,
Will eliminate the coroner:
You may be a native in your habitat,
But to foreigners you're just a foreigner.

THE PARENT

Children aren't happy with nothing to ignore,
And that's what parents were created for.

FAMILY COURT

One would be in less danger
From the wiles of the stranger
If one's own kin and kith
Were more fun to be with.

THE LIFE OF THE PARTY

Lily, there isn't a thing you lack,
Your effect is simply stunning.
But Lily, your gown is low in the back,
So conduct yourself with cunning.
Some of your charm is charm of face,
But some of your charm is spinal;
Losing your looks is no disgrace,
But losing your poise is final.
Ridicule's name is Legion,
So look to your dorsal region.

For Artie,
Old Artie,
The life of the party,
Is practically perfect tonight;
He's prettily, properly tight;
He's never appeared so bright.
Have you ever seen Artie
Enliven a party?
You've never seen Artie —
Why Lord love a duck!
At present old Artie is running amuck.
There's a wink in his eye
And a smile on his lips
For the matron he tickles,
The waiter he trips.
There's a rubber cigar,
And a smoking-room jest,
To melt the reserve
Of the clerical guest.
There's a pin for the man who stoops over,
And a little trained flea for Rover.
So Lily, beware of your back!
More daring than duller and older blades,

Artie is hot on the track.
I've noticed him eying your shoulder blades.
And maybe it's salad,
And maybe it's ice,
But I fear he has planned
Some amusing device,
For the laughter is slack
And he's taking it hard —
He's eying your back —
And Artie's a card —
He's forming a plan —
May I fetch you a shawl?
That inventive young man —
There is one in the hall.
Though your back is divine
In its natural state,
May I curtain your spine? —
Dear Heaven, I'm late!
Aren't you glad that you came to the party?
And weren't you amused by Artie?

Horace, the moment that you appeared,
I admired your manly beauty,
But I feel that a word about your beard
Is only my bounden duty.
Your tailor's craft is a dandy's dream,
Your suavity leaves me lyrical,
But escaping tonight with your self-esteem
Will require a minor miracle.
Fun is a gay deceiver,
So look to your kingly beaver.

For Artie,
Old Artie,
The life of the party,
Is hitting his stride tonight.

No bushel obscures his light.
He's knocking them left and right.
Have you ever seen Artie
Enliven a party?
You've never seen Artie —
My lad, you're in luck,
For Artie, old Artie, is running amuck.
At Artie's approach
Lesser wags droop.
Have you seen the tin roach
He drops in your soup?
Is a spoon in your pocket?
Or gum in your chair?
It's Artie, old Artie,
Who magicked them there.
And of those who complain, there's a rumor
That they're lacking in sense of humor.
So Horace, beware of your beard!
I scent some fantastic flubdubbery!
Old Artie has just disappeared
And I've noticed him eying your shrubbery.
And maybe it's syrup,
And maybe it's mice,
But I fear he has planned
Some amusing device.
His conceptions are weird,
And nothing is barred —
He was eying your beard —
And Artie's a card —
When Artie returns,
The fun will begin —
May I fetch you a bag
To put on your chin?
Just a small paper bag
To envelop the bait?
For Artie's a wag —

Sorry, Horace, I'm late!
Aren't you glad that you came to the party?
And weren't you amused by Artie?

THE GERM

A mighty creature is the germ,
Though smaller than the pachyderm.
His customary dwelling place
Is deep within the human race.
His childish pride he often pleases
By giving people strange diseases.
Do you, my poppet, feel infirm?
You probably contain a germ.

ONE THIRD OF A CALENDAR

In January everything freezes.
We have two children. Both are she'ses.
This is our January rule:
One girl in bed, and one in school.

In February the blizzard whirls.
We own a pair of little girls.
Blessings upon of each the head —
The one in school and the one in bed.

March is the month of cringe and bluster.
Each of our children has a sister.
They cling together like Hansel and Gretel,
With their noses glued to the benzoin kettle.

April is made of impetuous waters
And doctors looking down throats of daughters.
If we had a son too, and a thoroughbred,

We'd have a horse,
And a boy,
And two girls
In bed.

MORE ABOUT PEOPLE

When people aren't asking questions
They're making suggestions
And when they're not doing one of those
They're either looking over your shoulder or stepping on your toes
And then as if that weren't enough to annoy you
They employ you.
Anybody at leisure
Incurs everybody's displeasure.
It seems to be very irking
To people at work to see other people not working,
So they tell you that work is wonderful medicine,
Just look at Firestone and Ford and Edison,
And they lecture you till they're out of breath or something
And then if you don't succumb they starve you to death or some-
    thing.
All of which results in a nasty quirk:
That if you don't want to work you have to work to earn enough
    money so that you won't have to work.

THE COW

The cow is of the bovine ilk;
One end is moo, the other, milk.

LINES TO A THREE–NAME LADY

Mrs. Hattie Boomer Spink,
You puzzle me a lot.

Do you, I wonder, ever think?
And, if you do, of what?

Oh, solons bow like slender reeds
Beneath your firm resolve.
Your words I know, I know your deeds —
But whence do they evolve?

Do you employ a cerebrum,
And eke a cerebellum?
Or do you simply let 'em come,
With Gabriel at the hellum?

Your native mental processes
Imply some secret canker;
Instead of thoughts, antipathies;
Instead of reason, rancor.

The ripple in your skull that spreads
From some primeval pebble,
How quickly washes o'er the heads
Of prophet and of rebel!

You three-name women, Mrs. Spink,
You puzzle me a lot.
Do you, I wonder, ever think?
And if you do, of what?

When gossip first began to link
Your name with that of Mr. Spink,
O Hattie Boomer, did you think?
— And what's become of Mr. Spink?

LITTLE FEET

Oh, who would live in a silent house,
As still as a waltz left unwritten by Strauss,

As undisturbed as a virgin dewdrop,
And quiet enough to hear a shoe drop?
Who would dwell
In a vacuum cell,
In a home as mute as a clapperless bell?
Oh, a home as mute as a bell that's clapperless
Is forlorn as an Indian in Indianapolis.

Then ho! for the patter of little feet,
And the childish chatter of voices sweet,
For the ringing laughter and prancing capers
That soothe your ear as you read the papers,
For the trumpets that blow and the balls that bounce
As you struggle to balance your old accounts,
For the chubby arms that encircle your neck,
And the chubby behinds that your lap bedeck,
And sirens who save their wiliest wooing
For the critical spot in whatever you're doing.

Shakespeare's, I'm sure, was a silent house,
And that of Good King Wenceslaus,
And Napoleon's dwelling, and Alexander's,
And whoever's that wrote *The Dog of Flanders.*
Yes, Shelley and Keats
And other élites,
They missed the patter of little feets,
For he who sits and listens to pattering
Will never accomplish more than a smattering.

Then ho! for the patter of little feet!
Some find these footfalls doubly sweet,
Subjecting them to the twofold use
Of paternal pride and a good excuse.
You say, for instance, my modest chanteys
Are not so fine as Pope's or Dante's?
My deeds do not compare with those

Of Nelson, or Michelangelo's?
Well, my life is perpetual Children's Hour,
Or boy! would immortal genius flower!

GENEALOGICAL REFLECTION

No McTavish
Was ever lavish.

THE MIND OF PROFESSOR PRIMROSE

My story begins in the town of Cambridge, Mass.,
Home of the Harvard Business and Dental Schools,
And more or less the home of Harvard College.
Now, Harvard is a cultural institution,
Squandering many a dollar upon professors,
As a glance at a Harvard football team makes obvious;
Professors wise and prowling in search of wisdom,
And every mother's son of them absent-minded.
But the absentest mind belonged to Professor Primrose.
He had won a Nobel award and a Pulitzer Prize,
A Guggenheim and a leg on the Davis Cup,
But he couldn't remember to shave both sides of his face.
He discharged the dog and took the cook for an airing;
He frequently lit his hair and combed his cigar;
He set a trap for the baby and dandled the mice;
He wound up his key and opened the door with his watch;
He tipped his students and flunked the traffic policeman;
He fed the mosquitoes crumbs and slapped at the robins;
He always said his prayers when he entered the theater,
And left the church for a smoke between the acts;
He mixed the exterminator man a cocktail
And told his guests to go way, he had no bugs;
He rode the streets on a bicycle built for two,
And he never discovered he wasn't teaching at Yale.

At last one summer he kissed his crimson flannels
And packed his wife in camphor, and she complained.
She had always hated camphor, and she complained.
"My dear," she ordered, "these *contretemps* must cease;
You must bring this absent mind a little bit nearer;
You must tidy up that disorderly cerebellum;
You must write today and enroll in the Pelman Institute."
He embraced his pen and he took his wife in hand,
He wrinkled a stamp and thoughtfully licked his brow,
He wrote the letter and mailed it, and what do you know?
In a couple of days he disappeared from Cambridge.
"For heaven's sake, my husband has disappeared,"
Said Mrs. Primrose. "Now isn't that just like him?"
And she cut the meat and grocery orders in half,
And moved the chairs in the living room around,
And settled down to a little solid comfort.
She had a marvelous time for seven years,
At the end of which she took a train to Chicago.
She liked to go to Chicago once in a while
Because of a sister-in-law who lived in Cambridge.
Her eye was caught at Schenectady by the porter;
She noticed that he was brushing off a dime,
And trying to put the passenger in his pocket.
"Porter," she said, "aren't you Professor Primrose?
Aren't you my husband, the missing Professor Primrose?
And what did you learn at the Pelman Institute?"
"Good Lawd, Maria," the porter said, "good Lawd!
Did you say *Pelman*? Ah wrote to de *Pullman* folks!"

REFLECTION ON INGENUITY

Here's a good rule of thumb:
Too clever is dumb.

THE TURTLE

The turtle lives 'twixt plated decks
Which practically conceal its sex.
I think it clever of the turtle
In such a fix to be so fertile.

AFTER THE CHRISTENING

Come along, everybody, see the pretty baby,
Such a pretty baby ought to be adored.
Come along, everybody, come and bore the baby,
See the pretty baby, begging to be bored.

Hurry, hurry, Aunt Louise,
Silly names are sure to please.
Bother what the baby thinks!
Call her Kitchy-kitch and Binks,
Call her Wackywoo and Snookums,
Just ignore her dirty lookums,
Who than she is fairer game
For every kind of silly name?
Baby cannot answer back,
Or perhaps an aunt she'd lack.

Come along, everybody, isn't she a darling?
Such a little darling ought to be enjoyed.
Come along, everybody, let's annoy the baby,
Such a darling darling begs to be annoyed.

Goodness Gracious, Uncle George!
Home at last from Valley Forge?
Won't you try on her the whoops
That cheered the Continental troops?
Stand a little closer, please;
That will put her at her ease;

And babies find it hard to hear,
So place your mouth against her ear —
I guess she heard it, Uncle George;
I'm sure they did at Valley Forge.

Come along, everybody, see the little lady,
Isn't she adorable and kissable and pleasing?
Come along, everybody, come and tease the baby,
Here's a lady baby available for teasing!

Cousin Charles was always chummy;
He's about to poke her tummy.
Grandpa almost chokes on chuckles,
Tickling with his beard her knuckles;
All of Granny's muscles ache
From half an hour of patty-cake;
God-mamma with glee begins
A noisy count of baby's chins;
God-papa with humor glows
Playing piggie with her toes.
See the happy prideful parents,
Do they think of interference?
Certainly not, while baby gives
Such wholesome fun to relatives.

Up and at her, everybody, at the pretty baby,
Tell her she's a dumpling, tell her she's a dear.
Everybody knows the way to woo a baby —
Tickle her and pinch her and yodel in her ear.

ASIDE TO HUSBANDS

What do you do when you've wedded a girl all legal and lawful,
And she goes around saying she looks awful?
When she makes deprecatory remarks about her format,

And claims that her hair looks like a doormat?
When she swears that the complexion of which you are so fond
Looks like the bottom of a dried-up pond?
When she for whom your affection is not the least like Plato's
Compares her waist to a badly tied sack of potatoes?
Oh, who wouldn't rather be on a flimsy bridge with a hungry lion
    at one end and a hungry tiger at the other end and hungry
    crocodiles underneath
Than confronted by their dearest making remarks about her own
    appearance through clenched teeth?
Why won't they believe that the reason they find themselves the
    mother of your children is because you think of all the looks
    in the world, their looks are the nicest?
Why must we continue to be thus constantly ordealed and crisised?
I think it high time these hoity-toity ladies were made to realize
    that when they impugn their face and their ankles and their
    waist
They are thereby insultingly impugning their tasteful husbands'
    impeccable taste.

THE FISH

The fish, when he's exposed to air,
Displays no trace of *savoir-faire,*
But in the sea regains his balance
And exploits all his manly talents.
The chastest of the vertebrates,
He never even sees his mates,
But when they've finished, he appears
And O.K.'s all their bright ideas.

TELL IT TO THE ESKIMOS
or
TELL IT TO THE ESQUIMAUX

Jonathan Jukes is full of health,
And he doesn't care who knows it.
Others may exercise by stealth,
But he with a cry of *Prosit!*
Others put up with coated tongues,
And shoulders narrow and droopy;
Jonathan overinflates his lungs
With a thundering shout of Whoopee!
Jonathan's noise is healthy noise,
Jonathan's joys are healthy joys,
Jonathan shuns the primrose path,
And starts the day with an icy bath.

I might forgive the super-physique
Contained in the Jukes apparel;
The apple glowing in either cheek;
The chest like an oyster barrel;
The muscles that flow like a mountain stream
And the nose that needs no Kleenex,
The rigorous diet, the stern régime
Of arduous calistheenex;
I can pardon most of the healthy joys,
I can pardon most of the healthy noise,
But Heaven itself no pardon hath
For the man who boasts of an icy bath.

If the Missing Links were vigorous chaps
And their manly deeds were myriad,
Must civilization then relapse
Back to the glacial period?
Humanity learns at a fearful price;
Must the lessons all be lost?

Does the locomotive feed on ice?
Is the liner propelled by frost?

One constant truth mankind has found
Through fire and flood and slaughter:
The thing that makes the wheels go round
Is plenty of good hot water.
And therefore, therefore, Jonathan Jukes,
You deserve the harshest of harsh rebukes;
You and your frigid daily bath
Are blocking civilization's path.
You think of yourself as Spartan and spunky?
So, Jonathan, is the old brass monkey.

REFLECTION ON CAUTION

Affection is a noble quality;
It leads to generosity and jollity.
But it also leads to breach of promise
If you go around lavishing it on red-hot momise.

TURNS IN A WORM'S LANE

I've never bet on a so-called horse
That the horse didn't lose a leg.
I've never putted on a golfing course
But the ball behaved like an egg.
I've never possessed three royal kings
But somebody held three aces;
In short, I'm a lad whose presence brings
The joy to bankers' faces.

And everybody says, "What a splendid loser!"
Everybody says, "What a thoroughgoing sport!"
And I smile my smile like an amiable Duse,

[85]

I leer like a lawyer in the presence of a tort.
And I crack my lips,
And I grin my grin,
While someone else
Rakes my money in.
Yes, I smile a smile like the Mona Lisa,
Though my spirits droop like the Tower of Pisa.
Yes, I chortle like a military march by Sousa
And everybody says, "What a splendid loser!"

I'll buy a tome, an expensive tome,
On the art of double dealing,
And I'll wrap it up and I'll take it home,
While the bells of Hell are pealing.
I'll stealthily study the ebony arts
Of men like the great Houdini,
Till both in foreign and local parts
I'm known as a darned old meany.

And everyone will say, "What a nasty winner!"
And everyone will say, "What a dreadful sport!"
And they'll all stop inviting me to come to dinner,
For I used to be a dimple and I want to be a wart.
But I won't care,
And I'll win with a scowl,
Foul means or fair,
But preferably foul.

I'll jeer my victims every time I vanquish,
And if I lose I shall scream with anguish.
And people will say, "What a dreadful sport!"
And I'll say, "Phooie!" or something of the sort.

ELECTION DAY IS A HOLIDAY

People on whom I do not bother to dote
Are people who do not bother to vote.
Heaven forbid that they should ever be exempt
From contumely, obloquy and various kinds of contempt.
Some of them like Toscanini and some like Rudy Vallée,
But all of them take about as much interest in their right to ballot
    as their right to ballet.
They haven't voted since the heyday of Miss Russell (Lillian)
And excuse themselves by saying What's the difference of one vote
    in fifty million?
They have such refined and delicate palates
That they can discover no one worthy of their ballots,
And then when someone terrible gets elected
They say, There, that's just what I expected!
And they go around for four years spouting discontented criticisms
And contented witticisms,
And then when somebody to oppose the man they oppose gets
    nominated
They say Oh golly golly he's the kind of man I've always abomi-
    nated,
And they have discovered that if you don't take time out to go to
    the polls
You can manage very nicely to get through thirty-six holes.
Oh let us cover these clever people very conspicuously with loath-
    ing,
For they are un-citizens in citizens' clothing.
They attempt to justify their negligence
On the grounds that no candidate appeals to people of their in-
    tegligence,
But I am quite sure that if Abraham Lincoln (Rep.) ran against
    Thomas Jefferson (Dem.)
Neither man would be appealing enough to squeeze a vote out
    of them.

THE RHINOCEROS

The rhino is a homely beast,
For human eyes he's not a feast.
Farewell, farewell, you old rhinoceros,
I'll stare at something less prepoceros.

SEPTEMBER MORN

Oh, what in the world could be more fun
Than to have your holiday over and done;
Than to stand in a rural railway station
With fifty weeks till your next vacation!
Ah me, what jovial words are spoken
When you find the suitcase handle is broken.
You juggle golf bags and tennis rackets,
And ludicrous bulging paper packets,
You count your paraphernalia twice
From the children themselves to their milk and ice.
A whistle announces the train is coming;
You drop the children's portable plumbing;
The train draws up with a jerk and a wiggle
From the engineer's convulsive giggle,
And every window flattens the nose
Of a passenger reveling in your woes,
And the only car with an open door
Is a hundred yards behind or before.
Heave up the bags, the ice, the milk,
Heave up your struggling youthful ilk!
Heave up, heave up, and keep on heaving;
This good old train will soon be leaving.
The grim conductor, watch in hand,
Glares angrily on your hapless band.
Oh when was order e'er restored
By disgusted cries of All aboard?

This luggage on the platform piled
May well conceal a favorite child.
Conductor, cease your cry disgusted;
Distracted parents can't be trusted,
In times of stress they have been known
To ship their offspring off alone;
Not unprotected, not at large,
But in the kind conductor's charge.
Farewell, farewell to the sand and foam,
You are getting yourself and your family home.
Oh, I think there is no such capital fun
But having your teeth out one by one.

FROM A MANHATTAN TOMB

I know that a little verse is a versicle but I don't know if a little
    phrase is a phrasicle

But I do know that at the moment I feel too too alas and alacka-
    daisicle.

What though around me is the hustle and bustle of a great city at
    its labors?

What though I am hemmed in by the most industrious and ingen-
    ious kind of neighbors?

What though young people are joining forever or parting forever
    with each tick of the clock?

What though Mr. Belloc admires Mr. Chesterton or Mr. Chester-
    ton admires Mr. Belloc?

What though to produce the Sunday papers thousands of square
    miles of Canada are deforested?

What though in an attempt to amuse the public thousands of
    writers and actors and things are utterly exhorested?

What though young humans are getting born and old humans are
    getting deceased and middle-aged humans are getting used
    to it?

What though a Bronxville husband has discovered that he can put
    the baby to sleep by reading Proust to it?

[89   ]

All these things may be of great moment to those who are con-
cerned with them in any way,
But how are they going to help me to get through the day?
For I have had to eat luncheon while I was still sorry I had eaten
breakfast and I shall have to eat dinner while I am still sorry
I ate luncheon
And my spirit has been put through the third degree and thrown
into a very dark dank dismal dungeon.
Why do people insist on bringing me anecdotes and allegories and
alcohol and food?
Why won't they just let me sit and brood?
Why does the population swirl around me with vivacious violence
When all I want to do is sit and suffer in siolence?
Everybody I see tries to cheer me up
And I wish they would stop.

REFLECTION ON BABIES

A bit of talcum
Is always walcum.

EPSTEIN, SPARE THAT YULE LOG!

When I was but a boy,
'Twas my once-a-yearly joy
To arise of a Yuletide morning,
And eagerly behold
The crimson and the gold
Of the messages the mantelpiece adorning.
There were angels, there were squires,
There were steeples, there were spires,
There were villagers, and mistletoe and holly,
There were cozy English inns
With the snow around their chins,

And I innocently thought them rather jolly.
I blush for me, but by your leave,
I'm afraid that I am still naïve.

Oh, give me an old-fashioned Christmas card,
With mistletoe galore, and holly by the yard,
With galumptious greens and gorgeous scarlets,
With crackling logs and apple-cheeked varlets,
With horses prancing down a frosty road,
And a stagecoach laden with a festive load,
And the light from the wayside windows streaming,
And a white moon rising and one star gleaming.

Departed is the time
Of Christmases sublime;
My soprano is now a mezzo-basso;
And the mantelpiece contains
The angular remains
Of a later representative Picasso.
There are circles, there are dots,
There are corners, there are spots,
There are modernistic snapshots of the city;
Or, when the artist lags,
They are livened up with gags.
You must choose between the arty and the witty.
I blush for me, but I must say
I wish you'd take them all away.

Oh, give me an old-fashioned Christmas card,
With hostlers hostling in an old inn yard,
With church bells chiming their silver notes,
And jolly red squires in their jolly red coats,
And a good fat goose by the fire that dangles,
And a few more angels and a few less angles.
Turn backward, Time, to please this bard,
And give me an old-fashioned Christmas card.

BIRTH COMES TO THE ARCHBISHOP

Ministers
Don't like bar sinisters.
They consider that sort of irregularity
As the height of vulgarity
And go around making remarks
About the need for patrolling the beaches and parks.
They hate to see any deadlock
Between sin and wedlock
And get very nervous
When people omit the marriage service.
They regard as villains
Owners of unauthorized chillains,
A point of view
Which of course doesn't embarrass me or you
But makes things very inconvenient
For many really quite nice girls who may have been just a bit
    lenient.

So although none of us is in danger
Of the arrival of an inexplicable little stranger
Still I think we ought to join with a lot of others
And wish the best of luck to the nation's unmarried mothers.

SOME OF MY BEST FRIENDS ARE CHILDREN

Ichneumons are fond of little ichneumons,
And lions of little lions,
But I am not fond of little humans;
I do not believe in scions.

Of course there's always our child,
But our child is different,
Our child appeals

[92]

To the cultivated mind.
Ours is a lady;
Boys are odoriferant;
Ladies are the sweetness;
Boys are the rind.

Whenever whimsy collides with whimsy
As parents compare their cherubs,
At the slightest excuse, however flimsy,
I fold my tent like the Arabs.

Of course there's always our child,
But our child is charminger,
Our child's eyes
Are a special kind of blue;
Our child's smile
Is quite a lot disarminger;
Our child's tooth
Is very nearly through.

Mankind, I consider, attained its zenith
The day it achieved the adult;
When the conversation to infants leaneth,
My horse is bridled and saddult.

Of course there's always our child,
But our child is wittier;
Our child's noises
Are the nicest kind of noise;
She has no beard
Like Tennyson or Whittier;
But Tennyson and Whittier
Began as little boys.

The Politician, the Parent, the Preacher,
Were each of them once a kiddie.

The child is indeed a talented creature.
Did I want one? Oh, heaven forbidde!

But now there's always our child,
And our child's adorable.
Our child's an angel
Fairer than the flowers;
Our child fascinates
One who's rather borable;
And incidentally,
Our child is ours.

OLD MEN

People expect old men to die,
They do not really mourn old men.
Old men are different. People look
At them with eyes that wonder when . . .
People watch with unshocked eyes;
But the old men know when an old man dies.

A DRINK WITH SOMETHING IN IT

There is something about a Martini,
A tingle remarkably pleasant;
A yellow, a mellow Martini;
I wish that I had one at present.
There is something about a Martini,
Ere the dining and dancing begin,
And to tell you the truth,
It is not the vermouth —
I think that perhaps it's the gin.

There is something about an old-fashioned
That kindles a cardiac glow;
It is soothing and soft and impassioned

[94]

As a lyric by Swinburne or Poe.
There is something about an old-fashioned
When dusk has enveloped the sky,
And it may be the ice,
Or the pineapple slice,
But I strongly suspect it's the rye.

There is something about a mint julep.
It is nectar imbibed in a dream,
As fresh as the bud of the tulip,
As cool as the bed of the stream.
There is something about a mint julep,
A fragrance beloved by the lucky.
And perhaps it's the tint
Of the frost and the mint,
But I think it was born in Kentucky.

There is something they put in a highball
That awakens the torpidest brain,
That kindles a spark in the eyeball,
Gliding singing through vein after vein.
There is something they put in a highball
Which you'll notice one day, if you watch;
And it may be the soda,
But judged by the odor,
I rather believe it's the Scotch.

Then here's to the heartening wassail,
Wherever good fellows are found;
Be its master instead of its vassal,
And order the glasses around.
For there's something they put in the wassail
That prevents it from tasting like wicker;
Since it's not tapioca,
Or mustard, or mocha,
I'm forced to conclude it's the liquor.

WATCHMAN, WHAT OF THE FIRST FIRST LADY?

Everybody can tell you the date of George Washington's birth,
But who knows the date on which Mrs. George Washington first
    appeared on earth?
Isn't there any justice
For the former Mrs. Custis?
It's a disgrace to every United State
That we don't know more about our first president's only mate.
We all know a lot of stories about the wife of King Arthur
But you never hear any about Martha.
And we have all read a lot of romantic tales about Catherine the
    Great,
But nobody even writes them about Washington's mate.
And we have all seen Katharine Cornell, or was it Helen Hayes
    or Ethel Barrymore,
Impersonate Cleopatra, who wasn't even anybody's real wife but
    nothing more or less than a promiscuous un-American parry-
    more,
But has anybody done anything about the mistress of the nation's
    whitest house?
No, and yet but for her the nation would be the child of a man
    without a spouse.

CHILDREN'S PARTY

May I join you in the doghouse, Rover?
I wish to retire till the party's over.
Since three o'clock I've done my best
To entertain each tiny guest;
My conscience now I've left behind me,
And if they want me, let them find me.
I blew their bubbles, I sailed their boats,
I kept them from each other's throats.
I told them tales of magic lands,

I took them out to wash their hands.
I sorted their rubbers and tied their laces,
I wiped their noses and dried their faces.
Of similarity there's lots
'Twixt tiny tots and Hottentots.
I've earned repose to heal the ravages
Of these angelic-looking savages.
Oh, progeny playing by itself
Is a lonely fascinating elf,
But progeny in roistering batches
Would drive St. Francis from here to Natchez.
Shunned are the games a parent proposes;
They prefer to squirt each other with hoses,
Their playmates are their natural foemen
And they like to poke each other's abdomen.
Their joy needs another's woe to cushion it;
Say a puddle, and somebody littler to push in it.
They observe with glee the ballistic results
Of ice cream with spoons for catapults,
And inform the assembly with tears and glares
That everyone's presents are better than theirs.
Oh, little women and little men,
Someday I hope to love you again,
But not till after the party's over,
So give me the key to the doghouse, Rover.

THE PANTHER

The panther is like a leopard,
Except it hasn't been peppered.
Should you behold a panther crouch,
Prepare to say Ouch.
Better yet, if called by a panther,
Don't anther.

THE VERY UNCLUBBABLE MAN

I observe, as I hold my lonely course,
That nothing exists without a source.
Thus, oaks from acorns, lions from cubs,
And health and wealth from the proper clubs.
There are yacht clubs, golf clubs, clubs for luncheon,
Clubs for flowing bowl and puncheon,
Clubs for dancing, clubs for gambling,
Clubs for sociable Sunday ambling,
Clubs for imbibing literature,
And clubs for keeping the cinema pure,
Clubs for friendship, clubs for snobbery,
Clubs for smooth political jobbery.
As civilization onward reels,
It's clubs that grease the speeding wheels.

Alas!

Oh, everybody belongs to something,
But I don't belong to anything;
No, I don't belong to anything, any more than the miller of Dee,
And everything seems to belong
To people who belong to something,
But I don't belong to anything,
So nothing belongs to me.

Racquet, Knickerbocker, Union League,
Shriners parading without fatigue,
Oddfellows, Red Men, Woodmen of the World,
Solvent Moose and Elks dew-pearled,
Tammany tigers, Temperance doves,
Groups of various hates and loves,
Success is the thing they all have an air of,
Theirs are the summonses taken care of,
Theirs are the incomes but not the taxes,

Theirs are the sharpest, best-ground axes;
Millions of members of millions of bands,
Greeting fellow members with helping hands;
Good fellows all in incorporated hordes,
Prosperity is what they are moving towards.

Alas!

Oh, everybody belongs to something,
But I don't belong to anything;
Yes, I belong to nothing at all, from Kiwanis to the R.F.C.,
And everything definitely belongs
To people who belong to lots of things,
But I don't belong to anything,
So nothing belongs to me.

PEDIATRIC REFLECTION

Many an infant that screams like a calliope
Could be soothed by a little attention to its diope.

GOOD–BY, OLD YEAR, YOU OAF
or
WHY DON'T THEY PAY THE BONUS?

Many of the three hundred and sixty-five days of the year are fol-
lowed by dreadful nights but one night is by far, oh yes, by
far the worst,
And that, my friends, is the night of December the thirty-first.
Man can never get it through his head that he is born to be not a
creditor but a debtor;
Man always thinks the annual thought that just because last year
was terrible next year is bound to be better.
Man is a victim of dope
In the incurable form of hope;
Man is a blemishless Pollyanna,

And is convinced that the advent of every New Year will place him
    in possession of a bumper crop of manna.
Therefore Man fills himself up with a lot of joie de vivre
And goes out to celebrate New Year's Ivre;
Therefore millions of respectable citizens who just a week before
    have been perfectly happy to sit at home and be cozily Christ-
    mas carolized
Consider it a point of honor to go out on the town and get them-
    selves paralyzed;
Therefore the whistles blow toot toot and the bells ring ding ding
    and the confetti goes confetti confetti at midnight on the
    thirty-first of December,
And on January first the world is full of people who either can't
    and wish they could, or can and wish they couldn't remem-
    ber.
They never seem to learn from experience;
They keep on doing it year after year from the time they are puling
    infants till they are doddering octogenerience.
My goodness, if there's anything in heredity and environment
How can people expect the newborn year to manifest any culture
    or refironment?
Every New Year is the direct descendant, isn't it, of a long line of
    proven criminals?
And you can't turn it into a philanthropist by welcoming it with
    cocktails and champagne any more successfully than with
    prayer books and hyminals.
Every new year is a country as barren as the old one, and it's no use
    trying to forage it;
Every new year is incorrigible; then all I can say is for Heaven's
    sakes, why go out of your way to incorrage it?

A CAROL FOR CHILDREN

God rest you, merry Innocents,
Let nothing you dismay,

Let nothing wound an eager heart
Upon this Christmas day.

Yours be the genial holly wreaths,
The stockings and the tree;
An aged world to you bequeaths
Its own forgotten glee.

Soon, soon enough come crueler gifts,
The anger and the tears;
Between you now there sparsely drifts
A handful yet of years.

Oh, dimly, dimly glows the star
Through the electric throng;
The bidding in temple and bazaar
Drowns out the silver song.

The ancient altars smoke afresh,
The ancient idols stir;
Faint in the reek of burning flesh
Sink frankincense and myrrh.

Gaspar, Balthazar, Melchior!
Where are your offerings now?
What greetings to the Prince of War,
His darkly branded brow?

Two ultimate laws alone we know,
The ledger and the sword —
So far away, so long ago,
We lost the infant Lord.

Only the children clasp his hand;
His voice speaks low to them,
And still for them the shining **band**
Wings over Bethlehem.

God rest you, merry Innocents,
While innocence endures.
A sweeter Christmas than we to ours
May you bequeath to yours.

SONG FOR A TEMPERATURE OF A
HUNDRED AND ONE

Of all God's creatures give me man
For impractical uniqueness,
He's hardly tenth when it comes to strenth,
But he leads the field in weakness.
Distemper suits the ailing dog,
The chicken's content with pip,
But the human race, which sets the pace,
Takes nothing less than Grippe.

THEN, hey for the grippe, for the goodly la grippe!
In dogs it's distemper, in chickens it's pip;
But the lords of creation insist at the least
On the germ that distinguishes man from the beast.

The mule with mange is satisfied,
They tell me in the South;
And the best-bred cows will drowse and browse,
Content with hoof-and-mouth;
Bubonic cheers the humble rat
As he stealthily leaves the ship;
When the horse gets botts he thinks it's lots,
But people hold out for grippe.

THEN, hey for the grippe, for the goodly la grippe,
For the frog in the throat and the chap on the lip;
For the ice on the feet and the fire on the brow,
And the bronchial tubes that moo like a cow.

And hey for the ache in the back of the legs,
And the diet of consommé, water and eggs,
For the mustard that sits on your chest like a cactus,
For the doctor you're kindly providing with practus;
And hey for the pants of which you're so fond,
And the first happy day they're allowed to be donned;
For the first day at work, all bundled in wraps,
And last but not least, for the splendid relapse.
So let man meet his Maker, a smile on his lip,
Singing hey, double hey, for the goodly la grippe.

WHAT'S THE USE?

Sure, deck your lower limbs in pants;
Yours are the limbs, my sweeting.
You look divine as you advance —
Have you seen yourself retreating?

I NEVER EVEN SUGGESTED IT

I know lots of men who are in love and lots of men who are
married and lots of men who are both,
And to fall out with their loved ones is what all of them are most
loth.
They are conciliatory at every opportunity,
Because all they want is serenity and a certain amount of impunity.
Yes, many the swain who has finally admitted that the earth is flat
Simply to sidestep a spat,
Many the masculine Positively or Absolutely which has been di-
luted to an If
Simply to avert a tiff,
Many the two-fisted executive whose domestic conversation is lim-
ited to a tactfully interpolated Yes,
And then he is amazed to find that he is being raked backwards
over a bed of coals nevertheless.

These misguided fellows are under the impression that it takes two
    to make a quarrel, that you can sidestep a crisis by nonag-
    gression and nonresistance,
Instead of removing yourself to a discreet distance.
Passivity can be a provoking *modus operandi;*
Consider the Empire and Gandhi.
Silence is golden, but sometimes invisibility is golder,
Because loved ones may not be able to make bricks without straw
    but often they don't need any straw to manufacture a bone
    to pick or blood in their eye or a chip for their soft white
    shoulder.
It is my duty, gentlemen, to inform you that women are dictators
    all, and I recommend to you this moral:
In real life it takes only one to make a quarrel.

THE KITTEN

The trouble with a kitten is
THAT
Eventually it becomes a
CAT.

DON'T GUESS, LET ME TELL YOU

Personally I don't care whether a detective-story writer was edu-
    cated in night school or day school
So long as they don't belong to the H.I.B.K. school.
The H.I.B.K. being a device to which too many detective-story
    writers are prone,
Namely the Had I But Known.
Sometimes it is the Had I But Known what grim secret lurked be-
    hind that smiling exterior I would never have set foot within
    the door,
Sometimes the Had I But Known then what I know now I could
    have saved at least three lives by revealing to the Inspector

the conversation I heard through that fortuitous hole in the floor.

Had-I-But-Known narrators are the ones who hear a stealthy creak at midnight in the tower where the body lies, and, instead of locking their door or arousing the drowsy policeman posted outside their room, sneak off by themselves to the tower and suddenly they hear a breath exhaled behind them,

And they have no time to scream, they know nothing else till the men from the D.A.'s office come in next morning and find them.

Had I But Known-ers are quick to assume the prerogatives of the Deity,

For they will suppress evidence that doesn't suit their theories with appalling spontaneity,

And when the killer is finally trapped into a confession by some elaborate device of the Had I But Known-er some hundred pages later than if they hadn't held their knowledge aloof,

Why they say Why Inspector I knew all along it was he but I couldn't tell you, you would have laughed at me unless I had absolute proof.

Would you like a nice detective story for your library which I am sorry to say I didn't rent but owns?

I wouldn't have bought it had I but known it was impregnated with Had I But Knowns.

THE CARIBOU

Among the forests of the North,
The caribou walks back and forth.
The North is full of antlered game,
But none so pervious to fame.
For sportsmen on a sporting quest,
The caribou leads all the rest.
I hardly dare to tell you, madam,
I call him Caribou Ben Adhem.

PLEASE LEAVE FATHER ALONE

Mother's Day is a very fine day,
And mothers are very fine people,
And the human race by them is crowned
As the church is crowned by the steeple.
We often refer to mother love;
To mother hate, less often;
To fathers we hardly refer at all,
But once a year we soften.

It's Father's Day, it's Father's Day,
The eager mothers cry.
And what of that? And what of that?
The fathers make reply.
Well, here's a collar, and here's a stud,
The mothers murmur low,
And fathers avoid each other's glance,
Meaning, I told you so.

Oh, Mother's Day is a very fine day,
And not alone for mothers.
The florist finds it to his taste,
And so do a lot of others.
The candy people jump for joy,
The jeweller rubs his hands,
And the new coupé is shining proof
That Father understands.

It's Mother's Day, it's Mother's Day,
The eager fathers cry,
And, Red-hot diggety ziggety dog,
The mothers make reply.
Well, here's a wrap of sable fur,
The fathers murmur low,

And mothers catch each other's glance,
Meaning, I told you so.

Oh, Father's Day is a dreadful day,
And therefore fathers dread it;
For better a cycle of calm neglect
Than a day of grudging credit.
Oh why not leave the fathers be?
Their point of view is stoic;
So let them lurk in their niche in life,
Essential but not heroic.

LEGAL REFLECTION

The postal authorities of the United States of America
Frown on Curiosa, Erotica and Esoterica,
Which is a break, I guess,
For stockholders of the American Railway Express.

WHAT'S THE MATTER, HAVEN'T YOU GOT
ANY SENSE OF HUMOR?

There is at least one thing I would less rather have in the neighborhood than a gangster,
And that one thing is a practical prankster.
I feel that we should differ more sharply than Montagues and Capulets or York and Lancaster,
Me and a practical prancaster.
If there is a concentration camp in limbo, that is the spot for which I nominate them,
Not because I don't like them, but simply because I abominate them.
The born practical prankster starts out in early youth by offering people a chair,
And when they sit down it isn't there,

And he is delighted and proceeds to more complicated wheezes,
Such as ten cent X-rays to see through people's clothes with and
     powders to give them itches and sneezes,
And his boutonnière is something that people get squirted in the
     eye out of,
And their beds are what he makes apple pie out of.
Then as he matures he widens his scope,
And he is no longer content to present people with exploding ci-
     gars and chocolate creams with centers of soap.
I have recently read with complete satisfaction of a practical prank-
     ster two of whose friends had just been married,
Which was of course in itself simply a challenge to be harried,
And it was a challenge he was eager to meet,
And he went to the roof of their hotel and tied a rope around his
     waist and a colleague lowered him to where he could clash
     a pair of cymbals outside the window of the nuptial suite,
And he weighed two hundred and eighty pounds and the rope
     broke,
And that to my mind is the perfect practical joke.

LUCY LAKE

Lawsamassy, for heaven's sake!
Have you never heard of Lucy Lake?
Lucy is fluffy and fair and cosy,
Lucy is like a budding posy.
Lucy speaks with a tiny lisp,
Lucy's mind is a will-o'-the-wisp.
Lucy is just as meek as a mouse,
Lucy lives in a darling house,
With a darling garden and darling fence,
And a darling faith in the future tense.
A load of hay, or a crescent moon,
And she knows that things will be better soon.
Lucy resigns herself to sorrow

In building character for tomorrow.
Lucy tells us to carry on,
It's always darkest before the dawn.
A visit to Lucy's bucks you up,
Helps you swallow the bitterest cup.
Lucy Lake is meek as a mouse.
Let's go over to Lucy's house,
And let's lynch Lucy!

THE OYSTER

The oyster's a confusing suitor:
It's masc., and fem., and even neuter.
At times it wonders, may what come,
Am I husband, wife, or chum.

HOW LONG HAS THIS BEEN GOING ON? OH, QUITE LONG

Some people think that they can beat three two's with a pair of
     aces,
And other people think they can wind up ahead of the races,
And lest we forget,
The people who think they can wind up ahead of the races are ev-
     erybody who has ever won a bet.
Yes, when you first get back five-sixty for two, oh what a rosy-toed
     future before you looms,
But actually your doom is sealed by whoever it is that goes around
     sealing people's dooms,
And you are lost forever
Because you think you won not because you were lucky but be-
     cause you were clever.
You think the race ended as it did, not because you hoped it,
But because you doped it,

And from then on you withdraw your savings from the bank in
　　ever-waxing wads
Because you are convinced that having figured out one winner you
　　can figure out many other winners at even more impressive
　　odds,
And pretty soon overdrawing your account or not betting at all is
　　the dilemma which you are betwixt
And certainly you're not going to not bet at all because you are sure
　　you will eventually wind up ahead because the only reason
　　the races haven't run true to form, by which you mean your
　　form, is because they have been fixed,
So all you need to be a heavy gainer
Is to bet on one honest race or make friends with one dishonest
　　trainer.
And I don't know for which this situation is worse,
Your character or your purse.
I don't say that race tracks are centers of sin,
I only say that they are only safe to go to as long as you fail to be-
　　gin to win.

A WATCHED EXAMPLE NEVER BOILS

The weather is so very mild
That some would call it warm.
Good gracious, aren't we lucky, child?
Here comes a thunderstorm.

The sky is now indelible ink,
The branches reft asunder;
But you and I, we do not shrink;
We love the lovely thunder.

The garden is a raging sea,
The hurricane is snarling;
Oh happy you and happy me!
Isn't the lightning darling?

Fear not the thunder, little one.
It's weather, simply weather;
It's friendly giants full of fun
Clapping their hands together.

I hope of lightning our supply
Will never be exhausted;
You know it's lanterns in the sky
For angels who are losted.

We love the kindly wind and hail,
The jolly thunderbolt,
We watch in glee the fairy trail
Of ampere, watt, and volt.

Oh, than to enjoy a storm like this
There's nothing I would rather.
Don't dive beneath the blankets, Miss!
Or else leave room for Father.

THE WAPITI

There goes the Wapiti,
Hippety-hoppity!

HEARTS AND FLOWERS
or
WHAT I KNOW ABOUT BOLIVAR BLACK

I do not care for Bolivar Black,
And I think that I never shall;
A shiver goes rippling up my back
When Bolivar calls me Pal.
I am commonly captain of my soul,

But my head is bowed and bloody,
No joy can I find in human kind,
When Bolivar calls me Buddy.

His smile is broad as the Golden West
From Olympia, Wash., to Texas,
And a heart as warm as a desert storm
Sizzles his solar plexus.
Bolivar's love for his fellow man
Is deep as the rolling ocean,
And the favorite scent of the Orient
Enlivens his shaving lotion.

He's wild about kiddies, people say,
And devoted to widows and orphans;
When he speaks as he should of motherhood
His sonorous accent sorftens.
He scatters crumbs for our feathered friends,
He is kind to kittens and puppies,
And his salary check is at the beck
Of a prodigal tribe of guppies.

The beggars gamble among themselves
For the right to beg of Bolivar;
And the yeggmen go with a tale of woe
Instead of a big revolivar.
He lavishes fruit on his travelling friends,
And flowers upon the ill;
When a dozen dine and order wine,
Why, Bolivar grabs the bill.

His virtues bloom like the buds in May,
His faults, I believe, are few,
But whether you find him gold or clay
Depends on the point of view.
So you may care for Bolivar Black,

And his generous actions quote;
My praise is checked when I recollect
My name on Bolivar's note.

SPRING COMES TO MURRAY HILL

I sit in an office at 244 Madison Avenue,
And say to myself You have a responsible job, havenue?
Why then do you fritter away your time on this doggerel?
If you have a sore throat you can cure it by using a good goggeral,
If you have a sore foot you can get it fixed by a chiropodist,
And you can get your original sin removed by St. John the Bopo-
dist,
Why then should this flocculent lassitude be incurable?
Kansas City, Kansas, proves that even Kansas City needn't always
be Missourible.
Up up my soul! This inaction is abominable.
Perhaps it is the result of disturbances abdominable.
The pilgrims settled Massachusetts in 1620 when they landed on
a stone hummock.
Maybe if they were here now they would settle my stomach.
Oh, if I only had the wings of a bird
Instead of being confined on Madison Avenue I could soar in a
jiffy to Second or Third.

NOTHING BUT NATURE

Ha ha ha! the sun is shining!
Yo ho ho! the sky is blue!
See the earth in peace reclining!
See the ocean reclining, too!
Tra la la! the birds are chirruping!
Fields are green and flowers are gay!
Maples swell with sap a-syruping!
Nature is spreading herself today!

[113]

Well, let's go out and trample on a violet,
Let's steal candy from a curly-headed tot,
Take a wrong number and deliberately dial it,
Let's plant thistles under squatters when they squat,
Let's throw pepper on the robins on their nests,
Let's tell Altman's we prefer to buy at Best's,
Let's cry Boo! at golfers as they putt,
Let's open windows that people want shut,
Let's step on somebody's nice white shoes,
Let's join a club and not pay dues,
Let's send bills and let's raise rents,
Let's put mosquitoes in campers' tents,
Let's teach Nature not to spread so free
On a day when my love is off of me.

Yah yah yah! the rain is raining!
Zut alors! the wild waves boil!
Hear the homeless wind complaining!
Watch the shrubbery bite the soil!
Nya nya nya! come sleet, come icicles!
The world is a welter of freezing spray!
Pity the acrobats on high-wheeled bicycles!
Nature is having a tantrum today!

Well, let's buy lace from a visiting Armenian,
Let's give a beggar a nickel for a bath,
Let's praise Homer to a Homer-sick Athenian,
Let's spread sunbeams all along the path,
Let's go listen to the neighborhood bores,
Let's help mothers through revolving doors,
Let's go to church and fill the plate with money,
Let's tell the minister the sermon was a honey,
Let's teach whales to avoid harpooners,
Let's be kind to congressmen and crooners,
Let's make hunters make friends with moose,
Let's buy songbirds and turn them loose,

And that will teach Nature to tantrum when
My love is speaking to me again.

TWO SONGS FOR A BOSS NAMED
MR. LONGWELL

I

Put it there, Mr. Longwell, put it there!
You're a bear, Mr. Longwell, you're a bear!
It's our verdict
That your service is perfect.
You're a regular American crusader
And you'll lick old H. L. Mencken's Armada.
You know life isn't all a picnic
But it hasn't made you a cynic.
From first to last
As the banner goes past
We'll sing our favorite air.
Our choice always narrows
To the man you can't embarrass,
So put it there, Mr. Longwell, put it there!

II

L for loyalty to his grand old firm,
O for his eyes of blue,
N for his ideals and his spirit of co-operation,
G for his influence on me and you.
W for his ability to collect and co-ordinate facts,
E–L–L for the laborsaving card-index system he put through.
Put them all together, they spell LONGWELL,
Which is about what you might expect them to do.

A WARNING TO WIVES

"The outcome of the trial is another warning that if you must kill someone, you should spare the person possessing life insurance. . . . Figures
are available to show that convictions are much more common in 'insurance
murders' than in other types of homicides." — BOSTON HERALD.

Speak gently to your husband, ma'am,
And encourage all his sneezes;
That nasty cough may carry him off,
If exposed to draughts and breezes.
And suppose the scoundrel lingers on,
And insists on being cured;
Well, it isn't a sin if a girl steps in —
Unless the brute's insured.

Oh, the selfishness of men, welladay, welladay!
Oh the sissies, oh the softies, oh the mice!
Egotistically they strive to keep themselves alive,
And insurance is their scurviest device.
Insurance!
It's insurance
That tries a lady's temper past endurance.
Yet it's safer, on the whole,
To practice self-control
If there's apt to be a question of insurance.

Arsenic soup is a dainty soup,
But not if he's paid his premium.
Or a .32 in a pinch will do,
If you're bored with the epithalemium.
But to make acquittal doubly sure —
No maybes, no perhapses —
You'll do well to wait to expunge your mate
Until his policy lapses.

The hypocrisy of men, welladay, welladay!
Whited sepulchers are much to be preferred.

They claim it's for their wives they evaluate their lives,
But it's fatal if you take them at their word.
Insurance!
Oh, insurance!
What holds potential widows fast in durance?
Not the Adlers and the Freuds,
But the Mutuals and Lloyds,
And the jury's evil mind about insurance.

SONG TO BE SUNG BY THE FATHER OF
INFANT FEMALE CHILDREN

My heart leaps up when I behold
A rainbow in the sky;
Contrariwise, my blood runs cold
When little boys go by.
For little boys as little boys,
No special hate I carry,
But now and then they grow to men,
And when they do, they marry.
No matter how they tarry,
Eventually they marry.
And, swine among the pearls,
They marry little girls.

Oh, somewhere, somewhere, an infant plays,
With parents who feed and clothe him.
Their lips are sticky with pride and praise,
But I have begun to loathe him.
Yes, I loathe with a loathing shameless
This child who to me is nameless.
This bachelor child in his carriage
Gives never a thought to marriage,
But a person can hardly say knife
Before he will hunt him a wife.

I never see an infant (male),
A-sleeping in the sun,
Without I turn a trifle pale
And think Is *he* the one?
Oh, first he'll want to crop his curls,
And then he'll want a pony,
And then he'll think of pretty girls
And holy matrimony.
He'll put away his pony,
And sigh for matrimony.
A cat without a mouse
Is he without a spouse.

Oh, somewhere he bubbles bubbles of milk,
And quietly sucks his thumbs.
His cheeks are roses painted on silk,
And his teeth are tucked in his gums.
But alas, the teeth will begin to grow,
And the bubbles will cease to bubble;
Given a score of years or so,
The roses will turn to stubble.
He'll sell a bond, or he'll write a book,
And his eyes will get that acquisitive look,
And raging and ravenous for the kill,
He'll boldly ask for the hand of Jill.
This infant whose middle
Is diapered still
Will want to marry
My daughter Jill.

Oh sweet be his slumber and moist his middle!
My dreams, I fear, are infanticiddle.
A fig for embryo Lohengrins!
I'll open all of his safety pins,
I'll pepper his powder, and salt his bottle,
And give him readings from Aristotle.

Sand for his spinach I'll gladly bring,
And Tabasco sauce for his teething ring.
Then perhaps he'll struggle through fire and water
To marry somebody else's daughter.

THE PHŒNIX

Deep in the study
Of eugenics
We find that fabled
Fowl, the Phœnix.
The wisest bird
As ever was,
Rejecting other
Mas and Pas,
It lays one egg,
Not ten or twelve,
And when it's hatched it,
Out pops itself.

LINES INDITED WITH ALL THE
DEPRAVITY OF POVERTY

One way to be very happy is to be very rich
For then you can buy orchids by the quire and bacon by the flitch.
And yet at the same time
People don't mind if you only tip them a dime.
Because it's very funny
But somehow if you're rich enough you can get away with spend-
    ing water like money
While if you're not rich you can spend in one evening your salary
    for the year
And everybody will just stand around and jeer.
If you are rich you don't have to think twice about buying a judge
    or a horse,

Or a lower instead of an upper, or a new suit, or a divorce,
And you never have to say When,
And you can sleep every morning until nine or ten,
All of which
Explains why I should like very, very much to be very, very rich.

MALICE DOMESTIC

A Mrs. Shepherd of Danbury, Conn.,
She tried to steal our cook,
She may have thought to stay anon.,
But now she's in a book!
Oh — Mrs. — Shepherd,
OH! Mrs. SHEPHERD!
I'll hunt you hither, I'll hunt you yon.
Did you really hope to remain anon.?
Didn't you know the chance you took
Making a pass at a poet's cook?

Oh, Mrs. S. of the Nutmeg State,
No human shame she knew,
Her carnal appetites to sate,
Our home she walked into.
Oh — Mrs. — Shepherd!
OH! Mrs. SHEPHERD!
By hook and by crook and by telephone
You attempted to rape us of our own.
You ruptured the laws of God and man
And made a pass at Matilda Ann.

Then here's a health to Matilda Ann
Whose soups are soundly peppered,
Whose commonest meats are godlike feats,
Who resisted Mrs. Shepherd.
But — Oh — Mrs. — Shepherd!

OH! Mrs. SHEPHERD!
You ruptured the laws of man and God
When in our kitchen you softly trod.
You tiptoed hither, you tiptoed yon,
You fondly hoped to remain anon.,
But householders all, the nation over,
Shall hear the name of the lawless rover
Who by telephone and by hook and crook
Attempted to alienate our cook.
Go back to your home in Danbury, Conn.,
And carry this curse to ponder on:
I hope that your soup is washy-wishy,
Your salad sandy, your butter fishy,
Your oatmeal scorched and your sirloins boiled,
Your soufflé soggy, your sherbet oiled,
Till all your neighbors in Danbury, Conn.,
As they watch the Shepherds grow feeble and wan,
Say: "She should have thought of the chance she took,
Making a pass at a poet's cook."

MACHINERY DOESN'T ANSWER, EITHER, BUT YOU AREN'T MARRIED TO IT

Oh Daddy, look at that man, excuse my pointing, but just look at him!

He is in a frenzy or something, as if a red rag or something had been shook at him!

His eyes are rolling like a maniac's,

Oh isn't it shocking how insaniacs!

Oh Daddy, he is talking to thin air,

He is having a long conversation with somebody who isn't there!

He is talking to himself, he must be under the influence of either Luna or Bacchus;

Oh Daddy, Daddy, I think we had better go a long way away from him immediately because one in his condition might at any moment have an impulse to attacchus!

Nay, hush ye, hush ye, do not fret ye, my little white manchild,
Who if your parents hadn't been Caucasian would have been an
ebony or copper or tan child,
Life will teach you many things, chief of which is that every man
who talks to himself isn't necessarily out of his wits;
He may have a wife who knits.
Probably only he and his Maker
Know how many evenings he has spent trying to raise a conversa-
tion while his beloved created sweaters by the acre.

Ah, my inquiring offspring, you must learn that life can be very
bitter,
But never quite so much so as when trying to pry a word out of
a knitter.
Sometimes she knits and sits,
Sometimes she sits and knits,
And you tell her what you have been doing all day and you ask
what she has been doing all day and nothing happens, and
you tell her what you would like to do this evening and ask
her what she would like to do this evening and nothing
happens, and you think you will disintegrate if you don't get
some response, and you speak tenderly of your courtship and
your bridal,
And you might just as well try to get a response out of an Oriental
idol,
And you notice a spasmodic movement of her lips,
And you think she is going to say something but she is only counting the number of stitches it takes to surround the hips;
And she furrows her beautiful brow, which is a sign that something is wrong somewhere and you keep on talking and dis-
regard the sign,
And she casts a lethal glance, as one who purls before swine,
And this goes on for weeks
At the end of which she lays her work down and speaks,
And you think now maybe you can have some home life but she
speaks in a tone as far off as Mercury or Saturn,

And she says thank goodness that is finished, it is a sight and she
    will never be able to wear it, but it doesn't matter because she
    can hardly wait to start on an adorable new pattern,
And when this has been going on for a long time, why that's the
    time that strong men break down and go around talking to
    themselves in public, finally,
And it doesn't mean that they are weak mentally or spinally,
It doesn't mean, my boy, that they ought to be in an asylum like
    Nijinsky the dancer,
It only means that they got into the habit of talking to themselves
    at home because they themselves were the only people they
    could talk to and get an answer.

A CHILD'S GUIDE TO PARENTS

Children, I crave your kind forbearance;
Our topic for today is Parents.

Parents are generally found in couples,
Except when divorce their number quadruples.

Mostly they're married to each other.
The female one is called the mother.

Paternal pride being hard to edit,
The male, or father, claims the credit,

But children, hark! Your mother would rather,
When you arrived, have been your father.

At last on common ground they meet:
Their child is sweetest of the sweet.

But burst not, babe, with boastful glee;
It is themselves they praise, not thee.

[123]

The reason Father flatters thee, is —
Thou must be wonderful, aren't thou his?

And Mother admires *her* offspring double,
Especially after all that trouble.

The wise child handles father and mother
By playing one against the other.

Don't! cries this parent to the tot;
The opposite parent asks, Why not?

Let baby listen, nothing loth,
And work impartially on both.

In clash of wills, do not give in;
Good parents are made by discipline;

Remember the words of the wise old senator:
Spare the tantrum, and spoil the progenitor,

But joy in heaping measure comes
To children whose parents are under their thumbs.

THE TURKEY

There is nothing more perky
Than a masculine turkey.
When he struts he struts
With no ifs or buts.
When his face is apoplectic
His harem grows hectic,
And when he gobbles
Their universe wobbles.

THE SEVEN SPIRITUAL AGES OF
MRS. MARMADUKE MOORE

Mrs. Marmaduke Moore, at the age of ten
(Her name was Jemima Jevons then),
Was the quaintest of little country maids.
Her pigtails slapped on her shoulderblades;
She fed the chickens, and told the truth
And could spit like a boy through a broken tooth.
She could climb a tree to the topmost perch,
And she used to pray in the Methodist church.

At the age of twenty her heart was pure,
And she caught the fancy of Mr. Moore.
He broke his troth (to a girl named Alice),
And carried her off to his city palace,
Where she soon forgot her childhood piety
And joined in the orgies of high society.
Her voice grew English, or, say, Australian,
And she studied to be an Episcopalian

At thirty our lives are still before us,
But Mr. Moore had a friend in the chorus.
Connubial bliss was overthrown
And Mrs. Moore now slumbered alone.
Hers was a nature that craved affection;
She gave herself up to introspection;
Then, finding theosophy rather dry,
Found peace in the sweet Bahai and Bahai.

Forty! and still an abandoned wife.
She felt old urges stirring to life.
She dipped her locks in a bowl of henna
And booked a passage through to Vienna.
She paid a professor a huge emolument
To demonstrate what his ponderous volume meant.

[125]

Returning, she preached to the unemployed
The gospel according to St. Freud.

Fifty! she haunted museums and galleries,
And pleased young men by augmenting their salaries.
Oh, it shouldn't occur, but it does occur,
That poets are made by fools like her.
Her salon was full of frangipani,
Roumanian, Russian and Hindustani,
And she conquered par as well as bogey
By reading a book and going Yogi.

Sixty! and time was on her hands —
Maybe remorse and maybe glands.
She felt a need for a free confession,
To publish each youthful indiscretion,
And before she was gathered to her mothers,
To compare her sinlets with those of others,
Mrs. Moore gave a joyous whoop,
And immersed herself in the Oxford Group.

That is the story of Mrs. Moore,
As far as it goes. But of this I'm sure —
When seventy stares her in the face
She'll have found some other state of grace.
Mohammed may be her Lord and master,
Or Zeus, or Mithros or Zoroaster.
When a lady's erotic life is vexed
God knows what God is coming next.

EVERYBODY TELLS ME EVERYTHING

I find it very difficult to enthuse
Over the current news.
Just when you think that at least the outlook is so black that it can
   grow no blacker, it worsens,

And that is why I do not like the news, because there has never been an era when so many things were going so right for so many of the wrong persons.

THE WOMBAT

The wombat lives across the seas,
Among the far Antipodes.
He may exist on nuts and berries,
Or then again, on missionaries;
His distant habitat precludes
Conclusive knowledge of his moods.
But I would not engage the wombat
In any form of mortal combat.

LOOK FOR THE SILVER LINING

I can't say that I feel particularly one way or the other towards bell-boys,
But I do admit that I haven't much use for the it's-just-as-well boys,
The cheery souls who drop around after every catastrophe and think they are taking the curse off
By telling you about somebody who is even worse off.
No matter how deep and dark your pit, how dank your shroud,
Their heads are heroically unbloody and unbowed.
If you have just lost the one love of your life, there is no possible doubt of it,
They tell you there are as good fish in the sea as ever came out of it.
If you are fined ten dollars for running past a light when you didn't but the cop says you did,
They say Cheer up think of the thousand times you ran past them and didn't get caught so you're really ten thousand bucks ahead, Hey old kid?

If you lose your job they tell you how lucky you are that you've
    saved up a little wealth
And then when the bank folds with the savings they tell you you
    sure are lucky to still have your health.
Life to them is just one long happy game,
At the conclusion of which the One Great Scorer writes not
    whether you won it or lost it, but how you played it, against
    your name.
Kismet, they say, it's Fate. What is to be, will be. Buck up! Take
    heart!
Kismet indeed! Nobody can make me grateful for Paris Green in
    the soup just by assuring me that it comes that way Allah
    carte.

OH TO BE ODD!

Hypochondriacs
Spend the winter at the bottom of Florida and the summer on top
    of the Adirondriacs.
You go to Paris and live on champagne wine and cognac
If you're a dipsomognac.
If you're a manic-depressive
You don't go anywhere where you won't be cheered up, and peo-
    ple say "There, there!" if your bills are excessive.
But you stick around and work day and night and night and day
    with your nose to the sawmill
If you're normal.

MY DEAR, HOW EVER DID YOU THINK UP
THIS DELICIOUS SALAD?

This is a very sad ballad,
Because it's about the way too many people make a salad.
Generally they start with bananas,
And they might just as well use Gila monsters or iguanas.

[128]

Pineapples are another popular ingredient,
Although there is one school that holds preserved pears or peaches
　　　more expedient,
And you occasionally meet your fate
In the form of a prune or a date.
Rarely you may chance to discover a soggy piece of tomato looking
　　　very forlorn and Cinderella-ry,
But for the most part you are confronted by apples and celery,
And it's not a bit of use at this point to turn pale or break out in a
　　　cold perspiration,
Because all this is only the foundation,
Because if you think the foundation sounds unenticing,
Just wait until we get to the dressing, or rather, the icing.
There are various methods of covering up the body, and to some,
　　　marshmallows are the pall supreme,
And others prefer whipped cream,
And then they deck the grave with ground-up peanuts and mara-
　　　schinos
And you get the effect of a funeral like Valentino's,
And about the only thing that in this kind of salad is never seen
Is any kind of green,
And oil and vinegar and salt and pepper are at a minimum,
But there is a maximum of sugar and syrup and ginger and nutmeg
　　　and cinnamum,
And my thoughts about this kind of salad are just as unutterable
As parsnips are unbutterable,
And indeed I am surprised that the perpetrators haven't got around
　　　to putting buttered parsnips in these salmagundis,
And the salad course nowadays seems to be a month of sundaes.

WHAT ALMOST EVERY WOMAN KNOWS
SOONER OR LATER

Husbands are things that wives have to get used to putting up with,
And with whom they breakfast with and sup with.

They interfere with the discipline of nurseries,

And forget anniversaries,

And when they have been particularly remiss

They think they can cure everything with a great big kiss,

And when you tell them about something awful they have done they just look unbearably patient and smile a superior smile,

And think, Oh she'll get over it after a while.

And they always drink cocktails faster than they can assimilate them,

And if you look in their direction they act as if they were martyrs and you were trying to sacrifice, or immolate them.

And when it's a question of walking five miles to play golf they are very energetic but if it's doing anything useful around the house they are very lethargic,

And then they tell you that women are unreasonable and don't know anything about logic,

And they never want to get up or go to bed at the same time as you do,

And when you perform some simple common or garden rite like putting cold cream on your face or applying a touch of lipstick they seem to think you are up to some kind of black magic like a priestess of Voodoo,

And they are brave and calm and cool and collected about the ailments of the person they have promised to honor and cherish,

But the minute they get a sniffle or a stomach-ache of their own, why you'd think they were about to perish,

And when you are alone with them they ignore all the minor courtesies and as for airs and graces, they utterly lack them,

But when there are a lot of people around they hand you so many chairs and ash trays and sandwiches and butter you with such bowings and scrapings that you want to smack them.

Husbands are indeed an irritating form of life,

And yet through some quirk of Providence most of them are really very deeply ensconced in the affection of their wife.

PRIDE GOETH BEFORE A RAISE
or
AH, THERE, MRS. CADWALLADER–SMITH!

The Cadwallader-Smiths
Are People with Poise;
I consider them one of the minor joys,
Though frequently wishing
That I could share
Their imperturbable *savoir-faire.*

Madame is a modishly youthful matron,
Artfully dyed and I think enameled;
Monsieur is a generous opera patron,
A Man-about-Town, by trade untrammeled.
Oh the dapper dandies,
The haughty dames,
In the phalanx of hy-
Phenated names!
(Have you ever observed
That the name of Smith
Is the oftenest hy-
Phenated with?)
Now come the junior Cadwallader-Smiths,
Those perennial rotogravurian myths,
Maidens who scale the Alps and Rockies,
Debutantes with the world in tow,
Polo players and gentleman jockeys,
And athletes tailored in Savile Row.
Oh glamorous girls and golden boys,
They practically palpitate with poise!
Say me a word. It's a word they've got.
So what?

Well, though hardly copy for a great biographer,
They know how to twinkle for a news photographer.

They don't go to work, but they wallow in shekels,
And they sit on beaches and don't get freckles.
They exchange divorces without bearing malice,
And they all get presented at Buckingham Palace.
They receive reporters with a nonchalant air,
And they're dignified even in the barber chair,
They are dignified even in their testimonials
To beautifying lotions for the crude Colonials.
They take a paper and they read the headlines,
So they've heard of unemployment and they've heard of breadlines,
And they philanthropically cure them all
By getting up a costume charity ball.
They tipple nectar and they nibble lotus,
And they pay no attention to a jury notus,
And they don't get a summons when they run past stop-lights,
So they have the point of view of true cosmopolites.
They could all pay taxes, but they'd rather not.
So what?
Well, they're People with Poise,
The Cadwallader-Smiths,
With the sensitive senses of monoliths,
Which I freely admit
I could use myself,
Had I all I desire of profit and pelf.

THE SQUIRREL

A squirrel to some is a squirrel,
To others, a squirrel's a squirl.
Since freedom of speech is the birthright of each,
I can only this fable unfurl:
A virile young squirrel named Cyril,
In an argument over a girl,
Was lambasted from here to the Tyrol
By a churl of a squirl named Earl.

ARE YOU A SNODGRASS?

It is possible that most individual and international social and
   economic collisions
Result from humanity's being divided into two main divisions.
Their lives are spent in mutual interference,
And yet you cannot tell them apart by their outward appearance.
Indeed the only way in which to tell one group from the other
   you are able
Is to observe them at the table,
Because the only visible way in which one group from the other
   varies
Is in its treatment of the cream and sugar on cereal and berries.
Group A, which we will call the Swozzlers because it is a very suit-
   able name, I deem,
First applies the sugar and then swozzles it all over the place pour-
   ing on the cream,
And as fast as they put the sugar on they swozzle it away,
But such thriftlessness means nothing to ruthless egotists like they,
They just continue to scoop and swozzle and swozzle and scoop,
Until there is nothing left for the Snodgrasses, or second group.
A Snodgrass is a kind, handsome intelligent person who pours the
   cream on first,
And then deftly sprinkles the sugar over the cereal or berries after
   they have been properly immersed,
Thus assuring himself that the sugar will remain on the cereal and
   berries where it can do some good, which is his wish,
Instead of being swozzled away to the bottom of the dish.
The facts of the case for the Snodgrasses are so self-evident that it
   is ridiculous to debate them,
But this is unfortunate for the Snodgrasses as it only causes the sinister and vengeful Swozzlers all the more to hate them.
Swozzlers are irked by the superior Snodgrass intelligence and no-
   bility
And they lose no opportunity of inflicting on them every kind of
   incivility.

If you read that somebody has been run over by an automobile
You may be sure that the victim was a Snodgrass, and a Swozzler
was at the wheel.
Swozzlers start wars and Snodgrasses get killed in them,
Swozzlers sell water-front lots and Snodgrasses get malaria when
they try to build in them.
Swozzlers invent fashionable diets and drive Snodgrasses crazy
with tables of vitamins and calories,
Swozzlers go to Congress and think up new taxes and Snodgrasses
pay their salaries,
Swozzlers bring tigers back alive and Snodgrasses get eaten by ana-
condas,
Snodgrasses are depositors and Swozzlers are absconders,
Swozzlers hold straight flushes when Snodgrasses hold four of a
kind,
Swozzlers step heavily on the toes of Snodgrasses' shoes as soon as
they are shined.
Whatever achievements Snodgrasses achieve, Swozzlers always
top them;
Snodgrasses say Stop me if you're heard this one, and Swozzlers
stop them.
Swozzlers are teeming with useful tricks of the trade that are not
included in standard university curricula;
The world in general is their oyster, and Snodgrasses in particular.
So I hope for your sake, dear reader, that you are a Swozzler, but
I hope for everybody else's sake that you are not,
And I also wish that everybody else was a nice amiable Snodgrass
too, because then life would be just one long sweet harmoni-
ous mazurka or gavotte.

A PARABLE FOR SPORTS WRITERS, SOCIETY COLUMNISTS, BOND SALESMEN AND POETS

or

GO GET A REPUTATION

I

Ezra Æsop, at eighty-eight,
He published a volume of verse.
The rhymes were ragged,
The meter wilted,
The prosody prosy,
The stanzas stilted.
But other poets at eighty-eight,
Patriarchal or celibate,
Might — conceivably —
Might — believably —
Might — finally, irretrievably —
Have seized the muse by the horns and tail,
And written a volume worse.
So the red fires burned,
And the banners flew,
And the fat nymphs danced
In the pagan dew,
And the mountains skipped like little lambs,
And editors squandered telegrams,
And over deserts,
And under oceans,
Through Rotary, Red Men, Elks and Yosians,
The word flew East and the word flew West,
Flew with the wings of a drummer's jest,
That the book of the era, beyond debate,
Was the book by the poet of eighty-eight.
O, Excellent Ezra! the people cried,
He might have doddered,
He might have died,

He might have entered a monastery,
He might have adopted his secretary.
But what did he do?
He studied at home,
Then up and published a slender tome.
So they borrowed early and purchased late
The book by the poet of eighty-eight,
And El Dorado had no bonanzas
Like Ezra Æsop's elderly stanzas.

II

Rosalie Ransome, going on six,
She published a volume, too,
And Heaven pity the heretics
Who neglected to read it through.
For the word was out,
In palace and cot,
Of the teensy, weensy, talented tot,
And gangsters gossiped of Rosalie Ransome,
Who lisped iambics,
And lisped 'em handsome.
The public panted,
The press grew giddy,
At the very thought
Of a lyrical kiddy,
And professors pawned their Shelley and Keats
To purchase Rosalie's youthful feats.

III

A regular poet published a book,
And an excellent book it was,
But nobody gave it a second look,
As nobody often does.
He was going on half-past thirty-five,
So it didn't keep him long alive.

REFLECTION OF THE FALLIBILITY
OF NEMESIS

He who is ridden by a conscience
Worries about a lot of nonscience;
He without benefit of scruples
His fun and income soon quadruples.

RAVEN, DON'T STAY AWAY FROM MY
DOOR
— A CHANT FOR APRIL FIRST

What pleasanter task for All Fools' Day than going over all the
    things you have done before
And don't want to do again never no more, never no more, never
    no more?
Oh softer than the lap of ripples on Innisfree's poetically described
    shore
Is never no more.
Sweeter than the prospect of encountering a dozen ladies each as
    exquisite as Mr. Poe's lost Lenore
Is never no more.
More alluring than an invitation to visit rich and charming friends
    on the Côte d'Or
Is never no more.
Oh let us toy with the comforting but untrue tenet that the burnt
    child dreads the fire that burned him;
Let us each of us dream that the last lesson he had was a lesson
    that really learned him.
I at least refuse to be dissudaded by anyone, even Mrs. Luce or
    Mrs. Post or Dorothy Dix or Petrarch's Laura;
On this day of days I shall be a hard-shell, shouting fundamental-
    ist never no maura.
Never no more will I escort a lady home downtown when I am
    sleepy and want to go up;

Or drink buttermilk, or sauerkraut juice; or anything at all out of
    a paper cup;
Or see anybody off on a boat;
Or expect anybody else to like a book or a play on which I happen
    to particularly dote.
Or underestimate a Slav;
Or say politely No I haven't heard a story, when as a matter of fact
    I have;
Or let any parent tell me what Sister said to Sonny;
Or play bridge for love, or if it comes to that, for money;
Or get flustered into accepting an invitation I don't want to accept
    just because I can't think quickly at the telephone;
Or believe that something is better than something else just be-
    cause it's wrapped in cellophane.
Also, commuting and eating out of doors —
These belong on any list of ideal never no mores.
In conclusion may I say that if this were not a song for the First
    of April I'd feel very guilty
At daring even to contemplate such a devastatingly delightful im-
    possibility.

DRAGONS ARE TOO SELDOM

To actually see an actual marine monster
Is one of the things that do before I die I wonster.
Should you ask me if I desire to meet the bashful inhabitant of
    Loch Ness,
I could only say yes.
Often my eye with moisture dims
When I think that it has never been my good fortune to gaze on
    one of Nature's whims.
Far from ever having seen a Gorgon
I haven't even seen the midget that sat in the lap of Mr. Morgan.
Indeed it is my further ill fortune or mishap

That far from having seen the midget that sat in it I have never
    even seen Mr. Morgan's lap.
Indeed I never much thought about Mr. Morgan's having a lap
    because just the way you go into churches and notice the
    stained glass more than the apses
When you think about multi-millionaires you don't think about
    their laps as much as their lapses;
But it seems that they do have laps which is one human touch that
    brings them a little closer to me and you,
And maybe they even go so far as to sometimes have hiccups too.
But regular monsters like sea serpents don't have laps or hiccups
    or any other characteristic that is human,
And I would rather see a second-rate monster such as a mermaid
    than a first-rate genius such as John Bunyan or Schiaparelli
    or Schubert or Schumann;
Yes, I would rather see one of the sirens
Than two Lord Byrons,
And if I knew that when I got there I could see Cyclops or Scylla
    and Charybdis or Pegasus
I would willingly walk on my hands from here to Dallas, Texas,
Because I don't mean to be satirical,
But where there's a monster there's a miracle,
And after a thorough study of current affairs, I have concluded
    with regret
That the world can profitably use all the miracles it can get,
And I think life would be a lot less demoralizing,
If instead of sitting around in front of the radio listening to tor-
    ture singers sing torture songs we sat around listening to the
    Lorelei loreleising.

SUPPOSE I DARKEN YOUR DOOR

It seems to me that if you must be sociable it is better to go and see
    people than to have people come and see you,
Because then you can leave when you are through.

Yes, the moment you begin to nod

You can look at your watch and exclaim Goodness gracious, it is ten o'clock already, I had no idea it was so late, how very odd!

And you politely explain that you have to get up early in the morning to keep an important engagement with a man from Alaska or Siam,

And you politely thank your host and hostess for the lovely time and politely say good night and politely scram,

But when you yourself are the home team and the gathering is under your own roof,

You haven't got a Manchurian's chance of being aloof.

If you glance at your watch it is grievous breach of hospitality and a disgrace,

And if you are caught in the midst of a yawn you have to pretend you were making a face and say Come on everybody, let's see who can make the funniest face.

Then as the evening wears on you feel more and more like an unsuccessful gladiator,

Because all the comfortable places to sit in are being sat in by guests and you have to repose on the window sill or the chandelier or the radiator,

And somebody has always brought along a girl who looks like a loaf of raisin bread and doesn't know anybody else in the room,

And you have to go over to the corner where she is moping and try to disperse her gloom,

And finally at last somebody gets up and says they have to get back to the country or back to town again,

And you feebly say Oh it's early, don't go yet, so what do they do but sit down again,

And people that haven't said a word all evening begin to get lively and people that have been lively all evening get their second wind and somebody says Let's all go out in the kitchen and scramble some eggs,

And you have to look at him or her twice before you can convince yourself that anybody who would make a suggestion like that hasn't two heads or three legs,

And by this time the birds are twittering in the trees or looking in the window and saying Boo,

But nobody does anything about it and as far as I know they're all still here, and that's the reason I say that it is better to go and see people than to have people come and see you.

LOOK WHAT YOU DID, CHRISTOPHER!

In fourteen hundred and ninety-two,
Somebody sailed the ocean blue.
Somebody borrowed the fare in Spain
For a business trip on the bounding main,
And to prove to people, by actual test,
You could get to the East by traveling West.
Somebody said, Sail on! Sail on!
And studied China and China's lingo,
And cried from the bow, There's China now!
And promptly bumped into San Domingo.
Somebody murmured, Oh dear, oh dear!
I've discovered the Western Hemisphere.

And that, you may think, my friends, was that.
But it wasn't. Not by a fireman's hat.
Well enough wasn't left alone,
And Columbus was only a cornerstone.
There came the Spaniards,
There came the Greeks,
There came the Pilgrims in leather breeks.
There came the Dutch,
And the Poles and Swedes,
The Persians, too,
And perhaps the Medes,
The Letts, the Lapps and the Lithuanians,

Regal Russians, and ripe Roumanians.
There came the French
And there came the Finns,
And the Japanese
With their formal grins.
The Tartars came,
And the Terrible Turks —
In a word, humanity shot the works.
And the country that should have been Cathay
Decided to be
The U.S.A.

And that, you may think, my friends, was that.
But it wasn't. Not by a fireman's hat.
Christopher C. was the cornerstone,
And well enough wasn't left alone.
For those who followed
When he was through,
They burned to discover something, too.
Somebody, bored with rural scenery,
Went to work and invented machinery,
While a couple of other mental giants
Got together
And thought up Science.
Platinum blondes
(They were once peroxide),
Peruvian bonds
And carbon monoxide,
Tax evaders
And Vitamin A,
Vice crusaders,
And tattletale gray —
These, with many another phobia,
We owe to that famous Twelfth of Octobia.
O misery, misery, mumble and moan!
Someone invented the telephone,

And interrupted a nation's slumbers,
Ringing wrong but similar numbers.
Someone devised the silver screen
And the intimate Hollywood magazine,
And life is a Hades
Of clicking cameras,
And foreign ladies
Behaving amorous.
Gags have erased
Amusing dialog,
As gas replaced
The crackling firelog.
All that glitters is sold as gold,
And our daily diet grows odder and odder,
And breakfast foods are dusty and cold —
It's a wise child
That knows its fodder.
Someone invented the automobile,
And good Americans took the wheel
To view American rivers and rills
And justly famous forests and hills —
But somebody equally enterprising
Had invented billboard advertising.
You linger at home
In dark despair,
And wistfully try the electric air.
You hope for a program controversial,
And what do they give you?
A beer commercial.
Oh, Columbus was only a cornerstone,
And well enough wasn't left alone,
For the Inquisition was less tyrannical
Than the iron rules of an age mechanical,
Which, because of an error in '92,
Are clamped like corsets on me and you,
While Children of Nature we'd be today

If San Domingo
Had been Cathay.

And that, you may think, my friends, is that.
But it isn't — not by a fireman's hat.
The American people,
With grins jocose,
Always survive the fatal dose.
And though our systems are slightly wobbly,
We'll fool the doctor this time, probly.

FIRST PAYMENT DEFERRED

Let us look into the matter of debt
Which is something that the longer you live, why the deeper into
it you get,
Because in the first place every creditor is his debtor's keeper,
And won't let you get into debt in the first place unless you are
capable of getting in deeper,
Which is an unfortunate coincidence
Because every debtor who is capable of getting deeper into debt is
attracted only to creditors who will encourage him to get
deeper into debt, which is a most fabulous and unfair You-
were-a-creditor-in-Babylon-and-I-was-a-Christian-debtor Eli-
nor Glyncidence.
Some debtors start out with debts which are little ones,
Such as board and lodging and victual ones;
Other debtors start out by never demanding that their bills be
itemized,
Which means that they are bitten by little creditors upon the backs
of bigger creditors and are so on ad infinitumized.
Veteran debtors dabble in stocks,
Or their families get adenoids or appendicitis or pox,
Any of which means that debt is what they get beneather and be-
neather,

Either to them who told them about the stocks or to them who administer the chloroform and ether.
Some debts are fun while you are acquiring them,
But none are fun when you set about retiring them,
So you think you will reform, you think instead of sinking into debt you will ascend into credit,
So you live on a budget and save twenty-five per cent of your salary and cut corners and generally audit and edit,
And that is the soundest idea yet,
Because pretty soon your credit is so good that you can charge anything you want and settle down for eternity into peaceful and utterly irremediable debt.

HUSH, HERE THEY COME

Some people get savage and bitter when to backbiters they refer,
But I just purr.
Yes, some people consider backbiters to be rankest of the rank,
But frankly, I prefer them to people who go around being frank,
Because usually when you are backbitten behind your back you don't know about it and it doesn't leave a trace,
But frankness consists of having your back bitten right to your face,
And as if that weren't enough to scar you,
Why you are right there in person to scotch the defamation, and if you don't happen to be able to scotch it, why where are you?
Frank people are grim, but genuine backbiters are delightful to have around,
Because they are so anxious that if what they have been saying about you has reached your ears you shouldn't believe it, that they are the most amiable companions to be found;
They will entertain you from sunset to dawn,
And cater encouragingly to all your weaknesses so that they can broadcast them later on,

So what if they do gnaw on your spine after enjoying your beer
    and skittles?
I don't blame them the least of jots or tittles,
Because certainly no pastime such diversion lends
As talking friends over analytically with friends,
So what if as they leave your house or you leave theirs backbiters
    strip your flesh and your clothes off,
At least it is your back that they bite, and not your nose off.
I believe in a place for everything and everything in its place,
And I don't care how unkind the things people say about me so
    long as they don't say them to my face.

BIOLOGICAL REFLECTION

A girl whose cheeks are covered with paint
Has an advantage with me over one whose ain't.

I YIELD TO MY LEARNED BROTHER
or
IS THERE A CANDLESTICK MAKER IN
THE HOUSE?

The doctor gets you when you're born,
The preacher, when you marry,
And the lawyer lurks with costly clerks
If too much on you carry.
Professional men, they have no cares;
Whatever happens, they get theirs.

You can't say When
To professional men,
For it's always When to they;
They go out and golf
With the big bad wolf
In the most familiar way.

[146]

Hard times for them contain no terrors;
Their income springs from human errors.

The noblest lord is ushered in
By a practicing physician,
And the humblest lout is ushered out
By a certified mortician.
And in between, they find their foyers
Alive with summonses from lawyers.

Oh, would my parents long ago
Had memorized this motto!
For then might I, their offspring, buy
A Rolls or an Isotto.
But now I fear I never can,
For I am no professional man.

You can't say When
To professional men,
For it's always When to they;
They were doing fine
In '29,
And they're doing fine today.
One beacon doth their paths illumine,
To wit: To err is always humine.

I HAD NO IDEA IT WAS SO LATE

Consider the man without a watch.
He is like a soda without Scotch.
Of the male character I can quickly give you the gist;
It is the reach for the pocket or the glance at the wrist.
From the moment they are fledglings
Males discipline themselves with timings and schedulings.
Be they lovers, golfers, or railroad engineers,

Time is the essential ingredient in their careers,
And there is nothing more surly
Than a watchless man who doesn't know whether he is late or
early,
And clocks are no good to him because he can't take them along,
And anyhow a clock is only something that you compare with
your watch and find the clock is several minutes wrong.
If there is one thing that every man thinks how sublime it is,
It is to know what time it is.
Women don't like watches, they only tolerate them when they are
embedded in brooches or bracelets or belts,
Or in some way disguised to look like something else.
Yes, it's obvious that women don't like them or need them,
Because with women's watches you need a microscope and a map
to read them.
Time is something they resent, and they fight it with peculiarly
feminine resistance;
They refuse to acknowledge its existence.
In this sexual conflict in attitude toward time who am I to tip
the scales?
I only know that more males wait for females than females wait
for males.

REFLECTION ON THE PASSAGE OF TIME, ITS INEVITABILITY AND ITS QUIRKS

In nineteen hunderd
Jeunes filles wondered.

GRASSHOPPERS ARE VERY INTELLIGENT

Ah woe, woe, woe, man was created to live by the sweat of his
brow,
And it doesn't make any difference if your brow was moist yester-

day and the day before, you've still got to get it moist again right now,

And you know deep in your heart that you will have to continue keeping it dewy

Right up to the time that somebody at the club says, I suppose we ought to go to what's-his-name's funeral, who won the fifth at Bowie?

That's a nasty outlook to face,

But it's what you get for belonging to the human race.

So far as I know, mankind is the only section of creation

That is doomed to either pers- or ex-piration.

Look at the birds flying around, and listen to them as their voices in song they hoist;

No wonder they sing so much, that haven't got any brows, and if they had they couldn't be bothered keeping them moist.

And bees don't do anything either, bees just have a reputation for industry because they are sharp enough to buzz,

And people hear a bee buzzing and don't realize that buzzing isn't any trouble for a bee so they think it is doing more than it actually does,

So next time you are about to expend some enthusiasm on the bee's wonderful industrial powers,

Just remember that that wonderful bee would die laughing if you asked it to change places with you and get its brow moist while you went around spending the day smelling flowers.

But if you are humanity, it is far from so,

And that is why I exclaim Woe woe woe,

Because I don't see much good in being the highest form of life

If all you get out of it is a brow moist from perpetual struggle and strife.

Indeed sometimes when my brow is particularly moist I think I would rather be a humble amœba

Than Solomon in all his glory entertaining the Queen of Sheba.

HEARTS OF GOLD
or
A GOOD EXCUSE IS WORSE THAN NONE

There are some people who are very resourceful
At being remorseful,
And who apparently feel that the best way to make friends
Is to do something terrible and then make amends.
They come to your party and make a great hit with your Victorian
aunt and with her freely mingle,
And suddenly after another drink they start a lot of *double enten-
dre* the *entendre* of which is unfortunately not *double* but
single,
And if you say anything to them they take umbrage,
And later when you are emptying the ash trays before going to
bed you find them under the sofa where they have crept for
a good night's slumbrage.
Then next day they are around intoning apologies
With all the grace and conviction of a high-paid choir intoning
doxologies.
There are people in every group
Who will jog your elbow at table just when you are lifting a spoon-
ful of very hot soup,
Or at a musicale or something while you're listening to a ravish-
ing obbligato
Will forget their cigarettes and burn a hole in your clothes the size
of a medium-sized tomato.
And then you are presented with a lot of form-fitting apologies
Quite good enough, I am sure, for inclusion in one of the higher-
class anthologies.
Everybody says these people have hearts of gold,
But nevertheless they are always talking when you're putting, or
splashing mud on you from their car, or giving you a cold,
And they are always sure that today you don't mind their inflicting
on you any sorrow,

Because they'll give you so much pleasure when they smilingly
　　apologize tomorrow,
But I myself would rather have a rude word from someone who
　　has done me no harm
Than a graceful letter from the King of England saying he's sorry
　　he broke my arm.

INTROSPECTIVE REFLECTION

I would live all my life in nonchalance and insouciance
Were it not for making a living, which is rather a nouciance.

I'm a Stranger Here Myself

CURL UP AND DIET

Some ladies smoke too much and some ladies drink too much and
some ladies pray too much,
But all ladies think that they weigh too much.
They may be as slender as a sylph or a dryad,
But just let them get on the scales and they embark on a doleful
jeremiad;
No matter how low the figure the needle happens to touch,
They always claim it is at least five pounds too much;
No matter how underfed to you a lady's anatomy seemeth,
She describes herself as Leviathan or Behemoth;
To the world she may appear slinky and feline,
But she inspects herself in the mirror and cries, Oh, I look like a
sea lion.
Once upon a time there was a girl more beautiful and witty and
charming than tongue can tell,
And she is now a dangerous raving maniac in a padded cell,
And the first indication her friends and relatives had that she was
mentally overwrought
Was one day when she said, I weigh a hundred and twenty-seven,
which is exactly what I ought.
Oh, often I am haunted
By the thought that somebody might some day discover a diet that
would let ladies reduce just as much as they wanted,
Because I wonder if there is a woman in the world strong-minded
enough to shed ten pounds or twenty,
And say There now, that's plenty;
And I fear me one ten-pound loss would only arouse the craving
for another,
So it wouldn't do any good for ladies to get their ambition and look
like somebody's fourteen-year-old brother,
Because, having accomplished this with ease,
They would next want to look like somebody's fourteen-year-old
brother in the final stages of some obscure disease,
And the more success you have the more you want to get of it,

So then their goal would be to look like somebody's fourteen-year-
old brother's ghost, or rather not the ghost itself, which is
fairly solid, but a silhouette of it,
So I think it is very nice for ladies to be lithe and lissome,
But not so much so that you cut yourself if you happen to embrace
or kissome.

I HAVE IT ON GOOD AUTHORITY

There are two kinds of people who blow through life like a breeze,
And one kind is gossipers, and the other kind is gossipees,
And they certainly annoy each other,
But they certainly enjoy each other,
Yes, they pretend to flout each other,
But they couldn't do without each other,
Because gossipers are lost without a thrill and a shock,
Because they like to sit in rocking chairs and gossip and rock and
rock and gossip and gossip and rock,
And if the gossipees weren't there to give them a thrill and a shock
their life would be all rocking and no gossip,
Which would be as flat as music without people named Sacha and
Yehudi and Ossip,
While on the other hand everybody errs
If they think the gossipees could be happy without the gossipers,
Because you don't have to study under Freud or Adler or Coué
To know that it isn't any fun being a roué if nobody notices that
you are a roué,
And indeed connoisseurs agree
That even gossipers don't know anything about gossip until they
have heard one gossipee gossiping about another gossipee.
Another good thing about gossip is that it is within everybody's
reach,
And it is much more interesting than any other form of speech,
Because suppose you eschew gossip and just say Mr. Smith is in
love with his wife,

Why that disposes of the Smiths as a topic of conversation for the rest of their life,

But suppose you say with a smile, that poor little Mrs. Smith thinks her husband is in love with her, he must be very clever,

Why then you can enjoyably talk about the Smiths forever.

So a lot of people go around determined not to hear and not to see and not to speak any evil,

And I say Pooh for them, are you a man or a mouse, are you a woman or a weevil?

And I also say Pooh for sweetness and light,

And if you want to get the most out of life why the thing to do is to be a gossiper by day and gossipee by night.

THE MIDDLE OF THE MONTH

Oh, some people grieve for New Year's Eve,
And some for the dog days fiddle;
My moment sublime is the restful time
When the month is at the middle.

Sing tirra lirra loo for the middle of the month,
Which wipes out woes like chamois!
The middle of the month is honey and milk!
The middle of the month is mammy!
Now let us exult,
For the bills of ult.
Are limbo's laughing stocks;
At Fate we scoff,
For a fortnight off
Are the impotent bills of prox.
The first of the month is oyster-gray,
The last of the month is clammy,
But it's tirra lirra loo for the middle of the month,
For the middle of the month is mammy!

Time, fly not back upon thy track!
The past is merely tedium,
And the future, too, so stand still, do,
While the month is at the medium!

Then tirra lirra loo for the middle of the month
And gambol it in like May Day!
The ravenous wolves are toothless now,
The lambs are in their heyday.

Now turn not pale
At the morning mail
Nor shrink when the telephone shrills,
No evil betides
On the blessed Ides,
The lull between the bills!
Oh, the first of the month is oyster-gray
And the last of the month is clammy,
But it's tirra lirra loo for the middle of the month,
For the middle of the month is mammy!

FIRST FAMILIES, MOVE OVER!

Carry me back to Ole Virginny,
And there I'll meet a lot of people from New York,
There the Ole Marsa of the Hounds is from Smithtown or Peapack
    or Millbrook,
And the mocking bird makes music in the sunshine accompanied
    by the rattling shaker and the popping cork.

All up and down the old plantation
Socialites are riding hell-for-leather like witches and warlocks,
And there is only one thing that keeps the squirearchy from being
    a genuine reproduction,
Which is that the peasantry's hair is kinky so they haven't any
    forelocks so they can't tug their forelocks.

In the evening by the bright light you can hear those darkies sing-
ing,
How the white folks do enjoy it and call the attention of their
friends from Piping Rock to the natural musical talent of
the dusky proletariat.
You can hear those banjos ringing because the hands have been or-
dered to exchange their saxophones for banjos,
And they wish they were singing Lookie lookie lookie, here comes
Cookie, but their instructions are to sing Swing Low Sweet
Chariot.

Oh what is more beautiful and more Southern than a Southern
beauty from Philadelphia or Rumson,
And indeed where was Southern beauty before the advent of Ru-
binstein and Elizabeth Arden?
And what is more gracious than a hostess calling you you-all in the
singular and plural indiscriminately,
And what has more local color than a lovely girl in jodhpurs telling you about her gyarrrden?

Oh the long happy days spent huntin' or shootin' or fishin',
Or in any other sport provided it's lackin' in g's!
Oh the long happy evenings spent sniffing jasmine and poring over
the shiny new family Bible,
And figuring out that after all this is really your home because
great grandmother Wilkins was a Filkins and the Filkinses
were related by marriage to the Randolphs or the Lees!

So please somebody carry me back to Ole Virginny,
Where gentlemen are gentlemen and a lady is known by the prod-
uct she endorses,
Where the atmosphere is as Southern as an advertisement for a
medium-priced rye whiskey,
And where the Virginians from Virginia have to ride automobiles
because the Virginians from Long Island are the only ones
who can afford to ride horses.

A CLEAN CONSCIENCE NEVER RELAXES

There is an emotion to which we are most of us adduced,
But it is one which I refuse to boost.
It is harrowing, browbeating, and brutal,
Besides which it is futile.
I am referring, of course,
To remorse.
Remorse is a violent dyspepsia of the mind,
But it is very difficult to treat because it cannot even be defined,
Because everything is not gold that glisters and everything is not
    a tear that glistens,
And one man's remorse is another man's reminiscence,
So the truth is that as far as improving the world is concerned, re-
    morse is a duffer,
Because the wrong people suffer,
Because the very fact that they suffer from remorse proves they are
    innocuous,
Yes indeed, it is the man remorse passes over completely who is the
    virulent streptococcuous.
Do you think that when Nero threw a martyr to the lions remorse
    enveloped him like an affinity?
Why, the only remorse in the whole Colosseum was felt by the mar-
    tyr who was reproaching himself for having dozed through
    the sermon on the second Sunday after Trinity.
So I think remorse ought to stop biting the consciences that feed it,
And I think the Communist Party ought to work out some plan
    for taking it away from those who have it and giving it to
    those who need it.

BANKERS ARE JUST LIKE ANYBODY ELSE, EXCEPT RICHER

This is a song to celebrate banks,
Because they are full of money and you go into them and all you
    hear is clinks and clanks,

Or maybe a sound like the wind in the trees on the hills,

Which is the rustling of the thousand dollar bills.

Most bankers dwell in marble halls,

Which they get to dwell in because they encourage deposits and discourage withdralls,

And particularly because they all observe one rule which woe betides the banker who fails to heed it,

Which is you must never lend any money to anybody unless they don't need it.

I know you, you cautious conservative banks!

If people are worried about their rent it is your duty to deny them the loan of a single penny, even though it be worth only $3\frac{7}{10}$ francs.

Yes, if they request fifty dollars to pay for a baby you must look at them like the English looking at Joan of Arc,

And tell them what do they think a bank is, anyhow, they had better go get the money from their friendly neighborhood shark.

But suppose people come in and they have a million and they want another million to pile on top of it,

Why, you brim with the milk of human kindness and you urge them to accept every drop of it,

And you lend them the million so then they have two million and this gives them the idea that they would be better off with four,

So they already have two million as security so you have no hesitation in lending them two more,

And all the vice-presidents nod their heads in rhythm,

And the only question asked is do the borrowers want the money sent or do they want to take it withm.

But please do not think that I am not fond of banks,

Because I think they deserve our appreciation and thanks,

Because they perform a valuable public service in eliminating the jackasses who go around saying that health and happiness are everything and money isn't essential,

Because as soon as they have to borrow some unimportant money to maintain their health and happiness they starve to death so they can't go around any more sneering at good old money, which is nothing short of providential.

PRAYER AT THE END OF A ROPE

Dear Lord, observe this bended knee,
This visage meek and humble,
And heed this confidential plea,
Voiced in a reverent mumble.

I ask no miracles nor stunts,
No heavenly radiogram;
I only beg for once, just once,
To not be in a jam.

One little moment thy servant craves
Of being his own master;
One placid vale between the waves
Of duty and disaster.

Oh, when the postman's whistle shrills,
Just once, Lord, let me grin:
Let me have settled last month's bills
Before this month's come in.

Let me not bite more off the cob
Than I have teeth to chew;
Please let me finish just one job
Before the next is due.

Consider, too, my social life,
Sporadic though it be;
Why is it only mental strife
That pleasure brings to me?

For months, when people entertain,
Me they do not invite;
Then suddenly invitations rain,
All for the self-same night.

R.S.V.P.'s I pray thee send
Alone and not in bunches,
Or teach me I cannot attend
Two dinners or two lunches.

Let me my hostess not insult,
Not call her diamonds topaz;
Else harden me to the result
Of my fantastic faux pas.

One little lull, Lord, that's my plea,
Then loose the storm again;
Just once, this once, I beg to be
Not in a jam. Amen.

MIRIAM'S LUCKY DAY

Once there was a girl named Miriam,
And she spent part of her time in a delirium,
And she said, I wish the world were a little less mysterious,
Because I do like to know when I am delirious,
But I have discovered that whenever I regard the world and judge
  it logical and normal and headed for the millennium at a
  mile a minute,
Why that's the time I ought to be enclosed in a spacious park with
  an asylum in it,
But whenever everybody else seems to be running around in a de-
  lirium,
Why that's the time when somebody may be fuzzy-minded, but it
  isn't Miriam.

So finally she convened an enormous convention, national and international,

And she said, Please I wish everybody would help me to determine when I am delirious and when I am rational,

Because, she said, at present I am just a bit hazy,

Because when I am crazy you all seem perfectly sane, but when I am sane you all seem perfectly crazy,

So, she said, forgive me if I am too personal or informal,

But I hope from now on you will all behave so that I will think you are delirious if I am delirious, and normal if I am normal,

So they all said, What a good idea, hurrah for Miriam!

Who are we? Who are we? We are the boys and girls of the Eastern and Western hemispheres, and we are going to help her with her delirium!

So from then on manias were declared reprehensible,

And everybody tried to be sensible,

And there wasn't any more war,

And there were only as many people dancing at night clubs as could comfortably get on the floor,

And all the rich people cried Soak the rich, and all the poor people cried No that would retard recovery, soak the poor!

And the tailors made men's and women's coats with the buttons on the same side, and that stopped a lot of argument between husbands and wives as to the comparative intelligence of men and women, you may be sure.

And what with one thing and another everybody was sensible and lived happily ever after and they said they owed it all to Miriam,

So they offered her the dictatorship of the world, but she never used it, only in a delirium.

WOMAN PULLS THE WIRES

I have been idly leafing through the Book of Proverbs and the Book of Deuteronomy,

But I have failed to find what I was seeking, which was a few pithy
    words on the subject of lovely woman and her weakness for
    peculiar economy,
And at first I couldn't understand the omission and then I thought,
    Why of course!
The Book of Proverbs and the Book of Deuteronomy were written
    before the days of Marconi and Morse,
And to appreciate lovely woman really entangled in the coils of
    economy you are unable
Until you have seen her in the coils of composing a telegram or a
    radiogram or a cable.
The occasion may be one of life and death, but she does not wire
    at once, she frugally decides to wait,
Because she is determined to save the pennies that are saved by
    getting the night or week-end rate,
So suppose you are out of town and your wife wants to tell you
    that the children have turned into wart hogs and somebody
    will give you a million dollar contract if you call them up
    right away and she has shot the minister's wife and eloped
    with the minister,
She will not squander money on a rush message, no, she sends it
    creeping overnight, thus saving a sum so tidy that you can't
    see it even in these days when the financial outlook is pretty
    sinister.
Or suppose that she instead of you is out of town and she decides
    that she should have brought along a certain dress,
Why then she sends you a costly rush wire but she is still econom-
    ical and the instructions are so terse that you have nothing
    to act on but a wrong guess,
So it takes about twenty dollars worth of electricity to get straight-
    ened out and you are quite broke and burst,
All of which could have been avoided if she had spent an extra
    thirty cents at first.
Oh I often think that most of the misery in the world is caused by
    the telegraph companies who make you pay extra for all words
    over ten,

And I realize they have a right to a profit, but I wish they would
　　abolish all their present special rates and start all over again
　　with just one for lovely economical woman, and one for men.

SONG BEFORE BREAKFAST

Hopeful each morning I arise
And splash the cobwebs from my eyes.
I brush my teeth and scrape my chin
And bravely at the mirror grin.
Sternly I force myself to say,
Huzza! huzza! another day!
Oh happy me! oh lucky I!
Another chance with life to vie!
Another golden opportunity
To rise and shine in this community!
Another target for my aim!
Another whack at wealth and fame!
Almost I feel within me stir
A budding force of character.
Who knows, indeed, but what I might
Perhaps have altered overnight?
Today may be the day, who knows,
That sees me triumph o'er my foes:
Gluttony, simony, and sloth,
And drawing on the table cloth;
Perjury, arson, envy, pride,
And renting tales of homicide;
Barratry, avarice and wrath
And blowing bubbles in the bath.
The differences this day may bring!
Perhaps I'll work like anything;
I'll travel to my tasks on foot,
And in the bank the carfare put,
And buy a haircut when I need it,

And if I get a letter, read it,
And every eve improve myself
By inching through the Five Foot Shelf.
The things I want to do, I won't,
And only do the things I don't.
What lordly aspirations dawn
The while I draw my trousers on!
Oh beamish morning, big with hope
And noble tasks with which to cope,
If I should fail you, do not sorrow;
I'll be a better man tomorrow.

THE UNSELFISH HUSBAND

Once upon a time there was a man named Orlando Tregennis and
he was in love with his wife,

And he thought he would express his love by serenading her but
his serenade wasn't very successful because his playing inter-
fered with his singing because all he could play was the fife,

So then he said, I will climb the highest mountain in the world and
name it after my wife and then she will give me a look of
love, so he climbed the highest mountain in the world and
his wife was indeed whom he named it after,

But she didn't give him a look of love, she gave him a look of
laughter,

And not only a look of laughter but a look of menace,

Because he named it after his wife by naming it Mt. Mrs. Orlando
Tregennis,

So then he said that he certainly was sorry that during the great
war he had absent-mindedly forgotten to join the army,

Because he said if he had been entitled to a bonus he would have
given her every penny even though she was already so en-
trancing that no amount of mere money could make her a jot
or tittle more allury or charmy,

And she greeted this remark with ribald merriment,

And she said that possibly money wouldn't get her any further
    than she was, but she'd like a chance to try the experiment,
So then Mr. Tregennis said, Well, I haven't any gold,
But I will give you my most precious possession, I will give you my
    cold,
And he gave her his cold and first of all she tried to spurn it,
And then she tried to return it,
But he said No darling, now it's your very own cold,
It is yours to have and to hold,
Because if you reckon I don't give gifts for keeps you made a mis-
    take when you reckoned,
Because there hasn't been an Indian-giver in the Tregennis family
    since my great-great-grandfather, old Hiawatha Tregennis II.
But she wouldn't take no for an answer, but he wouldn't say yes,
    and Mr. Tregennis's precious cold went shuttling back and
    forth between them for the rest of their lives,
And I hope everybody will turn out to be such self-sacrificing hus-
    bands and wives.

THE COMMON COLD

Go hang yourself, you old M.D.!
You shall no longer sneer at me.
Pick up your hat and stethoscope,
Go wash your mouth with laundry soap;
I contemplate a joy exquisite
In never paying you for your visit.
I did not call you to be told
My malady is a common cold.

By pounding brow and swollen lip;
By fever's hot and scaly grip;
By these two red redundant eyes
That weep like woeful April skies;
By racking snuffle, snort, and sniff;

By handkerchief after handkerchief;
This cold you wave away as naught
Is the damnedest cold man ever caught.

Give ear, you scientific fossil!
Here is the genuine Cold Colossal;
The Cold of which researchers dream,
The Perfect Cold, the Cold Supreme.
This honored system humbly holds
The Super-cold to end all colds;
The Cold Crusading for Democracy;
The Führer of the Streptococcracy.

Bacilli swarm within my portals
Such as were ne'er conceived by mortals,
But bred by scientists wise and hoary
In some Olympian laboratory;
Bacteria as large as mice,
With feet of fire and heads of ice
Who never interrupt for slumber
Their stamping elephantine rumba.

A common cold, forsooth, gadzooks!
Then Venus showed promise of good looks;
Don Juan was a budding gallant,
And Shakespeare's plays show signs of talent;
The Arctic winter is rather coolish,
And your diagnosis is fairly foolish.
Oh what derision history holds
For the man who belittled the Cold of Colds!

SPLASH!

Some people are do-it-some-other-timers and other people are do-
it-nowers,

And that is why manufacturers keep on manufacturing both bath-
tubs and showers,
Because some bathers prefer to recline
On the cornerstone of their spine,
While others, who about their comfort are less particular,
Bathe perpendicular.
Thus from the way people lave themselves
You can tell how under other circumstances they will behave
themselves.
Tubbers indulge in self-indulgence,
And they loll soaking until they are a moist mass of warm rosy
effulgence,
And finally they regretfully hoist themselves up and shiver and say
Brrrr! even though the atmosphere is like an orchid-house
and the mirror is coated with steam,
And they pat at their moistness with a towel as soft as whipped
cream,
So it is obvious that the tubber is a sybaritic softie,
And will never accomplish anything lofty.
How different is the showerer, whose chest is often festooned with
hair such as bedecked our ancestors arboreal!
He has no time to waste on luxuriousness, but skims through the
spray with the speed of a Democratic politician skimming
through a Republican editorial,
After which he grates himself on something which he calls a
towel,
But which anybody covered with human skin instead of cowhide
would call a file or a spur or a rowel,
And thus at the same time he avoids procrastination
And improves his circulation,
So we see that the showerer is a Spartan,
And sternly guides his ambitious life along the lines laid down by
baccalaureate preachers and Bruce Barton,
And this is the reason that in the game of life although occasional
points are won by the tubber,
The showerer always gets game and rubber.

Sometimes tubbers and showerers get into arguments about tubs
and showers and become very warlike and martial,
But I myself have always been strictly impartial,
Yes, I am neutrally anchored halfway between Calais and Dover,
And all I will impartially and neutrally say is that there are three
things you can't do in a shower, and one is read, and the
other is smoke, and the other is get wet all over.

I'LL GET ONE TOMORROW

Barber, barber, come and get me;
Hairy torrents irk and fret me.
Hair and hair again appears,
And climbs like ivy round my ears;
Hair across my collar gambols;
Down my neck it wayward ambles;
Ever down it trips and trickles,
Yes, and where it trips, it tickles.
Barber dear, I wish I knew
Why I do not visit you,
Why I grudge the minutes ten
In your sanitary den,
Why I choose to choke on hair
Rather than to mount your chair.
Men no busier than I
Weekly to your office hie;
Men no braver than myself
Confront the armory on your shelf;
Men no wealthier than me
Gladly meet your modest fee,
And for a multiple of a dollar
Keep the jungle off their collar.
I alone am shy and flustered,
A solitary, cowardly custard,
Shaggy as a prize Angora,

[171]

Overrun with creeping flora.
Barber, barber, you're in luck;
The bell has rung, the hour has struck.
Sloth is strong, but hair is stronger;
I cannot stand it any longer.
Barber, barber, here I come;
Shake up the odorous bay rum;
Bring on your shears, your scythes, your snippers,
Bring on your crisp, electric clippers;
Employ a dozen extra sweepers;
Bring giant harvesters and reapers;
I warn you that a bumper crop
Waits to overwhelm your shop.
Barber, barber, be verbose,
Be anything, but clip me close;
Leave me razored, leave me scissored,
Leave me hairless as a lizard;
Barber, barber, singe and scald;
Barber, can't you make me bald?
I'd be the happiest of men,
And never think of you again.

THE JAPANESE

How courteous is the Japanese;
He always says, "Excuse it, please."
He climbs into his neighbor's garden,
And smiles, and says, "I beg your pardon";
He bows and grins a friendly grin,
And calls his hungry family in;
He grins, and bows a friendly bow;
"So sorry, this my garden now."

THE FRIENDLY TOUCH

You go into a store and select half-a-dozen shirts and charge them,
And finally you get them paid for along about the time you either
      have to give them away or enlarge them,
And you don't go back to the store because although it has nice
      shirts, still, for your modest budget it's rather expensive,
And the possibilities of a charge account are too extensive,
You need some more shirts,
But your conscience hurts;
Your bureau drawer is emptied
But you refuse to be temptied;
You say, No, they have nice shirts but they look on any purchase
      under two hundred dollars with boredom,
And I simply can't afforedom.
Well, everything is simply splendid,
And suddenly you get a letter from them saying they have been
      looking over their accounts and note that they have not
      served you since April 15th, 1931, and in what way have
      they offended?
This is followed by other letters even more imploring,
Indeed the tone becomes positively adoring;
They beg you to purchase something from them,
They egg you to purchase something from them;
They hint that if their plea you ignore,
Why, they will simply close up their store,
And you succumb to their appealings,
And buy half-a-dozen shirts just so as not to hurt their feelings.
Well, their feelings seem to recover all right from the wreck,
Because around the middle of the following month you get a let-
      ter from them saying they have been looking over their ac-
      counts and how about favoring them with a check?
This is followed by other letters even more suggestive of lovers'
      meetings ending in journeys,
And in about two weeks they turn over their share of the corre-
      spondence to their attorneys,

So you send the check and the affair is ended,

And you swear off and in about a year you get a letter from them saying they have been looking over their accounts and note that they have not served you since October 2nd, 1936, and in what way have they offended?

Some people chase their own coattails in revolving doors,

And other people write letters for stores.

DON'T GRIN, OR YOU'LL HAVE TO BEAR IT

It is better in the long run to possess an abscess or a tumor

Than to possess a sense of humor.

People who have senses of humor have a very good time,

But they never accomplish anything of note, either despicable or sublime,

Because how can anybody accomplish anything immortal

When they realize they look pretty funny doing it and have to stop to chortle?

Everybody admits that Michelangelo's little things in the Sistine Chapel are so immortal they have everybody reeling,

But I'll bet he could never have dashed them off if he had realized how undignified he looked lying up there with his stomach on the ceiling.

Yes, fatal handicaps in life are fortunately few,

But the most fatal of all is the faculty of seeing the other person's point of view,

And if your devoted mother suggests that you will some day be rich and famous, why perish the suggestion;

That is, perish it if you are afflicted with the suspicion that there are two sides to every question.

Good gracious, how could anybody corner wheat

If they were sissy enough to reflect that they were causing a lot of other people to be unable to afford to eat?

Look at mayors and congressmen and presidents, always excepting college presidents, such as Harvard's Conant;

Do you think they could get elected if they admitted even to them-
       selves that there was anything to be said for their opponent?
No, no, genius won't get you as far as common everyday facility
Unless it is accompanied by a conviction of infallibility,
And people who have a sense of humor are extremely gullible,
But not enough so, alas, to believe that they are infullible.

SONG FOR DITHERERS

I journey not whence nor whither,
I languish alone in a dither;
I journey not to nor fro,
And my dither to me I owe.
I could find a pleasanter name for it
Had I somebody else to blame for it,
But alas that beneath the sun
Dithers are built for one.
This is the song of the dither,
For viol, bassoon or zither,
Till the greenest simpletons wither
This is the song of the dither;
When regular troubles are wrong with you,
Others are guilty along with you;
Dithers are private trouble
Where you privately stew and bubble.
Come hither, somebody, come hither,
Would you care for a share of my dither?
I want somebody else to be mad at;
"Have at you!" to cry, and be had at.
I am tired of being angry at me,
There is room in my dither for three,
There is room in my dither for two;
We could butt at each other and moo;
We could hiss like the serpent, and slither
Through the tropical depths of my dither;

[175]

Like bees we could fight along beelines,
Or spit at each other like felines;
I care not who gaineth the laurel,
All I want is a foe and a quarrel.
Alone in my dither I pine.
For the sake of the days of lang syne,
For your white-haired old feyther and mither,
Come along, come along to my dither.
With no foe in my dither but me,
I swoon, I lay doon, and I dee.

THE STRANGE CASE OF MR. DONNYBROOK'S BOREDOM

Once upon a time there was a man named Mr. Donnybrook.

∽

He was married to a woman named Mrs. Donnybrook.

∽

Mr. and Mrs. Donnybrook dearly loved to be bored.

∽

Sometimes they were bored at the ballet, other times at the cinema.

∽

They were bored riding elephants in India and elevators in the Empire State Building.

∽

They were bored in speakeasies during Prohibition and in cocktail lounges after Repeal.

∽

They were bored by Grand Dukes and garbagemen, debutantes and demimondaines, opera singers and operations.

∽

They scoured the Five Continents and the Seven Seas in their mad pursuit of boredom.

∽

This went on for years and years.

∽

One day Mr. Donnybrook turned to Mrs. Donnybrook.

∽

My dear, he said, we have reached the end of our rope.

∽

We have exhausted every yawn.

∽

The world holds nothing more to jade our titillated palates.

∽

Well, said Mrs. Donnybrook, we might try insomnia.

∽

So they tried insomnia.

∽

About two o'clock the next morning Mr. Donnybrook said, My, insomnia is certainly quite boring, isn't it?

∽

Mrs. Donnybrook said it certainly was, wasn't it?

∽

Mr. Donnybrook said it certainly was.

∽

Pretty soon he began to count sheep.

∽

Mrs. Donnybrook began to count sheep, too.

∽

After awhile Mr. Donnybrook said, Hey, you're counting my sheep!

∽

Stop counting my sheep, said Mr. Donnybrook.

∽

Why, the very idea, said Mrs. Donnybrook.

∽

I guess I know my own sheep, don't I?

∽

How? said Mr. Donnybrook.

∽

They're cattle, said Mrs. Donnybrook.

∽

They're cattle, and longhorns at that.

૱

Furthermore, said Mrs. Donnybrook, us cattle ranchers is shore
tired o' you sheepmen plumb ruinin' our water.

૱

I give yuh fair warnin', said Mrs. Donnybrook, yuh better git them
woolly Gila monsters o' yourn back across the Rio Grande
afore mornin' or I'm a goin' to string yuh up on the nearest
cottonwood.

૱

Carramba! sneered Mr. Donnybrook. Thees ees free range, no?

૱

No, said Mrs. Donnybrook, not for sheepmen.

૱

She strung him up on the nearest cottonwood.

૱

Mr. Donnybrook had never been so bored in his life.

EXPERIENCE TO LET

Experience is a futile teacher,
Experience is a prosy preacher,
Experience is a fruit tree fruitless,
Experience is a shoe-tree bootless.
For sterile wearience and drearience,
Depend, my boy, upon experience.
The burnt child, urged by rankling ire,
Can hardly wait to get back at the fire,
And, mulcted in the gambling den,
Men stand in line to gamble again.
Who says that he can drink or not?
The sober man? Nay nay, the sot.
He who has never tasted jail
Lives well within the legal pale,
While he who's served a heavy sentence,

Renews the racket, not repentance.
The nation bankrupt by a war
Thinks to recoup with just one more;
The wretched golfer, divot-bound,
Persists in dreams of the perfect round.
Life's little suckers chirp like crickets
While spending their all on losing tickets.
People whose instinct instructs them naught
But must by experience be taught,
Will never learn by suffering once,
But ever and ever play the dunce.
Experience! Wise men do not need it!
Experience! Idiots do not heed it!
I'd trade my lake of experience
For just one drop of common sense.

THE MAN WITH TWO NEW SUITS

Who is that well-dressed handsome man?
Is everybody's eager cry,
I make response, for the fleeting nonce:
Excuse me, it is I!
The clangorous bells their homage pay,
The jubilant whistle toots,
And the murmur grows, Look, there he goes,
The man with two new suits!

The first is a tasteful quiet gray,
The second is a quiet brown;
One wouldn't suppose such reticent clothes
Would so excite the town.
The coats display no waspish waist,
The trousers boast no pleats,
But the collars fit like Glyn and It,
And Oh the lordly seats!

On the gleaming steps of the City Hall
The Mayor takes his stand,
With welcoming teeth, and a laurel wreath
And a gold key in his hand.
The city is yours, the Mayor cries,
And the guard of honor salutes,
And the gaping crowd cheers long and loud
For the man with two new suits.

The brown one has a single breast,
And the breast of the gray is double,
And they mold the form to the perfect norm
Where the scapulae cease to trouble.
The trousers nestle around the hips,
Then flow like a weeping willow —
Oh as gay am I as a butterfly,
Yet snug as the armadillo!

The old suit bagged across the knees,
And it also bagged behind;
The foraging moth had pierced its cloth,
And the nap was neatly shined.
I gave that suit to a shabby tramp,
I thought his poverty earned it,
And he said What's that? And then he spat,
And he took it out and burned it.

But now bring forth your noblest malt,
Your noblest barley and grape,
Triumphal parade and cavalcade
And torrent of ticker tape!
Now man and child shall work no more,
But seize their zithers and lutes,
And spend their days in endless praise
Of the man with two new suits!

IT'S SNUG TO BE SMUG

Oh, sometimes I wish I had the wings of an angel because then I could fly through the air with the greatest of ease,

And if I wanted to be somewhere else I could get there without spending any money on taxis or railroad tickets or tips or fees,

Yes, I could fly to Paris and do as a Parisian, or fly to Rome and do as a Roman,

But on the other hand wings would necessitate my sleeping on my abdomen,

So I don't really wish I had the wings of an angel, but sometimes I wish I had the sweet voice of a thrush,

And then if I sang an Indian Love Lyric why thousands of beautiful beauties would harken and quiver and blush,

And it would be a treat to hear my rendition of Sweet Alice Ben Bolt,

But on the other hand who would go to harken to anybody who was known to eat insects and moult?

So I don't really wish I had the sweet voice of a thrush, but sometimes I wish I had the courage of a lion,

And then I could look life in the eye with a will of iron,

And to a goose, or a burglar, or even a butler, I wouldn't hesitate to say Boo!

But on the other hand I might encounter a goose or a burglar or a butler who had the courage of a lion too,

So I don't really wish I had the courage of a lion but sometimes I wish I had the innocence of a lamb,

And then I would never wake up crying Fie on me! and Damn!

But on the other hand innocence is a security on which it is hard to borrow,

Because all it means is that either you get eaten by a wolf today or else the shepherd saves you from the wolf so he can sell you to the butcher tomorrow,

So I do not really wish I had the innocence of a lamb,

I guess I'll stay just as I am.

TO A LADY PASSING TIME BETTER LEFT
UNPASSED

O lady of the lucent hair,
Why do you play at solitaire?
What imp, what demon misanthrope,
Prompted this session of lonely hope?
What boredom drives you, and great Lord!
How can such as you be bored?
The gleaming world awaits your eye
While you essay futility.
That mouth is shaped for livelier sport
Than paging of a pasteboard court —
Why, even the Red Knave longing lingers,
While Black Queens wait, in those white fingers. —
See now the joy that lights your face
Squandered on some fortuitous ace,
Where formerly dark anger burned
When a five perverse would not be turned.
O, know you not, that darkling frown
Could topple Caesar's empire down;
That quick, bright joy, if flashed on men,
Could sudden build it up again?
Get up! Get up! Throw down the pack!
Rise in your gown of shining black!
Withdraw, my dear, while you are able
The slender feet from 'neath the table;
Remove from the regretful baize
The elbows curved in cunning ways.
Is there no game that pleasure brings
But fretting over painted things?
No gay, ecstatic end in view
But shuffle and begin anew?
Get up, I tell you, girl, get up!
Wine keeps not ever in the cup;
Even Love immortal, love undying,

Finds the loved one's Patience trying.
Let two-and-fifty rivals hiss me —
For God's sake, girl, come here and kiss me.

THE STRANGE CASE OF THE BLACKMAILING DOVE

Once upon a time there was a flock of doves.

༄

They used to sit around the dovecote and coo.

༄

The littlest dove was named Daingerfield.

༄

Daingerfield could coo like the dickens, but he never got anything to eat.

༄

Whenever anything to eat turned up, the buxom doves elbowed him out of the way.

༄

The buxom doves got buxomer and buxomer.

༄

Daingerfield got tenuouser and tenuouser.

༄

Meanwhile he kept on cooing.

༄

One day his mind was weakened by starvation and he forgot his lines.

༄

He didn't say Coo.

༄

He said Boo.

༄

The buxom doves were panic-stricken. They fluttered around him like doves.

༄

Daingerfield knows all, said the buxom doves. But good old Daingerfield won't tell, will you Daingerfield?

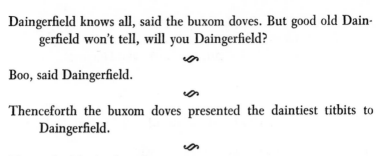

Boo, said Daingerfield.

Thenceforth the buxom doves presented the daintiest titbits to Daingerfield.

This is the life, he thought.

Boo, he said. Who's holding out on a titbit? Boo!

After awhile the doves were invited to a society wedding.

It was the wedding of Felise Bankery, only child of Mrs. Liz Bankery Brokery Buttery and the late Reginald Bankery, the noted runner-up.

Felise was to marry the dashing Borogavian mixed triples runner-up, Baron Von Luciano.

Mrs. Liz Bankery Brokery Buttery thought a flock of doves in the church would be nice.

Different, she said, and sort of symbolic.

The doves were released as the happy pair stood at the altar.

The cathedral echoed with their cooing.

Daingerfield couldn't see a thing. He sulked until the cooing stopped.

Boo! said Daingerfield clearly.

The bride jumped. So did the groom. Then they beckoned to Daingerfield.

∽

This is soft, thought Daingerfield. He approached, booing mellifluously.

∽

Why do you boo? asked Felise. Is it because of the brace and a half of twins ensuing from my secret marriage to the chauffeur?

∽

Boo, said Daingerfield with a smirk.

∽

Why do you boo? asked Baron Von Luciano. Is it because the social position of a baron in Borogavia is that of an extra waiter at a banquet?

∽

Boo, said Daingerfield with another smirk.

∽

The bride turned to the groom.

∽

After all, she said simply, a baron is a baron, and we don't have to go to Borogavia, do we?

∽

The groom turned to the bride.

∽

After all, he said, a hundred million is a hundred million, and we can fire the chauffeur, can't we?

∽

No indeed, said the bride.

∽

Coo, said Daingerfield.

NINE MILES TO THE RAILROAD

The country is a funny place,
I like to look it in the face.

[185   ]

And everywhere I look I see
Some kind of animal or tree.

Indeed, I frequently remark
The country is rather like a park.

The country cows give milk, and moo,
Just like their sisters in the zoo.
The rural squirrel in his rage
Chirks like a squirrel in a cage.

Animals, in their joys and passions,
Like women, follow city fashions.

The horses here pull plows and carts
All day until the sun departs.
In summer, or when fields are frosted,
They work until they are exhausted.

Next, to the track themselves they hie
To be bet upon by the likes of I.

As through the countryside you pass
You look at grass and still more grass.
Grass leers at you where'er you turn
Until your tired eyelids burn.

They ought to break it up, or soften it,
With pretty signs saying, please keep offen it.

I like the country very much.
It's good to hear and smell and touch.
It makes you feel akin with Nature,
Though wobbly on her nomenclature.

I'd free my lungs of city air
If I didn't feel much more important there.

EVERY DAY IS MONDAY

Monday is the day that everything starts all over again,
Monday is the day when just as you are beginning to feel peaceful
you have to get up and get dressed and put on your old gray
bonnet and drive down to Dover again,
It is the day when life becomes grotesque again,
Because it is the day when you have to face your desk again;
When the telephone rings on Saturday or Sunday you are pleased
because it probably means something pleasing and you take
the call with agility,
But when it rings on any other day it just usually means some ad-
ditional responsibility,
And if in doubt,
Why the best thing to do is to answer it in a foreign accent or if
you are a foreigner answer it in a native accent and say you
are out.
Oh, there is not a week-day moment that can't wring a sigh from
you,
Because you are always being confronted with people who want
to sell you something, or if they don't want to sell you something, there is something they want to buy from you,
And every shining hour swaggers arrogantly up to you demanding to be improved,
And apparently not only to improve it, but also to shine it, is what
you are behooved.
Oh for a remedy, oh for a panacea, oh for a something, oh yes, oh
for a coma or swoon,
Yes indeed, oh for a coma that would last from nine A.M. on
Monday until Saturday noon.

POOR MR. STRAWBRIDGE

Once there was a man who lived by the ocean named Mr. Strawbridge,
And all he wanted was a drawbridge,

But when people asked him what kind
He couldn't make up his mind.
His fingernails he would bite and his thumbs he would twiddle
Trying to decide whether he wanted one that revolved on a pivot
     or one that went up in the middle,
So finally everybody went to Mr. Strawbridge
And asked him why he wanted a drawbridge.
And Mr. Strawbridge smiled a smile seraphic
And said he wanted it because he wanted to interfere with traffic.
He said it gave him great satisfaction
To sit on his veranda and watch the Atlantic Ocean in action
But he said sometimes on Sundays and holidays he couldn't see
     the Atlantic for the motorists,
And he said he'd rather see the former than the latter even though
     they were handsome and respectable Kiwanians and Lions
     and Rotarists,
And he said maybe he was a silly old goose,
But it always gave him a pain to see a line of automobiles practi-
     cally hooked up together like freight cars on a long freight
     train, particularly when the freight train was ten miles long
     and you never seemed to get to the caboose,
And he said that doubtless all the gipsying was most romantic,
But he still preferred looking at the Atlantic
And he said he didn't see why people went out in one automobile
     between a lot of other automobiles, because they didn't get
     any air or scenery,
No, they just got a view of the license plate in front and a lot of
     annoyance and dust and gasolinery,
And therefore, said Mr. Strawbridge,
Everybody else would see just as much and I would see much
     more if they were all held up somewhere by an open draw-
     bridge,
So all his friends said he was a genius,
And they gave him a lot of orchids and gardenius,
But they never gave him a drawbridge,
And that is why I call him poor Mr. Strawbridge.

COFFEE WITH THE MEAL

A gentlemanly gentleman, as mild as May,
Entered a restaurant famed and gay.
A waiter sat him in a draughty seat
And laughingly inquired what he'd like to eat.
"Oh I don't want venison, I don't want veal,
But I do insist on coffee with the meal.
Bring me clams in a chilly group,
And a large tureen of vegetable soup,
Steak as tender as a maiden's dream,
With lots of potatoes hashed in cream,
And a lettuce and tomato salad, please
And crackers and a bit of Roquefort cheese,
But waiter, the gist of my appeal,
Is coffee with, coffee with, coffee *with* the meal."
The waiter groaned and he wrung his hands;
"Perhaps da headwaiter onderstands."
Said the sleek headwaiter, like a snobbish seal,
"What, monsieur? Coffee with the meal?"
His lip drew up in scornful laughter;
"Monsieur desires a demi-tasse after!"
Monsieur's eyes grew hard as steel,
He said, "I'm ordering coffee with the meal.
Hot black coffee in a great big cup,
Fuming, steaming, filled right up.
I don't want coffee iced in a glass,
And I don't want a miserable demi-tasse,
But what I'll have, come woe, come weal,
Is coffee with, coffee with, coffee *with* the meal."
The headwaiter bowed like a poppy in the breeze;
"Monsieur desires coffee with the salad or the cheese?"
Monsieur said, "Now you're getting warmer;
Coffee with the latter, coffee with the former;
Coffee with the steak, coffee with the soup,
Coffee with the clams in a chilly group;

Yes, and with a cocktail I could do,
So bring me coffee with the cocktail, too.
I'll fight to the death for my bright ideal,
Which is coffee with, coffee with, coffee *with* the meal."
The headwaiter swiveled on a graceful heel;
"Certainly, certainly, coffee with the meal!"
The waiter gave an obsequious squeal,
"Yes sir, yes sir, coffee with the meal!"
Oh what a glow did Monsieur feel
At the warming vision of coffee with the meal.
One hour later Monsieur, alas!
Got his coffee in a demi-tasse.

THE QUEEN IS IN THE PARLOR

Let's go over to Lily's,
And we'll all play games;
We'll act like regular sillies,
We'll assume ridiculous names,
We'll embarrass the butler,
And shock the maids,
With some of our subtler
Sly charades.
Come along, come along to Lily's,
Effervescent incessantly Lily's,
Come along, come along to Lily's,
And we'll all play games.

Lily is loaded with strictures
And many a palpable hit
For people who won't draw pictures,
For people who won't be IT.
There are sharpened pencils
And **virgin** papers,

All the utensils
For mental capers.
Here's a new one! You're going to love it!
Just enter into the spirit of it!
The name of the game is, Who Is Whom?
Harold, you have to leave the room;
I hope a few minutes alone won't bore you;
We'll whistle when we are ready for you.
Amanda, sit on the chandelier;
You represent Eternity, dear;
Now let me think — oh yes, Louise,
Stand on the sofa — on one leg, please;
You're Nelson — oh, it was Nelson's arm!
Well, a change of limbs lends whimsical charm.
George and Edward are Scrooge and Marley;
Pincus, you be Bonnie Prince Charlie.
Now, do I dare be Cleopatra?
No, really I don't! Why George, you flattra!
Everyone ready? This is fun!
Harold must guess us, every one,
And portray us all in a cartoon trim
While we each write a sonnet on him.
Hoo hoo, Harold! Hoo hoo! Hoo hoo!
Come in now, Harold, we're ready for you!
Hoo hoo, Harold! — Oh no! Not that!
Harold is missing, and so's his hat.

Let's go over to Lily's,
We'll all play games;
We'll bloom like daffy-down-dillies
And romp like Colonial Dames.
Anne, think of a number!
George, pick a card!
But I shall slumber
And slumber hard.
Come along, come along to Lily's,

Energetic aesthetically Lily's
Come along, come along to Lily's,
The Queen of the Parlor Games!

THE EIGHT O'CLOCK PERIL

Breakfast is an institution that I don't know who commenced it,
But I am not for it, I am against it.
It is a thoroughly inedible repast,
And the dictionary says it is derived from the words *break,* mean-
    ing *to break,* and *fast,* meaning a *fast,* so to breakfast means
    to break your fast.
Well that just shows how far you can trust a dictionary,
Because I never saw a definition that was more utterly fictionary.
The veriest child could see it doesn't check,
Because if the first syllable of breakfast means *to break,* why is it
    pronounced *brek?*
Shame on you, you old lexicographers, I shall call you laxicogra-
    phers because you have grown very lax,
Because it is perfectly obvious that the first syllable in breakfast is
    derived from the far-famed Yale football cheer, which is
    Brekekekex co-ax co-ax,
And did you even get the second syllable right? Why a thousand
    times No,
Because the *fast* in *breakfast* doesn't mean fast, *abstinence from
    food,* it means *fast,* not *slow.*
So with that in mind we can peek behind the scenes
And then we can see what *break-fast* really means,
It means that if you wake up in the morning feeling unappetized
    and sickly,
Why you are confronted by a meal and the entire Yale football
    team coaxes you with an axe to eat it quickly.

[192]

THE STRANGE CASE OF MR. BALLANTINE'S VALENTINE

Once upon a time there was an attorney named Mr. Ballantine.

✧

He lived in the spacious gracious days of the nineteenth century.

✧

Mr. Ballantine didn't know they were spacious and gracious.

✧

He thought they were terrible.

✧

The reason he thought they were terrible was that love had passed him by.

✧

Mr. Ballantine had never received a valentine.

✧

He said to his partner, My name is Mr. Ballantine and I have never received a valentine.

✧

His partner said, Well my name is Mr. Bogardus and I have received plenty of valentines and I just as soon wouldn't.

✧

He said Mr. Ballantine didn't know when he was well off.

✧

Mr. Ballantine said, I know my heart, I know my mind, I know I long for a valentine.

✧

He said here it was St. Valentine's day and when he sat down at his desk what did he find?

✧

Valentines?

✧

No.

✧

I find affidavits, said Mr. Ballantine.

✧

That's the kind of valentine get, said Mr. Ballantine.

⌇

Mr. Bogardus said that affidavit was better than no bread.

⌇

Mr. Ballantine said that affidavit, affidavit, affidavit onward, into the valley of death rode the six hundred.

⌇

Mr. Bogardus said that any man who would rhyme "onward" with "six hundred" didn't deserve any affidavits at all.

⌇

Mr. Ballantine said coldly that he was an attorney, not a poet, and Mr. Bogardus had better take the matter up directly with Lord Tennyson.

⌇

Mr. Bogardus said Oh all right, and speaking of lords, he couldn't remember who was the king before David, but Solomon was the king affidavit.

⌇

Mr. Ballantine buried Mr. Bogardus in the cellar and went out in search of love.

⌇

Towards evening he encountered a maiden named Herculena, the Strongest Woman in the World.

⌇

He said, Madam my name is Mr. Ballantine and I have never received a valentine.

⌇

Herculena was delighted.

⌇

She said, My name is Herculena the Strongest Woman in the World, and I have never received a valentine either.

⌇

Mr. Ballantine and Herculena decided to be each other's valentine.

⌇

All was merry as a marriage bell.

⌇

Mr. Ballantine nearly burst with joy.

〜

Herculena nearly burst with pride.

〜

She flexed her biceps.

〜

She asked Mr. Ballantine to pinch her muscle.

〜

Mr. Ballantine recovered consciousness just in time to observe the vernal equinox.

〜

He thought she said bustle.

EPILOGUE TO MOTHER'S DAY, WHICH IS TO BE PUBLISHED ON ANY DAY BUT MOTHER'S DAY

Mothers! Mothers! It was visions of mothers that had been relentlessly haunting me,

Wherever I turned I saw misty mothers sitting around taunting me.

It was battalions of irritated spectres that blanched my face and gave me this dull and lustre-lack eye,

Night and day I was surrounded by mothers, from Mrs. Whistler, Senior, to Mrs. Dionne and from Yale the mother of men to Niobe and the mother of the Gracchi.

I resented this supernatural visitation, these are not the dark ages, these are the days of modernity,

I wilted before this intrusion of miasmic maternity.

Mothers, I cried, oh myriads of mothers, I can stand it no longer, what can I do for you?

Do you want me to have you exorcised, do you want me to pray for you, do you want me to say Boo for you?

I know you are major figures in history's Who's Whom,

But I wish you would go away because your company is flattering but I would rather have your room.

Then they replied in hollow chorus,

We have thought of something that we want to have published but we can't write so you will have to write it for us,

And if you write it we will leave you alone,

And if you don't write it we will haunt you brain from skull and flesh from bone,

So I acquiesced and the ghastly horde dictated to me and I wrote it,

And a promise is a promise and an army of ghostly mothers is an army of ghostly mothers, so I quote it: —

M is for the preliminary million-dollar advertising appropriation,

O means that she is always white-haired, bespectacled and at least eighty-five years old,

T is for Telegraph message number 31B which contains a tastefully blended expression of sentiment and congratulation,

H is for the coast-to-coast questionnaire which proved conclusively that seven-and-one-half citizens out of every ten with incomes of $5000 a year or better would rather have their mother than gold.

E is for the Elephants which everybody is very glad didn't sit down on their mothers,

R is for Rosemary which is for Remembrance of the fact that a mother is one thing that you will never have more than one of,

Put them all together and before you can say H. Wellington Carruthers, they spell what everybody who loves their mother only once a year and then only at the instigation of the Chamber of Commerce is a son of.

ENGLAND EXPECTS

Let us pause to consider the English,

Who when they pause to consider themselves they get all reticently thrilled and tinglish.

Englishmen are distinguished by their traditions and ceremonials,

And also by their affection for their colonies and their condescension to their colonials.

When foreigners ponder world affairs, why sometimes by doubts they are smitten,

But Englishmen know instinctively that what the world needs most is whatever is best for Great Britain.

English people disclaim sparkle and verve,

But speak without reservations of their Anglo-Saxon reserve.

After listening to little groups of English ladies and gentlemen at cocktail parties and in hotels and Pullmans, of defining Anglo-Saxon reserve I despair,

But I think it consists of assuming that nobody else is there.

All good young Englishmen go to Oxford or Cambridge and they all write and publish books before their graduation,

And I often wondered how they did it until I realized that they have to do it because their genteel accents are so developed that they can no longer understand each other's spoken words so the written word is their only means of intercommunication.

England is the last home of the aristocracy, and the art of protecting the aristocracy from the encroachments of commerce has been raised to quite an art,

Because in America a rich butter-and-egg man is only a rich butter-and-egg man or at most an honorary LL.D. of some hungry university, but in England why before he knows it he is Sir Benjamin Buttery, Bart.

Anyhow, I think the English people are sweet,

And we might as well get used to them because when they slip and fall they always land on their own or somebody else's feet.

THIS WAS TOLD ME IN CONFIDENCE

Oh, I do like a little bit of gossip
In the course of a cozy little chat,
And I often wonder why

My neighbors all imply
I'm a pussy, I'm a tabby, I'm a cat.
Mrs. Dooley murmured meow at me this morning;
Mrs. Cohen would have cut me if she could;
But my feelings aren't so filmy
That names are going to kill me,
And a little bit of gossip does me good.

Oh, I do like a little bit of gossip;
I am pleased with Mr. Moffet's double life.
It's provocative to watch
Mr. Taylor guzzle Scotch;
I wonder if he knows about his wife?
The sheriff wants a word with Mrs. Walker;
She doesn't pay her bills the way she should;
Yet I hear from several sources
That she gambles on the horses —
Oh, a little bit of gossip does me good.

Oh, I do like a little bit of gossip;
It seems to lend a savor to my tea;
The deplorable mistakes
That everybody makes
Are calories and vitamins to me.
If I tell you Mrs. Drew is off to Reno,
You are not to breathe a word, that's understood;
For I said to Mrs. Drew
That I heard it all from you —
Oh, a little bit of gossip does me good.

Oh, I do like a little bit of gossip,
But for scandal or for spite there's no excuse;
To think of Mrs. Page
Telling lies about my age!
Well, her tongue is like her morals, rather loose.
Mrs. Murgatroyd eats opium for breakfast,

And claims I'm running after Mr. Wood;
That sort of vicious slander
Arouses all my dander —
But a little bit of gossip does me good.

UNANSWERED BY REQUEST

There are several things in life that keep me guessing,
And one of them is what are the French words for French leave
and French fried potatoes and French dressing,
And I am also a trifle vague
About how you ask people to a Dutch treat or talk to them like a
Dutch uncle in The Hague.
And why do restaurants put signs in their windows advertising
REAL HOME COOKING and expect the customers to come
rushing in all panting and overjoyed
When the reason that half the people who eat in restaurants are
eating in restaurants is because with home cooking they have
become cloyed?
And when is a violin a fiddle?
And when the tide goes out here does it go in somewhere else or
does it just pile up and make the ocean deeper in the middle?
And who is the brownie whose duty it is to see that the theater curtain never goes up on time except the one evening that you
are late?
And who is the railroad dispatcher who arranges his dispatching so
that every time you are about to see something interesting out
of your train window your view is cut off by a hundred-car
freight?
These are the kind of riddles and conundrums with which life
Is far too rife,
But fortunately for the human race thinking people eventually discover that there is only one satisfactory way of dealing with a
riddle or a conundrum.
And that is to stop worrying about the answers and just get clean
out from undrum.

CAT NAPS ARE TOO GOOD FOR CATS

Oh, early every afternoon
I like a temporary swoon.
I do not overeat at luncheon,
I do not broach the bowl or puncheon;
Yet the hour from two to three
Is always sleepy-time to me.

Bolt upright at my desk I sit,
My elbows digging into it,
My chin into my hands doth fit,
My careful fingers screen my eyes,
And all my work before me lies,
Which leads inquisitive passer-bys
Who glance my way and see me nod,
To think me wide awake, if odd.

I would not sell my daily swoon
For all the rubies in Rangoon.
What! sell my swoon? My lovely swoon?
Oh, many and many's the afternoon
I've scoured the woods with Daniel Boone,
And sipped a julep with Lorna Doone
And former Governor Ruby Laffoon.
I'll sell my soul before my swoon,
It's not for sale, my swoon's immune.

From two to three each afternoon
Mine are the Mountains of the moon,
Mine a congenital silver spoon.
And I can lead a lost platoon
Or dive for pearls in a haunted lagoon,
Or guide a stratosphere balloon.
Oh, where the schooner schoons, I schoon,
I can talk lion, or baboon,

Or make a crooner cease to croon.
I like to swoon, for when I swoon
The universe is my macaroon.
Then blessings on thee, my afternoon torpor,
Thou makest a prince of a mental porpor.

THE CITY

This beautiful ditty
Is, for a change, about the city,
Although ditties aren't very popular
Unless they're rural and not metropular.

Sentimentalists object to towns initially
Because they are made artificially,
But so is vaccination,
While smallpox is an original creation.

Artists speak of everything urban
As the W.C.T.U. speaks of rye and bourbon,
And they say cities are only commercial marts,
But they fail to realize that no marts, no arts.

The country was made first,
Yes, but people lived in it and rehearsed,
And when they finally got civilization down,
Why, they moved to town.

Take country people, they suffer stoically,
But city people prefer to live unheroically;
Therefore city dentistry is less painful,
Because city dentists find it more gainful.

City people are querulous and queasy,
And they'd rather die than not live easy

And if they did die, they'd find fault
If they weren't put in an air-conditioned vault.

Yes, indeed, they are certainly sissies,
Not at all like Hercules or Ulysses,
But because they are so soft,
City life is comfortable, if not perpetually, at least oft.

NATURE KNOWS BEST

I don't know exactly how long ago Hector was a pup,
But it was quite long ago, and even then people used to have to
    start their day by getting up.
Yes, people have been getting up for centuries,
They have been getting up in palaces and Pullmans and peniten-
    tiaries.
The caveman had to get up before he could go out and track the
    brontosaurus,
Verdi had to get up before he could sit down and compose the
    Anvil Chorus,
Alexander had to get up before he could go around being domi-
    nant,
Even Rip Van Winkle had to get up from one sleep before he
    could climb the mountain and encounter the sleep which
    has made him prominent.
Well, birds are descended from birds and flowers are descended
    from flowers,
And human beings are descended from generation after genera-
    tion of ancestors who got up at least once every twenty-four
    hours,
And because birds are descended from birds they don't have to be
    forced to sing like birds, instead of squeaking like rats,
And because flowers are descended from flowers they don't have
    to be forced to smell like flowers, instead of like burning rub-
    ber or the Jersey flats,

But you take human beings, why their countless generations of
  ancestors who were always arising might just as well have
  spent all their lives on their mattresses or pallets,
Because their descendants haven't inherited any talent for getting
  up at all, no, every morning they have to be forced to get up
  either by their own conscience or somebody else's, or alarm
  clocks or valets.
Well, there is one obvious conclusion that I have always held to,
Which is that if Nature had really intended human beings to get
  up, why they would get up naturally and wouldn't have to
  be compelled to.

SUMMERGREEN FOR PRESIDENT

Winter comes but once a year but it lasts for most of it,
And you may think there is a chance it may be a mild one, but
  there isn't a ghost of it.
Some people still say ice is nicer than slush,
And to those people I say Hush.
Some people still say snow is nicer than rain,
Which is like being still unreconciled to the defeat of James G.
  Blaine.
Some people still say a freeze is nicer than a thaw,
And I hope they find cold storage Japanese beetles in their slaw.

Slush is much nicer than ice because when you step in it you simply go splash, instead of immediately depositing either your
  posterior or your pate on it,
And also you don't have to skate on it.
Rain is much nicer than snow because you don't have to have
  rain plows piling rain up in six-foot piles exactly where you
  want to go,
And you don't have to build rain-men for the kiddies and frolic in
  sleighs and sleds, and also rain is nicer because it melts the
  snow.
A thaw is obviously much nicer than a freeze,

[203   ]

Because it annoys people with skis.

And in all my life I have only known one man who honestly liked winter better than summer,

Because every summer he used to have either his tonsils or his appendix or something out, and every winter he was a plumber.

THE STRANGE CASE OF THE DEAD DIVORCEE

Once upon a time there was a beautiful woman named Mrs. Geraldine McGregor Hamilton Garfinkle Boyce.

⁓

Her first husband, Mr. McGregor, divorced her for infidelity.

⁓

That wasn't his real reason, but he didn't want to blast her reputation.

⁓

Her second husband, Mr. Hamilton, divorced her for infidelity, too.

⁓

He had better grounds, which he was too chivalrous to mention.

⁓

Her third husband, Mr. Garfinkle, was a cad.

⁓

He prepared a statement for the press setting forth his actual motives for divorcing her.

⁓

Her white-haired old mother pled tearfully with him for seven hours, pausing only to telephone her maid to bring over a dozen clean handkerchiefs.

⁓

Mr. Garfinkle, if a cad, was a soft-hearted cad.

⁓

He destroyed his original damaging statement and informed the press that he was divorcing his wife for infidelity.

⁓

It was in June that Mrs. Geraldine McGregor Hamilton Garfinkle
became Mrs. Geraldine McGregor Hamilton Garfinkle Boyce.

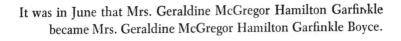

It was in July that Mr. Boyce slaughtered her with a priceless heirloom, an ice-pick.

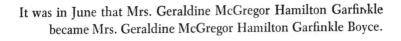

At the trial, Mr. Boyce pled guilty.

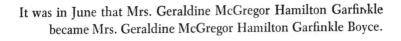

She was infidelitous, said Mr. Boyce, and I saw red.

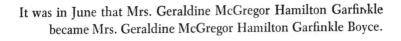

Mr. Boyce's lawyer asked him if he didn't have a better excuse.

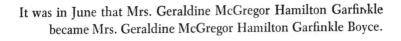

Maybe I have, said Mr. Boyce, but my lips are sealed.

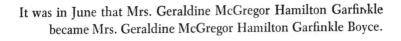

De mortuis, you know, said Mr. Boyce.

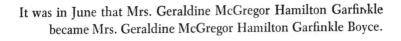

I will only say that she was infidelitous.

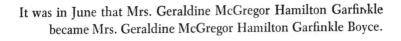

Mr. Boyce was convicted and condemned to die.

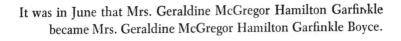

Came Mr. Boyce's Execution Eve.

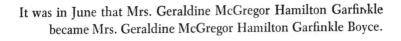

The reporters were already strapping their cameras to their ankles
when a delegation waited upon the Governor.

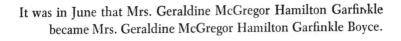

The delegation consisted of Mr. McGregor, Mr. Hamilton and
Mr. Garfinkle.

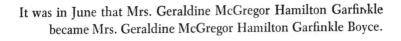

There are extenuating circumstances in the case of Mr. Boyce, said
Mr. McGregor.

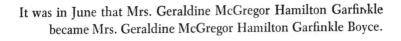

It is time the truth about Geraldine McGregor Hamilton Garfinkle
Boyce were told, said Mr. Hamilton.

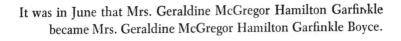

I would have told it long ago but for my soft heart, said Mr. Garfinkle.

&

Geraldine McGregor Hamilton Garfinkle Boyce was a juleper-in-the-manger, said Mr. McGregor, Mr. Hamilton and Mr. Garfinkle.

&

She never drank but half a mint julep, they said.

&

But when she was offered a mint julep, did she quietly drink half of it and quietly give the other half to her husband when he had finished his?

&

Not Geraldine McGregor Hamilton Garfinkle Boyce! they said.

&

She said No thank you, I only want half of one, I'll drink half of my husband's, they said.

&

Other women's husbands get a julep and a half, they said.

&

Geraldine McGregor Hamilton Garfinkle Boyce's husbands get half a julep, they said.

&

The Governor pardoned Mr. Boyce forthwith.

&

Ten minutes later the Governor's butler discovered the body of the Governor's lady on the veranda.

&

The ice-pick that protruded from her heart was a priceless heirloom.

EVERYBODY EATS TOO MUCH ANYHOW

You gulp your breakfast and glance at the clock,
Through eleventh hour packing you gallop amok
You bundle your bags in the back of the car,

You enter, she enters, and there you are.
It's au revoir to your modest abode,
You're gipsies, away on the open road;
The conversation is sweet as clover,
With breakfast practically hardly over.
"Darling, light me a cigarette?"
"At once and with all my heart, my pet;
"And by the way, we are off the track;
"We should have turned left a half-mile back."
You swing around with a cheery smile,
Thus far, a mile is only a mile.
The road is romance, so let it wind,
With breakfast an hour or so behind.
Under the tires the pebbles crunch,
And through the dust creep thoughts of lunch
The speedometer sits on a steady fifty
And more and more does lunch seem nifty.
Your eyes to the road ahead are glued,
She glances about in search of food.
She sees a place. She would like to try it.
She says so. Well, you're already by it.
Ignoring the road, you spot an eatery;
The look of it makes her interior teetery.
She sees a beauty. It's past and gone.
She's simmering now, like a tropical dawn.
She snubs the excuse as you begin it:
That there'll be another one any minute,
She says there won't. It must be a plot;
She's absolutely correct. There's not.
You finally find one. You stop and alight.
You're both too annoyed to eat a bite.
Oh, this is the gist of my gipsy song:
Next time carry your lunch along.

YES AND NO

Oh would I were a politician,
Or else a person with a mission.
Heavens, how happy I could be
If only I were sure of me.

How would I strut, could I believe
That, out of all the sons of Eve,
God had granted this former youth
A binding option on His truth.

One side of the moon we've seen alone;
The other she has never shown.
What dreamless sleep, what sound digestion,
Were it the same with every question!

Sometimes with secret pride I sigh
To think how tolerant am I;
Then wonder which is really mine:
Tolerance, or a rubber spine?

COLUMBUS

Once upon a time there was an Italian,
And some people thought he was a rapscallion,
But he wasn't offended,
Because other people thought he was splendid,
And he said the world was round,
And everybody made an uncomplimentary sound,
But his only reply was Pooh,
He replied, Isn't this fourteen ninety-two?
It's time for me to discover America if I know my chronology,
And if I discover America you owe me an apology,
So he went and tried to borrow some money from Ferdinand

But Ferdinand said America was a bird in the bush and he'd rather
      have a berdinand,
But Columbus' brain was fertile, it wasn't arid,
And he remembered that Ferdinand was unhappily married,
And he thought, there is no wife like a misunderstood one,
Because her husband thinks something is a terrible idea she is
      bound to think it a good one,
So he perfumed his handkerchief with bay rum and citronella,
And he went to see Isabella,
And he looked wonderful but he had never felt sillier,
And she said, I can't place the face but the aroma is familiar,
And Columbus didn't say a word,
All he said was, I am Columbus, the fifteenth-century Admiral
      Byrd,
And just as he thought, her disposition was very malleable,
And she said, Here are my jewels, and she wasn't penurious like
      Cornelia the mother of the Gracchi, she wasn't referring to
      her children, no, she was referring to her jewels, which were
      very very valuable,
So Columbus said, somebody show me the sunset and somebody
      did and he set sail for it,
And he discovered America and they put him in jail for it,
And the fetters gave him welts,
And they named America after somebody else,
So the sad fate of Columbus ought to be pointed out to every child
      and every voter,
Because it has a very important moral, which is, Don't be a dis-
      coverer, be a promoter.

A NECESSARY DIRGE

Sometimes it's difficult, isn't it, not to grow grim and rancorous
Because man's fate is so counter-clockwise and cantankerous.
Look at all the noble projects that die a-borning,
Look how hard it is to get to sleep at night and then how hard it is
      to wake up in the morning!

How easy to be unselfish in the big things that never come up and
      how hard in the little things that come up daily and hourly,
      oh yes,
Such as what heroic pleasure to give up the last seat in a lifeboat
      to a mother and babe, and what an irritation to give some
      housewife your seat on the Lexington Avenue Express!
How easy for those who do not bulge
To not overindulge!
O universe perverse, why and whence your perverseness?
Why do you not teem with betterness instead of worseness?
Do you get your only enjoyment
Out of humanity's annoyment?
Because a point I would like to discuss
Is, why wouldn't it be just as easy for you to make things easy for
      us?
But no, you will not listen, expostulation is useless,
Home is the fisherman empty-handed, home is the hunter caribou-
      less and mooseless.
Humanity must continue to follow the sun around
And accept the eternal run-around.
Well, and if that be the case, why come on humanity!
So long as it is our fate to be irked all our life let us just keep our
      heads up and take our irking with insouciant urbanity.

ONE MAN'S MEED IS ANOTHER MAN'S OVEREMPHASIS

I salute the section of our lordly Sunday journals which is entitled
      Scores of College Football Games Continued from Page One,
Because there a flock of not very notorious institutions of learning
      find their annual place in the sun.
Yes, the football season is a kindly time of year,
And during it we read of campuses of which at other times we do
      not often hear.

Would a playwright, for instance, ordinarily select Aurora as the Alma Mater for his hero?

Yet it is here recorded that Aurora one week held Wright Jr. to a six-to-six tie and the next week took the measure of Wartburg, nineteen to zero.

Yes, and the St. Cloud Teachers are an aggregation that no college-lover can conscientiously shelve,

Because they nosed out the Bemidji Teachers thirteen to twelve.

Oh ye of little faith who take Yale and Notre Dame for your Alpha and Omega,

What about Hiwassee, which outscored Biltmore, and Dillard, which engaged in a Homeric deadlock with Talladega?

When better endowments are offered,

Well, what's the matter with Augustana and Millsaps and Spearfish and Gustavus Adolphus and Wofford?

So if anybody makes derogatory remarks about the football season let us answer with scornful defiance,

And meanwhile let us not forget that Huron beat Yankton six to nothing on the very same day that Jamestown smothered Wahpeton Science.

THE STRANGE CASE OF THE PLEASING
TAXI–DRIVER

Once upon a time there was a taxi-driver named Llewellyn Abdullah — White — Male — $5-10\frac{1}{2}$ — 170.

Llewellyn had promised his mother he would be the best taxi-driver in the world.

His mother was in Heaven.

At least, she was in a Fool's Paradise because her boy was the best taxi-driver in the world.

He was, too.

✑

On rainy nights his flag was always up.

✑

He knew not only how to find the Waldorf, but the shortest route to 5954 Gorsuch Avenue.

✑

He said Thank you when tipped, and always had change for five dollars.

✑

He never drove with a cigar in his mouth, lighted or unlighted.

✑

If you asked him to please not drive so fast, he drove not so fast, and didn't get mad about it, either.

✑

He simply adored traffic cops, and he was polite to Sunday drivers.

✑

When he drove a couple through the park he never looked back and he never eavesdropped.

✑

My boy is the best taxi-driver in the world and no eavesdropper, said his mother.

✑

The only trouble was that the bad taxi-drivers got all the business.

✑

Llewellyn shrank from White — Male — 5–10½ — 170 to Sallow — Male — 5–9¾ — 135.

✑

Cheest, Llewellyn, said his mother.

✑

Cheest, Mother, replied Llewellyn.

✑

Llewellyn and his mother understood each other.

✑

He took his last five dollars in dimes and nickels which he had been
    saving for change and spent it on cigars at two for a nickel.

✍

The next day he insulted seven passengers and a traffic cop, tore
    the fender off a car from Enid, Oklahoma, and passed
    through 125th Street while taking a dear old lady from 52nd
    to 58th.

✍

That evening he had forty dollars on the clock.

✍

Llewellyn is no longer the best taxi-driver in the world, but his
    license reads White — Male — 5–11 — 235.

✍

In the park he is the father of all eavesdroppers.

✍

Couples who protest find him adamant.

✍

Since he is the father of all eavesdroppers and adamant, I think we
    might call him an Adam-ant-Evesdropper and there leave
    him.

✍

Good-by, Llewellyn.

EVERYBODY MAKES POETS

Poets aren't very useful,
Because they aren't very consumeful or very produceful.
Even poets of great promise
Don't contribute much to trade and commerce,
To which, indeed, even poets of great achievement
Are a positive bereavement,
Because they aren't very sensible,
Because they think buying and selling are cheap and lousy and
    reprehensible,
And this is a topic about which poets are people to whom you can-
    not tell anything,

[213]

Because they are people who cannot afford to buy anything and are
    seldom glib enough to sell anything.
Some poets are bitter,
But they are preferable to the poets who are all of a twitter,
But even the poets who are all of a twitter are as dependable as
    Rotary
Compared to what each of them has around him which is a raptur-
    ous coterie,
Because every poet is threatened constantly by one disaster,
Which is that a lot of otherwise thwarted male and female ladies
    will go around calling him Master,
And then there is nothing to do but surrender,
And then it is good-by old poetry, hello old theosophy and gender,
And yet on the other hand if a poet isn't fed by a lot of male and
    female ladies who are affected,
Why, until long after he is dead or gets the Pulitzer Prize, why he
    is neglected.
So my advice to mothers is if you are the mother of a poet don't
    gamble on the chance that future generations may crown
    him.
Follow your original impulse and drown him.

NO WONDER OUR FATHERS DIED

Does anybody mind if I don't live in a house that is quaint?
Because, for one thing, quaint houses are generally houses where
    plumbing ain't,
And while I don't hold with fanatical steel-and-glass modernistic
    bigots,
Still, I do think that it simplifies life if you live it surrounded by
    efficient pipes and faucets and spigots.
I admit that wells and pumps and old oaken buckets are very nice
    in a poem or ode,
But I feel that in literature is where they should have their perma-
    nent abode,

Because suppose you want a bath,
It is pleasanter to be able to take it without leaving a comfortable
    stuffy room and going out into the bracing fresh air and
    bringing back some water from the end of a path.
Another thing about which I am very earnest,
Is that I do like a house to be properly furnaced,
Because if I am out in the bracing fresh air I expect to be frozen,
But to be frigid in a stuffy room isn't what I would have chosen.
And when you go to bed in a quaint house the whole house grum-
    bles and mutters,
And you are sure the walls will be shattered by clattering shutters.
At least you hope it's the shutters but you fear it's a gang of quaint
    ghosts warming up for twelve o'clock,
And you would lock yourself snugly in but the quaint old key won't
    turn in the quaint old lock,
So you would pull the bedclothes snugly up over your head and lie
    there till a year from next autumn,
Were it not a peculiarity of bedclothes in quaint houses that if you
    pull them up on top, why your feet stick out at the bautum,
But anyhow you find a valley among the hilltops of your mattress
    and after a while slumber comes softly stealing,
And that is when you feel a kiss on your cheek and you think
    maybe it is a goodnight kiss from your guardian angel, but it
    isn't, it's a leak in the ceiling.
Oh, I yield to none in my admiration of the hardy colonists and
    their hardy spouses,
But I still feel that their decadent descendants build more com-
    fortable houses.

MIDSUMMER'S DAYMARE

Mumbo jumbo, what have we here?
Why we have the longest day in the year.
This is the rarest day of June,
And it's weeks and weeks from dawn to noon.

This is the calendar's blazing highlight,
It's months and months from noon to twilight.
Lucky are they who retain their friends
Through the day that seldom if ever ends.
Take a modest date, like December twenty,
And still the telephone jangles plenty,
Still you encounter bores enough,
Obligations and chores enough,
Visitors to avoid enough
Like something out of Freud enough,
Creditors, editors, tears and combats,
Newsreel beauties embracing wombats,
Feeble coffee and vanishing waiters,
Newsreel girls riding alligators,
Traffic and taxes and dues and duties
And candidates kissing newsreel beauties.
Oh, man has need of all his strength
To survive a day of medium length;
What wonder, then, that man grows bitter
On a day that sits like a flagpole-sitter?
Mumbo jumbo, noon infernal,
This, my dears, is the day eternal.
You toil for a dollar or two per diem,
You mope and hope for the blessed P.M.,
You look at the clock, you're ready for mayhem;
Is it P.M. yet? No, it's still the A.M.!
On farm and field, in office and park,
This is the day that won't get dark.
Dusk is an exile, night has fled,
Never again shall we get to bed,
The sun has swallowed the moon and stars,
Midnight lies with the buried Czars.
This is the guerdon of prayer and fasting:
Glorious day, day everlasting!

THE STRANGE CASE OF THE IRKSOME PRUDE

Once upon a time there was a young man named Harold Scrutiny.

❧

Harold had many virtues and practically no vices.

❧

He smoked, to be sure.

❧

Also he drank and swore.

❧

Moreover, he was a pickpocket.

❧

But, for all that, Harold was no prude.

❧

I am no prude, Harold often said.

❧

But Detective Guilfoyle of the Pickpocket Squad is a prude, the old prude, said Harold.

❧

One day Harold went into the subway to pick some pockets.

❧

There was a man on the platform penciling a beard on the lady on the toothpaste placard.

❧

Hey, said Harold.

❧

Hey who, said the man.

❧

Hey you, that's hey who, said Harold.

❧

Aren't you going to give her a moustache?

❧

Sure I'm going to give her a moustache, said the man.

❧

What do you think I am?

❧

I think you're somebody that puts the beard on ladies on toothpaste placards before they put on the moustache, said Harold.

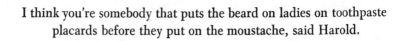

Don't you know enough to put the moustache on first?

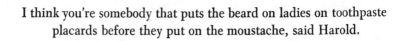

You put the moustache on first, why then you can turn it up or turn it down, whichever you want, said Harold.

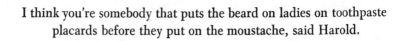

You try to turn a moustache down after the beard's on, it runs into the beard, said Harold.

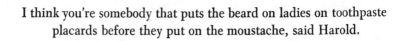

It don't look like a moustache, only like a beard grows up and down both.

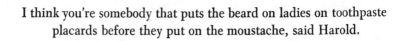

Go on, said the man, go on and pick some pockets.

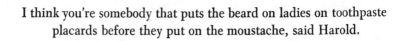

Harold turned to his work, but his mind was elsewhere.

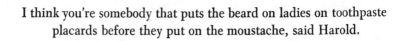

Suddenly the lady on the toothpaste placard got off the toothpaste placard and arrested him.

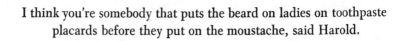

It was Detective Guilfoyle of the Pickpocket Squad all the time.

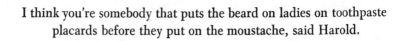

You got a beard grows up and down both, said Harold.

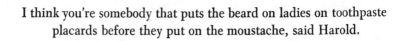

Detective Guilfoyle searched Harold.

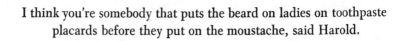

He certainly was surprised at what he found.

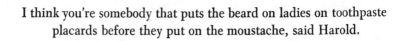

So was Harold.

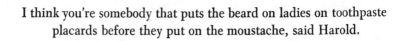

Harold hadn't picked any pockets at all because his mind was elsewhere.

He had picked a peck of pickled peppers.

Detective Guilfoyle wanted to call Harold a name, but he couldn't
because he was a prude.

꘏

Harold picked his pocket and later became the smokingest swear-
ingest, drinkingest Assistant District Attorney the county ever
had.

꘏

Don't be a prude.

A WORD ON WIND

Cows go around saying Moo,
But the wind goes around saying Woooo.
Ghosts say Woooo to you, too,
And sometimes they say Boo to you, too,
But everybody has heard the wind and few people have heard a
ghost,
So it is commonly supposed that the wind says Woooo the most.
Scientists try to tell us that wind is caused by atmospheric condi-
tions at the North Pole or over distant Canadian ranches,
But I guess scientists don't ever get to the country because every-
body who has ever been in the country knows that wind is
caused by the trees waggling their branches.
On the ocean, where there are no trees, they refer to the wind as
gales,
And it is probably caused by whales,
And in the Sahara, where there are no trees or whales either, they
call the wind a simoom or something,
And it is the result of the profanation of Tutankhamen's tomb or
something.
Ill winds blow nobody good and they also blow new hats into mud
puddles and voracious clouds of mosquitoes into propinquity
with your hide,
And they make your cigarette burn down on just one side.
Some people are very refined,

And when they recite poetry or sing songs they pronounce wind,
wined.

Well, dear wined, every time you say Wooooo,

Why I wish you would say it to people who say wined, right after
you have said it somewhere where somebody is making fer-
tilizer or glue.

A STITCH TOO LATE IS MY FATE

There are some people of whom I would certainly like to be one,

Who are the people who get things done.

They balance their checkbooks every month and their figures always agree with the bank's,

And they are prompt in writing letters of condolence or thanks.

They never leave anything to chance,

But always make reservations in advance.

When they get out of bed they never neglect to don slippers so they
never pick up athlete's foot or a cold or a splinter,

And they hang their clothes up on hangers every night and put
their winter clothes away every summer and their summer
clothes away every winter.

Before spending any money they insist on getting an estimate or a
sample,

And if they lose anything from a shoelace to a diamond ring it is
covered by insurance more than ample.

They have budgets and what is more they live inside of them,

Even though it means eating things made by recipes clipped from
the Sunday paper that you'd think they would have died of
them.

They serve on committees

And improve their cities.

They are modern knight errants

Who remember their godchildren's birthdays and the anniversaries
of their godchildren's parents,

And in cold weather they remember the birds and supply them
with sunflower seed and suet,

And whatever they decide to do, whether it's to save twenty-five
per cent of their salary or learn Italian or write a musical
comedy or touch their toes a hundred times every morning
before breakfast, why they go ahead and do it.
People who get things done lead contented lives, or at least I guess
so,
And I certainly wish that either I were more like them or they were
less so.

SPRING SONG

Listen, buds, it's March twenty-first;
Don't you know enough to burst?
Come on, birds, unlock your throats!
Come on, gardeners, shed your coats!
Come on zephyrs, come on flowers,
Come on grass, and violet showers!
And come on, lambs, in frisking flocks!
Salute the vernal equinox!
Twang the cheerful lute and zither!
Spring is absolutely hither!
Yester eve was dark despair,
With winter, winter, everywhere;
Today, upon the other hand,
'Tis spring throughout this happy land.
Oh, such is Nature's chiaroscuro,
According to the Weather Bureau.

Then giddy-ap, Napoleon! Giddy-ap, Gideon!
The sun has crossed the right meridian!
What though the blasts of Winter sting?
Officially, at least, it's Spring,
And be it far from our desire
To make the Weather Man a liar!

So, blossom, ye parks, with cozy benches,
Occupied by blushing wenches!
Pipe, ye frogs, while swains are sighing,
And furnaces unwept are dying!
Crow, ye cocks, a little bit louder!
Mount, ye sales of paint and powder!
Croon, ye crooner, yet more croonishly!
Shine, ye moon, a lot more moonishly!
And oh ye brooklets, burst your channels!
And oh ye camphor, greet ye flannels!
And bloom, ye clothesline, bloom with wash,
Where erstwhile squudged the grim galosh!
Ye transit lines, abet our follies
By turning loose your open trolleys!
And ye, ye waking hibernators,
Drain anti-freeze from your radiators!
While ye, ye otherwise useless dove,
Remember, please, to rhyme with love.

Then giddy-ap, Napoleon! Giddy-ap, Gideon!
The sun has crossed the right meridian!
What though the blasts of Winter sting?
Officially, at least, it's Spring!

SHRINKING SONG

Woollen socks, woollen socks!
Full of color, full of clocks!
Plain and fancy, yellow, blue,
From the counter beam at you.
O golden fleece, O magic flocks!
O irresistible woollen socks!
O happy haberdasher's clerk
Amid that galaxy to work!
And now it festers, now it rankles

Not to have them round your ankles;
Now with your conscience do you spar;
They look expensive, and they are;
Now conscience whispers, You ought not to,
And human nature cries, You've got to!
Woollen socks, woollen socks!
First you buy them in a box.
You buy them several sizes large,
Fit for Hercules, or a barge.
You buy them thus because you think
These lovely woollen socks may shrink.
At home you don your socks with ease,
You find the heels contain your knees;
You realize with saddened heart
Their toes and yours are far apart.
You take them off and mutter Bosh,
You up and send them to the wash.
Too soon, too soon the socks return,
Too soon the horrid truth you learn;
Your woollen socks can not be worn
Unless a midget child is born,
And either sockless you must go,
Or buy a sock for every toe.
Woollen socks, woollen socks!
Infuriating paradox!
Hosiery wonderful and terrible,
Heaven to wear, and yet unwearable.
The man enmeshed in such a quandary
Can only hie him to the laundry,
And while his socks are hung to dry,
Wear them once as they're shrinking by.

THE DROP OF A HAT

Darling, what is that?
That, angel, is a hat.

Are you positive? Are you certain?
Are you sure it's not a curtain?
Shall you really place your head in it?
How's for keeping cake or bread in it?
Do not wear it on your head;
Find some other use instead.
Say a cloth for drying dishes,
Or a net for catching fishes.
Darling, what is that?
Are you sure it is a hat?
And if so, what was the matter
With the hatter?
Was he troubled? Was he ill?
Was he laughing fit to kill?
Oh, what was on his mind
As he designed?
Had he gone without his supper?
Was he dressing in an upper?
Did he plot a wily plan
To annoy his fellow man?
Is its aspect, rear and frontal,
Intended to disgruntle,
Or was it accidental
And is he now repental?
Are memories of the brim
Now agony to him?
Do visions of the crown
Drag his spirits down?
Oh, may the Furies batter
That eleven-fingered hatter!
May doom and gloom enswaddle
The creator of this model!
I hope he made a lot of them,
That dozens he has got of them;
I hope he has a harem,
And all his spouses warem.

THE STRANGE CASE OF MR. FORTAGUE'S DISAPPOINTMENT

Once upon a time there was a man named Mr. Lionel Fortague.

∽

He didn't have very much to talk about.

∽

In summer he used to ask people if it was hot enough for them.

∽

It always was.

∽

In winter he used to ask people if it was cold enough for them.

∽

It always was.

∽

Mr. Lionel Fortague got pretty sick of people it was hot enough for.

∽

He got pretty sick of people it was cold enough for, too.

∽

He decided he would arise and go now.

∽

He decided he would go to Innisfree.

∽

The people of Innisfree are different, thought Mr. Lionel Fortague.

∽

As soon as he got to Innisfree he asked the people if it was cold
enough for them.

∽

They asked him What? Was what cold enough for who?

∽

Mr. Lionel Fortague was delighted.

∽

I knew Innisfree would be different, he said to himself.

∽

He could hardly wait for summer to verify his conclusion.

∽

As soon as summer came he asked everybody if it was hot enough for them.

꙳

Everybody said the question was familiar but they couldn't remember the answer.

꙳

Mr. Lionel Fortague said he would settle down on Innisfree, the home of iridescent chitchat.

꙳

He said he would a small cabin build there, of clay and wattles made.

꙳

Everybody said did he mean he would build a small cabin there, made of clay and wattles?

꙳

Mr. Lionel Fortague said yes, but his way of putting it was more poetic.

꙳

Everybody said maybe, but they were all out of wattles.

꙳

Mr. Lionel Fortague grew very angry at the people of Innisfree.

꙳

He a small cabin built there, of clay and beaverboard made.

꙳

He a fierce-looking dog at an annual clearance sale bought, and it the people of Innisfree one by one to bite he instructed.

꙳

My, he was disappointed.

꙳

He had forgotten that a bargain dog never bites.

UNDER THE FLOOR

Everybody knows how the waters come down at Lodore,
But what about voices coming up through the floor?
Oh yes, every time that into a task you set your teeth

[226]

Something starts talking in the room underneath,
And no matter how many authorities you quiz,
You can never find out who or what it is;
You know one thing about it and nothing more,
That it is just something that goes around making noises that come
    up through the floor.
Sometimes it sings the Indian Love Call and sometimes it sings
    Lead, Kindly Light, by Cardinal Newman,
But even then it doesn't sound human,
And sometimes it just gobbles,
And the sound wibbles and wobbles,
And sometimes it snarls like a ghoul interrupted at its unholy feast,
And sometimes it just mutters like blood going down the drain of a
    tub after a murderer has finished dismembering the deceased;
It cackles, it crackles, it drones, it buzzes, it chortles,
It utters words but in no tongue spoken by mortals,
Yes, its language is a mystery for evermore,
The language of whatever it is that makes the noise that comes up
    through the floor,
And you shiver and quiver and wonder,
What's under?
Is it banshees or goblins or leprechauns, or trolls or something?
Or pixies or vampires or lost souls or something?
What is it below?
Better not, better not know.
Don't let it upset you,
But also don't overlook the possibility that someday whatever it is
    that makes the noises that come up through the floor may
    come up through the floor and get you.

THE STRANGE CASE OF THE AMBITIOUS CADDY

Once upon a time there was a boy named Robin Bideawee.

He had chronic hiccups.

❦

He had hay fever, too.

❦

Also, he was learning to whistle through his teeth.

❦

Oh yes, and his shoes squeaked.

❦

The scoutmaster told him he had better be a caddy.

❦

He said, Robin, you aren't cut out for a scout, you're cut out for
a caddy.

❦

At the end of Robin's first day as a caddy the caddymaster asked
him how he got along.

❦

Robin said, I got along fine but my man lost six balls, am I ready
yet?

❦

The caddymaster said No, he wasn't ready yet.

❦

At the end of the second day the caddymaster asked him again how
he got along.

❦

Robin said, My man left me behind to look for a ball on the fourth
hole and I didn't catch up to him till the eighteenth, am I
ready yet?

❦

The caddymaster said No, he wasn't ready yet.

❦

Next day Robin said, I only remembered twice to take the flag on
the greens and when I did take it I wiggled it, am I ready
yet?

❦

The caddymaster said No, he wasn't ready yet.

❦

Next day Robin said, My man asked me whether he had a seven or an eight on the waterhole and I said an eight, am I ready yet?

⚬

The caddymaster said No, he wasn't ready yet.

⚬

Next day Robin said, Every time my man's ball stopped on the edge of a bunker I kicked it in, am I ready yet?

⚬

The caddymaster said No, he wasn't ready yet.

⚬

Next day Robin said, I never once handed my man the club he asked for, am I ready yet?

⚬

The caddymaster said No, he wasn't ready yet.

⚬

Next day Robin said, I bet a quarter my man would lose and told him so, am I ready yet?

⚬

The caddymaster said, Not quite.

⚬

Next day Robin said, I laughed at my man all the way round, am I ready yet?

⚬

The caddymaster said, Have you still got hiccups, and have you still got hay fever, and are you still learning how to whistle through your teeth and do your shoes still squeak?

⚬

Robin said, Yes, yes, a thousand times yes.

⚬

Then you are indeed ready, said the caddymaster.

⚬

Tomorrow you shall caddy for Ogden Nash.

KIND OF AN ODE TO DUTY

O Duty,
Why hast thou not the visage of a sweetie or a cutie?
Why displayest thou the countenance of the kind of conscientious
  organizing spinster
That the minute you see her you are aginster?
Why glitter thy spectacles so ominously?
Why art thou clad so abominously?
Why art thou so different from Venus
And why do thou and I have so few interests mutually in com-
  mon between us?
Why art thou fifty per cent martyr
And fifty-one per cent Tartar?
Why is it thy unfortunate wont
To try to attract people by calling on them either to leave undone
  the deeds they like, or to do the deeds they don't?
Why art thou so like an April post mortem
On something that died in the autumn?
Above all, why dost thou continue to hound me?
Why art thou always albatrossly hanging around me?
Thou so ubiquitous,
And I so iniquitous.
I seem to be the one person in the world thou art perpetually
  preaching at who or to who;
Whatever looks like fun, there art thou standing between me and
  it, calling yoo-hoo.
O Duty, Duty!
How noble a man should I be hadst thou the visage of a sweetie or
  a cutie!
Wert thou but houri instead of hag
Then would my halo indeed be in the bag!
But as it is thou art so much forbiddinger than a Wodehouse hero's
  forbiddingest aunt
That in the words of the poet, When Duty whispers low, Thou
  must, this erstwhile youth replies, I just can't.

BOOP–BOOP–ADIEUP, LITTLE GROUP!

There are several generally recognized grounds for divorce,

And there are moments when stealing is a starving man's only recourse;

There are gatherings when it is perfectly proper to tell a dubious story if there is sufficient wit in it,

And there are provocations under which it is allowable to pull away an old lady's chair as she is about to sit in it,

But there is one unpardonable sin and in extenuation of it let us quote no Ballads of Reading Gaol and in praise of it let us chant no merry madrigals,

And that is amateur theadrigals.

Now, the urge to dress up and pretend to be somebody else is a universal human weakness,

Like never going to church except on Easter and then crowding out all the people who have been there the other fifty-one Sundays of the year, or never going to the races except for the Belmont or the Preakness.

So if some alternate All-Eastern left tackle who has been told he looks like Noel Coward wants to toss badinage back and forth like a medicine ball with a Junior Leaguer who has been told that with her glasses off she looks like Gertrude Lawrence,

Why that's their business, like drinking sidecars in bed or putting maple walnut ice cream on their oysters, and if they kept it to themselves it could be viewed with tolerance as well as abhorrence,

But the trouble is that they refuse to indulge their depraved appetites in the privacy of deserts or cloisters,

The kick is missing unless a lot of people are on hand to watch them drink sidecars in bed or put maple walnut ice cream on their oysters,

So they inveigle all their friends and relatives and all the relatives of their friends and all the friends of their relatives, in the name of various worthy charities,

Into paying for the privilege of sitting for three hours on piano
stools and watching them project their personalities across
the footlights with the gusto and élan of Oriental beggars ex-
hibiting their physical peculiarities.
Tonight I am being taken to see the Troubadour Players do the
Merchant of Venice.
I shall go with the same eagerness with which, if I weren't me, I
should pay three-thirty to watch me play tennis.

MAN BITES DOG–DAYS

In this fairly temperate clime
Summertime is itchy time.
O'er rocks and stumps and ruined walls
Shiny poison ivy crawls.
Every walk in woods and fields
Its aftermath of itching yields.
Hand me down my rusty hatchet;
Someone murmured, Do not scratch it.

Reason permeates my rhyme:
Summertime is itchy time.
Beneath the orange August moon
Overfed mosquitoes croon.
After sun-up, flies and midges
Raise on people bumps and ridges.
Hand me down my rusty hatchet;
Someone murmured, Do not scratch it.

Lo, the year is in its prime;
Summertime is itchy time.
People loll upon the beaches
Ripening like gaudy peaches.
Friends, the beach is not the orchard,
Nor is the peach by sunburn tortured.

Hand me down my rusty hatchet;
Someone murmured, Do not scratch it.

Now the menu is sublime;
Summertime is itchy time.
Berries, clams, and lobsters tease
Our individual allergies.
Rash in rosy splendor thrives,
Running neck-and-neck with hives.
Hand me down my rusty hatchet;
Someone murmured, Do not scratch it.

The bluebells and the cowbells chime;
Summertime is itchy time.
Despite cold soup, and ice, and thermoses
Garments cling to epidermises.
That fiery-footed centipede,
Prickly heat prowls forth to feed.
Hand me down my rusty hatchet;
Someone murmured, Do not scratch it.

Hatchet-killings ain't a crime:
Summertime is itchy time.

I'M TERRIBLY SORRY FOR YOU, BUT I CAN'T HELP LAUGHING

Everybody has a perfect right to do what they please,
But one thing that I advise everybody not to do is to contract a
    laughable disease.
People speak of you respectfully if you catch bubonic,
And if you get typhus they think you have done something posi-
    tively mastodonic;
One touch of leprosy makes the whole world your kin,
And even a slight concussion earns you an anxious inquiry and
    not a leering grin.

Yes, as long as people are pretty sure you have something you are
    going to be removed by,
Why they are very sympathetic, and books and flowers and visits
    and letters are what their sympathy is proved by.
But unfortunately there are other afflictions anatomical,
And people insist on thinking that a lot of them are comical,
And if you are afflicted with this kind of affliction people are
    amused and disdainful,
Because they are not bright enough to realize that an affliction can
    be ludicrous and still be ominous and painful.
Suppose for instance you have a dreadful attack of jaundice, what
    do they do?
They come around and smile and say Well well, how are you to-
    day, Dr. Fu-Manchu?
The early martyrs thought they knew what it was to be taken over
    the jumps,
But no martyr really ought to get his diploma until he has under-
    gone his friends' witticisms during his mumps.
When you have laryngitis they rejoice,
Because apparently the funniest thing in the world is when you
    can't chide them for laughing at your lost voice, because you
    have lost your voice.
So I advise you, at the risk of being pedantic,
If you must be sick, by all means choose a sickness that is prefer-
    ably fatal and certainly romantic,
Because it is much better to have that kind of sickness and be sick
    unto death or anyway half to death,
Than to have the other kind and be laughed to death.

WHERE THERE'S A WILL, THERE'S VELLEITY

Seated one day at the dictionary I was pretty weary and also pretty
    ill at ease,
Because a word I had always liked turned out not to be a word at
    all, and suddenly I found myself among the v's,

And suddenly among the v's I came across a new word which was
    a word called *velleity,*
So the new word I found was better than the old word I lost, for
    which I thank my tutelary deity,
Because velleity is a word which gives me great satisfaction,
Because do you know what it means, it means *low degree of voli-*
    tion not prompting to action,
And I always knew I had something holding me back but I didn't
    know what,
And it's quite a relief to know it isn't a conspiracy, it's only velleity
    that I've got,
Because to be wonderful at everything has always been my ambi-
    tion,
Yes indeed, I am simply teeming with volition,
So why I never was wonderful at anything was something I
    couldn't see
While all the time, of course, my volition was merely volition of a
    low degree,
Which is the kind of volition that you are better off without it,
Because it puts an idea in your head but doesn't prompt you to do
    anything about it.
So you think it would be nice to be a great pianist but why bother
    with practicing for hours at the keyboard,
Or you would like to be the romantic captain of a romantic ship
    but can't find time to study navigation or charts of the ocean
    or the seaboard;
You want a lot of money but you are not prepared to work for it,
Or a book to read in bed but you do not care to go into the noctur-
    nal cold and murk for it;
And now if you have any such symptoms you can identify your
    malady with accurate spontaneity;
It's velleity,
So don't forget to remember that you're velleitous, and if anybody
    says you're just lazy,
Why, they're crazy.

THE STRANGE CASE OF THE GIRL
O' MR. SPONSOON'S DREAMS

Once upon a time there was a man named Mr. Sponsoon who was highly ineffectual.

∽

He always looked as if he were growing a moustache.

∽

His singing voice was pretty fair except for the high notes.

∽

Oh yes, and the low notes, too.

∽

One day he was driving along the street when he saw a beautiful girl.

∽

My, what a beautiful girl, said Mr. Sponsoon. I wish I knew her name.

∽

If I asked her her name, said Mr. Sponsoon, she might think me a brazen cad.

∽

But if I don't know her name, she will go out of my life forever.

∽

Mr. Sponsoon thought and thought.

∽

Suppose I run over her gently, he thought at last.

∽

With one wheel, say.

∽

Certainly with no more than two.

∽

Then I can read her name in the morning paper and all will be hotsy-totsy.

∽

Mr. Sponsoon pointed his car at the beautiful girl.

∽

The beautiful girl leaped like a thoroughbred gazelle.

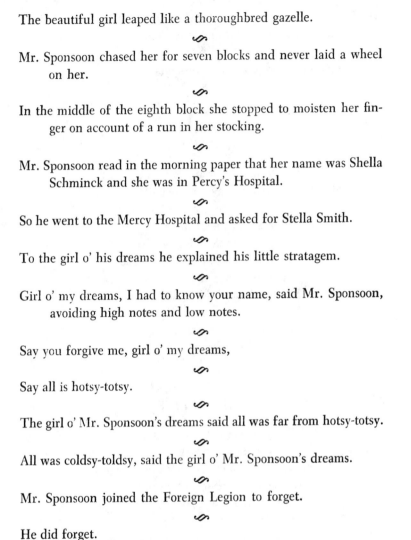

Mr. Sponsoon chased her for seven blocks and never laid a wheel
on her.

In the middle of the eighth block she stopped to moisten her finger on account of a run in her stocking.

Mr. Sponsoon read in the morning paper that her name was Shella
Schminck and she was in Percy's Hospital.

So he went to the Mercy Hospital and asked for Stella Smith.

To the girl o' his dreams he explained his little stratagem.

Girl o' my dreams, I had to know your name, said Mr. Sponsoon,
avoiding high notes and low notes.

Say you forgive me, girl o' my dreams,

Say all is hotsy-totsy.

The girl o' Mr. Sponsoon's dreams said all was far from hotsy-totsy.

All was coldsy-toldsy, said the girl o' Mr. Sponsoon's dreams.

Mr. Sponsoon joined the Foreign Legion to forget.

He did forget.

He forgot it was the Foreign Legion.

He thought it was the American Legion.

Mr. Sponsoon applied a battery tickler-upper to the person of the favorite wife of an intransigent Sheikh.

*

And so we bid farewell to Mr. Sponsoon.

THE CALF

Pray, butcher, spare yon tender calf!
Accept my plea on his behalf;
He's but a babe, too young by far
To perish in the abattoir.
Oh, cruel butcher, let him feed
And gambol on the verdant mead;
Let clover tops and grassy banks
Fill out those childish ribs and flanks.
Then may we, at some future meal,
Pitch into beef, instead of veal.

THE PURIST

I give you now Professor Twist,
A conscientious scientist.
Trustees exclaimed, "He never bungles!"
And sent him off to distant jungles.
Camped on a tropic riverside,
One day he missed his loving bride.
She had, the guide informed him later,
Been eaten by an alligator.
Professor Twist could not but smile.
"You mean," he said, "a crocodile."

THE ANT

The ant has made himself illustrious
Through constant industry industrious.
So what?
Would you be calm and placid
If you were full of formic acid?

THE HIPPOPOTAMUS

Behold the hippopotamus!
We laugh at how he looks to us,
And yet in moments dank and grim
I wonder how we look to him.
Peace, peace, thou hippopotamus!
We really look all right to us,
As you no doubt delight the eye
Of other hippopotami.

THE CENTIPEDE

I objurgate the centipede,
A bug we do not really need.
At sleepy-time he beats a path
Straight to the bedroom or the bath.
You always wallop where he's not,
Or, if he is, he makes a spot.

JANGLE BELLS

Man is said to want but little here below,
And I have an idea that what he wants littlest of is snow.
Snow is all right while it is snowing;
It is like inebriation because it is very pleasing when it is coming,
        but very unpleasing when it is going,

But any further resemblance between the two has escaped this
    Old Master,
Because certainly everybody would rather be sozzled than snow-
    bound, except maybe Mrs. Ella Boole and Lady Astor.
Snow is what you are up to your neck in when people send you
    post cards from Florida saying they wish you were there, and
    I wish they might sit on a burr,
Because they don't wish anything of the kind, no, they are secretly
    glad you are not there, otherwise they couldn't send the post
    card saying they wish you were.

UP FROM THE WHEELBARROW

Some people understand all about machinery,
And to them it is just like beautiful poetry or beautiful scenery,
Because they know how to control and handle it,
Because they understandle it,
Yes, when they are confronted with a complicated piece of ma-
    chinery,
Why, they are as cool and collected as a dean sitting in his dean-
    ery,
And I certainly wish I were among them because if there is one
    thing that makes me terrified and panical,
It is anything mechanical and nowadays everything is mechanical.
O thrice unhappy home
Whose master doesn't know the difference between a watt and an
    ohm!
O radio glum and silent as a glum and silent burial
When no one knows what to do about the grounding or the aerial!
O four-door sedan cantankerous and stubborn and Mad Hattery,
With none to give a thought to occasionally changing the oil or
    once in a while checking on the battery!
O telephone and vacuum cleaners and cameras and electric toast-
    ers and streamlined locomotives and artificial refrigeration,
O thermostats and elevators and cigarette-lighters and air-condi-

tioning units and all ye other gadgets that make ours a mighty
    nation,
I think you are every one a miracle,
And you do wonderful things and it's probably only because I don't
    see how you do what you do that when I think of you I be-
    come hystirical,
And of course that is silly of me because what does it matter how
    you function so long as all I have to do to get you to function
    is push a button or throw a switch,
Always assuming that I can remember which is which,
So keep on functioning, please,
Because if you don't I shall starve or freeze.

AWAY FROM IT ALL

I wish I were a Thibetan monk
Living in a monastery.
I would unpack my trunk
And store it in a tronastery;
I would collect all my junk
And send it to a jonastery;
I would try to reform a drunk,
And pay his expenses at a dronastery.
And if my income shrunk
I would send it to a shronastery.

THE SAGE OF DARIEN

Upon a peak in Darien
The Sage surveys his fellow men,
Exerting to its full capacity
His preternatural sagacity.
Sore eyes and empty stomach mutiny;
The Sage confines himself to scrutiny,
Occasionally sniffing through a tube

The vapor of a bouillon cube.
Thus, all his grosser instincts chastening,
He thinks to bring the vision hastening.
The truth about his fellow men,
He hopes, will bloom within his ken.
At last appears a tiny truth,
A sliver like a baby's tooth.
Now fast it grows, it swells, it waxes,
It multiplies itself like taxes.
The ultimate truth, for what it's worth,
Crowds minor truthlets off the earth.
The Sage cries Bother! through his beard;
Says he, Exactly what I feared.
I needn't have come to Darien
To scrutinize my fellow men;
It seems I've scaled this natural steeple
To learn what I've always known about people;
To confirm through sacrifice intense
The fact that people have no sense.
People are born in pain and woe,
In woe and pain through life they go,
Harpies attend their to-and-froing,
And yet the blockheads keep on going.
Republics rob them, monarchies milk them,
Revolutions unfailingly bilk them;
Tyrants imprison them and slaughter them;
Promoters take their stocks and water them;
Statements and bills pile high around them;
Sheriffs and credit departments hound them;
By ten-ton trucks they are forced from the roads;
Every October they change their abodes;
Frequent expensive diseases smite them;
Sunbeams burn them, mosquitoes bite them;
Employers jeer at their shiny diplomas;
Advertisers insult their aromas;
People are born in pain and woe,

In woe and pain through life they go;
They have no cause at all for thanksgiving.
And yet the idiots keep on living.
Upon a peak in Darien
The Sage renounced his fellow men.
His fellow men he did renounce,
And leapt, and lit, and didn't bounce.

PIPE DREAMS

Many people have asked me what was the most beautiful sight I
      saw during the recent summer,
And I think the most beautiful sight was the day the water
      wouldn't stop running and in came the plumber,
Because your cottage may be very cunning,
But you don't appreciate it when the water won't stop running,
And you would almost rather submit to burgling
Than to consistent gurgling.
And then the other most beautiful sight I saw during the summer
Was the day the water wouldn't run at all and in came the
      plumber,
Because one thing even less enticing than a mess of pottage
Is a waterless cottage,
So apparently all my beautiful memories of the summer
Are beautiful memories of the plumber,
And I am sorry they aren't more romantic,
I am sorry they are not memories of the moonlight rippling on the
      Atlantic,
Oh my yes, what wouldn't I give for some beautiful memories of
      the fields and the sky and the sea,
But they are not for the likes of me,
Nay, if you want to have beautiful memories of the summer,
Why the thing to do is to be a plumber,
Because then you can have some really beautiful beauties to re-
      member,

Because naturally plumbers wouldn't think plumbers were the
     most beautiful thing they saw between June and September.
And that's the great advantage plumbers have over me and you,
They don't have to think about plumbers, so they can concentrate
     on the view.

ABSENCE MAKES THE HEART GROW
HEART TROUBLE

I know a girl who is in Paris, France,
And I fear that every evening she goes out to dance,
And she ought to be pining for the undersigned,
But I fear that nothing is further from her mind,
And what is very suspicious, her letters say that she is being very
     quiet,
But my nerves deny it,
And I am unhappily sure that she is drinking champagne with
     aristocrats,
And exchanging cynicisms with sophistocrats.
She goes walking in the *Bois*
With elegant young men who are not *moi*.
She is receiving compliments from ambassadors,
And riding in *fiacres* with foreign agents who cry that for her they
     would betray the secrets of their lords and massadors.
Artists to have her pose for them are clamoring,
Tenors and symphony conductors tempt her with their entire rep-
     ertoire from Pagliacci to Götterdämmerung;
Argentines and Brazilians
Seek to dazzle her with their dazzling millions;
Men of the world with etchings and monocles
Plead with her to become part of their personal chronicles;
Aides and equerries try to explain without too much bluntness and
     yet without too much shyness
The advantages a girl or a tailor enjoys when he or she is entitled
     to the subtitle of By Appointment to His Royal Highness.

Trips abroad are very nice for Davis Cup teams and Olympic
    teams, and that's about all you can say for them,
Because I think that when you are fond of somebody you would
    rather be with them than away from them,
So I wish that time would suddenly advance,
Because I want to be standing on the dock trying to find some-
    body on deck who will undoubtedly be wearing a terribly
    smart and perfectly terrible hat which she bought in Paris,
    France.

OUT IS OUT

Come in, dear guests, we've got a treat for you,
We've prepared a different place to eat for you!
Guess where we're going to have our dinner!
Everyone guess! Who'll be the winner?
The dining room? Heavens! It's hereby stated
That dining rooms are dreadfully dated.
What in the world could be more plebeian
Than to eat in a place in which you can see in!
The living room? No, you're off the path;
No, not the bedroom; no, not the bath;
And not the cellar; and not the attic;
The kitchen? No, that's too democratic.
Do you all give up? Well, listen and hark:
We're going to dine outdoors, in the dark!
No lights, because there aren't any plugs,
And anyhow, lights attract the bugs.
Oh, it's drizzling a little; I think perhaps
The girls had better keep on their wraps;
Just strike a match and enjoy the way
The raindrops splash in the consommé.
You probably won't get botts or pellagra
From whatever lit on your pâté de foie gras.
Now, you're not expected to eat with skill,

And everybody's supposed to spill;
If your half-broiled chicken leaps about,
That's half the excitement of eating out;
If you dust it with sugar instead of salt,
It's everyone's fun and nobody's fault;
And if anything flies in your mouth, perchance,
Why, that is mystery, that's romance!
Such a frolic and such a lark
It is to eat outdoors in the dark!
The dandiest fun since I don't know when;
Would you eat in a stuffy old room again?
Oh yes you would, you lukewarm liars,
And I'll see you tomorrow at the cleaner's and dyer's.

ISN'T THAT A DAINTY DISH? NO!

I am tired of gadgets with cocktails,
I am awfully tired of gadgets with cocktails,
My heart leaps down when I behold gadgets with cocktails
With me they have outlived their popularity.
Gadgets with cocktails are stultified
Gadgets with cocktails are stertorous
Gadgets with cocktails are stark and stagnant
And for them I have no patience or charity.

I don't want any toast covered with vulcanized caviar
Or any soggy popcorn covered with cheesy butter or buttery cheese,
I don't want any potato chips or Tiny Tootsie pretzels or pretzel
     sticks,
And I don't want any crackers coated with meat paste or bargain
     pâté de foie gras particularly please.

Do not hand me that plate filled with olives unripe and overripe,
Anchovies whether curled or uncurled I have concluded not to
     abide,

Kindly mail all those salted peanuts and almonds to the Collector
     of Internal Revenue,
As well as all the little heart-shaped sandwiches filled with squashy
     stuff that when you pick them up they squirt out at the side.

Maybe somewhere there is somebody who would like the stuffed
     eggs and diminutive frankfurters,
Or who could look the stuffed celery in the eye and voluntarily
     chew it,
Maybe there is a Chinaman in China who would care for that slab
     of fumigated salmon,
And that thing whatever it is all rolled up with a toothpick sticking
     through it.

Hostesses never tire of gadgets with cocktails,
Hostesses sit around thinking up new gadgets with cocktails,
They prowl through the papers hunting tricky gadgets for cock-
     tails,
And if they don't serve more than other hostesses they are
     swamped with humiliation and grief;
Gadgets with cocktails to you, my dear Mrs. Marshmallow,
Gadgets with cocktails to you, Mrs. Rodney St. Rodney,
Gadgets with cocktails to you and all other hostesses,
And I'll take some bread and butter and a slice of rare roast beef.

OH, PLEASE DON'T GET UP!

There is one form of life to which I unconditionally surrender,
Which is the feminine gender.
I think there must be some great difference in the way men and
     women are built,
Because women walk around all day wearing shoes that a man
     would break his neck the first step he took in them because
     where a man's shoe has a heel a woman's shoe has a stilt.
Certainly a man shod like a woman would just have to sit down
     all day, and yet my land!

Women not only don't have to sit, but prefer to stand,
Because their pleasure in standing up is exquisite,
As everybody knows who has ever watched a woman pay a call
or a visit,
Because the proportions of feminine social chitchat are constant,
always;
One part of sitting down in the sitting room to four parts stand-
ing up saying good-by in foyers and hallways,
Which is why I think that when it comes to physical prowess,
Why woman is a wow, or should I say a wowess.

HOW NOW, SIRRAH? OH, ANYHOW

Oh, sometimes I sit around and think, what would you do if you
were up a dark alley and there was Caesar Borgia,
And he was coming torgia,
And brandished a poisoned poniard,
And looked at you like an angry fox looking at the plumpest
rooster in a boniard?
Why that certainly would be an adventure,
It would be much more exciting than writing a poem or selling a
debenture,
But would you be fascinated,
Or just afraid of being assassinated?
Or suppose you went out dancing some place where you generally
dance a lot,
And you jostled somebody accidentally and it turned out to be Sir
Lancelot,
And he drew his sword,
Would you say *Have at you!* or would you say *Oh Lord!?*
Or what if you were held up by a bandit,
And he told you to hand over your money, would you try to dis-
arm him and turn him over to the police, or would you over
just meekly hand it?

[248]

What would you do if you were in a luxurious cosmopolitan hotel
    surrounded by Europeans and Frenchmen,
And a beautiful woman came up to you and asked you to rescue
    her from some mysterious master mind and his sinister
    henchmen?
Would you chivalrously make her rescue your personal objective,
Or would you refer her to the house detective?
Yes, and what if you were on trial for murdering somebody whom
    for the sake of argument we might call Kelly or O'Connor,
And you were innocent but were bound to be convicted unless you
    told the truth and the truth would tarnish a lady's honor,
Would you elect to die like a gentleman or live like a poltroon,
Or put the whole thing in the hands of an arbitration committee
    headed by Heywood Broun?
Yes, often as through life I wander
This is the kind of question I ponder,
And what puzzles me most is why I even bother to ponder when I
    already know the answer,
Because anybody who won't cross the street till the lights are green
    would never get far as a Musketeer or a Bengal Lancer.

MR. BARCALOW'S BREAKDOWN

Once there was a man, and he was named Mr. Barcalow, to be
    exact,
And he prided himself on his tact,
And he said, One thing about an apple, it may have a worm in it,
    and one thing about a chimney, it may have soot in it,
But one thing about my mouth, I never put my foot in it.
Whenever he entered a community
He inquired of his host and hostess what topics he could discuss
    with impunity,
So no matter beside whom he was deposited,
Why, he could talk to them without disturbing any skeletons that
    should have been kept closeted,

But one dire day he went to visit some friends,

And he started asking tactful questions about untactful conversational trends,

And his host said that here was one place that Mr. Barcalow wouldn't need his tact,

Because taboos and skeletons were what everybody there lacked,

And his hostess said, That's right, but you'd better not mention bathrooms to Emily, who you will sit by at lunch,

Because her grandmother was scalded to death in a shower shortly after complaining that there was no kick in the punch,

And his host said, Oh yes, and steer away from education when you talk to the Senator,

Because somebody said his seventeen-year-old nephew would have to burn down the schoolhouse to get out of the third grade and his nephew overheard them and did burn down the schoolhouse, including the music teacher and the janitor,

And his hostess said, Oh yes, and if you talk about love and marriage to Mrs. Musker don't be surprised if her eye sort of wanders,

Because her daughter is the one who had the divorce suit with thirty-seven co-responders,

And Mr. Barcalow said, Well, can I talk about sports,

And his hostess said, Well maybe you'd better not because Louise's sister, the queer one, was asked to resign from the club because she went out to play moonlight tennis in shorts, and Mr. Barcalow said That's not so terrible is it, everybody wears shorts, and his hostess said, Yes, but she forgot the shorts.

So Mr. Barcalow said, The hell with you all, and went upstairs and packed,

And that was the last that was ever heard of Mr. Barcalow and his tact.

THE EVENING OUT

You have your hat and coat on and she says she will be right
  down,
And you hope so because it is getting late and you are dining on
  the other side of town,
And you are pretty sure she can't take long,
Because when you left her she already looked as neat and snappy
  as a Cole Porter song,
And so goes ten minutes, and then fifteen minutes, and then half
  an hour,
And you listen for the sound of water running because you sus-
  pect she may have gone back for a bath or a shower,
Or maybe she is taking a nap,
Or possibly getting up a subscription for the benefit of the children
  of the mouse that she said mean things about last night but
  she is now sorry got caught in a trap,
Or maybe she decided her hair was a mess and is now shampooing
  it,
But whatever she is up to, she is a long time doing it,
And finally she comes down and says she is sorry she couldn't find
  the right lipstick, that's why she was so slow,
And you look at her and she looks marvelous but not a bit more
  marvelous than she did when you left her forty-five minutes
  ago,
And you tell her she looks ravishing and she says No, she is a
  sight,
And you reflect that you are now an hour late, but at any rate she
  is now groomed for the rest of the night,
So you get to your destination and there's the ladies' dressing room
  and before you know it she's in it,
But she says she'll be back in a minute,
And so she is, but not to tarry,
No, only to ask you for her bag, which she has forgotten she had
  asked you to carry,
So you linger in the lobby

And wish you had a nice portable hobby,

And you try to pass the time seeing how much you can remember
of the poetry you learned in school, both good verse and bad
verse,

And eventually she re-appears just about as you have decided she
was in the middle of Anthony Adverse,

And she doesn't apologize, but glances at you as if you were Blue-
beard or Scrooge,

And says why didn't you tell her she had on too much rouge?

And you look to see what new tint she has acquired,

And she looks just the same as she did before she retired,

So you dine, and reach the theater in time for the third act, and
then go somewhere to dance and sup,

And she says she looks like a scarecrow, she has to go straighten up,

So then you don't see her for quite a long time,

But at last you see her for a moment when she comes out to ask if
you will lend her a dime,

The moral of all which is that you will have just as much of her
company and still save considerable on cover charges and
beverages and grub

If instead of taking her out on the town, you settle her in a nice
comfortable dressing room and then go off and spend the evening at the Club.

SONG FOR PIER SOMETHING OR OTHER

Steamer, steamer, outward bound,
Couldn't you, wouldn't you turn around?
Mightn't you double on your track?
Mightn't you possibly bring her back?
No, says the steamer, No, no, no!
We go, says the steamer, go, go, go!
Who, says the steamer, Who are you?
Boo! says the steamer.
Boo!

Steamer, steamer, are you sure
You can carry her secure?
Emerge from ice and storm and fog
With an uneventful log?
Chance, says the steamer, I am chance!
Chance, says the steamer, That's romance!
Who, says the steamer, Who are you?
Boo! says the steamer.
Boo!

Steamer, cogitate awhile,
Goddess unwittingly offended,
Are the males who prowl your decks
Attractive to the other sex?
Wait, says the steamer, Sit and wait.
Fate, says the steamer, I am Fate.
Who, says the steamer, Who are you?
Boo! says the steamer.
Boo!

Steamer, cogitate awhile,
Before you smile your final smile.
Seven days are yours to mock;
Steamer, wait until you dock.
Wait till she is safe ashore,
Steamer I do not adore!
Boo, says the steamer, and double boo!
Who, says the steamer,
Are you?

Steamer, steamer, I am he
Whose *raison d'être* you bore to sea.
Steamer, lightly you weighed your anchor.
Try so lightly to weigh my rancor.
As soon as she is safely off you
I'll curse you from Sandy Hook to Corfu.

You who carried her off so boldly
Shall pay for it hotly, pay for it coldly,
With fog and howling hurricanes,
And icebergs in the shipping lanes,
And strikes of longshoremen and tugs,
And a passenger list of jitter bugs —
Pooh! says the steamer, Pooh for you!
Toodle-de-oodle-de-oo!

THE INTRODUCTION

This is Mr. Woolley, Mrs. Dixon;
This is Mrs. Dixon, Mr. Woolley;
Mr. Woolley, Mrs. Dixon is a vixen;
Mrs. Dixon, Mr. Woolley is a bully.
Shake hands with Mr. Woolley, Mrs. Dixon;
Shake hands with Mrs. Dixon, Mr. Woolley;
And let the welkin shout that it's I who brought about
The meeting of the vixen and the bully.

Mrs. Dixon is one of those ladies
With a disposition acquired in Hades.
What! you exclaim. That placid blonde?
She's as shallow and calm as a lily pond!
I've seen her at parties, at dances, at teas,
Her crossest command is, If you please.
Well, give her a racquet and bulging shorts
And put her out on the tennis courts;
Then, if you care to behold your vixen,
Give her for partner Mr. Dixon.
Hark to her shrill and furious cries
As she damns his hands and feet and eyes.
It's mine! she shrieks. She swings and misses.
Why didn't you get it, you swine? she hisses.
She explains to the world her vagrant serves;

Her clumsy partner upsets her nerves.
He scores a placement. Says she, A miracle!
He doesn't. She rocks with mirth hystirical.
Over the backstop, into the net
She angrily lollops game and set,
And sweetly barks, when the match is through,
We're beaten again, dear, thanks to you.

Mr. Woolley, oh Mr. Woolley!
Hell will welcome him warmly, fully.
What! you exclaim. That genial fellow?
He's a chivalrous gentleman, mild and mellow.
Around the club, from lip to lip,
Run tales of his generous sportsmanship.
Well, if your stomach is strong and able,
Set him down at a contract table;
Then, if you care to behold your bully,
Give him for partner Mrs. Woolley.
She should have bid, or she shouldn't have bid,
She shouldn't have done whatever she did.
Does she hold a hand? He bids it away;
He'd rather go down than let her play.
A celluloid duck, he loudly avers,
Might boast of better brains than hers.
And oft, with polished wit sardonic,
He hails her as Poison, or Bubonic,
Or else with humor gay and easy,
Hope she's enjoying her parcheesi.
He roars, with the last lost rubber concluded;
We've lost ten dollars, and that's what you did.

Oh, this is Mr. Woolley, Mrs. Dixon,
And this is Mrs. Dixon, Mr. Woolley;
Mr. Woolley, Mrs. Dixon is a vixen;
Mrs. Dixon, Mr. Woolley is a bully.
Shake hands with Mr. Woolley, Mrs. Dixon;

Shake hands with Mrs. Dixon, Mr. Woolley;
To both of you more power, and may your meeting flower
In the slaughter of a vixen and a bully.

RIDING ON A RAILROAD TRAIN

Some people like to hitch and hike;
They are fond of highway travel;
Their nostrils toil through gas and oil,
They choke on dust and gravel.
Unless they stop for the traffic cop
Their road is a fine-or-jail road,
But wise old I go rocketing by;
I'm riding on the railroad.

I love to loll like a limp rag doll
In a peripatetic *salon;*
To think and think of a long cool drink
And cry to the porter, *allons!*
Now the clickety clack of wheel on track
Grows clickety clackety clicker:
The line is clear for the engineer
And it mounts to his head like liquor.
With a farewell scream of escaping steam
The boiler bows to the Diesel;
The Iron Horse has run its course
And we ride a chromium weasel;
We draw our power from the harnessed shower,
The lightning without the thunder,
But a train is a train and will so remain
While the rails glide glistening under.

Oh, some like trips in luxury ships,
And some in gasoline wagons,
And others swear by the upper air

And the wings of flying dragons.
Let each make haste to indulge his taste,
Be it beer, champagne or cider;
My private joy, both man and boy,
Is being a railroad rider.

JUST KEEP QUIET AND NOBODY WILL NOTICE

There is one thing that ought to be taught in all the colleges,
Which is that people ought to be taught not to go around always
    making apologies.
I don't mean the kind of apologies people make when they run
    over you or borrow five dollars or step on your feet,
Because I think that kind is sort of sweet;
No, I object to one kind of apology alone,
Which is when people spend their time and yours apologizing for
    everything they own.
You go to their house for a meal,
And they apologize because the anchovies aren't caviar or the par-
    tridge is veal;
They apologize privately for the crudeness of the other guests,
And they apologize publicly for their wife's housekeeping or their
    husband's jests;
If they give you a book by Dickens they apologize because it isn't
    by Scott,
And if they take you to the theater, they apologize for the acting
    and the dialogue and the plot;
They contain more milk of human kindness than the most capa-
    cious dairy can,
But if you are from out of town they apologize for everything local
    and if you are a foreigner they apologize for everything
    American.
I dread these apologizers even as I am depicting them,
I shudder as I think of the hours that must be spent in contradict-
    ing them,

Because you are very rude if you let them emerge from an argument victorious,

And when they say something of theirs is awful, it is your duty to convince them politely that it is magnificent and glorious,

And what particularly bores *me* with them,

Is that half the time you have to politely contradict them when you rudely agree with them,

So I think there is one rule every host and hostess ought to keep with the comb and nail file and bicarbonate and aromatic spirits on a handy shelf,

Which is don't spoil the denouement by telling the guests everything is terrible, but let them have the thrill of finding it out for themself.

PARSLEY FOR VICE–PRESIDENT!

I'd like to be able to say a good word for parsley, but I can't,

And after all what can you find to say for something that even the dictionary dismisses as a biennial umbelliferous plant?

Speaking of which, I don't know how the dictionary figures it as biennial, it is biennial my eye, it is like the poor and the iniquitous,

Because it is always with us, because it is permanent and ubiquitous.

I will not venture to deny that it is umbelliferous,

I will only add that it is of a nasty green color, and faintly odoriferous,

And I hold by my complaint, though every cook and hostess in the land indict me for treason for it,

That parsley is something that as a rhymer I can find no rhyme for it and as an eater I can find no reason for it.

Well, there is one sin for which a lot of cooks and hostesses are some day going to have to atone,

Which is that they can't bear to cook anything and leave it alone.

No, they see food as something to base a lot of beautiful dreams and romance on,

Which explains lamb chops with pink and blue pants on.

Everything has to be all decorated and garnished

So the guests will be amazed and astarnished,

And whatever you get to eat, it's sprinkled with a lot of good old
umbelliferous parsley looking as limp and wistful as Lillian
Gish,

And it is limpest, and wistfulest, and also thickest, on fish.

Indeed, I think maybe one reason for the disappearance of Enoch
Arden

Was that his wife had an idea that mackerel tasted better if instead of looking like mackerel it looked like a garden.

Well, anyhow, there's the parsley cluttering up your food,

And the problem is to get it off without being rude,

And first of all you try to scrape it off with your fork,

And you might as well try to shave with a cork,

And then you surreptitiously try your fingers,

And you get covered with butter and gravy, but the parsley lingers,

And you turn red and smile at your hostess and compliment her on
the recipe and ask her where she found it,

And then you return to the parsley and as a last resort you try to
eat around it,

And the hostess says, Oh you are just picking at it, is there something wrong with it?

So all you can do is eat it all up, and the parsley along with it,

And now is the time for all good parsleyphobes to come to the aid
of the menu and exhibit their gumption,

And proclaim that any dish that has either a taste or an appearance
that can be improved by parsley is *ipso facto* a dish unfit for
human consumption.

LINES TO BE SCRIBBLED ON SOMEBODY
ELSE'S THIRTIETH MILESTONE

Thirty today? Cheer up, my lad!
The good old thirties aren't so bad.

Life doesn't end at twenty-nine,
So come on in, the water's fine.
I, too, when thirty crossed my path,
Turned ugly colors with shame and wrath.
I kicked, I scratched, I bit my nails,
I indulged in tantrums the size of whales,
I found it hard to forgive my mater
For not having had me ten years later.
I struggled with reluctant feet
Where dotage and abdomens meet.
Like the tongue that seeks the missing tooth
I yearned for my extracted youth.
Since then some years have ambled by
And who so satisfied as I.
The thirties are things I wallow among,
With naught but pity for the young.
The less long ago that people were born
The more I gaze on them with scorn,
And each Thanksgiving I Thanksgive
That I'm slowly learning how to live.
So conquer, boy, your grief and rage,
And welcome to the perfect age!
I hope good fairies your footsteps haunt,
And bring you everything you want,
From cowboy suits and Boy Scout knives,
To beautiful, generous, wealthy wives.
If you play the horses, may you play good horses,
If you want divorces, may you get divorces,
Be it plenty of sleep, or fortune, or fame,
Or to carry the ball for Notre Dame,
Whatever it is you desire or covet,
My boy, I hope you get it and love it.
And you'll use it a great deal better, I know,
Than the child that you were a day ago.

LITTLE MISS MUFFET SAT ON A PROPHET —
AND QUITE RIGHT, TOO!

I am sure that if anybody into the condition of humanity cares to
probe,
Why they will agree with the prophet Job,
Because the prophet Job said that man that is born of woman is of
few days and full of trouble, that's what was said by the
prophet Job,
And the truth of that statement can be confirmed by anybody who
cares to probe.
So you would think that being born to trouble and woe, man would
be satisfied,
And indeed that just by being born at all his passion for trouble
would be gratisfied.
But is man content to leave bad enough alone?
Not so, he has to go out and create a lot more trouble and woe of
his own.
Man knows very well that rheumatism and measles and ice and
fog and pain and senility and sudden death are his for the
asking, and, indeed, his whether he asks for them or not,
But when it comes to agony, man is a glutton and a sot,
His appetite for punishment is immense,
And any torture that Nature overlooked, he invents.
There is no law of Nature that compels a man to drink too much,
Or even to think too much,
And when Nature looked at her handiwork, for purposes of her
own she certainly added gender to it,
But she didn't order everybody to dive overboard and surrender
to it,
Yes, it may have been Nature who induced two people to love each
other and end up by marrying each other,
But it is their own idea when they begin to lovingly torment and
harry each other.
And it may have been Nature who developed the mosquito and the
gnat and the midge,

But man developed golf and bridge,

And Nature may have thought up centipedes and ants,

But man all by himself thought up finance,

So this prophet will utter just one utterance instead of uttering them like the prophet Job in baker's twelves,

Which utterance is that people could survive their natural trouble all right if it weren't for the trouble they make for themselves.

THE PARTY NEXT DOOR

I trust I am not a spoil sport, but there is one thing I deplore,

And that is a party next door,

I am by nature very fond of everybody, even my neighbors,

And I think it only right that they should enjoy some kind of diversion after their labors,

But why don't they get their diversion by going to the movies or the Little Theater or the Comédie Française or the Commedia dell'arte?

Why do they always have to be giving a party?

You may think you have heard a noise because you have heard an artillery barrage or an avalanche or the subway's horrendous roar,

But you have never really heard anything until you have heard a party next door.

At a party next door the guests stampede like elephants in wooden shoes and gallop like desperate polo players,

And all the women are coloratura sopranos and all the men are train announcers and hogcallers and saxophone solo players.

They all have screamingly funny stories to tell to each other,

And half of them get at one end of the house and half of them get at the other end of the yard and then they yell to each other,

And even if the patrolman looks in from his beat they do not moderate or stop,

No, they just seduce the cop.

And at last you manage to doze off by the dawn's early light.

And they wake you up all over again shouting good night,
And whether it consists of two quiet old ladies dropping in for a game of bridge or a lot of revelers getting really sort of out-of-bounds-like,
That's what a party next door always sounds like,
So when you see somebody with a hoarse voice and a pallid face and eyes bleary and red-rimmed and sore,
It doesn't mean they've been on a party themselves, no, it probably means that they have experienced a party next door.

LOCUST–LOVERS, ATTENTION!

My attention has been recently focussed
Upon the seventeen-year locust.
This is the year
When the seventeen-year locusts are here,
Which is the chief reason my attention has been focussed
Upon the seventeen-year locust.
Overhead, underfoot, they abound,
And they have been seventeen years in the ground,
For seventeen years they were immune to politics and class war and capital taunts and labor taunts,
And now they have come out like billions of insect debutantes,
Because they think that after such a long wait,
Why they are entitled to a rich and handsome mate,
But like many another hopeful debutante they have been hoaxed and hocus-pocussed,
Because all they get is another seventeen-year locust.
Girl locusts don't make any noise,
But you ought to hear the boys.
Boy locusts don't eat, but it is very probable that they take a drink now and again, and not out of a spring or fountain,
Because they certainly do put their heads together in the treetops and render Sweet Adeline and She'll Be Comin' Round the Mountain.

I for one get bewildered and go all hot and cold

Everytime I look at a locust and realize that it is seventeen years old;

It is as fantastic as something out of H. G. Wells or Jules Verne or G. A. Henty

To watch a creature that has been underground ever since it hatched shortly previous to 1920,

Because locusts also get bewildered and go hot and cold because they naturally expected to find Jess Willard still the champ,

And Nita Naldi the vamp,

And Woodrow Wilson on his way to Paris to promote the perpetually not-yet-but-soon League,

And Washington under the thumb of Wayne B. Wheeler and the Anti-Saloon League.

Indeed I saw one locust which reminded me of a godmotherless Cinderella,

Because when it emerged from the ground it was whistling Dardanella.

Dear locusts, my sympathy for you is intense,

Because by the time you get adjusted you will be defunct, leaving nothing behind you but a lot of descendants who in turn will be defunct just as they get adjusted seventeen years hence.

TRAVELER'S REST

I know a renegade hotel.
I also know I hate it well.
An inn so vile, an inn so shameless,
For very disgust I leave it nameless,
Loathing the name I will not utter,
Whose flavor reeks of rancid butter.
Five stories tall this mantrap stands,
With steps outstretched like welcoming hands,
And travelers, weary of their mileage,
Respond to its bright electric smileage.

They park their cars, and praise the Lord
For downy bed and toothsome board.
They pass unwary through its portals,
And every imp in Hades chortles.
Behold the regulars in the lobby;
Expectoration is their hobby.
Behold the loftiest of clerks:
He's manicuring as he works,
And bridles into dapper wrath
At a mild request for a room and bath.
Behold the niftiest of collars
Which murmurs, "That will be sixteen dollars,"
The leer with innuendo rife,
Which says your wife is not your wife.
The doddering, halting elevator,
A contemporary of Poe or Pater.
The impudent boy with step that lags
Who snatches your coins and hides your bags;
The ill-fitting door to the musty room
That smells like a fairly empty tomb;
The bath you crave, being cramped and dusty
And the hot that turns out to be cold and rusty,
The towels clammy, the basin black,
And the bed that sags like a postman's back.
The dinner (ten dollars and a quarter)
For the porterhouse that tastes like the porter.
The sleepy ascent to the room once more,
And the drunken Lothario next door.
You see that the beds are not turned down,
And you know the bedclothes are dank and brown,
And there isn't a thing to hang your clothes on,
And the sheet you shudder to place your toes on.
You search in vain for a bedside lamp,
You lose your slippers, the rug is damp,
The bulb in the ceiling is all in all,
And the switch is set in the furtherest wall.

A century later the night is past,
And you stagger down to break your fast.
Fossil bacon and powdery eggs
And a cup of tepid water and dregs,
And you reach the desk and surrender your keys,
And the clerk sneers "Thirty-one dollars, please.
Fifteen for meals and sixteen for the room,
Do you know to who you are speaking to whom?
You can fry in Hell so long as you pay;
Stop in again when you pass our way!"
I know a renegade hotel.
I also know I hate it well.
To name its name I can't be induced
Because I'm sure it considers every knock a boost.

THE NAME IS TOO FAMILIAR

You go away for a trip, either business or pleasure,
And you think to settle down to a little anonymous leisure,
And the first thing you see on the train is a sign bearing the name
    of the porter,
And his name is Lafcadio Pauncefoote so you can't call him Boy
    or George, which eventually worries you into giving him an
    extra quarter,
And you go into the dining car a little later,
And there you are confronted with signs confiding to you the
    names of the steward and the waiter,
And the steward hovers over you like a hospitable owl,
And you can't call him Steward because now you think of him as
    Mr. Feeney your host, so when he asks you how your steak is
    you say Splendid instead of Foul,
And you get off the train and into a taxi,
And there's a picture to tell you that the driver's name is Maxie,
And you don't want to be hemmed in by names, you want to be
    alone,

But you think, At least it's other people's names that are hounding
    me and not my own,
And you go and register at a hotel and up comes the third assistant
    manager with a third assistant managerial gurgle,
And he looks at the register and then shakes hands and says We're
    mighty glad to have you with us, Mr. Alf B. Murgle,
We certainly hope you enjoy your stay, Mr. Murgle,
And the bellboy gets the idea and says Right this way, Mr. Murgle,
And the elevator boy gets the idea and says This is your floor, Mr.
    Murgle,
And the floor clerk gets the idea and says Good morning Mr. Mur-
    gle, there's your door, Mr. Murgle,
And the telephone girl gets the idea and says, Good morning Mr.
    Murgle, okay Plaza 3–8362, Mr. Murgle,
And the waiter gets the idea and says Will that be all, Mr. Mur-
    gle? Thank you, Mr. Murgle,
So your private life in the hotel is about as private as the private
    life of the Dionnes, but at first you are slightly flattered be-
    cause you think Somebody important must have sent them
    word of you,
And after they have Mr. Murgled you for the thousandth time you
    try to cash a two-dollar check and you discover they have
    never heard of you,
Yes, it's all a figure of speech,
Because they not only know you, but also don't know you, and
    combine the worst features of each.
That's the beauty about a name, whenever we want to anony-
    mously relax it pops up and prevents us,
And it is certainly nice to get home again and settle down as an ob-
    scure statistic in the census.

WHO UNDERSTANDS WHO ANYHOW?

There is one phase of life that I have never heard discussed in any
    seminar,

And that is that all women think men are funny and all men
    think that weminar.
Be the air the air of America or England or Japan,
It is full of husbands up in it saying, Isn't that just like a woman?
    And wives saying, Isn't that just like a man?
Well, it so happens that this is a unique fight,
Because both sides are right.
Each sex keeps on laughing at the other sex for not thinking the
    way they do,
Which is the cause of most domestic to-do and a-do,
Because breakfast is punctuated with spousely snorts,
Because husbands are jeering at their wives because they ignore
    the front page and read society and fashions, and wives are
    jeering at their husbands because they ignore the front page
    and read finance and sports,
And men think that women have an easy time because all they
    have to do is look after the household,
And what does that amount to but keeping an eye on the children
    and seeing that three meals a day are served and not allowing
    any litter to collect that would furnish a foothold for a
    mousehold?
And women think that men have an easy time because all they have
    to do is sit in an office all day long swapping stories and
    scratching up desks with their heels,
And going out to restaurants and ordering everything they like for
    their midday meals.
And oh yes, women like to resent the thought that they think men
    think they are toys,
And men like to bask in the thought that they think women think
    they are just big overgrown boys.
Well all these conflicting thoughts make for trouble at times but
    on the whole it is a sound idea for men and women to think
    different,
It is a topic upon which I am verbose and vociferant.
To it I dedicate my pen,
Because who would want to live in a world where the men all

thought like women and the women all thought like men?
No, no, kind sirs, I will take all my hard-earned money,
And I will bet it on the nose of the tribe whose men and women
    continue to think each other are funny.

THE BANQUET

Oh, here we are at the mammoth banquet
To honor the birth of the great Bosanquet!
Oh give a look at the snowy napery,
The costly flowers, the sumptuous drapery,
Row on row of silver utensils
Poised for action like salesmen's pencils,
Waiters gaudy as sugar plums,
Every waiter with seven thumbs,
Stream upon stream of gaudy bunting,
And lady commuters lion hunting,
The gleaming teeth at the speaker's table,
The clattering, chattering, battering babel.
Sit we here in the great unquiet
And brood awhile on the evening's diet.
As soggy and dull as good advice,
The butter floats in the melting ice.
In a neighboring morgue, beyond salvation,
The celery waits identification.
Huddled thick in an open vault,
Mummified peanuts moult their salt.
Out of the napkin peers a roll,
With the look of a lost and hardened soul.
The cocktail sauce, too weak to roister,
Fails to enliven the tepid oyster.
The consommé, wan as Elizabeth Barrett,
Washes over a drowning carrot.
Next, with its sauce of gummy tartar,
The sole, or flounder, or is it a garter?

And, be it Seattle or Cincinnati,
O'Sullivan's Rubber chicken patty;
Parsley potatoes, as tempting as soap,
String beans, hemp beans, and beans of rope.
And the waiter would sooner give you his daughter
Than give you another glass of water.
Pineapple salad next, by George!
That ought to raise your sunken gorge!
And green ice cream, sweet frozen suet,
With nuts and raisins sprinkled through it.
At sight of vari-colored *gâteaux*
The innards reel, as on a *bateau*.
At last the little cups belated
Of coffee dated, or inundated.
Chairs creak as half a thousand rumps
Twist them around with backward bumps.
A thousand eyes seek out, as one,
The beaming chairman on his throne.
He rises luminous through the smoke
Of banquet tobacco, or poison oak.
He bows, he coughs, he smiles a bit,
He sparkles with imitable wit —
Rabbi Ben Ezra, fly with me;
The almost worse is yet to be.
Let us arise and leave this banquet —
And by the way, Rabbi, who *was* Bosanquet?

DO SPHINXES THINK?

There is one thing I do not understand,
Which is how anybody successfully cuts the fingernails on their
     right hand,
Because it is easy to cut your left-hand fingernails, but with your
     right-hand fingernails, why you either have to let them grow
     ad infinitum,

Or else bitum.

Then there is another problem that keeps my brain working in two twelve-hour shifts,

Which is Why doesn't the fact that everything that goes up must come down, apply to elevators, or as the British say, lifts?

You have been standing on the tenth floor waiting to descend to the ground floor since Bob Son of Battle was a pup,

And all you see is elevators going up, up, up,

And first your impatience, and eventually your curiosity, grows keen,

When you see the same elevator going up a dozen times without having been down in between.

Is there a fourth dimension known only to elevator attendants,

Or do they, when they get to the top, glide across the roof to the next building and there make their descendance?

Whatever the secret is, to know it I should adore,

For I am tired of being marooned without my ten favorite movie actresses on the tenth floor.

An answer to the third baffler, however, would make the greatest difference in this dear old life o' mine,

Which is, ought I to hope to feel terrible, or to feel fine?

Because how can I tell which hope to nurse,

Because when I feel terrible I know that after a while I'll feel better, and when I feel fine I know that after a while I'll feel worse.

Is it better to feel terrible and know that pretty soon you'll feel fine or to feel fine and know that pretty soon you'll feel terrible, that is the question,

And I am open to suggestion,

And when you consider further that probably nobody can ever feel either fine or terrible anyhow, because how can you feel fine when you know that you're going to feel terrible or how can you feel terrible *et cetera* it all grows very confusing,

So let's leave everything in the hands of Dorothy Dix and Ted Husing.

WEDNESDAY MATINEE

Oh, yes, I'd love to go to the play,
But not the Wednesday matinee.
I'd rather stay home with *Lorna Doone*
Than go of a Wednesday afternoon,
I'd rather work on a crumbling levee
Than cope with a Wednesday theater bevy.
Women, women, and still more women;
A sea of drugstore perfume to swim in;
Tongues like sirens, and tongues like clappers,
And the ripping crackle of candy wrappers:
(A fudge-nut sundae was all their lunch,
They are dying for something sweet to munch;
And foreheads grow moist and noses glisten,
It's everyone talk, and nobody listen;
Voice beats on voice, and higher and higher
Screams and steams the anarchic choir.
The early-comers sit on the aisle
With their laps in a Himalayan pile,
Every corpulent knee a sentry
Denying to all the right of entry.
The usher glances at laps and knees,
And murmurs, Show me your tickets, please.
The aborigines clatter and clack,
But they're next aisle over and eight rows back.
Thither they march, with candy and wraps,
To be balked by other knees and laps.
The house lights fade, the footlights glow,
The curtain rises. This is the show;
This is the charm, the enchanted flame,
That drew them here from wherever they came.
Over the house no silence falls,
But shopper to shopper desperate calls;
Suburban ladies their tonsils gird,
Determined to have one final word,

Interrupting their own ripe rush
To squelch their neighbors with cries of Hush!
The dialogue dies upon the stage
At the rustle and swish of the program page.
With a wave of applause, terrific, tidal,
They recognize the star, their idol,
Undeterred by the sober fact
That she doesn't appear till the second act.
Now the whisper runs from row to row,
Doesn't the butler look like Joe?
And the mother's the image of Emily, kind of,
And who does the lover put you in mind of?
Now, like the drunkard scenting liquor,
The ladies sniff for dirt, and snicker;
Forgetting now their gum and fudge,
The ladies cackle and leer and nudge,
Rooting in every harmless line
For *double-entendre* and obscene design;
Yet prompt with handkerchief and tears
The moment a child or a dog appears.
The curtain falls; the play is ended.
Adorable! Dreadful! Stupid! Splendid!
They cry of the play that was unattended,
Unheard, unseen, and uncomprehended.
O matinee mænads, O bulging bacchantes,
I would my pen were as sharp as Dante's,
But as it isn't I simply say
You may keep your Wednesday matinee.

BARMAIDS ARE DIVINER THAN MERMAIDS

Fish are very good at swimming,
And the ocean with them is brimming.
They stay under water all year round,
And they never get drowned,

And they have a gift more precious than gold,
Which is that they never get cold.
No, they may not be as tasty as venison or mooseflesh,
But they never get gooseflesh.
They have been in the ocean since they were roe,
So they don't have to creep into it toe by toe,
And also they stay in it permanently, which must be a source of great satisfaction,
Because they don't have to run dripping and shivering up and down the beach waiting vainly for a healthy reaction.
Indeed when I think how uncomplicated the ocean is for fish my thoughts grow jealous and scathing,
Because when fish bump into another fish it doesn't wring from them a cry of Faugh! and ruin their day's bathing.
No, if it's a bigger fish than they are, they turn around and beat it,
And if it's littler, they eat it.
Some fish are striped and some are speckled,
But none of them ever heard of ultra-violet rays and felt it necessary to lie around getting sand in their eyes and freckled.
Oh, would it not be wondrous to be a fish? No, it would not be wondrous,
Because we unmarine humans are at the top of the animal kingdom and it would be very undignified to change places with anything under us.

SO PENSEROSO

Come, megrims, mollygrubs and collywobbles!
Come, gloom that limps, and misery that hobbles!
Come also, most exquisite melancholiage,
As dank and decadent as November foliage!
I crave to shudder in your moist embrace,
To feel your oystery fingers on my face.
This is my hour of sadness and of soulfulness,
And cursed be he who dissipates my dolefulness.
I do not desire to be cheered,

I desire to retire, I am thinking of growing a beard,
A sorrowful beard, with a mournful, a dolorous hue in it,
With ashes and glue in it.
I want to be drunk with despair,
I want to caress my care,
I do not wish to be blithe,
I wish to recoil and writhe,
I will revel in cosmic woe,
And I want my woe to show.
This is the morbid moment,
This is the ebony hour.
Aroint thee, sweetness and light!
I want to be dark and sour!
Away with the bird that twitters!
All that glitters is jitters!
Roses, roses are gray,
Violets cry Boo! and frighten me.
Sugar is stimulating,
And people conspire to brighten me.
Go hence, people, go hence!
Go sit on a picket fence!
Go gargle with mineral oil,
Go out and develop a boil!
Melancholy is what I brag and boast of,
Melancholy I mean to make the most of,
You beaming optimists shall not destroy it.
But while I am it, I intend to enjoy it.
Go, people, feed on kewpies and soap,
And remember, please, that when I mope, I mope!

COMPLAINT TO FOUR ANGELS

Every night at sleepy-time
Into bed I gladly climb.
Every night anew I hope
That with the covers I can cope.

Adjust the blanket fore and aft,
Swallow next a soothing draught;
Then a page of Scott or Cooper
May induce a healthful stupor.

O the soft luxurious darkness,
Fit for Morgan, or for Harkness!
Traffic dies along the street.
The light is out. So are your feet.

Adjust the blanket aft and fore,
Sigh, and settle down once more.
Behold, a breeze! The curtains puff.
One blanket isn't quite enough.

Yawn and rise and seek your slippers,
Which, by now, are cold as kippers.
Yawn, and stretch, and prod yourself,
And fetch a blanket from the shelf.

And so to bed again, again,
Cozy under blankets twain.
Welcome warmth and sweet nirvana
Till eight o'clock or so mañana.

You sleep as deep as Keats or Bacon;
Then you dream and toss and waken.
Where is the breeze? There isn't any.
Two blankets, boy, are one too many.

O stilly night, why are you not
Consistent in your cold and hot?
O slumber's chains, unlocked so oft
With blankets being donned or doffed!

The angels who should guard my bed
I fear are slumbering instead.
O angels, please resume your hovering;
I'll sleep, and you adjust the covering.

A PLEA FOR A LEAGUE OF SLEEP

Some people lead a feverish life,
For they with restlessness are rife.
They revel in labors energetic,
Their fare is healthful and ascetic,
Their minds are keen, their hands are earthy,
Each day they work on something worthy.
Something accomplished, something done,
Comprises their idea of fun.

My life with joy is sometimes fraught,
But mostly when I'm doing naught.
Yea, I could spend my whole career
A pillow underneath my ear.
How wise was he who wittily said
That there is nothing like a bed.
A mattress is what I like to creep on;
The right side is the one I sleep on.

Heroes who moil and toil and fight
Exist on eight hours' sleep a night.
I call this but a miserly budget,
Yet I assure you that they grudge it.
I've heard them groan, times without number,
At wasting a third of their lives in slumber.
All right, you Spartans who build and delve,
You waste eight hours, and I'll waste twelve.

No honester man is to be found
Than he who sleeps the clock around.

Of malice and ambition free,
The more he sleeps, the sleepier he.
No plots and schemes infest his head,
But dreams of getting back to bed.
His spirit bears no worldly taint;
Scratch a sluggard, and find a saint.

Stalin and Hitler while they sleep
Are harmless as a baby sheep;
Tyrants who cause the earth to quake
Are only dangerous when awake.
This world would be a happier place,
And happier the human race,
And all our pilots be less Pontius,
If people spent more time unconscious.

CAPTAIN JOHN SMITH

Captain John Smith was a full-blooded Briton,
The same as Boadicea and Bulwer-Lytton,
But his problem and theirs were not quite the same,
Because they didn't have to go around assuring everybody that that
     was their real name,
And finally he said, This business of everybody raising their eye-
     brows when I register at an inn is getting very boring,
So I guess I'll go exploring,
So he went and explored the River James,
Where they weren't as particular then as they are now about
     names,
And he went for a walk in the forest,
And the Indians caught him and my goodness wasn't he embor-
     rassed!
And he was too Early-American to write for advice from Emily
     Post,
So he prepared to give up the ghost,

And he prayed a prayer but I don't know whether it was a silent
    one or a vocal one,
Because the Indians were going to dash his brains out and they
    weren't going to give him an anaesthetic, not even a local one,
But along came Pocahontas and she called off her father's savage
    minions,
Because she was one of the most prominent Virginians,
And her eyes went flash flash,
And she said, Scat, you po' red trash,
And she begged Captain John Smith's pardon,
And she took him for a walk in the gyarden,
And she said, Ah reckon Ah sho' would have felt bad if anything
    had happened to you-all,
And she told him about her great-uncle Hiawatha and her cousin
    Sittin' Bull and her kissin' cousin King Philip, and I don't
    know who-all,
And he said you'd better not marry me, you'd better marry John
    Rolfe,
So he bade her farewell and went back to England, which adjoins
    Scotland, where they invented golf.

REQUIEM

There was a young belle of old Natchez
Whose garments were always in patchez.
When comment arose
On the state of her clothes,
She drawled, When Ah itchez, Ah scratchez!

INTER–OFFICE MEMORANDUM

The only people who should really sin
Are the people who can sin with a grin,
Because if sinning upsets you,
Why, nothing at all is what it gets you.

Everybody certainly ought to eschew all offences however venial
As long as they are conscience's menial.
Some people suffer weeks of remorse after having committed the
slightest peccadillo,
And other people feel perfectly all right after feeding their husbands arsenic or smothering their grandmother with a pillow.
Some people are perfectly self-possessed about spending their lives
on the verge of delirium tremens,
And other people feel like hanging themselves on a coathook just
because they took that extra cocktail and amused their fellow
guests with recitations from the poems of Mrs. Hemans.
Some people calmly live a barnyard life because they find monog-
amy dull and arid,
And other people have sinking spells if they dance twice in an
evening with a lady to whom they aren't married.
Some people feel forever lost if they are riding on a bus and the
conductor doesn't collect their fare,
And other people ruin a lot of widows and orphans and all they
think is, Why there's something in this business of ruining
widows and orphans, and they go out and ruin some more
and get to be a millionaire.
Now it is not the purpose of this memorandum, or song,
To attempt to define the difference between right and wrong;
All I am trying to say is that if you are one of the unfortunates
who recognize that such a difference exists,
Well, you had better oppose even the teensiest temptation with
clenched fists,
Because if you desire peace of mind it is all right to do wrong if it
never occurs to you that it is wrong to do it,
Because you can sleep perfectly well and look the world in the eye
after doing anything at all so long as you don't rue it,
While on the other hand nothing at all is any fun
So long as you yourself know it is something you shouldn't have
done.
There is only one way to achieve happiness on this terrestrial ball,
And that is to have either a clear conscience, or none at all.

TIME MARCHES ON

You ask me, brothers, why I flinch.
Well, I will tell you, inch by inch.
Is it not proper cause for fright
That what is day will soon be night?
Evenings I flinch the selfsame way,
For what is night will soon be day.
At five o'clock it chills my gore
Simply to know it isn't four.
How Sunday into Monday melts!
And every month is something else.
If Summer on the ladder lingers,
Autumn tramples upon her fingers,
Fleeing before the jostling train
Of Winter, and Spring, and Summer again.
Year swallows year and licks its lips,
Then down the gullet of next year slips.
We chip at Time with clocks and watches;
We flee him in love and double scotches;
Even as we scatter in alarm
He marches with us, arm in arm;
Though while we sleep, he forward rides,
Yet when we wake, he's at our sides.
Let men walk straight or let them err,
He never leaves them as they were.
While ladies draw their stockings on
The ladies they were are up and gone.
I pen my lines, I finish, I scan them,
I'm not the poet who began them.
Each moment Time, the lord of changers,
Stuffs our skins with ephemeral strangers.
Good heavens, how remote from me
The billion people I used to be!
Flinch with me, brothers, why not flinch,
Shirts caught in the eternal winch?

[281]

Come, let us flinch till Time stands still;
Although I do not think he will.
Hark brothers, to the dismal proof:
The seconds spattering on the roof!

Good Intentions

ALLOW ME, MADAM, BUT IT WON'T HELP

Adorable is an adjective and womankind is a noun,
And I often wonder why, although adorable womankind elects to
    talk standing up, it elects to put on its coat sitting down.
What is the outstanding characteristic of matinees, tea rooms
    and table d'hôtes?
Women, sitting firmly and uncomfortably on their coats;
Women at whose talents a contortionist would hesitate to scoff,
Because they also sat down on their coats to take them off.
What is *savoir-faire*?
It is the ability to pick up eighty-five cents in nickels and a lipstick
    with the right hand while the left hand is groping wildly
    over the back of a chair.
Yes, and if you desire *savoir-faire* that you could balance a cup on,
Consider the calmness of a woman trying to get her arm into the
    sleeve of a coat that she has sat down on too far up on.
Women are indeed the salt of the earth,
But I fail to see why they daily submit themselves voluntarily to
    an operation that a man only undergoes when he is trying to
    put on his trousers in an upper berth.

YOU AND ME AND P. B. SHELLEY

What is life? Life is stepping down a step or sitting in a chair,
And it isn't there.
Life is not having been told that the man has just waxed the floor,
It is pulling doors marked PUSH and pushing doors marked PULL
    and not noticing notices which say PLEASE USE OTHER
    DOOR.
It is when you diagnose a sore throat as an unprepared geography
    lesson and send your child weeping to school only to be re-
    turned an hour later covered with spots that are indubitably
    genuine,
It is a concert with a trombone soloist filling in for Yehudi Menu-
    hin.

[285   ]

Were it not for frustration and humiliation
I suppose the human race would get ideas above its station.
Somebody once described Shelley as a beautiful and ineffective
    angel beating his luminous wings against the void in vain,
Which is certainly describing with might and main,
But probably means that we are all brothers under our pelts,
And Shelley went around pulling doors marked PUSH and pushing
    doors marked PULL just like everybody else.

GLOSSINA MORSITANS, OR, THE TSETSE

A *Glossina morsitans* bit rich Aunt Betsy.
Tsk tsk, tsetse.

NOW TELL ME ABOUT YOURSELF

Everybody speaks of being patronized,
Yet nobody speaks of the truly irksome shambles which is, or are,
    being matronized,
By which I mean that there is nothing more impolitely and no-
    ticeably aloof
Than a woman of a certain sort sounding out a man of whose
    certain sort she hasn't yet got definite affidavits or proof.
She displays the great names of her acquaintance for his benefit
    like a *nouveau riche* displaying his riches.
And fixes him with the stare of a psychiatrist to see if there is one
    at which he twitches.
George Washington and George Sand and Lloyd George to her
    are Georgie,
And she would have addressed the Borgias behind their backs as
    Borgie.
She always wants to know, first, where do you come from, and
    second, do you of course know Babs and Bonzo Beaver there,
    which you never do, often for your own very good reasons,
    but you try to make your reply a polite one.

So you murmur, "Well I don't really know them, but I know *of* them," and she at once assigns you to your proper side of the tracks, and it is not the right one.

When she discusses national affairs she doesn't talk exactly treasonably.

But she refers to that part of the nation which lies outside of New York in the bright tone of one referring to a little tailor she has just discovered who does alterations very reasonably.

Please do not get the impression that a matronizing woman causes me to froth at the mouth or slaver;

I only wish to notify you that whenever you want her you can have her.

LATHER AS YOU GO

Beneath this slab
John Brown is stowed.
He watched the ads,
And not the road.

TIN WEDDING WHISTLE

Though you know it anyhow
Listen to me, darling, now,

Proving what I need not prove
How I know I love you, love.

Near and far, near and far,
I am happy where you are;

Likewise I have never learnt
How to be it where you aren't.

Far and wide, far and wide,
I can walk with you beside;

Furthermore, I tell you what,
I sit and sulk where you are not.

Visitors remark my frown
When you're upstairs and I am down,

Yes, and I'm afraid I pout
When I'm indoors and you are out;

But how contentedly I view
Any room containing you.

In fact I care not where you be,
Just as long as it's with me.

In all your absences I glimpse
Fire and flood and trolls and imps.

Is your train a minute slothful?
I goad the stationmaster wrothful.

When with friends to bridge you drive
I never know if you're alive,

And when you linger late in shops
I long to telephone the cops.

Yet how worth the waiting for,
To see you coming through the door.

Somehow, I can be complacent
Never but with you adjacent.

Near and far, near and far,
I am happy where you are;

Likewise, I have never learnt
How to be it where you aren't.

Then grudge me not my fond endeavor,
To hold you in my sight forever;

Let none, not even you, disparage
Such valid reason for a marriage.

THE SKINK

Let us do justice to the skink
Who isn't what so many think.
On consultation with a wizard
I find the skink a kind of lizard.
Since he is not a printer's whim,
Don't sniff and back away from him,
Or you may be adjudged too drunk
To tell a lizard from a skunk.

THE STRANGE CASE OF MR. ORMANTUDE'S BRIDE

Once there was a bridegroom named Mr. Ormantude whose in-
    tentions were hard to disparage,
Because he intended to make his a happy marriage,
And he succeeded for going on fifty years,
During which he was in marital bliss up to his ears.
His wife's days and nights were enjoyable
Because he catered to every foible;
He went around humming her favorite hymns
And anticipating her whims.
Many a fine bit of repartee died on his lips
Lest it throw her anecdotes into eclipse;
He was always silent when his cause was meritorious,

And he never engaged in argument unless sure he was so obviously wrong that she couldn't help emerging victorious,
And always when in her vicinity
He was careful to make allowances for her femininity;
Were she snappish, he was sweetish,
And of understanding her he made a fetish.
Everybody said his chances of celebrating his golden wedding looked good,
But on his golden wedding eve he was competently poisoned by his wife who could no longer stand being perpetually understood.

THE ABSENTEES

I'd ride a cock horse to Banbury Cross
For giblet gravy and cranberry sauce,
Two treats which are held in reserve by the waiter
Till you've finished your turkey and mashed potater.

APRIL YULE, DADDY!

Roses are things which Christmas is not a bed of them,
Because it is the day when parents finally realize that their children will always be a jump ahead of them.
You stay up all night trimming the tree into a veritable fairyland and then in the joyous morn you spring it on the children in a blaze of glory, and who says Ooh!?
You.
And you frantically point out the dictator's ransom in building sets and bicycles and embarrassingly lifelike dolls with which the room is checkered,
And the little ones pay about as much attention to them as they would to the punctuation in the *Congressional Record,*
Because they are fully occupied in withdrawing all the books from the bookcase to build a house to house the pup in,

Or pulling down the curtains to dress up in,

And you stand hangdoggedly around because you haven't any place to go,

And after a while they look casually over at the dictator's ransom and say, "Are those the presents? Oh."

And you console yourself by thinking Ah happy apathy, as long as we haven't had an emotional climax maybe we won't have an emotional anticlimax, maybe we'll get through the day without hysterics, ah happy apathy,

Ah may this Yuletide indeed turn out to be Yuletide without mishapathy.

Ah could this sensational lull but be permanent instead of pro tem;

Ah and doubly ah, if Christmas day could but end at eleven A.M.! —

But it doesn't, but the lull does, and here's something else you discover as you keep on living,

Which is that Christmas doesn't end for about two weeks after Christmas, but it starts all over again right after the following Thanksgiving.

I HAPPEN TO KNOW

Hark to the locusts in their shrill armadas.
Locusts aren't locusts. Locusts are cicadas.

To seals in circuses I travel on bee lines.
Seals aren't seals. Seals are sea lions.

I'm a buffalo hunter. Want to see my license?
Buffaloes aren't buffaloes. Buffaloes are bisons.

I'm too old to be pedantically hocus-pocused.
I'll stand on the buffalo, the seal and the locust.

I'M SURE SHE SAID SIX–THIRTY

One of the hardest explanations to be found
Is an explanation for just standing around.
Anyone just standing around looks pretty sinister,
Even a minister;
Consider then the plight of the criminal,
Who lacks even the protective coloration of a hyminal,
And as just standing around is any good criminal's practically daily
    stint,
I wish to proffer a hint.
Are you, sir, a masher who blushes as he loiters,
Do you stammer to passers-by that you are merely expecting a
    street car, or a dispatch from Reuter's?
Or perhaps you are a safeblower engaged in casing a joint;
Can you look the patrolman in the eye or do you forget all the
    savoir-faire you ever loint?
Suppose you are a shoplifter awaiting an opportunity to lift a shop,
Or simply a novice with a length of lead pipe killing time in a dark
    alley pending the arrival of a wealthy fop,
Well, should any official ask you why you are just standing around,
Do you wish you could simply sink into the ground?
My dear sir, do not be embarrassed, do not reach for your gun
    or your knife,
Remember the password, which, uttered in a tone of quiet despair,
    is the explanation of anyone's standing around anywhere at
    any hour for any length of time: "I'm waiting for my wife."

DO, DO, DO WHAT YOU DONE, DONE, DONE
BEFORE, BEFORE, BEFORE

There is a man whose name must be, I think, Mr. Oglethrip, and
    if you will bring me his head on a silver charger I will award
    you the hand of my daughter and a lien on my future salary,
And nobody has ever seen him but when you go to an amateur

performance of any kind he is always sitting in the upper left-hand corner of the gallery,

And he has the hands of a blacksmith and a heart full of enthusiasm,

And compared to the rest of the audience, well Mr. Oglethrip is not as chusiasm,

Because seasoned amateur performance attenders generally weigh their applause carefully so as not to be either a spendthrift or a hoarder,

Because unless the performers of any performance are your grandmother or your favorite cousin or something your aim is to applaud just enough to not hurt their feelings and not enough to induce them to duplicate the order,

And some girl who once handed you a cup of cocoa at a church supper appears and renders an imitation of Helen Hayes as Portia,

And your applause preserves the delicate balance between ecstasy and nausea,

And she is just about to resign the stage to the next performer and everything is as right as a couple of trivets,

When hark! What is that thunder in the upper left-hand corner of the gallery, can Mr. Oglethrip be driving rivets?

No, but he is clapping his horny hands and before you can catch your breath,

Why, the cocoa girl is back with an imitation of Judith Anderson's Lady Macbeth.

Mr. Oglethrip's cup has no brim,

Mr. Oglethrip is he to whom what is too much for anybody else is never enough for him,

If Mr. Oglethrip heard Conrad Hilton sing "Trees,"

He would want a reprise.

Do you know a picture program that Mr. Oglethrip would find simply peachy?

A double bill in which each picture contained a dual role for Don Ameche.

I think it would be nice

If when you cut off Mr. Oglethrip's head to bring to me on a
silver charger you would cut it off twice.

WHAT, NO OYSTERS?

There is no R in the month of May,
There's none in the month of June,
And the days of the dog, July and Aug.,
Glide past on R-less shoon.
Then where are you going, my pretty maid,
And what will you find to eat
While the oyster broods in inedible moods
In his lonely bridal suite?

"I'm going a-feasting, sir," she said,
"I am on my way to dine.
Let the succulent bivalve cling to its bed,
Methinks I am doing fine.
For the chowder laves the fragrant clam
In the old New England style,
And if corn on the cob with my teeth plays hob,
I'll remember not to smile.

The baby lobster scarlet gleams
Next a mound of fresh asparagus;
While the blue point dreams connubial dreams,
I'll munch till my veins are varacus.
Lo, luscious now as an infant's lisp,
The strawberry, tart and juicy,
And soft-shell crabs as sweet and crisp
As a nocturne by Debussy.

Though there is no R in the month of May,
And none in the month of June,
Nor the days of the dog, July and Aug.,

You can stuff till you're fit to swoon —
Who's that a-ringing the doorbell so,
Louder than doorbell ought to ring?
Why, it's half a dozen oysters, bowing low,
And their mouths are simply watering."

MS. FOUND IN A QUAGMIRE

Up, up, lad, time's a-wastin', press the ignition.
If relief is not forthcoming, consult your physician.
Winnow your symptoms, but never discard the chaff,
And consult your physician, your physician deserves a laugh.
Explain that when you swallow so much as a coddled egg it sticks
    like a fishbone
Somewhere behind your wishbone;
Inquire why your eyes of a sudden refuse to be focused,
And what is the sound in your ears like a courting locust.
Your physician's a man of talents;
Ask him whatever became of your sense of balance.
Don't be irked by his suavity;
Tell how you walk with your legs braced wide lest you trip over
    gravity;
Tell him, too, that your gaze is fixed on your shoes as you walk,
    and better to tell him why:
That a too long upward glance would send you headlong into
    the sky.
Tell him straight that on such and such a day
They took the difference between down and up away.
Give him your problem to solve,
Ask him what to hold onto when under your feet you can feel
    the earth revolve;
Every molehill a mountain, every wormhole a crater,
And every step like the step at the top of the escalator,
And don't forget
To reveal your discovery that hair can sweat.

Go ahead, tell him;
Release the cat from the bag, let the doctor bell him.
Give the doctor the chart, show him the map and the graph;
If relief is not forthcoming, it says right here on the label, consult
    your physician, your physician deserves a laugh.

THE SNIFFLE

In spite of her sniffle,
Isabel's chiffle.
Some girls with a sniffle
Would be weepy and tiffle;
They would look awful,
Like a rained-on waffle,
But Isabel's chiffle
In spite of her sniffle.
Her nose is more red
With a cold in her head,
But then, to be sure,
Her eyes are bluer.
Some girls with a snuffle,
Their tempers are uffle,
But when Isabel's snivelly
She's snivelly civilly,
And when she is snuffly
She's perfectly luffly.

WE DON'T NEED TO LEAVE YET, DO WE?
OR, YES WE DO

One kind of person when catching a train always wants to allow
    an hour to cover the ten-block trip to the terminus,
And the other kind looks at them as if they were verminous,
And the second kind says that five minutes is plenty and will even
    leave one minute over for buying the tickets,

And the first kind looks at them as if they had cerebral rickets.

One kind when theater-bound sups lightly at six and hastens off
to the play,

And indeed I know one such person who is so such that it frequently arrives in time for the last act of the matinee,

And the other kind sits down at eight to a meal that is positively
sumptuous,

Observing cynically that an eight-thirty curtain never rises till
eight-forty, an observation which is less cynical than bump-
tuous.

And what the first kind, sitting uncomfortably in the waiting room
while the train is made up in the yards, can never understand,

Is the injustice of the second kind's reaching their seat just as the
train moves out, just as they had planned,

And what the second kind cannot understand as they stumble over
the first kind's feet just as the footlights flash on at last

Is that the first kind doesn't feel the least bit foolish at having
entered the theater before the cast.

Oh, the first kind always wants to start now and the second kind
always wants to tarry,

Which wouldn't make any difference, except that each other is
what they always marry.

THE SMELT

Oh, why does man pursue the smelt?
It has no valuable pelt,
It boasts of no escutcheon royal,
It yields no ivory or oil,
Its life is dull, its death is tame,
A fish as humble as its name.
Yet — take this salmon somewhere else,
And bring me half a dozen smelts.

SLOW DOWN, MR. GANDERDONK, YOU'RE LATE

Do you know Mr. Ganderdonk, he is no Einstein, he has no theories of Time and Space,

But he is the only man I know can be both the hare and the tortoise in the same race.

Mr. Ganderdonk's proclivity

Is divoty Relativity.

Put him behind you in a twosome or a foursome,

His speed is awesome.

His relationship to your rear

Is that of a catamount to a deer,

And while you are still reaching for your putter

He is standing on the edge of the green going mutter mutter,

But once through you in his foursome or twosome,

His torpor is gruesome.

He is a golfer that the thought of other golfers simply hasn't occurred to;

He has three swings for every shot, the one he hopes to use, the
one he does use, and finally the one he would have preferred to.

His world from tee to cup

Consists of those behind him pressing him and those in front of
him holding him up,

Wherefore the rest of the world is his foe

Because the rest of the world is either too fast or too slow.

For Mr. Ganderdonk there is only one correct pace and that is his,

Whatever it is.

CREEPS AND CRAWLS

The insect world appealed to Fabre.
I find the insect world macabre.
In every hill of ants I see
A governed glimpse of what shall be,
And sense in every web contriver

Man's predecessor and survivor.
Someday, perhaps, my citronella
Will rank with Chamberlain's umbrella.

THE SCREEN WITH THE FACE WITH THE VOICE

How long
Is a song?
O Lord,
How long?
A second?
A minute?
An hour?
A day?
A decade?
A cycle of Cathay?
Press the ears
With occlusive fingers;
The whining melody
Lingers, lingers;
The mouthing face
Will not be hid,
But leers at the eye
From the inner lid.
With the sure advance of ultimate doom
The moaning adenoids larger loom;
The seven-foot eyebrows fall and rise
In roguish rapture or sad surprise;
Eyeballs roll with fine emotion,
Like buoys rocked by a treacle ocean;
Tugged like the bell above the chapel,
Tosses the giant Adam's apple;
Oozes the voice from the magic screen,
A slow Niagara of Grenadine;
A frenzy of ripe orgiastic pain,
Niagara gurgling down a drain.

How long
Is a song?
O Lord,
How long?
As long as Loew,
And Keith,
And Albee;
It Was,
And Is,
And Always Shall Be.
This is the string Time may not sever,
This is the music that lasts forever,
This is the Womb,
This is the Tomb,
This is Alpha, Omega, and Oom!
The eyes, the eyes shall follow you!
The throat, the throat shall swallow you!
Hygienic teeth shall wolf you!
And viscous voice engulf you!
The lolloping tongue itself answer your question!
The Adam's Apple dance at your ingestion!
And you shall never die, but live to nourish the bowels
Of deathless celluloid vowels.

A VISIT FROM DR. FELL

Dr. Fell is at the door and my *mens sana* is about to depart from
my *corpore sano,*
For this is the hour of the chocolate fingerprints in the books and
the coconut-marshmallow icing on the piano.
Dr. Fell is notable for the southern-central section of his silhouette,
And he lands in your frailest chair like somebody from the ninth
floor of a burning hotel landing in a net.
Hitherto, the plumbing has functioned as sweetly as a hungry
mosquito lapping up citronella,

But the plumbing is where Dr. Fell disposes of any unwanted object, from an old cigar to an old umbrella.
Dr. Fell's little finger projecting from his glass as he drinks couldn't possibly be genteeler or archer,
But whatever glasses you had a dozen of on his arrival you only have eleven of on his departure.
Every man but Dr. Fell has his own conception of enough;
Dr. Fell will not only nonchalantly knock a half-completed jigsaw puzzle onto the floor but nonchalantly carry off a key piece buried in his cuff.
Come on in Dr. Fell, you must take pot-luck with us, no, wait a minute, I forgot,
Today we can only offer you kettle-luck, last time you were here you ran the ice-pick through the pot.

HERE WE GO QUIETLY NUTS IN MAY

Do you hanker for April showers,
Or a rarefied day in June?
Give me a grade-A May day,
And please deliver it soon.
I am weary of branches naked,
Creaking like lovelorn cats;
The earth underfoot mud-cakèd,
And the sun overhead ersatz.
Send me a balmy zephyr
To play me a rigadoon,
And I'll gulp of my grade-A May day
Till my hiccups hammer the moon.

I WANT A DRINK OF WATER, BUT NOT FROM THE THERMOS

Have you ever lost your early start on a six-hundred-mile trip and had to spend the night in an individual wayside slum in-

stead of the cozy inn at which you had foresightedly engaged
rooms because child A couldn't find her absolutely favorite
doll, and when she did find it, child B hadn't finished plait-
ing her hair yet?

Then you will agree with me that an accurate definition of a millionth of a second is the interval between the moment when
you press the starter as you begin a six-hundred-mile trip
and the moment when two little tired voices inquire from
the back seat, "Are we nearly there yet?"

Then again, consider the other millionth of a second which lasts
a year, when Time stands still, and Eternity in the lap of
Infinity lingers,

Which is while you sit in helpless paralysis while child B carefully
slams the door on child A's fingers.

Take the battle royal whose results no bachelor need ever have
computed,

Which is the struggle to sit nearest to the open window, a struggle
the prize for which is the privilege of sticking the head and
arms out in just the right position to be immediately ampu-
tated.

Yes, for the father of none to thank his stars I think it only be-
hooving,

If merely because he has not to contend with little ones who will
descend from the car only on the traffic side, and preferably
quite some time before the car but not the traffic has stopped
moving.

Yes, he can roll along as confident as brass;

No restlessly whirling little leg will knock his spectacles off as he
confronts a bus, no little hand groping the floor for a vanilla
ice cream cone with chocolate thingamajigs on it will suddenly alight heavily upon the gas.

As the father of two there is a respectful question which I wish to
ask of fathers of five:

How do you happen to be still alive?

THE TROUBLE WITH WOMEN IS MEN

A husband is a man who two minutes after his head touches the
pillow is snoring like an overloaded omnibus,
Particularly on those occasions when between the humidity and
the mosquitoes your own bed is no longer a bed, but an in-
somnibus,
And if you turn on the light for a little reading he is sensitive to
the faintest gleam,
But if by any chance you are asleep and he wakeful, he is not slow
to rouse you with the complaint that he can't close his eyes,
what about slipping downstairs and freezing him a cooling
dish of pistachio ice cream.
His touch with a bottle opener is sure,
But he cannot help you get a tight dress over your head without
catching three hooks and a button in your coiffure.
Nor can he so much as wash his ears without leaving an inch of
water on the bathroom linoleum,
But if you mention it you evoke not a promise to splash no more
but a mood of deep melancholium.
Indeed, each time he transgresses your chance of correcting his
faults grows lesser,
Because he produces either a maddeningly logical explanation or
a look of martyrdom which leaves you instead of him feeling
the remorse of the transgressor.
Such are husbandly foibles, but there are moments when a foible
ceases to be a foible.
Next time you ask for a glass of water and when he brings it you
have a needle almost threaded and instead of setting it down
he stands there holding it out to you, just kick him fairly hard
in the stomach, you will find it thoroughly enjoible.

A BEGINNER'S GUIDE TO THE OCEAN

Let us now consider the ocean.
It is always in motion.

It is generally understood to be the source of much of our rain,
And ten thousand fleets are said to have swept over it in vain.
When the poet requested it to break break break on its cold gray rocks it obligingly broke broke broke,
Which as the poet was Alfred Lord Tennyson didn't surprise him at all but if it had been me I would probably have had a stroke.
Some people call it the Atlantic and some the Pacific or the Antarctic or the Indian or the Mediterranean Sea,
But I always say what difference does it make, some old geographer mumbling a few words over it, it will always be just the Ocean to me.
There is an immortal dignity about something like the Atlantic,
Which seems to drive unimmortal undignified human beings frustratedly frantic.
Just give them one foot on the beach and people who were perfectly normal formerly, or whilom,
Why, they are subject to whoops and capers that would get them blackballed from an asylum;
Yet be they never so rampant and hollerant,
The ocean is tolerant,
Except a couple of times a day it gives up in disgust and goes off by itself and hides,
And that, my dears, accounts for the tides.

THE GANDER

Be careful not to cross the gander,
A bird composed of beak and dander.
His heart is filled with prideful hate
Of all the world except his mate,
And if the neighbors do not err
He's overfond of beating her.
Is she happy? What's the use
Of trying to psychoanalyze a goose?

[304]

PUT BACK THOSE WHISKERS, I KNOW YOU

There is one fault that I must find with the twentieth century,
And I'll put it in a couple of words: Too adventury.
What I'd like would be some nice dull monotony
If anyone's gotony.
People have gone on for years looking forward hopefully to the
 beginning of every fresh anno Domini,
Full of more hopes than there are grits in hominy,
Because it is their guess that the Old Year has been so bad that
 the New Year cannot help being an improvement, and may
 I say that they would never make a living as guessers,
Because what happens, why the New Year simply combines and
 elaborates on the worst features of its predecessors.
Well, I know what the matter is, it stands out as clear as a chord
 in a symphony of Sibelius's,
The matter is that our recent New Years haven't been New Years
 at all, they have just been the same Old Year, probably 1914
 or something, under a lot of different aliases.
In my eagerness to encounter a New Year I stand ahead of most,
But only if it's a true New Year, not if it's merely the same Old
 Year with its beard shaved off and wearing a diaper labeled
 New Year just to get on the cover of the *Saturday Evening
 Post.*

BUGS

Some insects feed on rosebuds,
And others feed on carrion.
Between them they devour the earth.
Bugs are totalitarian.

NO DOCTORS TODAY, THANK YOU

They tell me that euphoria is the feeling of feeling wonderful, well,
 today I feel euphorian,

Today I have the agility of a Greek god and the appetite of a Victorian.
Yes, today I may even go forth without my galoshes,
Today I am a swashbuckler, would anybody like me to buckle any swashes?
This is my euphorian day,
I will ring welkins and before anybody answers I will run away.
I will tame me a caribou
And bedeck it with marabou.
I will pen me my memoirs.
Ah youth, youth! What euphorian days them was!
I wasn't much of a hand for the boudoirs,
I was generally to be found where the food was.
Does anybody want any flotsam?
I've gotsam.
Does anybody want any jetsam?
I can getsam.
I can play chopsticks on the Wurlitzer,
I can speak Portuguese like a Berlitzer.
I can don or doff my shoes without tying or untying the laces because I am wearing moccasins,
And I practically know the difference between serums and antitoccasins.
Kind people, don't think me purse-proud, don't set me down as vainglorious,
I'm just a little euphorious.

DANCE UNMACABRE

This is the witching hour of noon;
Bedlam breaks upon us soon.
When the stroke of twelve has tolled
What a pageant doth unfold.
Drawers slam on pads of notes,
Eager fingers clutch at coats;

[306]

Compact, lipstick, comb and hat,
Here a dab and there a pat;
The vital letter just begun
Can sulk in the machine till one.
Stenographers on clicking heels
Scurry forth in quest of meals;
Secretaries arm in arm
Fill the corridors with charm;
The stolid air with scent grows heavy
As bevy scuttles after bevy;
Like the pipers on the beach,
Calling shrilly each to each,
Sure as arrows, swift as skaters,
Converging at the elevators.
From the crowded lift they scatter
Bursting still with turbulent chatter;
The revolving door in rapture whirls
Its quarters full of pretty girls.
Soignée, comme il faut and *chic*
On forty or forty-five a week.
When One upon the dial looms
They hurry to their office tombs,
There to bide in dust till five,
When they come again alive.

IT'S A GRAND PARADE IT WILL BE,
MODERN DESIGN

Saint Patrick was a proper man, a man to be admired;
Of numbering his virtues I am never, never tired.
A handsome man, a holy man, a man of mighty deeds,
He walked the lanes of Erin, a-telling of his beads.
A-telling of his beads, he was, and spreading of the word.
I think that of Saint Patrick's Day, Saint Patrick hadn't heard.

[307]

The saint was born a subject of the ancient British throne,
But the Irish in their wisdom recognized him as their own.
A raiding party captured him, and carried him away,
And Patrick loved the Irish, and he lived to capture they,
A-walking of the valleys and a-spreading of the word.
I think that of Saint Patrick's Day, Saint Patrick hadn't heard.

He defied the mighty Druids, he spoke them bold and plain,
And he lit the Easter fire on the lofty hill of Shane.
He lit the Easter fire where the hill and heaven met,
And on every hill in Ireland the fire is burning yet.
He lit the Easter fire, a-spreading of the word.
I think that of Saint Patrick's Day, Saint Patrick hadn't heard.

Saint Patrick was a proper man before he was a saint,
He was shaky in his Latin, his orthography was quaint,
But he walked the length of Ireland, her mountains and her lakes,
A-building of his churches and a-driving out the snakes,
A-building of his churches and a-spreading of the word.
I think that of Saint Patrick's Day, Saint Patrick hadn't heard.

But the silver-tongued announcer is a coy, facetious rogue;
He ushers in Saint Patrick with a fine synthetic brogue,
He spatters his commercials with macushlas and colleens,
Begorras, worra-worras, and spurious spalpeens.
I hope one day Saint Patrick will lean down from Heaven's arch,
And jam the bloody air waves on the Seventeenth of March.

DOWN THE MOUSEHOLE, AND WHAT SCIENCE MISSED THERE

This is a baffling and forbidding world of disreputable international shakedowns,
And reputable scientists spending their lives trying to give mice nervous breakdowns.

[308]

Let us treat these scientists to a constructive suggestion on the house:

Have they thought to try their experiments on a married, or at least an engaged, mouse?

This suggestion is not frivolous or yeasty;

I want to tell them about a mouse I know, his name is Roger, who loses his mind at a twist of the wrist from his fiancée, later his wife, who first caught his eye because she seemed to him naught but, as he puts it, a wee sleekit cow'rin' tim'rous beastie.

Now, it is Roger's contention that to err is mouse-like, and being only mouse, though indeed his paternal grandmother was a mountain, he is all too often conscious of having erred not only as a mouse,

But as a mouse's spouse,

As a result of which when he is justly chastised,

He is, as a reasonable mouse, neither upset nor surprised.

It's a perfectly natural sequence, Roger says resignedly, that began with Adam and Eve in the garden:

Crime, punishment, apology, theater tickets, and eventual pardon.

What gets him down, he tells me, is when he has erred and doesn't know that he has erred,

When his conscience is clear as to thought, deed, misdeed, diet and word.

It is then, says Roger, that he is ready to pay the psychiatrist a lengthy visit,

Because he can't apologize without knowing what to apologize for, whereupon the coolness which chills him for whatever he has done that he doesn't know he has done grows all the cooler for the very reason that he has no idea what is it.

Worst of all, he adds in despair, is that while racking his brains to alight on what it can be that he erred about,

Why, he often loops an extra loop about his neck by apologizing for an error that if he hadn't apologized for it she would never have heard about.

So there you are, reputable scientists, it is in trying to recollect
   and expiate sins that it never knew were sins,
That is why a mouse is when it spins.

VISITORS LAUGH AT LOCKSMITHS, OR, HOSPITAL DOORS HAVEN'T GOT LOCKS ANYHOW

Something I should like to know is, which would everybody rather
   not do:
Be well and visit an unwell friend in the hospital, or be unwell in
   the hospital and have a well friend visit you?
This is a discussion which I am sorry that I ever commenced it,
For not only does it call up old unhappy memories, but each choice
   has so much to be said against it.
Take the sight of a visitor trying to entertain a patient or a patient
   trying to entertain a visitor,
It would bring joy to the heart of the Grand Inquisitor.
The patient either is too ailing to talk or is panting to get back to
   the chapter where the elderly spinster is just about to reveal
   to the Inspector that she now thinks she can identify the second voice in that doom-drenched quarrel,
And the visitor either has never had anything to say to the patient
   anyway or is wondering how soon it would be all right to
   depart for Belmont or Santa Anita or Laurel,
And besides, even if both parties have ordinarily much to discuss
   and are far from conversational mediocrities,
Why, the austere hygienic surroundings and the lack of ashtrays
   would stunt a dialogue between Madam de Staël and Socrates,
And besides, even if anybody did get to chatting glitteringly and
   gaudily,
They would soon be interrupted by the arrival of a nurse or an
   orderly.
It is a fact that I must chronicle with distress

That the repartee reaches its climax when the visitor finally spots
    the handle on the foot of the bed and cranks the patient's
    knees up and down and says, "That certainly is ingenious,"
    and the patient answers Yes.
How many times a day do I finger my pulse and display my tongue
    to the mirror while waiting for a decision to be elicited:
Whether to ignore my host of disquieting symptoms and spend my
    days visiting friends who have surrendered to theirs, or to
    surrender to my own and spend my days being visited.

LAMENT ON THE EVE OF PARTING

I shall grieve, I grieve, I am grieving.
Abel is leaving.
Abel, the wise and the clever,
Is leaving, is leaving forever.
He goes to a wealthy tycoon
For an extra five dollars a moon,
Abel, the kind and gentle
Whose faults, if any, were minor and incidental.
North Carolina was his native heath
And the gold in his heart ran all the way up to his teeth.
Abel, the courtly and portly
Is departing shortly.
Never were white shoes whitened or tan shoes tanned
As beneath his caressing hand,
Nor the silver and glass so luminous
As beneath those fingers bituminous.
Did a faucet leak, did the furnace refuse to function?
Abel had straightened it out between breakfast and luncheon.
Did a fuse blow, or a bulb flicker and die like the flame of plum-
    pudding brandy?
He had always a new one handy.
Did a guest request a harpoon, a harp, a tarpaulin, a tarpon, a
    turpentine hipbath, a hymnal, let the guest request what he
    would,

Abel would either produce, or rig up something as good.
He could string a radio aerial
Or lay out a person for burial.
His voice dark honey dripping from an olden golden pitcher,
Only smoother and richer.
Farewell, Abel, good-by,
You recede from my misty eye,
You have left to join your tycoon
For five more dollars a moon.
O Abel, no longer visible,
Abel, I'm misible!

SUPPOSE HE THREW IT IN YOUR FACE

Please don't anybody ask me to decide anything, I do not know a
    nut from a meg,
Or which came first, the lady or the tiger, or which came next, the
    chicken or the egg.
I am, alas, to be reckoned
With the shortstop who can't decide whether to throw to first or
    second,
Nor can I decide whether to put, except after c,
E before i, or i before e.
But where this twilight mind really goes into eclipse
Is in the matter of tips.
I stand stricken before the triple doom,
Whether, and How Much, and Whom.
Tell me, which is more unpleasant,
The look from him who is superior to a tip and gets it, or from him
    who isn't and doesn't?
I had rather be discovered playing with my toes in the Aquarium
Than decide wrongly about an honorarium.
Oh, to dwell forever amid Utopian scenery
Where hotels and restaurants and service stations are operated by
    untippable unoffendable machinery.

THE GRACKLE

The grackle's voice is less than mellow,
His heart is black, his eye is yellow,
He bullies more attractive birds
With hoodlum deeds and vulgar words,
And should a human interfere,
Attacks that human in the rear.
I cannot help but deem the grackle
An ornithological debacle.

NOW YOU SEE IT, NOW I DON'T

Some people look to the future and others look days of yore-wards,
But even they see more eye to eye than two people on a train one
    of whom is riding backwards and the other forwards.
I don't know how it does or when,
But anything interesting described by a forwards rider has van-
    ished by the time it should have swum into the backwards
    rider's ken,
While, through a freak twist of the current
The backwards rider gets to see a lot of interesting things that
    should have been there a moment ago for the forwards rider
    to see but somehow they just wurrent.
Travelers have told me and I have believed them,
That such noticeable objects as the Mississippi River and the Sierra
    Nevada mountains have disappeared between the time when
    the forwards rider pointed them out and the backwards rider
    should have perceived them.
There are those who in an effort to explain this phenomenon have
    developed a disturbing knack;
They sit forwards and look back,
While others to whom their vertebræ are dearer
Sit backwards and gaze on the fleeting landscape through a mirror.
But no matter what they describe

[313]

Their accounts never jibe.
When I eventually establish my Universal Travel Service and
    Guide Ways
I shall advise all my clients who really want to see anything just to
    sit at home and look sideways.

SO THAT'S WHO I REMIND ME OF

When I consider men of golden talents,
I'm delighted, in my introverted way,
To discover, as I'm drawing up the balance,
How much we have in common, I and they.

Like Burns, I have a weakness for the bottle,
Like Shakespeare, little Latin and less Greek;
I bite my fingernails like Aristotle;
Like Thackeray, I have a snobbish streak.

I'm afflicted with the vanity of Byron,
I've inherited the spitefulness of Pope;
Like Petrarch, I'm a sucker for a siren,
Like Milton, I've a tendency to mope.

My spelling is suggestive of a Chaucer;
Like Johnson, well, I do not wish to die
(I also drink my coffee from the saucer);
And if Goldsmith was a parrot, so am I.

Like Villon, I have debits by the carload,
Like Swinburne, I'm afraid I need a nurse;
By my dicing is Christopher out-Marlowed,
And I dream as much as Coleridge, only worse.

In comparison with men of golden talents,
I am all a man of talent ought to be;
I resemble every genius in his vice, however henious —
Yet I only write like me.

THERE'S ALWAYS AN UBBLEBUB

There are some fiestas that the moment you arrive at them you
    realize this is not your night to howl,
Because your hostess is still patting sofa cushions in the parlor and
    your host is upstairs applying the styptic pencil to his jowl,
And you apologize for being premature,
And when your hostess snarls "Oh that's all right," she is lying in
    her teeth, you may be sure,
And you wish she would keep on patting cushions and let you go
    out and walk around the block,
But she just sits there asking how you like their city and looking at
    the clock,
And at last in comes another guest whose name sounds like Miss
    Ubblebub, which seems highly improbable,
And she is wearing a dress that she wore first as a bridesmaid
    during the Harding administration and hair that hesitates
    between the waveable and the bobbable,
And you may not have suspected your hostess of craft,
But suddenly she is superintending appetizers and you and Miss
    Ubblebub are off in a corner as snug as two barnacles on a
    raft,
And an hour later when the last guest has been cocktailed and
    canapéed you have certainly run, as far as Miss Ubblebub is
    concerned, your conversational gamut,
And when at dinner you find yourself seated next to Miss Ubble-
    bub, I think you may be excused an ardent shucks, or even
    a quiet damut.

PLEASE PASS THE BISCUIT

I have a little dog,
Her name is Spangle.
And when she eats
I think she'll strangle.

[315]

She's darker than Hamlet,
Lighter than Porgy;
Her heart is gold,
Her odor, dorgy.

Her claws click-click
Across the floor,
Her nose is always
Against a door.

Like liquid gems
Her eyes burn clearly;
She's five years old,
And house-trained, nearly.

Her shame is deep
When she has erred;
She dreads the blow
Less than the word.

I marvel that such
Small ribs as these
Can cage such vast
Desire to please.

She's as much a part
Of the house as the mortgage;
Spangle, I wish you
A ripe old dortgage.

"TOMORROW, PARTLY CLOUDY"

Rainy vacations
Try people's patience.
To expect rain in the autumn
Experience has tautumn,
And rain in the spring and winter

Makes no stories for the printer,
But rain on summer colonies
Breeds misdemeanors and felonies.
Summer cottages are meant just to sleep in,
Not to huddle all day in a heap in,
And whether at sea level or in higher places
There are not enough fireplaces,
And the bookcase stares at you starkly
And seems to be full of nothing but Volume II of the life of Ruth-
        erford B. Hayes, and *The Rosary,* by Florence M. Barclay,
And everybody wishes they had brought woolens and tweeds in-
        stead of linens and foulards,
And if you succeed in lining up four for bridge the only deck turns
        out to have only fifty-one cards,
And tennis rackets grow frazzled and golf sticks rusty and bathing
        suits moldy,
And parents grow scoldy,
And on all sides you hear nothing but raindrops going sputter-sput,
        sputter-sput,
And bureau drawers won't open and bathroom doors won't shut,
And all attempts at amusement fail,
Even reading the previous tenants' jettisoned mail,
Although naturally it would never have been jettisoned
If it hadn't been reticent.
But you could stand everything if it wasn't for one malignant
        committee,
Which is the one that turns the sun on again just as you are leaving
        for the city.
Yes indeed, rainy vacations
Certainly try people's patience.

DR. FELL AND POINTS WEST

Your train leaves at eleven-forty-five and it is now but eleven-
        thirty-nine and a half,

And there is only one man ahead of you at the ticket window so
   you have plenty of time, haven't you, well I hope you enjoy
   a hearty laugh,
Because he is Dr. Fell, and he is engaged in an intricate maneuver,
He wants to go to Sioux City with stopovers at Plymouth Rock,
   Stone Mountain, Yellowstone Park, Lake Louise and Van-
   couver,
And he would like some information about an alternate route,
One that would include New Orleans and Detroit, with possibly
   a day or two in Minneapolis and Butte,
And when the agent has compiled the data with the aid of a slug
   of aromatic spirits and a moist bandanna,
He says that settles it, he'll spend his vacation canoeing up and
   down the Susquehanna,
And oh yes, which way is the bus terminal and what's playing at
   the Rivoli,
And how do the railroads expect to stay in business when their
   employees are incapable of answering a simple question accurately or civilly?
He then demands and receives change for twenty dollars and
   saunters off leaving everybody's jaw with a sag on it,
And when you finally get to buy your ticket not only has your train
   gone but you also discover that your porter has efficiently
   managed to get your bag on it.

LINES ON FACING FORTY

I have a bone to pick with Fate.
Come here and tell me, girlie,
Do you think my mind is maturing late,
Or simply rotted early?

ONE NIGHT IN OZ

O She whom I cannot abide,
Our hostess sat us side by side,

But must the heavy silence scream
Our heartfelt mutual disesteem?
Can we not mitigate our plight
If you turn left and I turn right?
This tasty fare will tastier taste
If by each other we are not faced;
Why shouldn't our acquaintance end,
Friend of a friend of a friend of a friend?
You do not love my way of life,
Myself, my children or my wife,
And too self-satisfied for tact,
Don't bother to conceal the fact,
While I my feelings may not hint
Till I can set them forth in print.
Our juxtaposition as we dine
Results from no intrigue of mine.
You'd wished yon titled refugee
Whose dollars jetted here with he,
While I, whose hopes are mild and mere,
Had but desired to not be here.
Discovering who sits next to who,
Your face fell one inch, mine fell two.
Yet o'er our hostess's well-meant food
Did I refrain from being rude,
A minor courtesy which I grieve
To note that you could not achieve.
Well, Madam, if you wish it so,
Hitch up your girdle, here we go.
O living sneer, poor painted peril,
Yours is the snobbery of the sterile.
Of hounds and huntin' you discourse
Who never sat upon a horse.
You, who have never penned a line
That would not shame a Bantu of nine,
Serve up the great as chummy nicknames
And little intimate make-you-sick names.

[319   ]

How glibly in your talk you glue
Bohemia to Park Avenue,
Unwitting that your gossipy speech
Stamps you a hanger-on in each.
Ah, let us our acquaintance end,
Friend of Hemingway's friend's friend's friend;
I'm just as glad as glad can be
To feel towards you as you towards me.

THOUGHTS THOUGHT ON AN AVENUE

There would be far less masculine gaming and boozing
But for the feminine approach to feminine fashions, which is distinctly confusing.
Please correct me if, although I don't think I do, I err;
But it is a fact that a lady wants to be dressed exactly like everybody else but she gets pretty upset if she sees anybody else dressed exactly like her.
Nothing so infuriates her as a similar hat or dress,
Especially if bought for less,
Which brings up another point which I will attempt to discuss in my guttural masculine jargon;
Her ideal raiment is costlier than her or her dearest friend's purse can buy, and at the same time her own exclusive and amazing bargain.
Psychologists claim that men are the dreamers and women are the realists,
But to my mind women are the starriest-eyed of idealists,
Though I am willing to withdraw this charge and gladly eat it uncomplaineously
If anyone can explain to me how a person can wear a costume that is different from other people's and the same as other people's, and more expensive than other people's and cheaper than other people's, simultaneously.

THOUGHTS THOUGHT WHILE WAITING FOR A PRONOUNCEMENT FROM A DOCTOR, AN EDITOR, A BIG EXECUTIVE, THE DE– PARTMENT OF INTERNAL REVENUE OR ANY OTHER MOMENTOUS PRONOUNCER

Is Time on my hands? Yes it is, it is on my hands and my face and
    my torso and my tendons of Achilles,
And frankly, it gives me the willies.
The quarter-hour grows to the half-hour as chime clings to the tail
    of the preceding chime,
And I am tarred and feathered with Time.
No matter how frantically I shake my hands the hours will not
    drop off or evaporate,
Nor will even the once insignificant minutes co-operate.
The clock has stopped at Now, there is no Past, no Future, and
    oddly enough also no Now,
Only the hot, moist, beaded seconds on the brow,
Only the days and nights in a gluey lump,
And the smothering weeks that stick like a swarm of bees to a
    stump.
Time stands still, or it moves forward or backward, or at least it
    exists, for Ex-Senator Rush Holt, for Doctor Dafoe, for Si-
    mon and Schuster, yes, and for Schiaparelli,
But for me it is limbo akimbo, an inverted void, a mouse with its
    tail pulled out of its mouth through its belly.
O, the world's most honored watch, I haven't been there, I've been
    here,
For how long, for one small seventeen-jeweled tick, or have I been
    sitting a year?
I'm a speck in infinite space,
Entombed behind my face.
Shall I suddenly start to gyrate, to rotate, to spiral, to expand
    through nebular process to a new universe maybe, or maybe
    only a galaxy?

But such a Goldbergian scheme to extinguish one lonely identity
  seems, well, undersimplified and, if I may say so, smart-alexy.
Oh, I shall arise and go now, preferably in a purple-and-gold
  palanquin,
Borne on the copper shoulders of a Seminole, an Apache, a Crow
  and an Algonquin,
And whatever be my heart's desire, be it a new understanding of
  Time or a cup of dew gathered from the spring's first jonquil,
Why if none of the other three will bring it to me, why perhaps the
  Algonquil.

SAMSON AGONISTES

I test my bath before I sit,
And I'm always moved to wonderment
That what chills the finger not a bit
Is so frigid upon the fundament.

SEEING EYE TO EYE IS BELIEVING

When speaking of people and their beliefs I wear my belief on my
  sleeve;
I believe that people believe what they believe they believe.
When people reject a truth or an untruth it is not because it is a
  truth or an untruth that they reject it,
No, if it isn't in accord with their beliefs in the first place they
  simply say, "Nothing doing," and refuse to inspect it.
Likewise when they embrace a truth or an untruth it is not for
  either its truth or its mendacity,
But simply because they have believed it all along and therefore
  regard the embrace as a tribute to their own fair-mindedness
  and sagacity.
These are enlightened days in which you can get hot water and
  cold water out of the same spigot,
And everybody has something about which they are proud to be

broad-minded but they also have other things about which
you would be wasting your breath if you tried to convince
them that they were a bigot,
And I have no desire to get ugly,
But I cannot help mentioning that the door of a bigoted mind
opens outwards so that the only result of the pressure of facts
upon it is to close it more snugly.
Naturally I am not pointing a finger at me,
But I must admit that I find any speaker far more convincing
when I agree with him than when I disagree.

THE STRANGE CASE OF MR. NIOBOB'S
TRANSMOGRIFICATION

Listen motorists, and learn:
Once there was a motorist named Mr. Niobob who took a trip from
which he didn't return.
His first five miles were simply seraphic
Because he was on a dual highway and there wasn't even a smat-
tering of traffic
But then he had to leave the dual highway because his destination
was merely New York,
And dual highways never go to anybody's destination, they all lead
to a deserted traffic circle in Yoakum Corners or Medicine
Fork,
So Mr. Niobob turned off the trafficless dual highway and with his
usual luck,
Well yes, he immediately found himself behind a truck,
And whenever to pass it he mustered his nerve
Well, naturally, they came to a curve,
And it also bored him
That whenever the road straightened out and he edged over for a
dash there would be another truck clattering toward him,
And he wished he had picked up a little voodoo on his cruise to
Haiti,

Because while the truck bogged down to three miles per hour on
the way uphill, why when he thought to overtake it on the
way down it accelerated to eighty,
And all of a sudden they again entered a dual highway,
And Mr. Niobob said, "By gum, now I can drive my way,"
And he stepped on the gas with all his might,
And just as he overtook the truck it turned down a side road on the
right.
Poor frustrated Mr. Niobob, his mind slipped quietly over the
brink,
He just sat down and cried and cried until a kind Commissioner
of Motor Vehicles took pity on him and transformed him into
a fountain, at which tired truck drivers often pause to drink.

AND THREE HUNDRED AND SIXTY–SIX
IN LEAP YEAR

Some people shave before bathing,
And about people who bathe before shaving they are scathing,
While those who bathe before shaving,
Well, they imply that those who shave before bathing are misbe-
having.
Suppose you shave before bathing, well the advantage is that you
don't have to make a special job of washing the lather off
afterwards, it just floats off with the rest of your accumula-
tions in the tub,
But the disadvantage is that before bathing your skin is hard and
dry and your beard confronts the razor like a grizzly bear
defending its cub.
Well then, suppose you bathe before shaving, well the advantage
is that after bathing your skin is soft and moist, and your
beard positively begs for the blade,
But the disadvantage is that to get the lather off you have to wash
your face all over again at the basin almost immediately after
washing it in the tub, which is a duplication of effort that
leaves me spotless but dismayed.

The referee reports, gentlemen, that Fate has loaded the dice,
Since your only choice is between walking around all day with a
      sore chin or washing your face twice.

JUST WRAP IT UP, AND I'LL THROW IT
AWAY LATER

Men think that men have more sense than women and women
      think that any woman has more sense than any man,
An issue which I eagerly evade, for who am I to pass judgment on
      the comparative reasoning processes of, say, Mr. Lunt and
      Miss Fontanne?
However, I ask you to visualize, please, a clear-thinking American
      male who needs a hat, or a left sock, or an ashtray in the form
      of the statue Civic Virtue by the sculptor MacMonnies,
And what does he do, he goes into the likeliest shop and buys it and
      returns to the regular evening race with the children for first
      go at the funnies.
Kindly contrast this with the procedure of his wife or sister or aunt
      who drops into a store for three ounces of flax for the spin-
      ning wheel or an extra minuet for the spinet,
And what happens, the doorstep is crawling for days with people
      delivering lampshades and bedspreads and dirndls and chairs
      that expand into bridge tables and bridge tables that expand
      into chaises longues, and husbands who can't bear it simply
      have to grin it.
Man's idea of shopping is to buy what he needs and get through
      with it.
Woman's idea is to have everything she has never needed sent
      home and then figure out what to do with it.
It is as true today as in the day of David and Goliath or Corbett
      and Fitzsimmons,
That men go into a shop to supply a want, and women principally
      to stimulate their imaginations, but men's imaginations need
      no extra stimulus as long as their world is filled with beauti-
      ful unanswerable womens.

Some people relate anecdotes about Samuel Goldwyn and Gregory
    Ratoff;
I sing of Dr. Fell, who slips in the only vacant barber chair while
    you are taking your hat off.
Does a young man go to a picture with a girl he hopes to make a
    bride of?
The immovable Dr. Fell is what the only two empty seats are one
    on each side of.
You are marooned downtown on a night when the rain is a Niagara
    and the wind is a bayonet,
And after twenty minutes of futile whistling you catch a taxi
    driver's eye and as he slows down Dr. Fell emerges miracu-
    lously from a hydrant, steps into the cab and drives away
    in it.
Dr. Fell obviously works with the assistance of a brownie or a
    malevolent dwarf,
For it is he who by monopolizing the middle of the road reaches
    the ferry ahead of you and slides into the last space, thus
    leaving you to two hours' uninterrupted contemplation of the
    wharf.
Yes, I fear that Dr. Fell is a monopolist and an obstructionist,
But I would not grudge him the obstructive monopoly of that por-
    tion of a whirlpool where the suction is the suctionest.

THE STRANGE CASE OF MR. PAUNCEFOOT'S
BROAD MIND

Once there was a man named Mr. Pauncefoot to whom Fate could
    not have been meaner,
Because he was a born in-betweener.
Yes, he was one whom in an argument nothing but woe ever be-
    tides,
Because he always thought that there was much to be said on both
    sides,

With the result that to his friends on the Left he was but a little
  capitalistic bee busy distributing Tory pollen,
While on the Right he was rumored to be in the pay of Stalin.
Mr. Pauncefoot lived in a suburb, which was inevitable but rather
  a pity,
Since the upshot was that he appeared as a city boy in the country
  and a country boy in the city.
He was never invited to sing either solo or in a convivial quartet by
  even the kindest Samaritan,
Because his voice was just a little too low for the tenor and just a
  little too high for the baritan.
Mr. Pauncefoot was miserable until one day he read about the
  donkey that starved to death between two haystacks because
  it couldn't decide which haystack to begin on, and he said,
  "That's an end of all my confusions,"
Only Mr. Pauncefoot didn't starve to death, quite the opposite, he
  spent the rest of his days very happily eating his own words
  between two conclusions.

SUMMER SERENADE

When the thunder stalks the sky,
When tickle-footed walks the fly,
When shirt is wet and throat is dry,
Look, my darling, that's July.

Though the grassy lawn be leather,
And prickly temper tug the tether,
Shall we postpone our love for weather?
If we must melt, let's melt together!

SO DOES EVERYBODY ELSE, ONLY NOT SO MUCH

O all ye exorcizers come and exorcize now, and ye clergymen draw
  nigh and clerge,

For I wish to be purged of an urge.

It is an irksome urge, compounded of nettles and glue,

And it is turning all my friends back into acquaintances, and all my acquaintances into people who look the other way when I heave into view.

It is an indication that my mental buttery is butterless and my mental larder lardless,

And it consists not of "Stop me if you've heard this one," but of "I know you've heard this one because I told it to you myself, but I'm going to tell it to you again regardless,"

Yes I fear I am living beyond my mental means

When I realize that it is not only anecdotes that I reiterate but what is far worse, summaries of radio programs and descriptions of cartoons in newspapers and magazines.

I want to resist but I cannot resist recounting the bright sayings of celebrities that everybody already is familiar with every word of;

I want to refrain but cannot refrain from telling the same audience on two successive evenings the same little snatches of domestic gossip about people I used to know that they have never heard of.

When I remember some titillating episode of my childhood I figure that if it's worth narrating once it's worth narrating twice, in spite of lackluster eyes and drooping jaws,

And indeed I have now worked my way backward from titillating episodes in my own childhood to titillating episodes in the childhood of my parents or even my parents-in-laws,

And what really turns my corpuscles to ice,

I carry around clippings and read them to people twice.

And I know what I am doing while I am doing it and I don't want to do it but I can't help doing it and I am just another Ancient Mariner,

And the prospects for my future social life couldn't possibly be barrener.

Did I tell you that the prospects for my future social life couldn't possibly be barrener?

DON'T EVEN TELL YOUR WIFE, PARTICULARLY

All good men believe that women would rather get rid of a piece
    of gossip than a bulge,
And all good women believe that gossip is a feminine weakness in
    which men never indulge.
Rather than give ear to scandalous rumors,
Why, men would rather play golf in bloomers,
And rather than talk behind each other's backs,
They would go shopping in a mink coat and slacks.
It is one of each sex's uniquenesses
That men's talk is all of humanity's aspirations, and women's all
    of their friends' weaknesses.
Yes, this is a universal credo that no amount of evidence can alter,
Including that of Petronius, Suetonius, Pepys, Boswell, the locker
    room of the country club, and Mrs. Winchell's little boy,
    Walter.
Allow me to ask and answer one question before departing for
    Mount Everest or Lake Ossipee:
Who says men aren't gossipy? — Men say men aren't gossipy.

THE JELLYFISH

Who wants my jellyfish?
I'm not sellyfish!

FRAILTY, THY NAME IS A MISNOMER

Once there was a couple named Mr. and Mrs. Pepperloaf and they
    were simply devoted,
Because each other was upon what they doted,
And in Mrs. Pepperloaf's eyes Mr. Pepperloaf could never err,
And he admitted only one flaw in her,
But it was a flaw which took many virtues to assuage,

[329   ]

Consisting in always asking him the date while she was reading
    the paper with the date clearly printed on every page,
And whenever he called her attention to this least admirable of
    her traits
She would retort that he didn't trust the paper's weather forecasts
    so then why should she trust its dates.
For eleven years his patience held
But finally he rebelled.
It was on the evening of Friday the seventh that she looked up
    from her paper and asked him the date,
And he replied firmly that she would find it at the top of the page
    so she looked at the top of the page and that was that, and
    presently they sat down to supper and ate,
And they were miserable because they had never disagreed and
    this contretemps was a beginner for them,
And at nine his employer's wife called up to ask where were they,
    she and eleven guests were waiting dinner for them,
And Mr. Pepperloaf asked Mrs. Pepperloaf how she could have
    so misreckoned,
And she said she knew that they had been invited out on the
    seventh but, according to the newspaper he had instructed
    her to consult, tonight was only the second,
And he picked up the paper and it was last week's, not today's,
And she said certainly, she had just been reading over some recipes
    for different delicious soufflés,
And now she found the first flaw in him because she had obeyed
    his order to look for the date in the paper, hadn't she, so
    his irritation was uncalled for and unseasonable.
Women would rather be right than reasonable.

THE CARAWAY SEED

The Abbé Voltaire, alias Arouet,
Never denounced the seed of the caraway;
Sufficient proof, if proof we need,
That he never bit into a caraway seed.

CELERY

Celery, raw,
Develops the jaw,
But celery, stewed,
Is more quietly chewed.

PLEASE KEEP ON FORWARDING

Some people are born simply to pay postage due,
Which is like being born simply to tread on the gum that other
people chew.
Anybody sensible
Knows that the demand for extra postage heralds the arrival of
tidings unconditionally dispensable;
There is no instance thus far
Of a postage-due envelope having contained either a check or a
confession of murder or an invitation to dine with Winston
Churchill and Hedy Lamarr;
It is postage-due mail that requests your presence at a benefit and
encloses two tickets that will be charged to you unless you
write a letter returning them to the requester;
It is postage-due mail that electrifies you with a full report of the
graduation exercises at the kindergarten that you attended,
while going on five, for one semester.
Yet such is the fascination of getting nothing for something that
whenever the postman whistles,
People hasten to proffer good money for misdirected and under-
stamped epistles.
I know a man whose moral sense is checkered,
And next to looking through keyholes he likes reading other people's mail, but not their postage-due mail, he says he'd
rather browse in the *Congressional Record*.

ASSORTED CHOCOLATES

If some confectioner were willing
To let the shape announce the filling,
We'd encounter fewer assorted chocs,
Bitten into and returned to the box.

THE PARSNIP

The parsnip, children, I repeat,
Is simply an anemic beet.
Some people call the parsnip edible;
Myself, I find this claim incredible.

I BURN MONEY

The song about the happy-go-lucky fellow who hasn't time to be a
    millionaire strikes me as pretty funny,
Because I am pretty happy-go-lucky myself but it isn't lack of
    time that keeps me from being a millionaire, it's lack of
    money,
But if anybody has a million that they're through with it,
Well, I know what I'd like to do with it.
My first acquisition would not be a lot of Old Masters or first
    editions or palatial palaces,
No, it would be to supply each of my pairs of pants with its own
    set of galluses.
I can also think of another extravagance with which to startle all
    beholders
Which is an attendant with no other duties than to apply anti-
    sunburn lotion to that vulnerable spot you can't get at your-
    self either by reaching over or under your shoulders.
Likewise I have an idea which should earn the gratitude of every
    regular-dinner eater alive,

[332]

Which is to promote a regular-dinner that when you order oysters
or clams on it you get six oysters or clams instead of five.
My next goal is one to reach which I should probably have to sink
into debt,
But it would be worth it because it is the development of a short,
hot, harsh, quick-burning, full-of-nicotine cigarette.
A million dollars could also be well spent in hiring somebody to invent some better rhymes for wife than rife and knife and
strife,
But I think what I would really do if I had a million would be to
buy a million dollars' worth of books written by me and then
besides having a lot of good books I could sit back and live
on the royalties for the rest of my life.

THE PORPOISE

I kind of like the playful porpoise,
A healthy mind in a healthy corpus.
He and his cousin, the playful dolphin,
Why they like swimmin like I like golphin.

THE SHARK

How many Scientists have written
The shark is gentle as a kitten!
Yet this I know about the shark:
His bite is worser than his bark.

THE CANTALOUPE

One cantaloupe is ripe and lush,
Another's green, another's mush.
I'd buy a lot more cantaloupe
If I possessed a fluoroscope.

THE OCTOPUS

Tell me, O Octopus, I begs,
Is those things arms, or is they legs?
I marvel at thee, Octopus;
If I were thou, I'd call me Us.

HAS ANYBODY SEEN MY NOUMENON *?

There is one point which I am more than human on,
And that's a noumenon.
On due reflection we are apt to find
That it is noumenons which lead us to believe that just this once
    two pair will beat three of a kind.
It is noumenons which whisper to our hearts that our futures will
    be brighter than our yores,
And noumenons which encourage us to laugh off the black clouds
    in the west and go ahead and move the supper table out of
    doors.
It is noumenons which, if you have no excuse for flouting natural
    laws, they supply it,
Such as kindling the hope that you can remain trim and lissome at
    forty without the nuisance of exercise or diet,
So now I shall go out and consume a hearty lunch,
But I know I shall remain trim and lissome in spite of it, because I
    have a strong noumenon, or overwhelming hunch.

THE MERMAID

Say not the mermaid is a myth,
I knew one once named Mrs. Smith.
She stood while playing cards or knitting;
Mermaids are not equipped for sitting.

* Noumenon, *n.*, an object known only by intuition, apart from any
evidence of the senses.

A BULLETIN HAS JUST COME IN

The rabbit's dreamy eyes grow dreamier
As he quietly gives you tularemia.

The parrot clashes his hooked proboscis
And laughs while handing you psittacosis.

In every swamp or wooded area
Mosquito witches brew malaria.

We risk at every jolly picnic
Spotted fever from a tick nick.

People perish of bubonic;
To rats, it's better than a tonic.

The hog converted into pork
Puts trichinosis on your fork.

The dog today that guards your babies
Tomorrow turns and gives them rabies.

The baby, once all milk and spittle,
Grows to a Hitler, and boy, can he hittle!

That's our planet, and we're stuck with it.
I wish its inheritors the best of luck with it.

THE EEL

I don't mind eels
Except as meals.

[335]

THE WASP

The wasp and all his numerous family
I look upon as a major calamily.
He throws open his nest with prodigality,
But I distrust his waspitality.

NOT GEORGE WASHINGTON'S, NOT
ABRAHAM LINCOLN'S, BUT MINE

Well, here I am thirty-eight,
Well, I certainly thought I'd have longer to wait.
You just stop in for a couple of beers,
And gosh, there go thirty-seven years.
Well, it has certainly been fun,
But I certainly thought I'd have got a lot more done.
Why if I had been really waked up and alive,
I could have been a Congressman since I was twenty-one or President since I was thirty-five.
I guess I know the reason my accomplishments are so measly:
I don't comprehend very easily.
It finally dawned on me that in life's race I was off to a delayed start
When at the age of thirty-three I had to be told that I could swim faster if I'd keep my fingers together instead of spreading them apart,
And I was convinced that precociousness was not the chief of my faults
When it was only last winter that I discovered that the name of that waltz that skaters waltz to is "The Skaters' Waltz."
After thirty-seven years I find myself the kind of man that anybody can sell anything to,
And nobody will ever tell anything to.
Whenever people get up a party of which I am to be a member to see some picture which I don't want to see because I am un-

interested in the situation that Scarlett and Mr. Chips are
    estranged over,
Why my head is what it is arranged over.
Contrariwise, I myself not only can't sell anybody anything,
I can't even ever tell anybody anything.
I have never yet had a good gossip bomb all poised and ready to
    burst
That somebody hasn't already told everybody first.
Yes, my career to date has certainly been a fiasco;
It would not have made a thrilling dramatic production for the
    late Oliver Morosco or the late David Belasco.
But in spite of the fact that my career has been a fiasco to date,
Why I am very proud and happy to be thirty-eight.

THE KANGAROO

O Kangaroo, O Kangaroo,
Be grateful that you're in the zoo,
And not transmuted by a boomerang
To zestful tangy Kangaroo meringue.

DON'T WAIT, HIT ME NOW!

If there are any wives present who wish to irritate their husbands
    or husbands who wish to irritate their wives,
Why I know an irritation more irritating than hives,
So if you think such an irritation expedient,
Here is the formula, in which the presence of a third person is the
    only essential extra ingredient;
Indeed is it beautifully simple,
But it is guaranteed to make a molehill out of a dimple
And what it consists of is that when you are annoyed with your
    husband or wife and want to do the opposite of woo them,
Why, you just talk at them instead of to them.
Suppose you think your Gregory danced too often with Mrs. Limb-
    worthy at the club, you don't say to him directly, "Gregory

I'll smack you down if you don't lay off that platinum-plated hussy,"

No, you wait till a friend drops in and then with a glance at Gregory say to her, "Isn't it funny what fools middle-aged men can make of themselves over anything blonde and slithery, do you understand how anybody sober and in their right mind could look twice at that Limbworthy job, but then of course darling, Gregory wasn't altogether in his right mind last night, was he?"

This is indeed more excruciating to Gregory than Shakespearean excursions and alarums,

Because there is no defense against caroms.

Or let us suppose you are irked by your Esmeralda's sudden passion for antiques.

Well you don't mention it for weeks,

No, you wait till a friend drops in and then with a glance at Esmeralda you say, "How anybody can be sucked in by this antique racket is beyond me, but there are some otherwise sensible women who'll mortgage their beauty treatments for a genuine early American paper doily or a guaranteed second-hand Killarney banshee,

But of course Esmeralda can't ever resist an opportunity to pick up some fossil to amaze her friends with, can she?"

And Esmeralda must sit quiet and take it with apparent docility,

Because the hit direct doesn't compare with the richochet in deadly unanswerability.

By this easy method can every Gregory score off every Esmeralda and every Esmeralda annihilate every Gregory,

And its only drawback besides eventual divorce is that it reduces all their friends to emotional beggary.

FURTHER REFLECTION ON PARSLEY

Parsley
Is gharsley.

I'LL WRITE THEIR NUMBER DOWN WHEN
WE GET HOME

Words, idle words, are what people's social life contains a goodly
store of,

And the idlest words are contained in the wishful phrase beginning, Why don't we see more of?

By the time your age is medium,

Well, your most exotic evenings are placid to the point of tedium,

Because whenever you step out you find yourself steping out amid
faces and ideas that are, to say the least, familiar,

Which is a situation which moves only from the willy-nilly to the
willy-nillier,

But once in every eleven blue moons you encounter a newcomer in
your little coterie,

And it doesn't matter whether he is a veteran or a veterinary or a
vestryman or a vegetarian or a notable or a Notogæan or a
notary,

Because his fresh point of view is as beneficial to anemic conversation as a transfusion or a tonic,

And his wife is equally attractive and stimulating, and the future
would be cute as a button if it weren't so inevitably ironic,

Because on the way home you say "My I like those people, why
don't we see more of them?" and it is agreed that Yes we certainly must, and from then on they might as well be living in
the ancient Anglian kingdom of Mercia,

Because you never see them again because you never do anything
about it except to murmur "Why don't we see more of them?"
and that is why the best definition I can think of for at least
one man's social life is simply inertia.

THE FLY

God in His wisdom made the fly
And then forgot to tell us why.

[339]

ASK DADDY, HE WON'T KNOW

Now that they've abolished chrome work
I'd like to call their attention to home work.
Here it is only three decades since my scholarship was famous,
And I'm an ignoramus.
I cannot think which goes sideways and which goes up and down,
    a parallel or a meridian,
Nor do I know the name of him who first translated the Bible into
    Indian, I see him only as an enterprising colonial Gideon.
I have difficulty with dates,
To say nothing of the annual rainfall of the Southern Central
    States.
Naturally the correct answers are just back of the tip of my tongue,
But try to explain that to your young.
I am overwhelmed by their erudite banter,
I am in no condition to differentiate between Tamerlane and Tam
    o' Shanter.
I reel, I sway, I am utterly exhausted;
Should you ask me when Chicago was founded I could only reply
    I didn't even know it was losted.

THE TERMITE

Some primal termite knocked on wood
And tasted it, and found it good,
And that is why your Cousin May
Fell through the parlor floor today.

FAHRENHEIT *GESUNDHEIT*

Nothing is glummer
Than a cold in the summer.
A summer cold
Is to have and to hold.

A cough in the fall
Is nothing at all,
A winter snuffle
Is lost in the shuffle,
And April sneezes
Put leaves on the treeses,
But a summer cold
Is to have and to hold.
Though golf course and beach
Slip beyond your reach,
By a fate grotesque
You can get to your desk,
And there is no rescue
From this germ grotesque.
You can feel it coming
In your nasal plumbing,
But there is no plumber
For a cold in the summer.
Nostrilly, tonsilly,
It prowls irresponsilly;
In your personal firmament
Its abode is permanent.
Oh, would it were curable
Rather than durable;
Were it Goering's or Himmler's,
Or somebody simlar's!
O Laval, were it thine!
But it isn't, it's mine.
A summer cold
Is to have and to hold.

Versus

I WILL ARISE AND GO NOW

In far Tibet
There live a lama,
He got no poppa,
Got no momma,

He got no wife,
He got no chillun,
Got no use
For penicillun,

He got no soap,
He got no opera,
He don't know Irium
From copra,

He got no songs,
He got no banter,
He don't know Hope,
He don't know Cantor,

He got no teeth,
He got no gums,
Don't eat no Spam,
Don't need no Tums.

He love to nick him
When he shave;
He also got
No hair to save.

Got no distinction,
No clear head,
Don't call for Calvert;
Drink milk instead.

[345]

He use no lotions
For allurance,
He got no car
And no insurance,

No Alsop warnings,
No Pearson rumor
For this self-centered
Nonconsumer.

Indeed, the
Ignorant Have-Not
Don't even know
What he don't got.

If you will mind
The box-tops, comma,
I think I'll go
And join that lama.

THE HUNTER

The hunter crouches in his blind
'Neath camouflage of every kind,
And conjures up a quacking noise
To lend allure to his decoys.
This grown-up man, with pluck and luck,
Is hoping to outwit a duck.

THOUGHTS THOUGHT AFTER A BRIDGE PARTY

All women are pets,
But most women shouldn't be allowed to open a package of cig-
    arettes.
I call down blessings on their bonny heads,

But they can't open a package of cigarettes without tearing it to
    shreds.
Of the two sexes, women are much the subtler,
But the way they open a package of cigarettes is comparable to
    opening a bottle of wine by cracking it on the butler.
Women are my inspiration and my queen,
But as long as they can rip the first cigarette from the package they
    don't care what happens to the other nineteen.
Women are my severest friend
But the last nineteen cigarettes in packages opened by them are
    not only bent but sere and withered and the tobacco is drib-
    bling out at either end.
Women are creatures of ingenuity and gumption,
Which is why when they finish one cigarette they leave the muti-
    lated nineteen cigarettes for some man and go to work on a
    fresh package, thus leaving thirty-eight mutilated cigarettes
    for masculine consumption.
Women are ethereal beings, subsisting entirely on chocolate marsh-
    mallow nut sundaes and cantaloupe,
But they open up a package of cigarettes like a lioness opening up
    an antelope.

ANY MILLENNIUMS TODAY, LADY?

As I was wandering down the street
With nothing in my head,
A sign in a window spoke to me
And this is what it said:

"Are your pillows a pain in the neck?
Are they lumpy, hard, or torn?
Are they full of old influenza germs?
Are the feathers thin and forlorn?
Bring 'em to us,
We do the trick;

[347   ]

Re-puff,
Replenish,
Re-curl,
Re-tick,
We return your pillows, spanned-and-spicked,
Re-puffed, replenished, re-curled, re-ticked."

As I was wandering down the street
With too much in my head,
The sign became a burning bush,
And this is what it said:

"Is the world a pain in the neck?
Is it lumpy, hard, or torn?
Is it full of evil ancestral germs
That were old before you were born?
Bring it to us,
We do the trick,
Re-puff,
Replenish,
Re-curl,
Re-tick,
In twenty-four hours we return the world
Re-puffed, replenished, re-ticked, re-curled."

As I was wandering down the street
I heard the trumpets clearly,
But when I faced the sign again
It spoke of pillows merely.
The world remains a derelict,
Unpuffed, unplenished, uncurled, unticked.

A WORD ABOUT WINTER

Now the frost is on the pane,
Rugs upon the floor again,

Now the screens are in the cellar,
Now the student cons the speller,
Lengthy summer noon is gone,
Twilight treads the heels of dawn,
Round-eyed sun is now a squinter,
Tiptoe breeze a panting sprinter,
Every cloud a blizzard hinter,
Squirrel on the snow a printer,
Rain spout sprouteth icy splinter,
Willy-nilly, this is winter.

Summer-swollen doorjambs settle,
Ponds and puddles turn to metal,
Skater whoops in frisky fettle,
Golf-club stingeth like a nettle,
Radiator sings like kettle,
Hearth is Popocatepetl.

Runneth nose and chappeth lip,
Draft evadeth weather strip,
Doctor wrestleth with grippe
In never-ending rivalship.
Rosebush droops in garden shoddy,
Blood is cold and thin in body,
Weary postman dreams of toddy,
Head before the heart grows noddy.

On the hearth the embers gleam,
Glowing like a maiden's dream,
Now the apple and the oak
Paint the sky with chimney smoke,
Husband now, without disgrace,
Dumps ash trays in the fireplace.

HOW DO YOU SAY HA–HA IN FRENCH?

There are several people who I can claim I am glad I am not, with-
    out being accused of pride and effrontery,
And one of them is the bartender of a French restaurant in an
    English-speaking country.
The conversation of the customers isn't calculated to keep a bar-
    tender young,
Even when they converse in their mother tongue;
How much more dispiriting it must be when after the second Mar-
    tini
They request a third because the first two are, not finished, but
    finis.
They select a *Maryland,* or cigarette,
And instead of Gotta light? it is *Avez-vous une allumette?*
When they cry *Garçon* after the school of Stratford atte Bowe or
    New Rochelle or Nineveh,
It is moot whether they want the waiter or Mrs. Miniver.
Somehow, in a *bistro,* or French eatery,
Everybody suddenly discovers they can talk like Sasha Guitry,
But they really can't,
And if I were the bartender I should poke them in the *œil* with
    the *plume de ma tante.*

LET'S NOT CLIMB THE WASHINGTON
MONUMENT TONIGHT

Listen, children, if you'll only stop throwing peanuts and bananas
    into my cage,
I'll tell you the facts of middle age.
Middle age is when you've met so many people that every new
    person you meet reminds you of someone else,
And when golfers' stomachs escape either over or under their belts.
It is when you find all halfbacks anthropoidal
And all vocalists adenoidal.

It is when nobody will speak loud enough for you to hear,
And you go to the ball game and notice that even the umpires are
    getting younger every year.
It's when you gulp oysters without bothering to look for pearls,
And your offspring cannot but snicker when you refer to your class-
    mates as boys and your bridge partners as girls.
It is when you wouldn't visit Fred Allen or the Aga Khan if it
    meant sleeping on a sofa or a cot,
And your most exciting moment is when your shoelace gets tangled
    and you wonder whether if you yank it, it will come clean or
    harden into a concrete knot.
Also, it seems simpler just to go to bed than to replace a fuse,
Because actually you'd rather wait for the morning paper than lis-
    ten to the eleven o'clock news,
And Al Capone and Babe Ruth and Scott Fitzgerald are as remote
    as the Roman emperors,
And you spend your Saturday afternoons buying wedding presents
    for the daughters of your contemporers.
Well, who wants to be young anyhow, any idiot born in the last
    forty years can be young, and besides forty-five isn't really
    old, it's right on the border;
At least, unless the elevator's out of order.

WHO DID WHICH?
or
WHO INDEED?

Oft in the stilly night,
When the mind is fumbling fuzzily,
I brood about how little I know,
And know that little so muzzily.
Ere slumber's chains have bound me,
I think it would suit me nicely,
If I knew one tenth of the little I know,
But knew that tenth precisely.

O Delius, Sibelius,
And What's-his-name Aurelius,
O Manet, O Monet,
Mrs. Siddons and the Cid!
I know each name
Has an oriflamme of fame,
I'm sure they all did something,
But I can't think what they did.

Oft in the sleepless dawn
I feel my brain is hominy
When I try to identify famous men,
Their countries and anno Domini.
Potemkin, Pushkin, Ruskin,
Velásquez, Pulaski, Laski;
They are locked together in one gray cell,
And I seem to have lost the passkey.

O Tasso, Picasso,
O Talleyrand and Sally Rand,
Elijah, Elisha,
Eugene Aram, Eugène Sue,
Don Quixote, Donn Byrne,
Rosencrantz and Guildenstern,
Humperdinck and Rumpelstiltskin,
They taunt me, two by two.

At last, in the stilly night,
When the mind is bubbling vaguely,
I grasp my history by the horns
And face it Haig and Haigly.
O, Snow-Bound was written by Robert Frost,
And Scott Fitzgerald wrote Paradise Lost,
Croesus was turned to gold by Minos,
And Thomas à Kempis was Thomas Aquinas.
Two Irish Saints were Patti and Micah,

The Light Brigade rode at Balalaika,
If you seek a roué to irk your aunt,
Kubla-Khan but Immanuel Kant,
And no one has ever been transmogrified
Until by me he has been biogrified.

Gently my eyelids close;
I'd rather be good than clever;
And I'd rather have my facts all wrong
Than have no facts whatever.

YOU BET TRAVEL IS BROADENING

Doctors tell me that some people wonder who they are, they don't
    know if they are Peter Pumpkin-eater or Priam,
But I know who I am.
My identity is no mystery to unravel,
Because I know who I am, especially when I travel.
I am he whom the dear little old ladies who have left their pocket-
    books on the bureau at home invariably approach,
And he whom the argumentative tippler oozes in beside though
    there are thirty empty seats in the coach.
I am he who finds himself reading comics to somebody else's chil-
    dren while the harassed mother attends to the youngest's
    needs,
Ending up with candy bar on the lapel of my previously faultless
    tweeds.
I am he in the car full of students celebrating victory with instru-
    ments saxophonic and ukulelean,
And he who, speaking only English, is turned to for aid by the
    non-English-speaking alien.
I am he who, finding himself the occupant of one Pullman space
    that has been sold twice, next finds himself playing Santa,
Because it was sold the second time to an elderly invalid, so there

is no question about who is going to sit in the washroom from Philadelphia to Atlanta.

I guess I am he who if he had his own private car

Would be jockeyed into sharing the master bedroom with a man with a five-cent cigar.

WHAT TO DO UNTIL THE DOCTOR GOES
or
IT'S TOMORROW THAN YOU THINK

Oh hand me down my old cigar with its Havana wrapper and its filling of cubeb,

Fill the little brown jug with bismuth and paregoric, and the pottle and cannikin with soda and rhubeb,

Lend me a ninety-nine piece orchestra tutored by Koussevitsky,

I don't want the ownership of it, I just want the usevitsky,

Bring me a firkin of Arkansas orators to sing me oratorios,

Remove these calf-clad Spenglers and Prousts and replace them with paper-covered Wodehouses and Gaboriaus,

Wrap up and return these secretarial prunes and prisms,

Let me have about me bosoms without isms.

Life and I are not convivial,

Life is real, life is earnest, while I only think I am real, and know I am trivial.

In this imponderable world I lose no opportunity

To ponder on picayunity.

I would spend either a round amount or a flat amount

To know whether a puma is only tantamount to a catamount or paramount to a catamount,

It is honey in my cup,

When I read of a sprinter sprinting the hundred in ten seconds flat, to think: Golly, suppose he stood up!

I guess I am not really reprehensible,

Just dispensable.

TWO DOGS HAVE I

For years we've had a little dog,
Last year we acquired a big dog;
He wasn't big when we got him,
He was littler than the dog we had.
We thought our little dog would love him,
Would help him to become a trig dog,
But the new little dog got bigger,
And the old little dog got mad.

Now the big dog loves the little dog,
But the little dog hates the big dog,
The little dog is eleven years old,
And the big dog only one;
The little dog calls him *Schweinhund,*
The little dog calls him Pig-dog,
She grumbles broken curses
As she dreams in the August sun.

The big dog's teeth are terrible,
But he wouldn't bite the little dog;
The little dog wants to grind his bones,
But the little dog has no teeth;
The big dog is acrobatic,
The little dog is a brittle dog;
She leaps to grip his jugular,
And passes underneath.

The big dog clings to the little dog
Like glue and cement and mortar;
The little dog is his own true love;
But the big dog is to her
Like a scarlet rag to a Longhorn,
Or a suitcase to a porter;
The day he sat on the hornet
I distinctly heard her purr.

[355]

Well, how can you blame the little dog,
Who was once the household darling?
He romps like a young Adonis,
She droops like an old mustache;
No wonder she steals his corner,
No wonder she comes out snarling,
No wonder she calls him *Cochon*
And even *Espèce de vache.*

Yet once I wanted a sandwich,
Either caviar or cucumber,
When the sun had not yet risen
And the moon had not yet sank;
As I tiptoed through the hallway
The big dog lay in slumber,
And the little dog slept by the big dog,
And her head was on his flank.

ON WAKING TO THE THIRD RAINY
MORNING OF A LONG WEEK END

Well, what shall I do today?
Shall I spend the day in the hay?
Shall I cover my head with the sheet,
Or go downstairs and eat?

If I leave my cozy nest
I will meet a fellow guest,
Or, what would irk me most,
I would meet my hostess and host,
While, if I stay upstairs,
My troubles are mine, not theirs.

I refuse to play Lotto or euchre
For either love or lucre;

[356]

I'm tired of discussing the arts,
And I've got bursitis from darts.
I am sick of people appearing
To announce that it looks like clearing;
Of games with pencil and paper,
And the girl who does Ruth Draper.

Today it would be as well,
I think, to lurk in my cell.
I'll refuse to speak to outsiders,
And only make friends with spiders;
I'll count the cracks in the floor,
And the steps between window and door;
I'll identify several stars
At night as I peer through the bars,
And when pastimes like these I exhaust,
I'll memorize *Paradise Lost*.

In closing, I'll mention, dear Auntie,
That the food here is wholesome but scanty;
If you'll send me a pie, when I open it
I'll hope for a file and a rope in it.

QUICK, HAMMACHER, MY STOMACHER!

Man is a glutton,
He will eat too much even though there be nothing to eat too much
    of but parsnips or mutton.
He will deprecate his paunch,
And immediately afterwards reach for another jowl or haunch.
People don't have to be Cassandras or Catos
To know what will happen to their paunches if they combine hot
    biscuits and strawberry shortcake and French fried potatoes,
Yet no sooner has a man achieved a one-pound loss

Than he gains two through the application to an old familiar dish
    of a new irresistible sauce.
Thus cooks aggravate men's gluttony
With capers and hollandaise and chutney,
They can take seaweed or pemmican
And do things to them in a ramekin,
Give them a manatee that has perished of exposure
And they will whip you up a casserole of ambrosia,
Which is why a man who digs his grave with his teeth's idea of life
    beyond the grave is definite,
There's a divine chef in it.
Men are gluttons,
And everybody knows it except tailors, who don't leave room
    enough at the edge to move over the buttons.

THE CHERUB

I like to watch the clouds roll by,
And think of cherubs in the sky;
But when I think of cherubim,
I don't know if they're her or him.

WHO CALLED THAT ROBIN
A PICCOLO PLAYER?

ROBINS GETTING LAZY. — Robins, now usually half tame and preferring
suburban to forest life, have become stupid and lazy in many cases. — NEW
YORK DAILY MIRROR

Hark hark the lark, no it is not a lark, it is a robin singing like a
    lark,
He is in disguise because he is now the target of a newspaper cru-
    sade like dirty books and vivisection and the man-eating
    shark.
He has been termed lethargic and fat,
It is said of him that he would rather live in Greenwich or Great
    Neck than in Medicine Hat,

It is rumored that at the Garden Club his wife once met an author,
And that he himself prefers a California Colonial bungalow to the
        tepee of Hiawatha,
And wears nylon instead of buckskin hosen,
And buys his worms at a super-market, cellophane-wrapped, and
        frozen.
In fact, the implication couldn't be clearer
That he is the spit and image of a reader of the *Mirror*.
Well for heaven's sake, how far can this scurrilous name-calling de-
        generate?
They are now attempting to besmirch a bird that I venerate.
His breast may be red, that is true,
But his heart is red, white and blue;
And as for being lazy, I know one robin that held down two jobs
        at once just so his younger brother (their parents had passed
        away uninsured) could get to be a transport pilot,
But if you mentioned it he was modest as a buttercup or vilot,
And the only reason he himself wasn't making those selfsame
        flights,
He had a bad head for heights.
If these editorial scandalmongers have to mong scandal about
        birds, let them leave the robin alone and turn their attention
        to the pelican;
It has an Oriental background and a triangular horny excrescence
        developed on the male's bill in the breeding season which
        later falls off without leaving trace of its existence, which for
        my money is suspicious and un-Amelican.

WHAT I KNOW ABOUT LIFE

I have recently been pondering the life expectancy which the Bible
        allots to man,
And at this point I figure I have worked my way through nine
        fourteenths of my hypothetical span.
I have been around a bit and met many interesting people and

made and lost some money and acquired in reverse order a
family and a wife,
And by now I should have drawn some valuable conclusions about
life.
Well I have learned that life is something about which you can't
conclude anything except that it is full of vicissitudes,
And where you expect logic you only come across eccentricities.
Life has a tendency to obfuscate and bewilder,
Such as fating us to spend the first part of our lives being embarrassed by our parents and the last part being embarrassed
by our childer.
Life is constantly presenting us with experiences which are un-
precedented and depleting,
Such as the friend who starts drinking at three in the afternoon
and explains it's only to develop a hearty appetite for dinner
because it's unhealthy to drink without eating.
Life being what it is I don't see why everybody doesn't develop an
ulcer,
Particularly Mrs. Martingale, the wife of a prominent pastry cook
from Tulsa.
He had risen to fame and fortune after starting as a humble pur-
veyor of noodles,
So he asked her what she wanted for her birthday and she said a
new Studebaker and he thought she said a new strudel baker
and she hated strudels.
So all I know about life is that it has been well said
That such things can't happen to a person when they are dead.

VERY FUNNY, VERY FUNNY

In this foolish world there is nothing more numerous
Than different people's senses of humorous,
And the difference between different sense of humors
Is as wide as the gap between shorts and bloomers.
This is what humor boils down unto —

Are you him who doeth, or him who it's done to?
If a friend is dogged by some awful hoodoo,
Why, naturally, he doesn't laugh, but you do;
If the puppy is sick on your new Tuxedo,
Why, naturally, you don't laugh, but he do.
Humor depends on the point of view,
It's a question of what is happening to who;
It's a question facing which I surrender,
It's also a question of What's your gender?
Strong men have squandered the best of their life
In trying to coax a smile from their wife.
I know a wag named Septimus Best;
His wife won't laugh at his merriest jest.
Under her bed he hides a skeleton;
He fills her bathtub with glue and gelatin;
He draws whiskers on pictures of Cleopatra,
And he's disrespectful to Frank Sinatra;
And she just sits in her gown of taffeta
And refuses to smile, either during or afeter.
I guess a sense of humor is what
Husbands tell each other their wives haven't got.

WE WOULD REFER YOU TO OUR SERVICE DEPARTMENT, IF WE HAD ONE

It fills me with elation
To live in such a mechanical-minded nation,
Surrounded not only by the finest scenery
But also the most machinery,
Where every prospect is attractive
And people are radioactive,
Reading books with show-how
Written by scientists with know-how.
Breathes there with soul so dead a fossil
Who never to himself hath said, Production is colossal?
Obviously civilization is far from a crisis

When the land teems with skilled craftsmen skillfully manufacturing gadgets and mechanical devices.
Millions of washing machines and electric refrigerators
Are shipped from the shipping rooms of their originators,
Streamlined dreamlined automobiles roll off the assembly lines in
battalions and droves,
Millions of radios pour from the factories for housewives to listen
to in the time they save through not having to slice their pre-
sliced loaves,
So when everybody has a houseful and a garageful of mechanical
perfection no one has any worries, but if you want a worry,
I will share one,
Which is, Why is it that when seemingly anybody can make an
automobile or a washing machine, nobody can repair one?
If you want a refrigerator or an automatic can opener or a razor
that plays "Begin the Beguine" you can choose between an
old rose or lavender or blue one,
But after you've got it, why if anything goes wrong don't think
you'll find anybody to fix it, just throw it away and buy a
new one.
Oh well, anyhow here I am nearly forty-five,
And still alive.

FIRST LIMICK

An old person of Troy
Is so prudish and coy
That it doesn't know yet
If it's a girl or a boy.

WHO TAUGHT CADDIES TO COUNT?
or
A BURNT GOLFER FEARS THE CHILD

I have never beheld you, O pawky Scot,
And I only guess your name,

Who first propounded the popular rot
That golf is a humbling game.
You putted perhaps with a mutton bone,
And hammered a gutty ball;
But I think that you sat in the bar alone,
And never played at all.

Ye hae spoken a braw bricht mouthfu', Jamie,
Ye didna ken ye erred;
Ye're richt that golf is a something gamie,
But humble is not the word.
Try arrogant, insolent, supercilious,
And if invention fades,
Add uppitty, hoity-toity, bilious,
And double them all in spades.

Oh pride of rank is a fearsome thing,
And pride of riches a bore;
But both of them bow on lea and ling
To the Prussian pride of score.
Better the beggar with fleas to scratch
Than the unassuming dub
Trying to pick up a Saturday match
In the locker room of the club.

The Hollywood snob will look you through
And stalk back into his clique,
For he knows that he is better than you
By so many grand a week;
And the high-caste Hindu's fangs are bared
If a low-caste Hindu blinks;
But they're just like one of the boys, compared
To the nabobs of the links.

Oh where this side of the River Styx
Will you find an equal mate

To the scorn of a man with a seventy-six
For a man with a seventy-eight?
I will tell you a scorn that mates it fine
As the welkin mates the sun:
The scorn of him with a ninety-nine
For him with a hundred and one.

And that is why I wander alone
From tee to green to tee,
For every golfer I've ever known
Is too good or too bad for me.
Indeed I have often wondered, Jamie,
Hooking into the heather,
In such an unhumble, contemptful gamie
How anyone plays together.

THERE WERE GIANTS IN THOSE DAYS
or
MAYBE THERE WEREN'T

When people bandy about bright sayings they like to attribute
    them to celebrities celebrated for their witticism,
Hoping thereby both to gain prestige and forestall criticism.
Thus many people in London have had their dispositions soured
By being cornered by other people and told stories attributed to
    Mr. Shaw or Noel Coward,
While over here, if people tell an anecdote either hygienic or
    spotty,
Why, they attribute it to Dorothy Parker, only they usually cozily
    refer to her as Dottie.
I have never heard an anecdote attributed to William Henry
    Harrison, or Rutherford B. Hayes,
So let us respectfully attribute the following titbits to their post-
    humous praise.

When William Henry Harrison faced a knotty problem he didn't
      wonder what would Gerald K. Smith or Earl Browder do,
He simply recounted the story of the two jealous Indian ranees who
      met on elephant-back and one ranee stroked her coiffure and
      said, Here's a pretty hair-do, and the other ranee stroked her
      elephant and said, Here's a pretty howdah-do;
And once when Rutherford B. Hayes found himself losing at
      backgammon,
Why, he casually upset the board and asked, Did you hear about
      Lord Louis Mountbatten, he asked a soldier in Burma, Are
      you Indo-Chinese? And the soldier said, No suh, I'se out-do'
      Alabaman.
Kindly do not attribute these anecdotes to the undersigned,
Kindly attribute them to these two hitherto unsung statesmen, who
      are dead and probably won't mind.

TARKINGTON, THOU SHOULD'ST BE LIVING
IN THIS HOUR

O Adolescence, O Adolescence,
I wince before thine incandescence.
Thy constitution young and hearty
Is too much for this aged party.
Thou standest with loafer-flattened feet
Where bras and funny papers meet.
When anxious elders swarm about
Crying "Where are you going?", thou answerest "Out,"
Leaving thy parents swamped in debts
For bubble gum and cigarettes.

Thou spurnest in no uncertain tone
The sirloin for the ice-cream cone;
Not milk, but cola, is thy potion;
Thou wearest earrings in the ocean,
Blue jeans at dinner, or maybe shorts,
And lipstick on the tennis courts.

Forever thou whisperest, two by two,
Of who is madly in love with who.
The car thou needest every day,
Let hub caps scatter where they may.
For it would start unfriendly talk
If friends should chance to see thee walk.

Friends! Heavens, how they come and go!
Best pal today, tomorrow foe,
Since to distinguish thou dost fail
Twixt confidante and tattletale,
And blanchest to find the beach at noon
With sacred midnight secrets strewn.

Strewn! All is lost and nothing found.
Lord, how thou leavest things around!
Sweaters and rackets in the stable,
And purse upon the drugstore table,
And cameras rusting in the rain,
And Daddy's patience down the drain.

Ah well, I must not carp and cavil,
I'll chew the spinach, spit out the gravel,
Remembering how my heart has leapt
At times when me thou didst accept.
Still, I'd like to be present, I must confess,
When thine own adolescents adolesce.

THE STRANGE CASE OF MR. PALLISER'S PALATE

Once there was a man named Mr. Palliser and he asked his wife,
    May I be a *gourmet?*
And she said, You sure may,
But she also said, If my kitchen is going to produce a Cordon Blue,
It won't be me, it will be you,

And he said, You mean *Cordon Bleu?*

And she said to never mind the pronunciation so long as it was
him and not *heu.*

But he wasn't discouraged; he bought a white hat and *The Cordon
Bleu Cook Book* and said, How about some *Huîtres en Robe
de Chambre?*

And she sniffed and said, Are you reading a cookbook or *Forever
Ambre?*

And he said, Well, if you prefer something more Anglo-Saxon,

Why suppose I whip up some tasty *Filets de Sole Jackson,*

And she pretended not to hear, so he raised his voice and said,
Could I please you with some *Paupiettes de Veau à la Grecque*
or *Cornets de Jambon Lucullus* or perhaps some nice *Moules
à la Bordelaise?*

And she said, Kindly lower your voice or the neighbors will think
we are drunk and *disordelaise,*

And she said, Furthermore the whole idea of your cooking anything fit to eat is a farce. So what did Mr. Palliser do then?

Well, he offered her *Œufs Farcis Maison* and *Homard Farci
St. Jacques* and *Tomate Farcie à la Bayonne* and *Aubergines
Farcies Provençales,* as well as *Aubergines Farcies Italiennes,*

And she said, Edward, kindly accompany me as usual to Hamburger Heaven and stop playing the fool,

And he looked in the book for one last suggestion and it suggested
Croques Madame, so he did, and now he dines every evening
on *Crème de Concombres Glacée, Côtelettes de Volaille Vi-
comtesse,* and *Artichauds à la Barigoule.*

WILL YOU HAVE YOUR TEDIUM
RARE OR MEDIUM?

Two things I have never understood: first, the difference between
a Czar and a Tsar,

And second, why some people who should be bores aren't, and
others, who shouldn't be, are.

I know a man who isn't sure whether bridge is played with a puck
   or a ball,
And he hasn't read a book since he bogged down on a polysyllable
   in the second chapter of *The Rover Boys at Putnam Hall.*
His most thrilling exploit was when he recovered a souvenir of
   the World's Fair that had been sent out with the trash,
And the only opinion he has ever formed by himself is that he
   looks better without a mustache.
Intellectually speaking, he has neither ears to hear with nor eyes
   to see with,
Yet he is pleasing to be with.
I know another man who is an expert on everything from witch-
   craft and demonology to the Elizabethan drama,
And he has spent a week end with the Dalai Lama,
And substituted for a mongoose in a fight with a cobra, and per-
   formed a successful underwater appendectomy,
And I cannot tell you how tediously his reminiscences affect me.
I myself am fortunate in that I have many interesting thoughts
   which I express in terms that make them come alive,
And I certainly would entertain my friends if they always didn't
   have to leave just when I arrive.

THE PORCUPINE

Any hound a porcupine nudges
Can't be blamed for harboring grudges.
I know one hound that laughed all winter
At a porcupine that sat on a splinter.

THERE'S NOTHING LIKE INSTINCT.
FORTUNATELY.

I suppose that plumbers' children know more about plumbing than
   plumbers do, and welders' children more about welding than
   welders,

Because the only fact in an implausible world is that all young
  know better than their elders.
A young person is a person with nothing to learn,
One who already knows that ice does not chill and fire does not
  burn.
It knows that it can read indefinitely in the dark and do its eyes
  no harm,
It knows it can climb on the back of a thin chair to look for a
  sweater it left on the bus without falling and breaking an
  arm.
It knows it can spend six hours in the sun on its first day at the
  beach without ending up a skinless beet,
And it knows it can walk barefoot through the barn without running a nail in its feet.
It knows it doesn't need a raincoat if it's raining or galoshes if it's
  snowing,
And knows how to manage a boat without ever having done any
  sailing or rowing.
It knows after every sporting contest that it had really picked the
  winner,
And that its appetite is not affected by eating three chocolate bars
  covered with peanut butter and guava jelly, fifteen minutes
  before dinner.
Most of all it knows
That only other people catch colds through sitting around in drafts
  in wet clothes.
Meanwhile psychologists grow rich
Writing that the young are ones parents should not undermine the
  self-confidence of which.

MARTHA'S VINEYARD

I live at the top of old West Chop
In a house with a cranky stove,
And when I swim I risk life and limb
On the pebbles that line the cove —

[369]

Where the waves wish-wash, and the foghorn blows,
And the blowfish nibble at your toes-oes-oes,
The blowfish nibble at your toes.

I lunch and sup on schrod and scup,
And once in a while on beans,
And the only news that I get to peruse
Is in last year's magazines —
Where the waves wish-wash, and the foghorn blows,
And the blowfish nibble at your toes-oes-oes,
The blowfish nibble at your toes.

When the sea gulls shout the lights go out,
And whenever the lights go on
I pursue the moth with a dusting cloth
Till the Bob White brings the dawn —
Where the waves wish-wash, and the foghorn blows,
And the blowfish nibble at your toes-oes-oes,
The blowfish nibble at your toes.

But when the breeze creeps through the trees
And the small waves shiver and shake,
Oh, I wouldn't swap my old West Chop
For a sizzling Western steak —
I want to wish-wash where the foghorn blows,
And the blowfish nibble at your toes-oes-oes,
The blowfish nibble at your toes.

THE PEOPLE UPSTAIRS

The people upstairs all practice ballet.
Their living room is a bowling alley.
Their bedroom is full of conducted tours.
Their radio is louder than yours.
They celebrate week ends all the week.

When they take a shower, your ceilings leak.
They try to get their parties to mix
By supplying their guests with Pogo sticks,
And when their orgy at last abates,
They go to the bathroom on roller skates.
I might love the people upstairs wondrous
If instead of above us, they just lived under us.

THE STRANGE CASE OF THE RENEGADE
LYRIC WRITER

Once there was a lyric writer named Mr. Amazon,
And being a lyric writer he spent most of his days with his pajamas on.
Since he wrote words for the music in musical comedies,
Why, he noted a great similarity between singers and the man-eating horses of Diomedes,
Because although the singers couldn't eat the tunes — you could always recognize the tunes as Chopin's or Rodgers's or Schumann's —
Well, they ate his lyrics the way the man-eating horses of Diomedes ate humans.
He was always complaining that Gee whiz,
Some people had to swallow their own words but singers only swallowed his;
And he swore that if he ever met a female singer who would pronounce his words he would offer her his heart and hand and undying loyalty
And 12½ per cent of his royalty.
Then one day he heard a new female singer in rehearsal
And his feelings underwent a reversal.
Her enunciation was fabulous,
He heard every one of his rhymes, even the most polysyllabulous;
So to show his admiration and confidence he wrote a new song especially for her, beginning "The Leith police releaseth us, releaseth us the police of Leith,"

And on opening night he sent her a perfect rose, but it seems she
	was a Spaniard and she sang the song with the rose between
	her teeth.
Mr. Amazon couldn't even distinguish a vowel,
It was like hearing a candidate with a loose tooth talking to a
	barber through a hot towel.
Mr. Amazon no longer writes lyrics, he writes radio commercials,
	because there is one fact on which he finally pounced:
When a writer rhymes sour stomach with kidney tubes it may not
	be prosody but boy, is it pronounced!

TABLEAU AT TWILIGHT

I sit in the dusk. I am all alone.
Enter a child and an ice-cream cone.

A parent is easily beguiled
By sight of this coniferous child.

The friendly embers warmer gleam,
The cone begins to drip ice cream.

Cones are composed of many a vitamin.
My lap is not the place to bitamin.

Although my raiment is not chinchilla,
I flinch to see it become vanilla.

Coniferous child, when vanilla melts
I'd rather it melted somewhere else.

Exit child with remains of cone.
I sit in the dusk. I am all alone,

Muttering spells like an angry Druid,
Alone, in the dusk, with the cleaning fluid.

THERE ARE MORE WAYS TO ROAST A PIG
THAN BURNING THE HOUSE DOWN
or
YOU CAN ALWAYS STICK YOUR HEAD
IN A VOLCANO

Poring over calendars is apt to give people round shoulders and
    a squint, or strabismus,
So I am perhaps fortunate in not needing a calendar to tell me
    when it's my birthday or Christmas.
I know that a year has rolled around once more
When I find myself thumbing a crisp new cigarette lighter just like
    the coven of other cigarette lighters strewn on a shelf in the
    garage along with the broken tire chains and the license plates
    for 1934.
It is only for myself that I presume to speak,
But I can light cigarettes with a cigarette lighter for exactly one
    week,
And then on the eighth day something comes up for renewal,
And sometimes it's the flint, and maybe the powder horn or ram-
    rod, and sometimes the fuel,
And if it's the flint you unscrew the little jigger at the bottom and
    the insides jump out at you like a jack-in-the-box and you
    can't get them back in without the services of an engineer
    and a gunsmith and a vet,
And if it's the fuel it gets everywhere except into the tank and
    when you spin the wheel the whole thing including your
    hand flares up like a crêpe Suzette.
Well, enough is enough,
And many less ingenious persons would turn to chewing cut plug,
    or sniffing snuff,
But in between birthdays and Christmases I have figured out a
    way to light cigarettes indoors and out in any kind of
    weather;
I just rub a match and a matchbox together.

SECOND LIMICK

A cook named McMurray
Got a raise in a hurry
From his Hindu employer
By favoring curry.

SEPTEMBER IS SUMMER, TOO
or
IT'S NEVER TOO LATE TO BE UNCOMFORTABLE

Well, well, well, so this is summer, isn't that *mirabile dictu,*

And these are the days when whatever you sit down on you stick to.

These are the days when those who sell four ounces of synthetic lemonade concocted in a theater basement for a quarter enter into their inheritance,

And Rum Collinses soak through paper napkins onto people's Hepplewhites and Sheratons,

And progressive-minded citizens don their most porous finery and frippery.

But it doesn't help, because underneath they are simultaneously sticky and slippery.

And some insomniacs woo insomnia plus pajamas and others minus,

And everybody patronizes air-conditioned shops and movies to get cool and then complains that the difference in temperature gives them lumbago and sinus,

And people trapped in doorways by thunderstorms console themselves by saying, Well, anyway this will cool it off while we wait,

So during the storm the mercury plunges from ninety-four to ninety-three and afterwards climbs immediately to ninety-eight,

And marriages break up over such momentous questions as Who ran against Harding — Davis or Cox?

And when you go to strike a match the head dissolves on the box,
But these estival phenomena amaze me not,
What does amaze me is how every year people are amazed to discover that summer is hot.

THE SECOND MONTH IT'S NOT ITEMIZED

I go to my desk to write a letter,
A simple letter without any frills;
I can't find space to write my letter,
My desk is treetop high in bills.

I go to my desk to write a poem
About a child of whom I'm afraid;
I can't get near it to write my poem
For the barrel of bills, and all unpaid.

I go to my desk for an asprin tablet,
For a handy bottle of syrup of squills,
I reach in the drawer for the trusty bicarbonate;
My fingers fasten on nothing but bills.

I go to my desk to get my checkbook
That checks may blossom like daffodils,
Hundreds of checks to maintain my credit;
I can't get through the bills to pay my bills.

I've got more bills than there are people,
I've got bigger bills than Lincoln in bronze,
I've got older bills than a Bangor & Aroostook day coach,
I've got bills more quintuplicate than Dionnes.

There's a man named Slemp in Lima, Ohio,
Since 1930 he has been constantly ill,
And of all the inhabitants of this glorious nation
He is the only one who has never sent me a bill.

The trouble with bills, it costs money to pay them,
But as long as you don't, your bank is full.
I shall now save some money by opening a charge account
With a fuller, a draper, and a carder of wool.

THE LION

Oh, weep for Mr. and Mrs. Bryan!
He was eaten by a lion;
Following which, the lion's lioness
Up and swallowed Bryan's Bryaness.

SOLILOQUY IN CIRCLES

Being a father
Is quite a bother.

You are free as air
With time to spare,

You're a fiscal rocket
With change in your pocket,

And then one morn
A child is born.

Your life has been runcible,
Irresponsible,

Like an arrow or javelin
You've been constantly travelin',

But mostly, I daresay,
Without a *chaise percée*,

To which by comparison
Nothing's embarison.

But all children matures,
Maybe even yours.

You improve them mentally
And straighten them dentally,

They grow tall as a lancer
And ask questions you can't answer,

And supply you with data
About how everybody else wears lipstick sooner and stays up later,

And if they are popular,
The phone they monopular.

They scorn the dominion
Of their parent's opinion,

They're no longer corralable
Once they find that you're fallible

But after you've raised them and educated them and gowned them,
They just take their little fingers and wrap you around them.

Being a father
Is quite a bother,
But I like it, rather.

ROLL ON, THOU DEEP AND DARK BLUE
COPY WRITER — ROLL!

I heard a pouting siren
Cry o'er a classic sea,
Please to remove, Lord Byron,
Your hand from off my knee!

No silver-tongued Don Juan
Shall henceforth do me wrong;
Though you sing like Mrs. Luhan,
I do not hear your song.

Go chant it to the lemming,
Go coo it to the dove;
I'm waiting for that Heming-
That Hemingway kind of love.

To think that Mr. Steinbeck
Once roused my amorous fires!
Now debutantes in Rhinebeck,
They read him to their sires.

And now my lip is bitten,
And now my heart makes moan,
With envy I am smitten
For Gregory and Joan.

A cinematic cordon
Is drawn around my heart,

[378]

So we'll go no more, George Gordon,
A-roving ere we part.

Though the heavens are a cup for
The pearly moon above,
Go away; I'm saving up for
That Hemingway kind of love.

THE STRANGE CASE OF THE
ENTOMOLOGIST'S HEART

Consider the case of Mr. Suggs.

He was an eminent entomologist, which is to say he knew nothing
but bugs.

He could tell the Coleoptera from the Lepidoptera,

And the Aphidae and the Katydididae from the Grasshoptera.

He didn't know whether to starve a cold or feed a fever, he was so
untherapeutical,

But he knew that in 1737 J. Swammerdam's *Biblia Naturae* had
upset the theories of Aristotle and Harvey by demonstrating
the presence of pupal structures under the larval cuticle.

His taste buds were such that he was always asking dining-car
stewards for their recipe for French dressing and mayonnaise,

But he was familiar with Strauss-Durckheim's brilliant treatise
(1828) on the cockchafer and that earlier (1760) but
equally brilliant monograph on the goat-moth caterpillar of
P. Lyonnet's.

He was so unliterary that he never understood the difference between *Ibid.* and *Anonymous*,

But he spoke of 1842 as the year in which Von Kölliker first described the formation of the blastoderm in the egg of the
midge *Chironomus*.

Mr. Sugg's specialty was fireflies, which he knew inside and out
and from stem to stern,

And he was on the track of why they blaze and don't burn,

And then one day he met a girl as fragrant as jessamine,
And he found her more fascinating than the rarest eleven-legged
    specimen,
But being a diffident swain he wished to learn how the land lay
    before burning his bridges,
So he bashfully asked her mother what she thought of his chances,
    and she encouragingly said, At sight of you my daughter
    lights up like a firefly, and Mr. Suggs stammered, Good gra-
    cious, what a strange place for a girl to light up!, and rapidly
    returned to his goat-moth caterpillars, blastoderms and
    midges.

THIRD LIMICK

Two nudists of Dover,
Being purple all over,
Were munched by a cow
When mistaken for clover.

POSSESSIONS ARE NINE POINTS OF CONVERSATION

Some people, and it doesn't matter whether they are paupers or
    millionaires,
Think that anything they have is the best in the world just because
    it is theirs.
If they happen to own a 1921 jalopy,
They look at their neighbor's new de luxe convertible like the
    wearer of a 57th Street gown at a 14th Street copy.
If their seventeen-year-old child is still in the third grade they
    sneer at the graduation of the seventeen-year-old children of
    their friends,
Claiming that prodigies always come to bad ends,
And if their roof leaks,
It's because the shingles are antiques.

Other people, and it doesn't matter if they are Scandinavians or Celts,
Think that anything is better than theirs just because it belongs to somebody else.
If you congratulate them when their blue-blooded Doberman pinscher wins the obedience championship, they look at you like a martyr,
And say that the garbage man's little Rover is really infinitely smarter;
And if they smoke fifteen-cent cigars they are sure somebody else gets better cigars for a dime.
And if they take a trip to Paris they are sure their friends who went to Old Orchard had a better time.
Yes, they look on their neighbor's ox and ass with covetousness and their own ox and ass with abhorrence,
And if they are wives they want their husband to be like Florence's Freddie, and if they are husbands they want their wives to be like Freddie's Florence.
I think that comparisons are truly odious, I do not approve of this constant proud or envious to-do;
And furthermore, dear friends, I think that you and yours are delightful and I also think that me and mine are delightful too.

POLTERGUEST, MY POLTERGUEST

I've put Miss Hopper upon the train,
And I hope to do so never again,
For must I do so, I shouldn't wonder
If, instead of upon it, I put her under.

Never has host encountered a visitor
Less desirabler, less exquisiter,
Or experienced such a tangy zest
In beholding the back of a parting guest.

[381]

Hoitiful-toitiful Hecate Hopper
Haunted our house and haunted it proper,
Hecate Hopper left the property
Irredeemably Hecate Hopperty.

The morning paper was her monopoly
She read it first, and Hecate Hopperly,
Handing on to the old subscriber
A wad of Dorothy Dix and fiber.

Shall we coin a phrase for "to unco-operate"?
How about trying "to Hecate Hopperate"?
On the maid's days off she found it fun
To breakfast in bed at quarter to one.

Not only was Hecate on a diet,
She insisted that all the family try it,
And all one week end we gobbled like pigs
On rutabagas and salted figs.

She clogged the pipes and she blew the fuses,
She broke the rocker that Grandma uses,
And she ran amok in the medicine chest,
Hecate Hopper, the Polterguest.

Hecate Hopper the Polterguest
Left stuff to be posted or expressed,
And absconded, her suavity undiminished,
With a mystery story I hadn't finished.

If I pushed Miss Hopper under the train
I'd probably have to do it again,
For the time that I pushed her off the boat
I regretfully found Miss Hopper could float.

PIANO TUNER, UNTUNE ME THAT TUNE

I regret that before people can be reformed they have to be sinners,
And that before you have pianists in the family you have to have
    beginners.
When it comes to beginners' music
I am not enthusic.
When listening to something called "An Evening in My Doll
    House," or "Buzz, Buzz, Said the Bee to the Clover,"
Why I'd like just once to hear it played all the way through, instead
    of that hard part near the end over and over.
Have you noticed about little fingers?
When they hit a sour note, they lingers.
And another thing about little fingers, they are always strawberry-
    jammed or cranberry-jellied-y,
And "Chopsticks" is their favorite melody,
And if there is one man who I hope his dentist was a sadist and all
    his teeth were brittle ones,
It is he who invented "Chopsticks" for the little ones.
My good wishes are less than frugal
For him who started the little ones going boogie-woogal,
But for him who started the little ones picking out "Chopsticks" on
    the ivories,
Well I wish him a thousand harems of a thousand wives apiece,
    and a thousand little ones by each wife, and each little one
    playing "Chopsticks" twenty-four hours a day in all the nurs-
    eries of all his harems, or wiveries.

PAPPY WANTS A POPPY

When I a winsome babe did creep,
I'm told that I was fond of sleep,
And later, as a handsome stripling,
Gave up my life to sleep and Kipling.
At thirty, proud and in my prime,

[383]

They found me sleeping half the time,
And now that I am forty-four,
Why, sleep I doubly do adore.
As headlines range from odd to oddest
My own requirements grow more modest;
I ask no cloud of daffodils,
But just a cask of sleeping pills.
Wrapped in a robe of rosy slumber
How happily my dreams I number:
Europe erupts in bumper crops;
Bubble Gum King swells up and pops;
Big hussy novel wilts on cob;
In Georgia, Negro lynches mob;
The Have-nots simply love the Haves,
And people understand the Slavs;
Good fairies pay my income taxes,
And Mrs. Macy shops at Saks's.
In an era opened by mistake
I'd rather sleep than be awake.
Indeed, at times I can't recall
Why ever I wake up at all.

NOT EVEN FOR BRUNCH

When branches bend in fruitful stupor
Before the woods break out in plaid,
The super-market talks more super,
The roadside stands go slightly mad.
What garden grew this goblin harvest?
Who coined these words that strike me numb?
I will not purchase, though I starvest,
The cuke, the glad, the lope, the mum.

In happier days I sank to slumber
Murmuring names as sweet as hope:

Fair gladiolus, and cucumber,
Chrysanthemum and cantaloupe.
I greet the changelings that awoke me
With warmth a little less than luke,
As farmer and florist crowd to choke me
With glad and lope, with mum and cuke.

Go hence, far hence, you jargon-mongers,
Go soak your head in boiling ads,
Go feed to cuttlefish and congers
Your mums and lopes, your cukes and glads.
Stew in the whimsy that you dole us;
I roam where magic casements ope
On cantemum spiced, and cuciolus,
On chrysanthecumber, and gladaloupe.

THE OUTCOME OF MR. BUCK'S SUPERSTITION

Let me tell you of Aloysius Buck
Who had a pathetic belief in luck.
While the soup was waiting for him to sup
He would see a pin and pick it up.
When eating fish he toyed with the fishbones,
Making believe that they were wishbones,
And his bedside table was leaning over
Under bushel baskets of four-leafed clover.
His wife was a model of patience and tact
But at last her pleasant nature cracked.
For a birthday present he gave her a horseshoe.
She said, My dear, I'm going to divorce you.
He promised that if she'd remain Mrs. Buck
He'd never again believe in luck.
I was a fool, said Aloysius,
I'll never again be superstitious.
He brought home the blackest cats he could catch

And lit three cigarettes upon one match,
He walked his wife underneath a ladder
And often trampled on his own shadder,
And to make his un-superstition clearer
He put his foot through his wife's best mirror.
His wife was a model of patience and tact.
But at last her pleasant nature cracked
Though she liked his face and admired his carriage
She went to court and dissolved their marriage
When he said, Let's have eleven children as fast as we're able,
Then we can always sit down thirteen at table.

MRS. PURVIS DREADS ROOM SERVICE
or
MR. PURVIS DREADS IT, TOO

Some say the fastest living creature is the cheetah,
Others nominate a duenna getting between a señor and a señorita,
Which goes to show that their knowledge of natural history is clear
    as a bell,
But they've never had their clothes off in a hotel.
Some hold out for the speed with which a Wagnerian quits an
    opera by Puccini,
Others for the speed with which an empty stomach is hit by a dry
    Martini.
These are speeds on whose superior speediness they persistently
    dwell,
Which simply proves that they've never had their clothes off in a
    hotel.
If you want to spite your face you can cut your nose off,
And if you want to spite people who think that cheetahs and du-
    ennas and dry Martinis are speedy, you can go to a hotel and
    take your clothes off,
Because some people can run the hundred in ten seconds and
    others would need only nine to circle the earth at the equator,

And they are the ones who knock on your triple-locked door just
as you're ready for the bath and before you can say Wait a
minute! they stalk in and if you're a man they're the maid
and if you're a woman they're the waiter.
So I say Hats off to our hotel managers,
I hope they all get mistaken for Japanese beetles by scarlet tanagers,
Because there are two dubious thrills they guarantee every guest,
And one is a fleet-footed staff that laughs at locksmiths, because
the other is a triple lock that will open only from the outside
and only if the inmate is completely undressed.

OH SHUCKS, MA'AM, I MEAN EXCUSE ME

The greatest error ever erred
Is a nice girl with a naughty word.
For naughty words I hold no brief,
They fill my modest heart with grief,
But since it's plainer every day,
That naughty words are here to stay,
At least let's send them back again
To where they come from: namely, men.
For men, although to language prone,
Know when to leave the stuff alone;
The stevedore, before each damn,
Stops to consider where he am;
The lumberjack is careful, too,
Of what he says in front of who;
And if surrounded by the young,
The taxi driver curbs his tongue.
The reason men speak softly thus is
That circumstances alter cusses,
And naughty words scream out like sirens
When uttered in the wrong environs.
But maidens who restrict their hips
Place no such limits on their lips;

Once they have learned a startling Verb,
No tactful qualms their heads disturb;
They scatter Adjectives hither and thence
Regardless of their audience,
And cannot hold a Noun in trust
But have to out with it, or bust,
And that's why men creep into crannies
When girls play cribbage with their grannies,
And nervous husbands develop hives
When ministers call upon their wives,
And fathers tie themselves in knots
When damsels stoop to caress their tots,
For who knows what may not be heard
From a nice girl with a naughty word?
One truth all womankind nonplusses:
That circumstances alter cusses.

ALWAYS MARRY AN APRIL GIRL

Praise the spells and bless the charms,
I found April in my arms.
April golden, April cloudy,
Gracious, cruel, tender, rowdy;
April soft in flowered languor,
April cold with sudden anger,
Ever changing, ever true —
I love April, I love you.

LISTEN TO THE LINOTYPE

In these days when we are living on the rim of a crater
I like the *New York Herald Tribune,* a paper that gets around to
    printing everything sooner or later.
Where else could I on October 2nd, 1947, have read or heard

[388   ]

That in 1929 the mockingbird was chosen by the Mississippi Federation of Women's Clubs to be Mississippi State bird?

Since this fact had seemingly lain dormant for seventeen years before receiving mention

I naturally wondered if it had ever been brought to the mockingbird's attention.

I was relieved to learn from a venerable Maryland mockingbird of my acquaintance that in 1930 a notification ceremony was held in Jackson,

Attended by hordes of citizens, running the gamut from white to Protestant and Anglo-Saxon.

The mockingbirds stated that the signal honor was far signaler than any they had anticipated,

They had never dreamed of being Mississississipated,

And then they scattered around a little suet and feed.

And voted the Mississippi Federation of Women's Clubs as the Federation of Women's Clubs most likely to succeed.

In gratitude for this information I showed my feathered friend an item from the same paper stating that the Tiber River, in Italy, is 253 miles long,

And he agreed with me when I said I wouldn't sell my subscription for a song.

LINES TO BE EMBROIDERED ON A BIB
or
THE CHILD IS FATHER OF THE MAN, BUT NOT FOR QUITE A WHILE

So Thomas Edison
Never drank his medicine;
So Blackstone and Hoyle
Refused cod-liver oil;
So Sir Thomas Malory
Never heard of a calory;
So the Earl of Lennox

Murdered Rizzio without the aid of vitamins or calisthenox;
So Socrates and Plato
Ate dessert without finishing their potato;
So spinach was too spinachy
For Leonardo da Vinaci:
Well, it's all immaterial,
So eat your nice cereal,
And if you want to name your own ration,
First go get a reputation.

FOURTH LIMICK

Three young Tennesseans
Whom snobs called plebeians
Cried, What do you mean?
We's married to we-uns.

I DO, I WILL, I HAVE

How wise I am to have instructed the butler to instruct the first
footman to instruct the second footman to instruct the door-
man to order my carriage;

I am about to volunteer a definition of marriage.

Just as I know that there are two Hagens, Walter and Copen,

I know that marriage is a legal and religious alliance entered into
by a man who can't sleep with the window shut and a woman
who can't sleep with the window open.

Moreover just as I am unsure of the difference between flora and
fauna and flotsam and jetsam

I am quite sure that marriage is the alliance of two people one of
whom never remembers birthdays and the other never for-
getsam,

And he refuses to believe there is a leak in the water pipe or
the gas pipe and she is convinced she is about to asphyx-
iate or drown,

And she says Quick get up and get my hairbrushes off the window
    sill, it's raining in, and he replies Oh they're all right, it's
    only raining straight down.
That is why marriage is so much more interesting than divorce,
Because it's the only known example of the happy meeting of the
    immovable object and the irresistible force.
So I hope husbands and wives will continue to debate and combat
    over everything debatable and combatable,
Because I believe a little incompatibility is the spice of life, par-
    ticularly if he has income and she is pattable.

THE GUPPY

Whales have calves,
Cats have kittens,
Bears have cubs,
Bats have bittens.
Swans have cygnets,
Seals have puppies,
But guppies just have little guppies.

I MUST TELL YOU ABOUT MY NOVEL

My grandpa wasn't salty,
No hero he of fable,
His English wasn't faulty,
He wore a coat at table.
His character lacked the color
Of either saint or satyr,
His life was rather duller
Than that of Walter Pater.

Look at Grandpa, take a look!
How can I write a book!

His temper wasn't crusty,
He shone not forth majestic
For barroom exploits lusty,
Or tyranny domestic.
He swung not on the gallows
But went to his salvation
While toasting stale marshmallows,
His only dissipation.

Look at Grandpa, take a look!
How can I write a book!

My Uncle John was cautious,
He never slipped his anchor,
His probity was nauseous,
In fact he was a banker.
He hubbed no hubba hubbas,
He wore two MacIntoshes,
Also a pair of rubbers
Inside of his galoshes.

Look at my uncle, take a look!
How can I write a book!

My other uncle, Herbie,
Just once enlarged his orbit,
The day he crushed his derby
While cheering James J. Corbett.
No toper he, or wencher,
He backed nor horse nor houri,
His raciest adventure
A summons to the jury.

Look at my uncles, take a look!
How can I write a book!

Round my ancestral menfolk
There hangs no spicy aura,
I have no racy kinfolk
From Rome to Glocca Morra.
Not nitwits, not Napoleons,
The mill they were the run of,
My family weren't Mongolians;
Then whom can I make fun of?

Look!
No book!

GOOD RIDDANCE, BUT NOW WHAT?

Come children, gather round my knee;
Something is about to be.

Tonight's December thirty-first,
Something is about to burst.

The clock is crouching, dark and small,
Like a time bomb in the hall.

Hark, it's midnight, children dear.
Duck! Here comes another year!

IS THIS SEAT TAKEN? YES
or
MY NECK IS STICKING IN

I hope that in my eldering age I'm not becoming noticeably queru-
    lous,
But I feel that conversations with strangers can be perilous.
Consider the case of the two strangers who met in a hotel dining
    room in Alabama,

And the menu was rather less than a panorama,

Indeed, it was as repetitious as a snore,

And the first stranger said, I'm a little sick of corn pone, and the second stranger, who was tall, tan, and turbaned, said, Glad to know you, I'm Mohammed Khan, a big Sikh of Cawnpore.

I am also disturbed by accounts of the two strangers, one male and one female, who met on the banks of the Congo and shared a bowl of semolina,

And presently he said, You've got eyes like a gazelle, and she giggled and said, Eyes like a gazelle? And he said, No, you's like a hyena.

This is the sort of experience for which I do not hanker,

So if you will excuse me, I shall now run over to the Banker's Trust Company and trust a banker.

I'LL TAKE THE HIGH ROAD COMMISSION

In between the route marks
And the shaving rhymes,
Black and yellow markers
Comment on the times.

All along the highway
Hear the signs discourse:

MEN
SLOW
WORKING
;
SADDLE
CROSSING
HORSE
.

Cryptic crossroad preachers
Proffer good advice,

Helping wary drivers
Keep out of Paradise.

Transcontinental sermons,
Transcendental talk:

SOFT
CAUTION
SHOULDERS
;
CROSS
CHILDREN
WALK

.

Wisest of their proverbs,
Truest of their talk,
Have I found that dictum:

CROSS
CHILDREN
WALK

.

When Adam took the highway
He left his sons a guide:

CROSS
CHILDREN
WALK
;
CHEERFUL
CHILDREN
RIDE

.

HAVE YOU TRIED STAYING AWAKE?
or
THEY'LL FIND A WAY TO STOP
THAT, TOO

Most people's downy couches have a footboard and a headboard,
And some people's downy couches also have a bed-board.
I must tell you before I forgets
That a bed-board is different from a bed *and* board, which is what
　　when your wife leaves it you are no longer responsible for her
　　debts,
But if you can't get to sleep because your couch is so downy that
　　you wallow and roll like a tug-boat off Cape Hatteras,
Why, you make it un-downy by slipping a bed-board under your
　　matteras,
Thereby earning, whether you wear pajamas or a gown,
The unusual privilege of getting to sleep by walking the plank lying
　　down.
O Civilization, O Progress, O Human Ingenuity!
O Fatuity in Perpetuity!
One genius chooses downy couches to set his mind upon,
And he spends a lifetime tinkering with Angeldust and Fogfoam
　　and Bubblemist until he has invented the downiest couch
　　ever reclined upon,
Whereupon another genius immediately invents a slab of wood
　　that you can put under it to harden it,
And up-and-coming dealers may now feature the most irresistible
　　of downy couches and the most immovable of bed-boards si-
　　multaneously, like the poison bottle with the antidote on the
　　label, so if I giggle in my hammock I hope you will pardon it.

THE ASP

Whenever I behold an asp
I can't suppress a startled gasp.
I do not charge the asp with matricide,
But what about his Cleopatricide?

GRIN AND BEAR LEFT

I don't want to be classed among the pedantics,
But next time I visit friends who have moved to the country I want
  to get together with them on terminology, or semantics.
When you ask them on the telephone how to get there they smil-
  ingly cry that it is simple,
In fact you can practically see them dimple,
You just drive on Route 402 to Hartley and then bear left a couple
  of miles till you cross a stream,
Which they imply is alive with tench, chub, dace, ide, sturgeon
  and bream,
And you go on till you reach the fourth road on the right,
And you can't miss their house because it is on a rise and it is
  white.
Well it's a neighborhood of which you have never been a fre-
  quenter,
But you start out on 402 and soon find yourself trying to disentan-
  gle Hartley from East Hartley, West Hartley, North and
  South Hartley, and Hartley Center,
And you bear left a couple of miles peering through the windshield,
  which is smattered with gnats and midges,
And suddenly the road is alive with bridges,
And your tires begin to scream
As you try to decide which bridge spans a rill, which a run, which
  a branch, which a creek, which a brook or river, and which
  presumably a stream;

And having passed this test you begin to count roads on the right,
     than which no more exhausting test is to be found,
For who is to say which is a road, which a lane, which a driveway
     and which just a place where somebody backed in to turn
     around?
But anyhow turning around seems a good idea so there is one
     thing I don't know still:
Whether that white house where the cocktails are getting warm
     and the dinner cold is on a ridge, a ledge, a knoll, a rise, or a
     hill.

HE DIGS, HE DUG, HE HAS DUG

Say not Eve needed Adam's pardon
For their eviction from the Garden;
I only hope some power divine
Gets round to ousting me from mine.
On bended knee, perspiring clammily,
I scrape the soil to feed my family,
Untaught, unteachable, undramatic,
A figure sorry and sciatic.
Although I've done the best I could,
Nothing comes up the way it should.
They're making playshoes of my celery,
It's rubbery, and purple-yellery,
My beets have botts, my kale has hives,
There's something crawly in my chives,
And jeering insects think it cute
To swallow my spray and spit out my fruit.
My garden will never make me famous,
I'm a horticultural ignoramus,
I can't tell a stringbean from a soybean,
Or even a girl bean from a boy bean.

THE ETERNAL VERNAL
or
IN ALL MY DREAMS MY FAIR FACE BEAMS

Forgive this singsong,
It's just my spring song.
All winter like the blossoms
I've been playing possums,
But with April adjacent
I'm a possum renascent.
I'm the Renaissance
In gabardine pants,
I'm a gossoon once more,
Not forty-five, but forty-four,
I drink my kumiss
With pepper and pumice,
I swim where the herring do
In search of derring-do,
I crouch in a pergola
To catch me a burgola,
I'm Gustavus Adolphus
Among tennis players and golphus,
Compared to me they're a tortoise
With advanced rigor mortis,
I combine the music of Götterdämmerung
With the words of the Decamerrung,
I woo nymphs like billy-o
With my well-known punctilio,
Which unless I've progressed
Is the punkest tilio by actual test,
I roll a one and a two at dice and consider them better than a good
　　cook or a good wife are,
Because one and two is free, and that's what the best things in life
　　are,
And if anyone disagrees they might just as well not have
　　done it,

Because I know this business backwards and that's the way I propose to run it.
In a word, it is spring,
And I can do any thing.

COUSIN EUPHEMIA KNOWS BEST
or
PHYSICIAN, HEAL SOMEBODY ELSE

Some people don't want to be doctors because they think doctors don't make a good living,
And also get called away from their bed at night and from their dinner on Christmas and Thanksgiving,
And other people don't want to be doctors because a doctor's friends never take their symptoms to his office at ten dollars a throw but insert them into a friendly game of gin rummy or backgammon,
And ask questions about their blood count just as the doctor is lining up an elusive putt or an elusive salmon.
These considerations do not influence me a particle;
I do not want to be a doctor simply because somewhere in the family of every patient is a female who has read an article.
You remove a youngster's tonsils and the result is a triumph of medical and surgical science,
He stops coughing and sniffling and gains eleven pounds and gets elected captain of the Junior Giants,
But his great-aunt spreads the word that you are a quack,
Because she read an article in the paper last Sunday where some Rumanian savant stated that tonsillectomy is a thing of the past and the Balkan hospitals are bulging with people standing in line to have their tonsils put back.
You suggest calamine lotion for the baby's prickly heat,
And you are at once relegated to the back seat,
Because its grandmother's cousin has seen an article in the "Household Hints" department of *Winning Parcheesi* that says the only remedy for prickly heat is homogenized streptomycin,

And somebody's sister-in-law has seen an article where the pathol-
ogist of *Better Houses and Trailers* says calamine lotion is
out, a conscientious medicine man wouldn't apply calamine
lotion to an itching bison.
I once read an unwritten article by a doctor saying there is only one
cure for a patient's female relative who has read an article:
A hatpin in the left ventricle of the hearticle.

CONSIDER THE LAPEL, SIR

Have you bought a suit at Spand and Spitz?
They won't let you wear it unless it fits.
That's what they warn you in all their ads,
And Spand and Spitz are scrupulous lads.
Spand and Spitz are intensely scrupulous,
You can't wear their suit if the seat is droopulous.
Do you want it for slumming, or tea at the Ritz?
They won't let you wear it unless it fits.
The pants they carry are envy arousers,
In fact, they are not pants, they are trousers.
You select a suit and you call it quits,
As far as you are concerned, it fits.
You put your money and keys and comb in it,
You prepare to pay, and walk on home in it,
When here comes Spitz and here comes Spand,
They look at you like a swollen gland,
Spitz swears to Spand, who swears to Spitz,
They won't let you wear it unless it fits.
You adore the suit, you appeal to Spand,
He jerks it apart with loving hand;
You wish to wear it, you cry to Spitz,
He rips it off, while Spand on you sits.
It may be the suit that you're who it's made for,
The suit you have fought for and bought and paid for;
But if Spand and Spitz don't admit it fits you,

To wear it away, you must learn jujitsu.
The hell with this esthetic palaver
When you just want to cover your threadbare cadaver.

HERE USUALLY COMES THE BRIDE

June means weddings in everyone's lexicon,
Weddings in Swedish, weddings in Mexican.
Breezes play Mendelssohn, treeses play Youmans,
Birds wed birds, and humans wed humans.
All year long the gentlemen woo,
But the ladies dream of a June "I do."
Ladies grow loony, and gentlemen loonier;
This year's June is next year's Junior.

I AM FULL OF PREVIOUS EXPERIENCE

Newspapermen say that of all work, newspaper work is the infernalist,
But nevertheless I am studying up to be a journalist.
I do not aspire to be a Pearson or a Pegler or a Gunther,
I don't think I will ever be selected as a Book-of-the-Monther,
I don't hope to score any scoops or beat any deadlines,
But after a careful ten-year examination of the press I do think I
have caught the knack of writing facetious little headlines.
Suppose a marmoset escapes in a saloon and mingles with the imbibers,
Why, "Monkey Business" is the heading expected by the subscrib·
ers,
And when a steer escapes on the way to the slaughterhouse and is
recaptured by a cowboy from Madison Square Garden my
cup is doubly full,
Because then I can write either "A Bum Steer" or "Throwing the
Bull."

[402]

What can be apter than "Fowl Play" when the minister's Rhode
    Island Reds disappear at dawn,
Or be it Mrs. Somebody-or-other's of 13 South Water Street's amo-
    rous Pekinese that is missing, what could be more appropri-
    ate than "Dog-Gone"?
My, my, in the names of animals how many cryptic little giggles
    are hidden;
Which of you could guess what type of creature is referred to in
    items entitled "A Cat-astrophe" or "Poor Fish" or "Gets Farm-
    er's Goat," or "No Kiddin' "?
No, I may never win any prizes from Mr. Pulitzer,
But when it comes to supplying the customers with little jokes for
    their breakfast table I will always be in there pitching hon-
    estly and trulitzer.

CONFESSION TO BE TRACED ON A
BIRTHDAY CAKE

Lots of people are richer than me,
Yet pay a slenderer tax;
Their annual levy seems to wane
While their income seems to wax.
Lots of people have stocks and bonds
To further their romances;
I've cashed my ultimate Savings Stamp —
But nobody else has Frances.

Lots of people are stronger than me,
And greater athletic menaces;
They poise like gods on diving boards
And win their golfs and tennises.
Lots of people have lots more grace
And cut fine figures at dances,
While I was born with galoshes on —
But nobody else has Frances.

Lots of people are wiser than me,
And carry within their cranium
The implications of Stein and Joyce
And the properties of uranium.
They know the mileage to every star
In the heaven's vast expanses;
I'm inclined to believe that the world is flat —
But nobody else has Frances.

Speaking of wisdom and wealth and grace —
As recently I have dared to —
There are lots of people compared to whom
I'd rather not be compared to.
There are people I ought to wish I was;
But under the circumstances,
I prefer to continue my life as me —
For nobody else has Frances.

IF HE SCHOLARS, LET HIM GO

I like to think about that great French critic and historian, Hippolyte Adolphe Taine.
I like to think about his great French critical and historical brain.
He died in 1893 at the age of sixty-five,
But previously he had been alive.
He wrote many books of outstanding worth,
But this was before his death, although following his birth.
He tried to interpret human culture in terms of outer environment,
And he knew exactly what the biographers of Rousseau and Shelley and Lord Byron meant.
His great philosophical work, *De l'intelligence,* in which he connected physiology with psychology, was written after meeting a girl named Lola,
And greatly influenced the pens of Flaubert, de Maupassant, and Zola.

He did much to establish positivism in France,
And his famous *History of English Literature* was written on purpose and not by chance.
Yes, Hippolyte Adolphe Taine may have been only five foot three, but he was a scholar of the most discerning;
Whereas his oafish brother Casimir, although he stood six foot seven in his bobby-socks, couldn't spell C–H–A–T, cat, and was pointed at as the long Taine that had no learning.

COMPLIMENTS OF A FRIEND

How many gifted pens have penned
That Mother is a boy's best friend!
How many more with like afflatus
Award the dog that honored status!
I hope my tongue in prune juice smothers
If I belittle dogs or mothers,
But gracious, how can I agree?
I know my own best friend is Me.
We share our joys and our aversions,
We're thicker than the Medes and Persians,
We blend like voices in a chorus,
The same things please, the same things bore us.
If I am broke, then Me needs money;
I make a joke, Me finds it funny.
I know what I like, Me knows what art is;
We hate the people at cocktail parties,
When I can stand the crowd no more,
Why, Me is halfway to the door.
I am a dodo; Me, an auk;
We grieve that pictures learned to talk;
For every sin that I produce
Kind Me can find some soft excuse,
And when I blow a final gasket,
Who but Me will share my casket?

[405]

Beside us, Pythias and Damon
We're just two unacquainted laymen.
Sneer not, for if you answer true,
Don't you feel that way about You?

CONFOUND YOU, DECEMBER TWENTY–SIXTH, I APOLOGIZE

December twenty-fifth is an exciting day because it is what people
    refer to when Merry Christmas they wish you;
But December twenty-sixth is just the day you spend tripping over
    ribbons and wading through green and scarlet tissue.
It is a day of such anticlimax as to frustrate the most ambitious,
It is lined with gray satin like a medium-priced casket, its atmos-
    phere is faintly morticious.
It is a day oppressive as asthma,
A day on which you want to call up the blood bank and ask them
    to return your plasma.
Its hours are as dilatory
As a ten-cent depilatory.
Indeed it is a day subject to such obsecration and obloquy
That I am beginning to feel sorry for it, my knees are getting wob-
    loquy as I strangle a sobloquy.
I am regretful that in discussing the reputation of December
    twenty-sixth I may have said anything to jeopardize it,
So by way of making amends I suggest that from now on we not
    necessarily lionize it, but couldn't we maybe just leopardize
    it?

THE MIDDLE

When I remember bygone days
I think how evening follows morn;
So many I loved were not yet dead,
So many I love were not yet born.

[406]

FOR A GOOD DOG

My little dog ten years ago
Was arrogant and spry,
Her backbone was a bended bow
For arrows in her eye.
Her step was proud, her bark was loud,
Her nose was in the sky,
But she was ten years younger then,
And so, by God, was I.

Small birds on stilts along the beach
Rose up with piping cry,
And as they flashed beyond her reach
I thought to see her fly.
If natural law refused her wings,
That law she would defy,
For she could do unheard-of things,
And so, at times, could I.

Ten years ago she split the air
To seize what she could spy;
Tonight she bumps against a chair,
Betrayed by milky eye.
She seems to pant, Time up, time up!
My little dog must die,
And lie in dust with Hector's pup;
So, presently, must I.

THE PERFECT HUSBAND

He tells you when you've got on too much lipstick,
And helps you with your girdle when your hips stick.

[407]

The Private Dining Room

THE PRIVATE DINING ROOM

Miss Rafferty wore taffeta,
Miss Cavendish wore lavender.
We ate pickerel and mackerel
And other lavish provender.
Miss Cavendish was Lalage,
Miss Rafferty was Barbara.
We gobbled pickled mackerel
And broke the candelabara,
Miss Cavendish in lavender,
In taffeta, Miss Rafferty,
The girls in taffeta lavender,
And we, of course, in mufti.

Miss Rafferty wore taffeta,
The taffeta was lavender,
Was lavend, lavender, lavenderest,
As the wine improved the provender.
Miss Cavendish wore lavender,
The lavender was taffeta.
We boggled mackled pickerel,
And bumpers did we quaffeta.
And Lalage wore lavender,
And lavender wore Barbara,
Rafferta taffeta Cavender lavender
Barbara abracadabra.

Miss Rafferty in taffeta
Grew definitely raffisher.
Miss Cavendish in lavender
Grew less and less stand-offisher.
With Lalage and Barbara
We grew a little pickereled,
We ordered Mumm and Roederer
Because the bubbles tickereled.

But lavender and taffeta
Were gone when we were soberer.
I haven't thought for thirty years
Of Lalage and Barbara.

PEEKABOO, I ALMOST SEE YOU

Middle-aged life is merry, and I love to lead it,
But there comes a day when your eyes are all right but your arm
    isn't long enough to hold the telephone book where you can
    read it,
And your friends get jocular, so you go to the oculist,
And of all your friends he is the joculist,
So over his facetiousness let us skim,
Only noting that he has been waiting for you ever since you said
    Good evening to his grandfather clock under the impression
    that it was him,
And you look at his chart and it says SHRDLU QWERTYOP, and
    you say Well, why SHRDNTLU QWERTYOP? and he says
    one set of glasses won't do.
You need two,
One for reading Erle Stanley Gardner's Perry Mason and Keats's
    "Endymion" with,
And the other for walking around without saying Hello to strange
    wymion with.
So you spend your time taking off your seeing glasses to put on your
    reading glasses, and then remembering that your reading
    glasses are upstairs or in the car,
And then you can't find your seeing glasses again because without
    them on you can't see where they are.
Enough of such mishaps, they would try the patience of an ox,
I prefer to forget both pairs of glasses and pass my declining years
    saluting strange women and grandfather clocks.

CORRECTION: *EVE* DELVED AND *ADAM* SPAN

The ladies of the garden club
Are in the other room,
And, fed on tea and sandwiches,
Their pretty fancies bloom,
I hear their gentle treble hubbub,
The ladies of the garden clubbub.

The ladies of the garden club,
Their words are firm and sure,
They know the lore of lime and mulch,
The poetry of manure.
Each spring they beautify our suburb,
The ladies of the garden cluburb.

Dear ladies of the garden club,
I love your natural zeal,
Your verdant thumbs, your canvas gloves,
The pads on which you kneel,
But I hear you making plans involving
Husbands in gardening instead of golfing.

Between the outer door and me
The flower ladies sit.
I'm frantic-footed, blind, and trapped,
Like mole in compost pit,
One timorous masculine minutia,
Caught between baby's-breath and fuchsia.

The air is sweet with talk of bulbs,
And phlox and mignonettes;
Arrangements drape the drawer that holds
My only cigarettes.
Would I had courage for an end run
Round herbaceous border and rhododendron!

Ranunculus can a prison make,
And hyacinth a cell;
I barely glimpse a patch of sky
Through wreath of immortelle.
And thus are fulfilled the baleful prophecies
Concerning men who are at home instead of their offices.

MY TRIP DAORBA

I have just returned from a foreign tour,
But ask me not what I saw, because I am not sure.
Not being a disciplinarian like Father Day,
I saw everything the wrong way,
Because of one thing about Father Day I am sure,
Which is that he would not have ridden backwards so that the little
Days could ride forwards on their foreign tour.
Indeed I am perhaps the only parent to be found
Who saw Europe, or eporuE, as I think of it, the wrong way round.
I added little to my knowledge of the countryside but much to my
reputation for docility
Riding backwards through ecnarF and ylatI.
I am not quite certain,
But I think in siraP I saw the ervuoL, the rewoT leffiE, and the
Cathedral of emaD ertoN.
I shall remember ecnerolF forever,
For that is where I backed past the house where etnaD wrote the
"onrefnI," or ydemoC eniviD, and twisted my neck admiring
the bridges across the onrA reviR.
In emoR I glimpsed the muroF and the nacitaV as in a mirror in
the fog,
While in ecineV I admired the ecalaP s'egoD as beheld from the
steerage of an alodnoG.
So I find conditions overseas a little hard to judge,
Because all I know is what I saw retreating from me as I rode
backwards in compartments in the niart and in carriages sitting on the taes-pmuj.

THE ANNIVERSARY

A marriage aged one
Is hardly begun;
A fling in the sun,
But it's hardly begun;
A green horse,
A stiff course,
And leagues to be run.

A marriage aged five
Is coming alive.
Watch it wither and thrive;
Though it's coming alive,
You must guess,
No or yes,
If it's going to survive.

A marriage aged ten
Is a hopeful Amen;
It's pray for it then,
And mutter Amen,
As the names
Of old flames
Sound again and again.

At twenty a marriage
Discovers its courage.
This year do not disparage,
It is comely in courage;
Past the teens,
And blue jeans,
It's a promising marriage.

Yet before twenty-one
It has hardly begun.

[415]

How tall in the sun,
Yet hardly begun!
But once come of age,
Pragmatically sage,
Oh, blithe to engage
Is sweet marri-age.

Tilt a twenty-first cup
To a marriage grown up,
Now sure and mature,
And securely grown up.
Raise twenty-one cheers
To the silly young years,
While I sit out the dance
With my dearest of dears.

ALL, ALL ARE GONE,
THE OLD FAMILIAR QUOTATIONS

Who was born too soon? I will tell you who was born too soon:
    Francis Bacon, Baron Verulam.
Therefore he could not ask his friends, *Why is Charles Lamb like*
    Baltimore, and supply his own answer, *Because he is deep in*
    the heart of Mary Lamb.
Who was born too late? I will tell you without further parley:
It was I, because I cannot remember whether it was Charles Lamb
    or who, who on the death of his last nearest and dearest pa-
    thetically exclaimed, *Now there is no one left to call me*
    Charlie.
I am always getting entangled in such mnemonic snarls,
But from internal evidence it was obviously someone named
    Charles,
So it couldn't have been Scrooge or Marley.
Nor could it have been Charles II, because there was always some-
    body to call him Charlie.

It would have been duck soup or pie or jam

If he had said, *There is no one left to call me Elia,* then I would
have known it was Lamb.

If I could but spot a conclusion, I should race to it,

But Charles is such a simple name that I can't put a face to it.

Still, I shouldn't complain, since it is its simplicity that gives it its
pathos;

There would be no poignancy in saying, *There is no one left to call
me Charlemagne or Lancelot or Athos.*

People prefer the simple to the grandiose,

And I do not believe that even in an antique land anybody would
sympathize with anybody who went around saying, *There is
no one left to call me Ozymandias.*

THE HAPPY ENDING OF MR. TRAIN

Once there was a man named Mr. Train who wasn't called Choo-
choo, which in itself is odd.

Furthermore, he knew a Mr. Rhodes who wasn't called Dusty, and
a Mr. Sloan who wasn't called Tod.

And they felt very unpopular not to be called Tod and Dusty and
Choo-choo,

Because this was back in the days when if you were popular you
were called Stinky or Baldy or the Tennessee Shad, and chicle
had just replaced tobacco as the new chew.

Well, of their unpopularity they grew wearier and wearier,

Until they got together and decided that they were unpopular because they were superior,

And Mr. Sloan was asked by Mr. Rhodes, and Mr. Train, who kept
going CHOO-choo, CHOO-choo, CHOO-choo, choo-CHOO,

Just how superior are YOU?

And Mr. Sloan replied that even as a child he had been familiar
with Homer's *Iliad* and Xenophon's *Anabasis,*

And he knew that the classical word for a clump of trees was coppice, so that he always went over the river and into the clump
of trees to play coppice and robberses,

And Mr. Rhodes and Mr. Train said You are still unpopular and
    alone,
You are not Tod, or even 's Liniment, you are still just Mr. Sloan.
And the aesthetic Mr. Rhodes boasted, I am superior because to
    my fiancée who to marry me was waiting until I got a steady
    job I said It's not too good, it's truly too bad you waited,
Because I did have a steady job teaching Art for seven years, but
    Art just graduated.
And Mr. Sloan retired at once to his coppices and bosky abodes,
Murmuring, No Dusty he, nor even the Colossus of, he was born,
    lived, and will die, as Mr. Rhodes.
But Mr. Train, he ain't say nuffin'
Just set on de sidin', a-tootin' and a-puffin'.

THE CALENDAR–WATCHERS
or
WHAT'S SO WONDERFUL ABOUT BEING
A PATRIARCH?

I'm like a backward berry
Unripened on the vine,
For all my friends are fifty
And I'm only forty-nine.

My friends are steeped in wisdom,
Like senators they go,
In the light of fifty candles,
And one on which to grow.

How can I cap their sallies,
Or top their taste in wine?
Matched with the worldly fifties,
What chance has forty-nine?

Behold my old companions,
My playmates and my peers,

Remote on the Olympus
Of half a hundred years!

These grave and reverend seniors,
They call me Little Man,
They pat my head jocosely
And pinch my cheek of tan.

Why must I scuff my loafers
And grin a schoolboy grin?
Is not my waist as ample?
Is not my hair as thin?

When threatened with a rumba,
Do I not seek the bar?
And am I not the father
Of a freshman at Bryn Mawr?

O, wad some pawky power
Gie me a gowden giftie,
I'd like to stop at forty-nine,
But pontificate like fifty.

I'M A PLEASURE TO SHOP FOR

Mine is a dauntless spirit, meaning a spirit that is hard to daunt;
Therefore, since nobody gives me Christmas presents any more, I
    shall console myself by compiling a list of Christmas pres-
    ents that I do not want.
I do not want a lamp made out of an umbrella stand, or a coffee
    table made out of an old wagon wheel, or a fire screen made
    out of a leftover piece of trellis,
Or, indeed, anything made out of, or to look like, anything ellis.
I do not want a novel written by a young genius in the earnest be-
    lief that nothing awful has ever happened before to anyone
    but him, certainly not to us dowdy duffers and stodgy codgers,

Nor tickets to the new musical by the smart boys who think they have discovered the secret of Hammerstein and Rodgers.

Since I am crazy about harshness and unpleasant aftertaste, I do not want a milder, less irritating cigarette, no matter how scientific the tests,

Nor an evening with friends watching the TV personality girls whom I can only think of irreverently as Community Chests.

I do not want a squirrel tail or a Confederate flag to dangle from the aerial of my car,

Or a picture window through which better to view my neighbor's picture window or the adjacent abattoir.

For me, please, no bottled Martinis,

No sweetbreads, no cottage cheese with or without chives, no blinis in sour cream, indeed, neither sour cream no blinis.

If you will just not come across with any one of the above, and make it snappy,

You will also make one dear old gentleman's Christmas very, very happy.

A CAUTION TO EVERYBODY

Consider the auk;

Becoming extinct because he forgot how to fly, and could only walk.

Consider man, who may well become extinct

Because he forgot how to walk and learned how to fly before he thinked.

I DIDN'T SAY A WORD
or
WHO CALLED THAT PICCOLO PLAYER
A FATHER?

A man could be granted to live a dozen lives,

And he still wouldn't understand daughters and wives.

It may be because sometimes their ears are pierced for earrings,

But they have the most eccentric hearings.
Their hearings are in fact so sensitive
That you frequently feel reprehensive.
At home, for instance, when near you,
Nobody can hear you.
After your most brilliant fireside or breakfast-table chats you can
count on two fingers the responses you will have got:
Either, Don't mumble, dear, or, more simply, What?
I suppose if you're male and parental
You get used to being treated mental,
But you'd feel less psychically distant
If they weren't so inconsistent,
Because if you open your mouth in a hotel or a restaurant their
eardrums quiver at every decibel,
And their embarrassment is almost, if not quite, inexprecibel.
Their eyes signal What's cooking? at you,
And their lips hiss, Shush, Daddy, everybody's looking at you!
Now, I realize that old age is a thing of beauty,
Because I have read Cicero's *De Senectute,*
But I prefer to approach senility in my own way, so I'll thank no-
body to rush me,
By which I mean specifically that my voice in a tearoom is no
louder than anybody else's, so why does everybody have to
shush me?

CALLING SPRING VII–MMMC

As an old traveler, I am indebted to paper-bound thrillers,
Because you travel faster from Cleveland to Terre Haute when
you travel with a lapful of victims and killers.
I am by now an authority on thumbprints and fingerprints and
even kneeprints,
But there is one mystery I have never been able to solve in certain
of my invaluable reprints.
I am happily agog over their funerals, which are always satisfac-
torily followed by exhumerals,

But I can't understand why so many of them carry their copyright
lines in Roman numerals.

I am just as learned as can be,

But if I want to find out when a book was first published, I have
to move my lips and count on my fingers to translate Copyright MCMXXXIII into Copyright 1933.

I have a horrid suspicion

That something lies behind the publisher's display of erudition.

I may be oversensitive to clues,

But I detect a desire to obfuscate and confuse.

Do they think that because a customer cannot translate
MCMXXXIII into 1933 because he is not a classical scholar,

He will therefore assume the book to have been first published yesterday and will therefore sooner lay down his XXV cents or
I/IV of a dollar?

Or do they, straying equally far from the straight and narrow,

Think that the scholarly will snatch it because the Roman copyright line misleads him to believe it the work of Q. Horatius
Flaccus or P. Virgilius Maro?

Because anybody can make a mistake when dealing with MCMs
and XLVs and things, even Jupiter, ruler of gods and men;

All the time he was going around with IO he pronounced it Ten.

EVERYBODY'S MIND TO ME A KINGDOM IS
or
A GREAT BIG WONDERFUL WORLD IT'S

Some melodies are popular as well as classical, which I suppose
makes them popsicles,

And some poems are part William Cullen Bryant and part Nick
Kenny which makes them thanatopsicles,

And to some people Wisconsin is what Guinevere was to Launce-
lot,

And if they are away from it they are Wisconsolate.

Some naturalists know why the sphinx is sphinxlike and the griffin
    is griffiny,
And some couples are so wealthy that even their tiffs are from
    Tiffany.
Some Angeleno socialites fine each other a dollar
If they say La Jolla,
And give each other a Picasso or a Goya
For pronouncing it La Hoya.
Why should not I pick up a masterpiece or a coin?
I will not longer say Des Moines,
I shall sail into the C. B. & Q. ticket office like a swan,
And ask for a lower to Day Mwahn.
This I shall do because I am a conscientious man, when I throw
    rocks at sea birds I leave no tern unstoned,
I am a meticulous man, and when I portray baboons I leave no
    stern untoned,
I am a man who values the fitness of things above notoriety and
    pelf,
Which is why I am happy I heard the cockney postmaster say to a
    doctor who was returning a leprechaun to Glocca Morra in
    an open envelope, Physician, seal thy h'elf.

NEXT!

I thought that I would like to see
The early world that used to be,
That mastodonic mausoleum,
The Natural History Museum.
At midnight in the vasty hall
The fossils gathered for a ball.
High above notices and bulletins
Loomed up the Mesozoic skeletons.
Aroused by who knows what elixirs,
They ground along like concrete mixers.
They bowed and scraped in reptile pleasure,
And then began to tread the measure.

There were no drums or saxophones,
But just the clatter of their bones,
A rolling, rattling carefree circus
Of mammoth polkas and mazurkas.
Pterodactyls and brontosauruses
Sang ghostly prehistoric choruses.
Amid the megalosauric wassail
I caught the eye of one small fossil.
Cheer up, old man, he said, and winked —
It's kind of fun to be extinct.

THEY WON'T BELIEVE, ON NEW YEAR'S EVE, THAT NEW YEAR'S DAY WILL COME WHAT MAY

How do I feel today? I feel as unfit as an unfiddle,
And it is the result of a certain turbulence in the mind and an un-
certain burbulence in the middle.
What was it anyway, that angry thing that flew at me?
I am unused to banshees crying Boo at me.
Your wife can't be a banshee,
Or can she?
Of course, some wives become less fond
When you're bottled in bond.
My Uncle George, in lavender-scented Aunt Edna's day,
If he had a glass of beer on Saturday night, he didn't dare come
home till the following Wednesday.
I see now that he had hit upon the ideal idea,
The passage of time, and plenty of it, is the only marital panacea.
Ah, if the passage of time were backward, and last night I'd been
a child again, this morning I'd be fragrant with orange juice,
Instead of reeking of pinch-bottle foreign juice;
But if I should turn out to be a child again, what would life hold
for me?
The woman I love would be too old for me.
There's only one solution to my problem, a hair of the dog, or
maybe a couple of hairs;

Then if she doesn't get mad at me life will be peaceful, and if she
   does, it will show she really cares.

CHANGE HERE FOR WICHITA FALLS
or
HAS ANYBODY SEEN MY WANDERLUST?

Luxury travel is something for which I pant;
But can I afford it? No, I can't.
Would I had studied Oriental languages as a pup;
I am always going to places where the timetable says Read UP.
Trains that me back to ole Virginny or ole Indianny carry,
They have always just dropped off the diner at Harrisburg or
   Wilkes-Barre, which I always get confused with John Wilkes-
   Barre.
Of streamliners and stratodomers I have heard gladsome tidings,
But to me they are simply blinding streaks to make way for which
   I have spent innumerable hours on rusty sidings.
To some people travel conjures up a picture of luggage plastered
   with glamorous labels and tags;
To me it is a picture of a remote station platform with no porters
   and taxis, just me and my sacroiliac and three heavy bags.
I am told that the comforts in modern hotels are stunning;
My experience is that a hotel is a place with the elevator out of or-
   der where you can only wash one hand at a time because
   there is no stopper for the drain and you have to keep squeez-
   ing the handles of the faucet to keep the water running.
That is the hard way to get an ablution;
It reminds me of the visitor to the Chinese zoo who asked what
   language the aquatic carnivora talked, Pidgin English? and
   the keeper replied, No, Otter Confucian.

DON'T LOOK FOR THE SILVER LINING, JUST WAIT FOR IT

The rabbit loves his hoppity and the wallaby loves his hippity.

I love my serendipity.

Let none look askance;

Serendipity is merely the knack of making happy and unexpected discoveries by chance.

Only yesterday I was bored by a bore — there is no topic that he isn't inept on it —

And when I pointed out a piece of chewing gum on the sidewalk, he was too busy talking to listen, so I soon made the happy and unexpected discovery that he had stepped on it.

It was serendipity when a recent hostess of mine in Philadelphia apologized for serving ham and eggs because she had forgotten to order scrapple,

Just as it was when I found a bow tie I could wear that didn't rise and fall with my Adam's apple.

Also when I found a hole in my pocket which I had tickets for a harp recital in, or in which I had tickets for a harp recital, to put it properer,

So instead of the harp recital we had to see the Marx Brothers in *A Night at the Opera.*

If your coat catches on a branch just as you are about to slip over a precipice precipitous,

That's serendipitous,

But when you happily and unexpectedly discover that you don't have to go to the dentist or the chiropodist,

That's serendopitist.

THE ASTIGMATIC NATURALIST

THE CATERPILLAR

I find among the poems of Schiller
No mention of the caterpillar,

[426]

Nor can I find one anywhere
In Petrarch or in Baudelaire,
So here I sit in extra session
To give my personal impression.
The caterpillar, as it's called,
Is often hairy, seldom bald;
It looks as if it never shaves;
When as it walks, it walks in waves;
And from the cradle to the chrysalis
It's utterly speechless, songless, whistleless.

THE TOUCAN

The toucan's profile is prognathous,
Its person is a thing of bathos.
If even I can tell a toucan
I'm reasonably sure that you can.

THE PLATYPUS

I like the duck-billed platypus
Because it is anomalous.
I like the way it raises its family,
Partly birdly, partly mammaly.
I like its independent attitude.
Let no one call it a duck-billed platitude.

THE HAMSTER

There is not much about the hamster
To stimulate the epigramster.
The essence of his simple story,
He populates the laboratory,
Then leaves his offspring in the lurch,
Martyrs to medical research.
Was he as bright as people am,
New York would be New Hamsterdam.

TWO GOES INTO TWO ONCE, IF YOU CAN
GET IT THERE

All my life I have been a witness of things,
Among which I keep witnessing the eternal unfitness of things.
Daily it is my wont
To notice how things that were designed to fit each other, don't.
Getting a cigarette into a cigarette-holder is like the round hole
    and the square peg,
And getting the cork back into the vermouth bottle is like reinsert-
    ing the cuckoo in the egg.
Why is the card-case always just a smidgin smaller than the deck?
Why does it take a $15\frac{3}{4}$ collar to encircle a $15\frac{1}{2}$ neck?
Experience is indeed a teacher, and I have learned this fact from
    it,
That no suitcase is large enough to recontain the clothes you just
    unpacked from it.
No wonder the grapes set on edge the teeth of the little foxes;
The minute you buy a dozen silver or brocade or leather match-
    box holders the match-box makers change the size of the
    boxes.
I am baffled, I weave between Scylla and Charybdis, between a
    writ of replevin and a tort;
I shall console myself with the reflection that even in this world,
    ever perverse and ever shifting, two pints still make one ca-
    vort.

WHY THE POSTMAN HAS TO RING TWICE
or
YELLOW ENVELOPE, WHERE HAVE YOU GONE?

Captain Ahab's desire was the White Whale.
My desire is to receive a telegram by telegraph messenger and not
    by telephone or mail.
If I should be asked, What hath God wrought? by Samuel F. B.
    Morse's ghost,

I should reply, He hath wrought the Telephone Company and the
United States Post,
And I am still trying to read the riddle
Of how the Telegraph Company got that cozy seat in the middle.
Oh Company uncertain, coy, and hard to please,
In the unprogressive olden times they relied on reliable elderly
boys with bicycles and puttees,
But now a telegram seems to be something that if they can't mail
it or phone it,
They disown it.
You stand convicted of impudence and effrontry
If you wish a telegram delivered, not mailed, to a person without
a telephone in either the city or, what they never heard of,
the country.
Do not try to appease me, I am unappeasable,
For every time I send an important telegram to be personally deliv-
ered I am inevitably notified just too late next day that deliv-
ery was impractical and unfeasible.
Telegraph Company, you are the darling of my heart, I adore you,
In token of which I present you with a new slogan: Don't write,
telegraph; we will mail it for you.

THE WILD JACKASS

Have ever you harked to the jackass wild,
Which scientists call the onager?
It sounds like the laugh of a backward child,
Or a hepcat on a harmonica.
But do not sneer at the jackass wild,
There is method in his hee-haw,
For with maidenly blush and accent mild
The jenny-ass answers, shee-haw.

THE TORTOISE

Come crown my brows with leaves of myrtle;
I know the tortoise is a turtle.
Come carve my name in stone immortal;
I know the turtoise is a tortle;
I know to my profound despair;
I bet on one to beat a hare.
I also know I'm now a pauper
Because of its tortley turtley torpor.

THE MULES

In the world of mules
There are no rules.

THE CUCKOO

Cuckoos lead Bohemian lives,
They fail as husbands and as wives,
Therefore they cynically disparage
Everybody else's marriage.

THE BIRDS

Puccini was Latin, and Wagner Teutonic,
And birds are incurably philharmonic.
The skylark sings a roundelay,
The crow sings "The Road to Mandalay,"
The nightingale sings a lullaby
And the sea gull sings a gullaby.
That's what shepherds listened to in Arcadia
Before some one invented TV's and radia.

THE SWAN

Scholars call the masculine swan a cob;
I call him a narcissistic snob.
He looks in the mirror over and over,
And claims to have never heard of Pavlova.

THE VOLUBLE WHEEL CHAIR

When you roll along admiring the view,
And everyone drives too fast but you;
When people not only ignore your advice,
But complain that you've given it to them twice;
When you babble of putts you nearly holed,
By gad, sir,
You are getting old.

When for novels you lose your appetite
Because writers don't write what they used to write;
When by current art you are unbeguiled,
And pronounce it the work of an idiot child;
When cacophonous music leaves you cold,
By gad, sir,
You are getting old.

When you twist the sheets from night to morn
To recall when a cousin's daughter was born;
When youngsters mumble and won't speak up,
And your dog dodders, who was a pup;
When the modern girl seems a hussy bold,
By gad, sir,
You are getting old.

When you scoff at feminine fashion trends;
When strangers resemble absent friends;
When you start forgetting the neighbors' names

And remembering bygone football games;
When you only drop in at the club to scold,
By gad, sir,
You are getting old.

But when you roar at the income tax,
And the slippery bureaucratic hacks,
And the ancient political fishlike smell,
And assert that the world is going to hell,
Why you are not old at all, at all;
By gad, sir,
You are on the ball.

THE CHILD IS FATHER TO THE MAN,
BUT WITH MORE AUTHORITY

Once there were some children and they were uninterested in
    chores,
And they never picked anything up or put anything back or brought
    anything in from out-of-doors.
They didn't want to take care of anything, just to play with it,
And their parents let them get away with it.
Little did they know that Nemesis
Was on the premises.
Their regrets were at first scant
When they were left alone on their island summer home because
    their parents were called away by the convalescence of a
    wealthy aunt.
They prepared to take advantage of nobody being around,
And this is what they found,
This is how they were hoist with their own petards,
There wasn't a deck with more than fifty-one cards,
And when they tried to play the handsome phonograph with which
    they were equipped,
The records were either lost, warped or chipped,

There were bows but no arrows, and bats and gloves but no ball,
And the untethered rowboat had drifted beyond recall,
And when they were wet the only towels were those strewn on the
    bathroom floor where moisture lingers,
And when they were cold they couldn't light a fire because all the
    matches had been used by people seeing how far down they
    would burn without burning their fingers.
Such experiences certainly taught them a lesson, and when their
    parents returned to their native heath,
Why, the first thing these children did was to leave the window
    open so it rained in on the piano, and go to bed without
    brushing their teeth.

THE VISIT

She welcomes him with pretty impatience
And a cry of Greetings and salutations!
To which remark, no laggard, he
Ripostes with a Long time no see.
Recovering her poise full soon,
She bids him Anyhoo, sit ye doon,
And settling by the fireside,
He chuckles, Thank you, kind sir, she cried.
Snug as a bug, the cup he waits
That cheers but not inebriates.
She offers him a truly ducal tea,
Whipped up, she says, with no diffewclty.
A miracle, if I didn't know you,
He says — It only shows to go you.
Eying her o'er the fragrant brew,
He tells her her smile is picturescue,
And now he whispers, a bit pajamaly,
That he's fed to the teeth with his whole fam damily,
Perhaps she'll forgive an old man's crotchet
And visit Bermuda on his yachat.

[433   ]

She says she might, despite Dame Rumor,
Because he is a who than whom none is whomer.
He sidles close, but no cigar —
Until the yachat, au reservoir.

A DOG'S BEST FRIEND IS HIS ILLITERACY

It has been well said that quietness is what a Grecian urn is the still
unravished bride of,
And that a door is what a dog is perpetually on the wrong side of.
I may add that a sachet is what many a housewife's linen is fra-
grantly entrusted to,
But that a cliché is what a dog owner must eventually get adjusted
to.
What does the visitor say when your dog greets him with South-
ern hospitality and salutes him all kissin'-cousiny?
He says, He smells my dog on me, doesn't he?
And he asks, How old is he, and you say Twelve, and he appraises
Spot with the eye of an antiquarian,
And says, Seven twelves are eighty something, why Spot in human
terms you're an octogenarian,
But these two bromides are just the rattle before the strike,
Because then he says it's funny but he's noticed how often dogs
and their masters look alike.
Such are the comments faced by dog owners from Peoria to Pesha-
war,
And frequently from a man who in canine terms is 322 years old,
and he is the spit and image of his own Chihuahua.
The only escape is to have something instead of dogs but whatever
I substituted I should probably err,
And if I ended up with raccoons every guest would turn out to be
a raccoonteur.

EHEU! FUGACES
or
WHAT A DIFFERENCE A LOT OF DAYS MAKE

When I was seventeen or so,
I scoffed at money-grubbers.
I had a cold contempt for dough,
And I wouldn't wear my rubbers.
No aspirin I took for pains,
For pests no citronella,
And in the Aprilest of rains
I carried no umbrella.

When I was young I was Sidney Carton,
Proudly clad in a Spartan tartan.
Today I'd be, if I were able,
Just healthy, wealthy, and comfortable.

When I was young I would not yield
To comforters and bed socks,
In dreams I covered center field
For the Giants or the Red Sox.
I wished to wander hence and thence,
From diamond mine to gold field,
Or piloting a Blitzen Benz,
Outdistance Barney Oldfield.

When I subscribed to *The Youth's Companion*
I longed to become a second D'Artagnan.
Today I desire a more modest label:
He's healthy, wealthy, and comfortable.

When I was pushing seventeen,
I hoped to bag a Saracen;
Today should one invade the scene,
I'd simply find it embaracen.

[435   ]

Ah, Postumus, no wild duck I,
But just a waddling puddle duck,
So here's farewell to the open sky
From a middle-aged fuddy-duddle duck.

When I was young I was Roland and Oliver,
Nathan Hale and Simón Bolívar.
Today I would rather side step trouble,
And be healthy, wealthy, and comfortubble.

EVERYBODY WANTS TO GET INTO
THE BAEDEKER

Most travelers eavesdrop
As unintentionally as autumn leaves drop,
Which brings up a question that confronts every conscientious
    traveler:
Should he, or should he not, of overheard misinformation be an
    unraveler?
The dear little old lady in front of you asks, What river is that, is
    it the Swanee or the Savannah?
And somebody who has no idea firmly says, It's the Potomac. It
    happens to be the Susquehanna.
The visiting Englishman asks, What is that mountain, and some-
    body yells, Pike's Peak! into his ear.
It isn't. It's Mt. Rainier.
Can one oneself of responsibility disembarrass
When one hears a fellow passenger being assured that the Île de
    France sails right up the Seine to Paris?
What is the etiquette
When one hears an eager sight-seer being informed that Green-
    wich Village is in Connecticut?
It is my experience that people who volunteer information are peo-
    ple who don't know the Eiffel Tower from the Tower of Pisa,
Or Desdemona from the Mona Lisa.

[436]

I am convinced that they have learned their geography through drawing mustaches on girls on travel posters,
And have done their own traveling exclusively on roller coasters.
What is that, madam? How do you get from 42nd Street and Broadway to Times Square?
Sorry, madam, but it's impossible to get from here to there.

THE WENDIGO *

The Wendigo,
The Wendigo!
Its eyes are ice and indigo!
Its blood is rank and yellowish!
Its voice is hoarse and bellowish!
Its tentacles are slithery,
And scummy,
Slimy,
Leathery!
Its lips are hungry blubbery,
And smacky,
Sucky,
Rubbery!
The Wendigo,
The Wendigo!
I saw it just a friend ago!
Last night it lurked in Canada;
Tonight, on your veranada!
As you are lolling hammockwise
It contemplates you stomachwise.
You loll,
It contemplates,
It lollops.
The rest is merely gulps and gollops.

* WENDIGO: In the mythology of the northern Algonquians, an evil spirit; one of a fabulous tribe of cannibals.
WEBSTER'S UNABRIDGED DICTIONARY

MR. BETTS'S MIND A KINGDOM IS

Do you know my friend Mr. Betts?
He claims he forgets.
When urged by Mrs. Betts to tell you about their trip to California
    he says he has no memory,
He is in a dilemma, he looks dilemmary.
He looks like a high-school music teacher substituting at the last
    minute for Iturbi,
And then he gives you a precise blow by blow, palm tree by palm
    tree, movie star by movie star account, starting at the Grand
    Central and finishing with an appreciation of the waitresses'
    rear elevation at the Brown Derby.
My friend Mr. Betts
Claims he forgets.
When asked by Mrs. Betts to tell you about that radio program
    that made her laugh, she thought she'd smother,
He says everything goes in one ear and out the other,
After which he takes the floor like Winston Churchill,
And re-creates the entire half hour from the first joke about the
    ungainly spinster who can't get a man to the final commer-
    chill.

Do you know my friend Mr. Betts?
I wish I could remember as accurately as he forgets.

THE STRANGE CASE OF THE CAUTIOUS
MOTORIST

Have you read the biography of Mr. Schwellenbach? You can miss
    it if you try.
Mr. Schwellenbach didn't have much to live for, but he didn't
    want to die.
Statistics of automobile fatalities filled his brain,
And he never drove over 25 miles an hour, and always, I regret to
    say, in the left-hand lane.

Whenever he stopped for a red light he cut off the ignition, put on
    the hand brake, locked all the doors, checked his license and
    registration cards, and looked in the glove compartment to
    see if he had mice,
So when the light turned green everybody behind him had to wait
    while he de-moused the car, reassured himself that he was
    driving legally, unlocked the doors, released the hand brake,
    reignited the ignition, pressed the wrong button and turned
    on Bing Crosby instead of the motor, and the light turned
    from green to red to green thrice.
Every autumn with the rains
Mr. Schwellenbach bought a new pair of chains.
He kept a record of every lethal blowout in the Western Hemi-
    sphere since 1921 in his files,
And he turned in his tires for new ones every 750 miles.
Well, he was driving on his new tires at 25 miles an hour in the
    left-hand lane of a dual highway last week, was Mr. Schwel-
    lenbach,
And a car coming the other way owned by a loan shark who had
    bought his old tires cheap had a blowout and jumped the di-
    viding line and knocked him to hellenbach.

THE UNWINGED ONES

I don't travel on planes.
I travel on trains.
Once in a while, on trains,
I see people who travel on planes.
Every once in a while I'm surrounded
By people whose planes have been grounded.
I'm enthralled by their air-minded snobbery,
Their exclusive hobnobbery.
They feel that they have to explain
How they happen to be on a train,
For even in Drawing Room A

They seem to feel déclassé.
So they sit with portentous faces
Clutching their attaché cases.
They grumble and fume about how
They'd have been in Miami by now.
By the time that they're passing through Rahway
They should be in Havana or Norway,
And they strongly imply that perhaps,
Since they're late, the world will collapse.
Sometimes on the train I'm surrounded
By people whose planes have been grounded.
That's the only trouble with trains;
When it fogs, when it smogs, when it rains,
You get people from planes.

WHAT IS BIBBIDI–BOBBIDI–BOO IN SANSKRIT?

When people tell me French is difficult, I show my dimple.
French is simple.
My pen is cosmopolitan, not parochial.
I am at home in French either classical or collochial.
I can pronounce *filet mignon* even while chewing it,
And I can and will fluently translate popular songs such as "Everybody's Doing It."
Tout le monde est faisant le, faisant le, faisant le,
Tout le monde est faisant le,
Faisant quoi?
Dindon pas!
Vois ce ragtime couple débonnaire,
Vois-les jeter leurs épaules en air,
C'est un hibou,
Un hibou, un hibou,
Où?
I think that even Mr. Berlin would agree that this has life and movement,

And that the few changes are an improvement.

That ragtime couple, for example, instead of just being vaguely over there,

They are now obviously in some expensive club, they are debonair.

And the substitution of *c'est un hibou, un hibou, un hibou* (it's an owl, it's an owl, it's an owl) for *c'est un ours, c'est un ours, c'est un ours* (it's a bear, it's a bear, it's a bear) —

That is a veritable *coup de tonnerre,*

That is a truly superior brand of merchandise,

Because in French *ours* (bear) might be confused with *oursin* (sea urchin) and what would a debonair owl-loving ragtime couple want with a fishy batch of sea-urchindise?

I feel I have built myself a monument of more than bricks and mortar,

And, having gained the gratitude of Mr. Berlin, I am now leafing through the works of Mr. Oscar Hammerstein and Mr. Cole Porter.

YOU CAN BE A REPUBLICAN, I'M A GENOCRAT

Oh, "rorty" was a mid-Victorian word
Which meant "fine, splendid, jolly,"
And often to me it has reoccurred
In moments melancholy.
For instance, children, I think it rorty
To be with people over forty.

I can't say which, come eventide,
More tedious I find;
Competing with the juvenile stride,
Or meeting the juvenile mind.
So I think it rorty, yes, and nifty,
To be with people over fifty.

The pidgin talk the youthful use
Bypasses conversation.

I can't believe the code they choose
Is a means of communication.
Oh to be with people over sixty
Despite their tendency to prolixty!

The hours a working parent keeps
Mean less than Latin to them,
Wherefore they disappear in jeeps
Till three and four A.M.
Oh, to be with people you pour a cup for
Instead of people you have to wait up for!

I've tried to read young mumbling lips
Till I've developed a slant-eye,
And my hearing fails at the constant wails
Of, If I can't, why can't I?
Oh, to be beside a septuagenarian,
Silent upon a peak in Darien!

They don't know Hagen from Bobby Jones,
They never heard Al Smith,
Even Red Grange is beyond their range,
And Dempsey is a myth.
Oh golly, to gabble upon the shoulder
Of someone my own age, or even older!

I'm tired of defining hadn't oughts
To opposition mulish,
The thoughts of youth are long long thoughts,
And Jingo! Aren't they foolish!
All which is why, in case you've wondered
I'd like a companion aged one hundred.

FABLES BULFINCH FORGOT

When Lord Byron wrote so glowingly of the isles of Greece
It was not mere coincidence or caprice.
Nobody than Lord Byron could have been sorrier
About the death of a heroic Grecian warrior,
But nobody after so short a period
Could find consolation in the company of a nymph or a Nereid,
So all praise to the nymphs of the isles of Greece.
May their tribe increase.
But their tribe won't increase if they all behave like a nymph
    named Chloë,
Who lived on the southernmost isle of Greece where it is swampy,
    not snowy.
Chloë caught the attention of Zeus,
And he slipped away from the banquet hall mumbling some ri-
    diculous excuse,
And when Hera called after him to come back, she knew what it
    meant when he got all skittish and scampery,
He said he'd be back for breakfast, he just had to see a mortal
    about a lamprey,
And he didn't want to tell a lie so he disguised himself as a
    lamprey-fisherman but he couldn't find his lamprey-fishing
    clothes,
So aside from his lamprey-spear he was as naked as a narcissus or
    a rose,
And he tracked Chloë through the swamp and offered her his
    heart and a golden chariot, a dandy four-wheeler,
But she refused because she was a Southern nymph, a Hellenic
    Dixiecrat, and she had been taught never to trust a nude
    eeler.

THE THIRTEENTH LABOR OF HERCULES

Some people think the nose of the Sphinx was flattened by Na-
    poleon's cannoneers,

But it wasn't, not by several thousand years.

Credit should go to a person who dressed like Adam and talked like Pericles,

This person being known to us as Hercules and to the illiterate Greeks as Heracles,

And Hercules performed twelve fabulous labors,

Which caused all the inhabitants of Ultima Thule to exclaim Begorra and Bejabers,

And just when he thought he was through with labors he was told by the gods, several of whom were his cousin,

That he must make it a baker's dozen.

They said that all brawn and no brain makes a dull demigod, so on immortality it was no dice

Unless he stumped the Sphinx thrice,

And Hercules said, Well I'll be a duck-billed platypus,

Here is a chance to avenge my friend Oedipus,

And he assumed an expression deceptively pleasant,

And he asked the Sphinx, Who is the heavyweight champion? and she said, Ezzard Charles, and he said, No it ezzant,

And he said, I'll give you another bone to pick at,

Why did Orpheus give up conducting and throw away his baton? and she said, I bet you don't know, either, and he said, Because there were more Bacchantes than he could shake a stick at,

And the Sphinx said, You can't stump me three times in a row, and he said, A house full, a hole full, you cannot catch a bowlful, can you riddle me that without straining?

And she said, Smoke? and Hercules said, No thank you, I'm in training.

From that point

The Sphinx's nose has been out of joint.

MEDUSA AND THE MOT JUSTE

Once there was a Greek divinity of the sea named Ceto and she married a man named Phorcus,

And the marriage must have been pretty raucous;

[444]

Their remarks about which child took after which parent must
 have been full of asperities,
Because they were the parents of the Gorgons, and the Graeae,
 and Scylla, and the dragon that guarded the apples of the
 Hesperides.
Bad blood somewhere.
Today the Gorgons are our topic, and as all schoolboys including
 you and me know,
They were three horrid sisters named Medusa and Euryale and
 Stheno,
But what most schoolboys don't know because they never get be-
 yond their Silas Marners and their Hiawathas,
The Gorgons were not only monsters, they were also highly tal-
 ented authors.
Medusa began it;
She wrote *Forever Granite.*
But soon Stheno and Euryale were writing, too, and they ad-
 dressed her in daily choruses,
Saying we are three literary sisters just like the Brontës so instead
 of Gorgons why can't we be brontësauruses?
Well, Medusa may have been mythical but she wasn't mystical,
She was selfish and egotistical.
She saw wider vistas
Than simply being the sister of her sisters.
She replied, tossing away a petrified Argonaut on whom she had
 chipped a molar,
You two can be what you like, but since I am the big *fromage* in
 this family, I prefer to think of myself as the Gorgon Zola.

LEDA'S FORTUNATE GAFFE

The Greeks called the king of the gods Zeus and the Romans
 called him Jupiter.
Not that the Romans were stupider,
Jupiter being Roman for Zeus Pater, or Zeus the Father,
Which was appropriate, rather.
Zeus Pater is not to be confused with Walter Pater,

Who flourished later.

I don't even know if Walter Pater had a wife,

But I bet he never poured into a lady's room disguised as a shower of gold in his life.

Zeus Pater, on the other hand, was so eager to escape the restraint of his jealous queen that once he nearly killed a guard,

And in order to forward his unsavory amours he impersonated just about everybody except Hildegarde.

One day he tiptoed out through heaven's portal

And picked up the handkerchief of a succulent mortal,

But when he wished to continue the acquaintance, he had run out of impersonations, he had nothing new to go as.

Juno always recognized him and followed him like Ruth after Boaz.

But this mortal happened to be Leda

And she was a great reader,

And when they were the equivalent of introduced,

Instead of Zeus, she thought the name was Proust,

And hey, hey!

The perplexing problem of what to impersonate was solved when she told him how much she admired *Swann's Way.*

HI–HO THE AMBULANCE–O

People on wheels hate people on feet,
It takes two to make a one-way street.
Traffic commissions plan and study,
And nearly every is a body.

EVERYTHING'S HAGGIS IN HOBOKEN
or
SCOTS WHA HAE HAE

That hero my allegiance earns
Who boldly speaks of Robert Burns.

[446]

I have an inexpensive hobby —
Simply not to call him Bobbie.
It's really just as easy as not
Referring to Sir Wally Scott,
But many, otherwise resolute,
When mentioning Burns go coy and cute.
Scholars hip-deep in Homer and Horace
Suddenly turn all doch-an-dorris;
Fine ladies who should pose and purr
Roll out a half-rolled Highland burr;
Conventioneers in littered lobby
Hoist their glasses in praise of Bobbie;
All, all Burns-happy and Bobbie-loopy,
They dandle him like a Scotian kewpie.
I'll brush away like gnats and midges
Those who quote from Bobbies Southey and Bridges;
I will not snap my Hopalong gun
At admirers of Bobbie Stevenson
(To be Bobbied is no worse, I guess,
Than being enshrined as R.L.S.);
I'd even attempt to save from drowning
Maidens who dream of Bobbie Browning;
But of Robert Burns I'm a serious fan,
He wrote like an angel and lived like a man,
And I yearn to shatter a set of crockery
On this condescending Bobbie-sockery.
Well, I'm off, before I break the law,
To read Tommy Hardy and Bernie Shaw.

FATHER, DEAR FATHER, GO JUMP IN THE LAKE
or
YOU'RE COSTLIER THAN YOU THINK

Once there was a man named Mr. Arents,
And he was the severest of parents.

Every time his seven children asked him when they could have a convertible he answered, bye and bye,
And he confiscated all their phonograph records that had songs with people singing, Aye yi aye yi.
He complained that they smoked too many cigarettes,
And he would neither feed nor bathe their pets.
He insulted all their friends at 4 A.M.
By standing at the head of the stairs in his pajamas and remarking, Ahem.
He insisted that they put on their shoes before they ate,
And objected when they scooped the middles out of the rolls and deposited the crust on their plate.
That was the erstwhile Mr. Arents,
The most unreasonable of parents.
You ought to see the new Mr. Arents,
He is a veritable model of forbearance.
He feels that whatever his seven children request,
It behooves him to behave at their behest.
Mr. Arents has had a warning,
Wherefore he brings them seven apples and seven convertibles each morning;
He is currying favor
Against the day his voice begins to quaver;
Any good will that his children may bear him, he wants to pad it,
He wants them to remember him as a right guy when he had it.
He knows that he is now an asset but he fears that all too soon
He will be an elderly liability in a chimney corner slurping porridge from a wooden spoon.
Mr. Arents has recently been told by an annuity salesman something that makes him feel so singular that he has shrunk to Mr. Arent:
Namely, it is easier for one parent to support seven children than for seven children to support one parent.

WHAT'S IN A NAME? SOME LETTER
I ALWAYS FORGET

Not only can I not remember anecdotes that are racy,

But I also can't remember whether the names of my Scottish
friends begin with M-c or M-a-c,

And I can't speak for you, but for myself there is one dilemma
with me in the middle of it,

Which is, is it Katharine with a K or Catherine with a C, and furthermore is it an A or is it an E in the middle of it?

I can remember the races between Man o' War and Sir Barton, and
Épinard and Zev,

But I can't remember whether it's Johnson or Johnston any more
than whether you address a minister as Mr. or Dr. or simply
Rev.

I know a cygnet from a gosling and a coney from a leveret,

But how to distinguish an I-double-T from an E-double-T Everett?

I am familiar with the nature of an oath,

But I get confused between the Eliot with one L and one T, and
the Elliot with two L's and one T, and the Eliott with one L
and two T's, and the Elliott with two of both.

How many of my friendships have lapsed because of an extra T or
a missing L;

Give me a simple name like Taliaferro or Wambsganss or Toporcer
or Joralemon or Mankiewicz that any schoolboy can spell,

Because many former friends thought I was being impolite to them

When it was only because I couldn't remember whether they were
Stuarts with a U or Stewarts with an E-W that I didn't write
to them.

THE STRANGE CASE OF MR. O'BANION'S
COME–UPPANCE

Once there was a man named Mr. O'Banion,
And he was a depressing companion.
He was so cynical

[449]

That it was practically clinical.

He was also a skeptic,

And would never eat a hamburger without first immersing it in antiseptic.

He believed that actresses exist on amours and marijuana,

And that St. George's dragon was really a large iguana.

He stated that every man has his price,

And he was sure that bartenders use the same olive twice.

He was especially derisive of the names of summer cottages,

He said they stuck in his craws, of which he had developed two, and in his epiglottages.

He said there was nothing more fraudulent than a summer cottage's cognomen,

And one day he pointed out to his Scout troup that there were three large opaque billboards between Seaview Villa and the ocean, and that everybody was restless at Dunroamin.

He hinted that at Lilac Lodge you couldn't even raise dandelions, and scoffed that Mon Repos and Beau Sejour would be the last place to find a French menu in,

And just as he remarked that Stuffed Sea Gull would be an apter name for Eagle's Eyrie, he was carried off by an eagle, and it was genuine.

HAND ME DOWN MY OLD SCHOOL
SLIDING PADS
or
THERE'S A HINT OF STRAWBERRY
LEAVES IN THE AIR

This is the outstretched, tentative toe,
The placid paddling into dotage:
To complement the radio
With the library of a summer cottage.

What calmer joy can life afford,
What more can fortune offer, or fame,

Than reading Mrs. Humphry Ward
While listening to the baseball game?

A glimpse of ducal silhouettes,
A flash of electronic science,
As kind hearts clash with coronets —
Also the Cardinals with the Giants.

The heroine's birth is most unusual —
It's three and two on Enos Slaughter.
What would she think of Stanley Musial,
And he of Lady Rose's daughter?

The code of stout King Edward's reign
Conceals outstanding hanky-panky,
Suggesting time and time again
The hidden ball of Eddie Stanky.

Beware, fair child, of how you stray;
Warkworth, that cad, is far too cuddly!
Ah! In the ninth, with two away,
She's rescued by the Duke of Chudleigh!

In a world where even umpires err,
Why scorn the Duchess's stumbling start?
"When she learned at last he needed her,
The dear knowledge filled and tamed her heart."

Oh, bury me where the blue begins,
Where ball meets bat as lord meets lord,
Out where the home team always wins
And virtue is its Humphry Ward.

THE STRANGE CASE OF THE LOVELORN
LETTER WRITER

Dear Miss Dix, I am a young lady of Scandinavian origin, and I
    am in a quandary.
I am not exactly broody, but I am kind of pondery.
I got a twenty-five waist and a thirty-five bust,
And I am going with a chap whose folks are very uppercrust.
He is the intellectual type, which I wouldn't want to disparage,
Because I understand they often ripen into love after marriage,
But here I am all set
For dalliance,
And what do I get?
Shilly-shalliance.
Just when I think he's going to disrobe me with his eyes,
He gets up off of the davenport and sighs.
Every time I let down my hair,
He starts talking to himself or the little man who isn't there.
Every time he ought to be worrying about me,
Why, he's worrying about his mother, that's my mother-in-law
    to be,
And I say let's burn that bridge when we come to it, and he says
    don't I have any sin sense,
His uncle and her live in incense.
Well, with me that's fine,
Let them go to their church and I'll go to mine.
But no, that's not good enough for Mr. Conscience and his mental
    indigestion,
He's got to find two answers for every question.
If a man is a man, a girl to him is a girl, if I correctly rememma,
But to him I am just a high pathetical dilemma.
What I love him in spite of
Is, a girl wants a fellow to go straight ahead like a locomotive and
    he is more like a loco-might-of.
Dear Miss Dix, I surely need your advice and solace.
It's like I was in love with Henry Wallace.

Well, while I eagerly await your reply I'm going down to the
river to pick flowers. I'll get some rosemary if I can't find a
camellia.
Yours truly, Ophelia.

HOW TO BE MARRIED WITHOUT A SPOUSE
or
MR. KIPLING, WHAT HAVE YOU DONE
WITH MR. HAUKSBEE?

Do any of you old fogies remember Mrs. Hauksbee? Without
Mrs. Hauksbee, Simla and Poona
Would have been just like Altoona.
At Mrs. Hauksbee's burra khanas
Nabobs pinned tails on donkeys and viceroys bobbed for bananas.
Mrs. Hauksbee disentangled subalterns and aides-de-camp
From shopworn maids-de-camp.
Under the deodars, whatever they may be, Mrs. Hauksbee was in
her glory,
But this is another story.
Mrs. Hauksbee was attended by a faithful old *amah,*
Which is the equivalent of in Alabama a faithful old *mamah,*
And this now *amah* was a conservative reactionary Hindu,
And she got tired of Mrs. Hauksbee all the time shifting her hem-
line and her hair-do and her skin-do,
And finally she asked Mrs. Hauksbee why she had dyed her hair
again and she got one of the usual answers.
Mrs. Hauksbee said she was changing her style to reform young
Slingsby of the Umpteenth Lancers,
And the *amah* (she had surreptitiously attended the Sorbonne)
Murmured, "*Plus ça change, plus c'est la memsahib,*" and wan-
dered on.

HAVE A SEAT BEHIND THE POTTED
PALM, SIR

I'm just an untutored traveling man,
And I only know as much as I can,
But ask me about itineraries,
And I'll tell you one factor that never varies:
All of the overnight trains arrive
In the dim-lit neighborhood of five.
Wherever you come, from wherever you've gone,
You always get into town at dawn.
You're reluctant to sway to the washroom once more
Between quivering curtain and quavering snore;
Why should one, when one in one's pocket hath
A hotel reservation for room and bath?
Detroit, Seattle, Dubuque, New Haven,
You descend at sunrise unbuttoned, unshaven,
In yesterday's socks and yesterday's shirt,
And yesterday's city's pervasive dirt,
But only a jiffy, you fondly suppose,
From a bath and a nap and a change of clothes,
Seeing you hold what is laughingly termed
A hotel reservation, confirmed.
You approach the desk with footstep glad,
And your reservation ironclad.
The clerk offhandedly waves you aside;
Your room is there, but it's occupied.
No use to wheedle, nobody to placate;
You're marooned till the squatter decides to vacate.
You retire to a crowded bench in the lobby,
And pretend that your beard is a lovable hobby.
By noon you're a vagrant, offensive and jailable;
You're finally told that your room is available.
You ascend to your castle among the stars,
And what do you find? Four dead cigars,
Towels and sheets in a crumpled bunch,

And word that the maid is out to lunch.
By confirmed reservations I'm stymied and bunkered;
I'd just as soon trust a confirmed drunkard.

THE BAT

Myself, I rather like the bat,
It's not a mouse, it's not a rat.
It has no feathers, yet has wings,
It's quite inaudible when it sings.
It zigzags through the evening air
And never lands on ladies' hair,
A fact of which men spend their lives
Attempting to convince their wives.

THE CHIPMUNK

My friends all know that I am shy,
But the chipmunk is twice as shy as I.
He moves with flickering indecision
Likes stripes across the television.
He's like the shadow of a cloud,
Or Emily Dickinson read aloud.

LET'S NOT PLAY LOTTO, LET'S JUST TALK

If anybody says conversation in our day is as good as it was in
    Dr. Johnson's,
Why, that's a lot of nonsense.
The art of conversation has been lost, or at least mislaid,
And no modern phrase-coiner can think of a fresher word for
    spade than spade.
Take the causerie of the most effervescent coterie,
It sounds like something sworn to before a notary.
Where are yesterday's epigrams, banter and badinage?

All you hear is who behaved scandalously at the club dance and
    how hard it is to get a new car into an old garage.
The maxim, the apothegm, yea, even the aphorism, die like echoes
    in the distance,
Overwhelmed by such provocative topics as clothes, beauticians,
    taxes and the scarcity of competent domestic assistants.
Come, sprinkle ashes and coffee substitutes upon my head,
I weep for the art of conversation, it is dead.
But wait a minute, the art of conversation is not dead, see it arise,
    vigorous, stimulating and untroubled,
Just as you start to play six spades, vulnerable, doubled and re-
    doubled.

TWEEDLEDEE AND TWEEDLEDOOM

Said the Undertaker to the Overtaker,
Thank you for the butcher and the candlestick-maker,
For the polo player and the pretzel-baker,
For the lawyer and the lover and the wife-forsaker,
Thank you for my bulging, verdant acre,
Said the Undertaker to the Overtaker.
Move in, move under, said the Overtaker.

I REMEMBER YULE

I guess I am just an old fogey.
I guess I am headed for the last roundup, so come along little
    dogey.
I can remember when winter was wintery and summer was
    estival;
I can even remember when Christmas was a family festival.
I can even remember when Christmas was an occasion for fireside
    rejoicing and general good will,
And now it is just the day that it's only X shopping days until.
What, five times a week at 8:15 P.M., do the herald angels sing?

That a small deposit now will buy you an option on a genuine
  diamond ring.
What is the message we receive with Good King Wencelaus?
That if we rush to the corner of Ninth and Main we can get that
  pink mink housecoat very inexpenceslaus.
I know what came upon the midnight clear to our backward par-
  ents, but what comes to us?
A choir imploring us to Come all ye faithful and steal a 1939 con-
  vertible at psychoneurotic prices from Grinning Gus.
Christmas is a sitting duck for sponsors, it's so commercial,
And yet so noncontroversial.
Well, you reverent sponsors redolent of frankincense and myrrh,
  come smear me with bear-grease and call me an un-American
  hellion,
This is my declaration of independence and rebellion.
This year I'm going to disconnect everything electrical in the
  house and spend the Christmas season like Tiny Tim and
  Mr. Pickwick;
You make me sickwick.

KIPLING'S VERMONT

The summer like a rajah dies,
And every widowed tree
Kindles for Congregational eyes
An alien suttee.

MAX SCHLING, MAX SCHLING, LEND
ME YOUR GREEN THUMB

A TRAVELOGUE OF FLOWERY CATALOGUES

Bobolink!
Bobolink!
Spink!
Spank!

Spink!
Bobbink!
Atkink!
Sprink!

Burpee.

IT'S ABOUT TIME

How simple was the relationship between the sexes in the days
of Francesca di Rimini;
Men were menacing, women were womeny.
When confronted with women, men weren't expected to under-
stand them;
Their alternatives were, if rejected, to un-hand, and if accepted,
to hand them.
I attribute much of our modern tension
To a misguided striving for intersexual comprehension.
It's about time to realize, brethren, as best we can,
That a woman is not just a female man.
How bootless, then, to chafe
When they are late because they have no watch with them, all
eleven of their watches are on the dressing table or in the
safe;
Give your tongue to the cat
When you ask what they want for their birthday and they say, Oh
anything, and you get anything, and then discover it should
have been anything but that.
Pocket the gold, fellows, ask not why it glisters;
As Margaret Fuller accepted the universe, so let us accept her
sisters.
Women would I think be easier nationalized
Than rationalized,
And the battle of the sexes can be a most enjoyable scrimmage
If you'll only stop trying to create woman in your own image.

MAYBE YOU CAN'T TAKE IT WITH YOU, BUT LOOK WHAT HAPPENS WHEN YOU LEAVE IT BEHIND

As American towns and cities I wander through,
One landmark is constant everywhere I roam;
The house that the Banker built in nineteen-two,
Dim neon tells me is now a funeral home.

THE CLUB CAR

Come, child, while rambling through the nation
Let's practice our pronunciation.
The liquid confluence here we see
Of r-i-b and a-l-d.
When first potato chips he nibbled,
That gentleman was merely ribald,
But now that he is four-rye-highballed,
We may properly pronounce him ribald.

LECTURER IN BOOKSTORE

Behold best-selling Mr. Furneval,
Behind a pile of books to autograph,
Like a bearded lady at a carnival
Hoping to sell her fly-specked photograph.

REFLECTION ON THE VERNACULAR

In cooking *petits pois,* or lesser peas,
Some use receipts, and some use recipes.
In spite of opposition warm,
I choose to use the former form.
In fact, though you may think me gossipy,

[459]

I plan to settle near Lake Ossipee,
And when my settlement is complete,
To change its name to Lake Osseipt.

THIS IS MY OWN, MY NATIVE TONGUE

Often I leave my television set to listen to my wireless,
So, often I hear the same song sung by the same singer many times
     a day, because at repeating itself the wireless is tireless.
There is one such song from which at sleepy time I can hardly
     bear to part,
A song in which this particular singer, who apparently has of-
     fended a nameless character in an undescribed way, states
     that he apawlogizes from the bawttom of his heart.
I am familiar with various accents — I know that in Indiana you
     stress the "r" in Carmen,
And that in Georgia if a ladybug's house is on far she sends for
     the farmen,
And I have paaked my caah in Cambridge, and elsewhere spoken
     with those who raise hawgs and worship strange gawds —
     but here I am, late in life's autumn,
Suddenly confronted with somebody's apawlogies and bawttom.
I tell you whawt,
Things were different when I was a tawddling tawt.
I may have been an indifferent schawlar,
Lawling around in my blue serge suit and doodling on my Eton
     cawllar;
In fact, I didn't even pick up much knawledge
In a year at cawllege;
I guess that of normal intelligence I had only about two thirds,
But, by gum, I was taught, or, by gum, was I tot, to pronounce
     my words.
And now they've gawt me wondering:
Was it the dawn or the don that from China cross the bay came
     up thundering?

As a tot, was I tawddling or was I toddling?
When I doodled, was I dawdling or was I dodling?
I have forgawtten oll I ever knew of English, I find my position
    as an articulate mammal bewildering and awesome.
Would God I were a tender apple blawssom.

LOVE ME BUT LEAVE MY DOG ALONE

Once there was a handsome man named Mr. Beamington and
    he was to good causes the most generous of donors,
And he was so popular with dogs that he couldn't understand why
    he was so unpopular with their owners.
He was bold as an eagle, a cock eagle, yet gentle as a dove, a hen-
    dove,
And the dog didn't live that he couldn't make a friend of.
If you had a brace of ferocious spaniels
Mr. Beamington would soon be romping with them through your
    annuals and peranniels.
He fondled schnauzers
With no scathe to his trousers.
At his voice the pit bull eschewed the manners of the bull pit,
And assumed those of the pulpit.
He could discuss Confucianism with a Pekingese,
And address the Boston terrier on Beacon Hill in purest Beaconese.
Yes, Mr. Beamington had a way with dogs, dogs simply adored
    him,
Yet their owners abhorred him,
Because he reckoned without the third law of Paracelsus,
Which clearly states that every dog-owner considers his dog a one-
    man dog, and its affection his own and nobody elsus.
So the only people who liked him were the owners of a Cairn,
Which frequently bit him, thus reassuring them that its heart was
    not hisn but theirn.

IT FIGURES

A lady from near Rising Sun,
She flattened her boy friend in fun,
Saying, Don't worry kid,
That's for nothing you did,
It's for something I dreamt that you done.

TUNE FOR AN ILL-TEMPERED CLAVICHORD

Oh, once there lived in Kankakee
A handy dandy Yankakee,
A lone and lean and lankakee
Cantankakerous Yankakee.
He slept without a blankaket,
And whiskikey, how he drankaket,
This rough and ready Yankakee,
The bachelor of Kankakee.
He never used a hankakee,
He jeered at hanky-pankakee;
Indeed, to give a frank account,
He didn't have a bank account.
And yet at times he hankakered
In marriage to be anchachored.
When celibacy rankakles,
One dreams of pretty ankakles.
He took a trip to Waikiki
And wooed a girl named Psycheche,
And now this rugged Yankakee
'S a married man in Kankakee.
Good night, dear friends, and thankakee.

You Can't Get There from Here

ANYBODY FOR MONEY?
or
JUST BRING YOUR OWN BASKET

Consider the banker.

He was once a financial anchor.

To pinch our pennies he would constantly implore us,

And if we wouldn't pinch them ourselves, he would pinch them
    for us.

Down to thrift he was always admonishing us to buckle,

Reminding us that many a mickle makes a muckle.

When with clients he was closeted,

He was attempting to convince them that everything ought to be
    made do, worn out, eaten up, or deposited.

In a word, if you wanted to catch up with the Joneses or bust,

You couldn't do either with the connivance of the First National
    Pablum Exchange & Trust.

Yes, bankers used to be like Scrooge before he encountered the
    ghost of Marley,

But along came TV and now they are Good-Time Charlie.

The jingle of coins multiplying at two per cent per annum has
    given way to the jingle of the singing commercial,

And their advertisements, implying that anyone who doesn't turn
    in his this year's car for a next year's model with all the latest
    excessories and borrow the difference from them is a frugal
    old fogy, range from the supplicatory to the coercial.

The way some people sing whiskily,

Bankers are singing fiscally.

Everything is hey-nonny-nonny,

Come in and get some money.

That bankers have only themselves to blame for the recent wave
    of holdups and embezzlements I think highly probable,

They are behaving so provocatively robbable.

BIRTHDAY ON THE BEACH

At another year
I would not boggle,
Except that when I jog
I joggle.

SO I RESIGNED FROM THE CHU CHIN
CHOWDER AND MARCHING CLUB

The thing about which I know the least
Is the inscrutable East.
Neither is my ignorance immutable,
I find that every hour the East grows more inscrutable.
Day by day
I memorize pithy witticisms beginning "Confucius say."
I retire to leafy bowers
And immerse myself in *Kai-Lung's Golden Hours,*
In the evening I beat assiduously on a gong,
Picking out "Slow Boat to China" and "Why Did I Tell You I Was
    Going to Shanghai?" and "Chong He Come from Hong
    Kong."
In a valiant effort the inscrutable Oriental mind to explore
I have lost a fortune at mah-jongg to an inscrutable Pekingese
    puppy who lives next door,
All to no avail;
Scrutably speaking, I am beyond the pale.
I have only one accomplishment about which I would write home
    to Mother:
I can tell at least one Celestial from at least one other;
I can tell you, for a modest price,
The difference between a mandarin waving his hat over a prostrate
    palanquin bearer and a mandarin sitting on a cake of ice.
Do you want to know, really and truly?
Well, the first mandarin is fanning his coolie.

NATURE–WALKS

or

NOT TO MENTION A DOPPING OF SHELDRAKES

1. THE SQUID

What happy appellations these
Of birds and beasts in companies!
A shrewdness of apes, a sloth of bears,
A sculk of foxes, a huske of hares.
An exaltation 'tis of larks,
And possibly a grin of sharks,
But I declare a squirt of squid
I should not like to be amid,
Though bachelors claim that a cloud of sepia
Makes a splendid hiding place in Leap Year.

2. THE OSTRICH

The ostrich roams the great Sahara.
Its mouth is wide, its neck is narra.
It has such long and lofty legs,
I'm glad it sits to lay its eggs.

3. THE PRAYING MANTIS

From whence arrived the praying mantis?
From outer space, or lost Atlantis?
I glimpse the grim, green metal mug
That masks this pseudo-saintly bug,
Orthopterous, also carnivorous,
And faintly whisper, Lord deliver us.

4. THE ABOMINABLE SNOWMAN

I've never seen an abominable snowman,
I'm hoping not to see one,
I'm also hoping, if I do,
That it will be a wee one.

5. THE MANATEE

The manatee is harmless
And conspicuously charmless.
Luckily the manatee
Is quite devoid of vanity.

6. THE SQUAB

Toward a better world I contribute my modest smidgin;
I eat the squab, lest it become a pigeon.

RING OUT THE OLD, RING IN THE NEW, BUT DON'T GET CAUGHT IN BETWEEN

1. FIRST CHIME

If there is anything of which American industry has a superfluity
It is green lights, know-how, initiative and ingenuity.
If there is one maxim to American industry unknown
It is, Let well enough alone.
Some people award American industry an encomium
Because it not only paints the lily, it turns it into a two-toned job
    with a forward look and backward fins and a calyx trimmed
    with chromium.
I don't propose to engage in a series of Lincoln-Douglas debates,
But take the matter of paper plates.
The future of many a marriage would have been in doubt
But for paper plates, which have imparted tolerability to picnics
    and the maid's day out,
But the last paper plates I handled had been improved into plastic
    and they are so artistic that I couldn't throw them away,
And I ended up by washing them against another day.
Look at the automotive industry, how it never relaxes;
It has improved the low-priced three so much that instead of a
    thousand dollars they now cost twenty-nine seventy-five,
    not including federal and local taxes.

Do you know what I think?

Ordinary mousetraps will soon be so improved that they will be too good for the mice, who will be elbowed out by mink.

2. SECOND CHIME

That low keening you hear is me bemoaning my fate;

I am out of joint, I was born either too early or too late.

As the boll said to the weevil,

Get yourself born before the beginning or after the end, but never in the middle of, a technological upheaval.

I am adrift, but know not whether I am drifting seaward or shoreward,

My neck is stiff from my head trying to turn simultaneously backward and forward.

One way I know I am adrift,

My left foot keeps reaching for the clutch when the car has an automatic shift.

Another way that I am adrift I know,

I'm in a car that I've forgotten has a clutch and I stall it when the light says STOP and again when the light says GO.

I find that when dressing I behave as one being stung by gallinippers

Because half my trousers are old style and half new and I am forever zipping buttons and buttoning zippers.

I can no longer enjoy butter on my bread;

Radio and TV have taught me to think of butter as "You know what" or "The more expensive spread."

I am on the thin ice of the old order while it melts;

I guess that perhaps in this changing world money changes less than anything else.

That is one reason money is to me so dear;

I know I can't take it wtih me, I just want the use of some while I am here.

MS. FOUND UNDER A SERVIETTE
IN A LOVELY HOME

. . . Our outlook is totally different from that of our American cousins,
who have never had an aristocracy. Americans relate all effort, all work,
and all of life itself to the dollar. Their talk is of nothing but dollars. The
English seldom sit happily chatting for hours on end about pounds.
— NANCY MITFORD in *Noblesse Oblige*

Dear Cousin Nancy:

You probably never heard of me or Cousin Beauregard or Cousin
    Yancey,

But since you're claiming kin all the way across the ocean, we fig-
    ure you must be at least partwise Southern,

So we consider you not only our kith and kin but also our kithin'
    couthern.

I want to tell you, when Cousin Emmy Lou showed us your piece
    it stopped the conversation flat,

Because I had twenty dollars I wanted to talk about, and Cousin
    Beauregard had ten dollars he wanted to talk about, and
    Cousin Yancey didn't have any dollars at all, and he wanted
    to talk about that.

But Cousin Emmy Lou looked over her spectacles, which the com-
    mon people call glasses,

And she offered us a dollar to stop talking about dollars and start
    talking about the English upper classes.

Cousin Beauregard wanted to know why the English aristocracy
    was called English when most of their names were French to
    begin with,

And now anybody with an English name like Hobbs or Stobbs has
    to accumulate several million of those pounds they seldom
    chat about, to buy his way in with.

Cousin Yancey said he could understand that — the St. Aubyns
    beat the hell out of the Hobbses in 1066 — but there was a
    more important point that he could not determine,

Which is why the really aristocratic English aristocrats have
    names that are translated from the German.

Cousin Emmy Lou is pretty aristocratic herself; in spite of her

[470]

weakness for hog jowl and potlikker, she is noted for her highborn pale and wan flesh,
And where most people get gooseflesh she gets swan flesh,
And she said she thought you ought to know that she had been over the royal roster
And she had spotted at least one impostor.
She noticed that the Wicked Queen said "Mirror, mirror on the wall" instead of "Looking glass, looking glass on the wall," which is perfectly true,
So the Wicked Queen exposed herself as not only wicked but definitely non-U.
After that, we all loosened our collars
And resumed our conversation about dollars.

DON'T BE CROSS, AMANDA

Don't be cross, Amanda,
Amanda, don't be cross,
For when you're cross, Amanda,
I feel an albatross
Around my neck, or dank gray moss,
And my eyes assume an impervious gloss.
Amanda,
Dear Amanda,
Don't be cross.

Do not frown, Amanda,
Amanda, do not frown,
For when you frown, Amanda,
I wamble like a clown,
My mouth is stuffed with eiderdown,
And I spatter coffee upon your gown.
Amanda,
Dear Amanda,
Do not frown.

Don't clam up, Amanda,
Amanda, do not clam,
For when you clam, Amanda,
I don't know where I am.
What is it that I did you damn?
Shall I make amends for a sheep, or a lamb?
Amanda,
Dear Amanda,
Do not clam.

Please be gay, Amanda,
Amanda, please be gay,
For when you're gay, Amanda,
The stars come out by day,
The police throw parking tags away,
And I want to kick up my heels and bray.
Amanda,
Dear Amanda,
Please be gay.

OAFISHNESS SELLS GOOD, LIKE AN ADVERTISEMENT SHOULD

I guess it is farewell to grammatical compunction,
I guess a preposition is the same as a conjunction,
I guess an adjective is the same as an adverb,
And "to parse" is a bad verb.
Blow, blow, thou winter wind,
Thou are not that unkind
Like man's ingratitude to his ancestors who left him the English
    language for an inheritance;
This is a chromium world in which even the Copley Plazas and
    the Blackstones and the Book Cadillacs are simplified into
    Sheratons.
I guess our ancient speech has gone so flat that we have to spike it;

Like the hart panteth for the water brooks I pant for a revival of
Shakespeare's *Like You Like It.*
I can see the tense draftees relax and purr
When the sergeant barks, "Like you were."
— And don't try to tell me that our well has been defiled by immi-
gration;
Like goes Madison Avenue, like so goes the nation.

SIC SEMPER MR. SHERMAN'S TEMPER
or
KINDLY PLACE YOUR ORDER IN ENGLISH

I have a friend named Mr. Sherman who is far from dodderin',
But he lives old-fashioned instead of moderun.
He believes that the terminology of drinking has long been com-
plete,
And it needs new wrinkles like Manhattan needs a hole in the
street.
He thinks the phrase whisky on ice
Is both descriptive and precise,
So of rocks he keeps a store
Which he gathered on the stern New England shore,
And when guests ask for bourbon on the rocks they get bourbon
on the rocks and they squint at their bourbon on the rocks
jitterily
Because he fulfills their request literally,
And when they clamor for that new favorite, bouillon on the rocks,
his eyes are so moist that he melts them with them,
And then he dips the rocks in bouillon and pelts them with them.
As for the folksy he-men who slap him on the back and bellow for
bourbon and branch water, they don't do it a second time or
a third,
He takes them at their word;
He has imported a dozen Mason jars of genuine branch water from

[473]

the Ozarks, and every serving contains three tadpoles and a crawfish,
After receiving which even a governor of Tennessee would switch to Scotch and soda and behave a little more standoffish.

AND HOW KEEN WAS
THE VISION OF SIR LAUNFAL?

Man's earliest pastime, I suppose,
Was to play with his fingers and his toes.
Then later, wearying of himself,
He devised the monster and the elf,
Enlivening his existence drab
With Blunderbore and Puck and Mab.
A modern man, in modern Maryland,
I boast my private gate to fairyland,
My kaleidoscope, my cornucopia,
My own philosopher's stone, myopia.
Except when rationalized by lenses,
My world is not what other men's is;
Unless I have my glasses on,
The postman is a leprechaun,
I can wish on either of two new moons,
Billboards are graven with mystic runes,
Shirts hung to dry are ragtag gypsies,
Mud puddles loom like Mississipsies,
And billiard balls resemble plums,
And street lamps are chrysanthemums.
If my vision were twenty-twenty,
I should miss miracles aplenty.

THE SOLITUDE OF MR. POWERS

Once there was a lonely man named Mr. Powers.
He was lonely because his wife fixed flowers.

[474]

Mr. Powers was a gallant husband, but whenever he wished to demonstrate his gal*lant*ry
His beloved was always out with six vases and a bunch of something or other in the pantry.
He got no conversation while they ate
Because she was always nipping dead blossoms off the centerpiece and piling them on her plate.
He could get no conversation after meals because if he happened to begin one
She would look at the mantel and wonder if she shouldn't switch the small fat vase with the tall thin one.
Yes, even when she wasn't actually fixing flowers there was no forgetting about them,
Because before fixing them she was busy cutting them, and after fixing them she was busy fretting about them.
Mr. Powers began to shave only once a week because no one cared whether his chin was scratchy;
He felt as lonely as *Cavalleria* without *Pagliacci*.
Finally he said Hey!
I might as well be alone with myself as alone with a lot of vases that have to have their water replenished every day,
And he walked off into the dawn,
And his wife just kept on refilling vases and never noticed that he was gone.
Beware of floral arrangements;
They lead to marital estrangements.

A BRIEF GUIDE TO RHYMING,
or
HOW BE THE LITTLE BUSY DOTH?

English is a language than which none is sublimer,
But it presents certain difficulties for the rhymer.
There are no rhymes for orange or silver
Unless liberties you pilfer.

I was once slapped by a young lady named Miss Goringe,
And the only reason I was looking at her that way, she represented
    a rhyme for orange.
I suggest that some painter do a tormented mural
On the perversity of the English plural,
Because perhaps the rhymer's greatest distress
Is caused by the letter *s*.
Oh, what a tangled web the early grammarians spun!
The singular verb has an *s* and the singular noun has none.
The rhymer notes this fact and ponders without success on it,
And moves on to find that his plural verb has dropped the *s* and
    his plural noun has grown an *s* on it.
Many a budding poet has abandoned his career
Unable to overcome this problem: that while the ear hears, the
    ears hear.
Yet he might have had the most splendiferous of careers
If only the *s*'s came out even and he could tell us what his ears
    hears.
However, I am happy to say that out from the bottom of this Pan-
    dora's box there flew a butterfly, not a moth,
The darling, four-letter word d-o-t-h, which is pronounced duth,
    although here we pronounce it doth.
Pronounce? Let jubilant rhymers pronounce it loud and clear,
Because when they can't sing that their ear hear they can legiti-
    mately sing that their ear doth hear.

CAN I GET YOU A GLASS OF WATER?
or
PLEASE CLOSE THE GLOTTIS AFTER YOU

One trouble with a cough,
It never quite comes off.
Just when you think you're through coughing
There's another cough in the offing.
Like the steps of a moving stair

[476]

There is always another cough there.
When you think you are through with the spasm
And will plunge into sleep like a chasm,
All of a sudden, quickly,
Your throat gets tickly.
What is this thing called a cough
That never quite comes off?
Well, the dictionary says it's an expulsion of air from the lungs
    with violent effort and noise produced by abrupt opening of
    the glottis,
To which I can only reply, Glottis — schmottis!
Not that I reject the glottis theory, indeed I pride myself on the
    artistry
Of my glottistry,
But there is a simpler definition with which I freely present you:
A cough is something that you yourself can't help, but everybody
    else does on purpose just to torment you.

CHACUN À SON BERLITZ

French is easy.
At speaking French I am the champ of the Champs Elysee,
And since I can speak Parisian without a flaw,
I will tell you why the crows, or les corbeaux, always win their
    battle against the scarecrows: it's on account of their esprit
    de caw.

I SPY
or
THE DEPRAVITY OF PRIVACY

My voice is a minor one, but I must raise it;
I come not only to bury privacy, but to praise it.
Yes, this is my long farewell to privacy;
Democracy seems to have turned into a sort of Lady Godivacy.
We are living in an era by publicity bewitched,

Where the Peeping Toms are not blinded, but enriched.

Keyhole-itis is contagious, and I fear that by our invasion of the privacy of the people who clamor for their privacy to be invaded,

Well, we are ourselves degraded;

And now that we can't leave the privacy of public personalities alone

We end up by invading our own.

What puts a neighbor's teeth on edge?

Your growing a hedge.

He is irked because he can't see what you're doing on your own lawn, raising tulips,

Or swigging juleps,

And curiosity is what he is in his knees up to,

And also exhibitionism, because he not only wants to know what *you* are doing, he wants you to know what *he's* up to,

So he has a picture window to look out through that he never lowers the blinds on, so you can't help looking in through it,

And you are forced to observe the nocturnal habits of him and his kin through it.

Things have reached a pretty pass; even my two goldfish, Jael and Sisera,

Complain that they have no more privacy than a candidate's viscera.

Well, privacy is a wall,

And something there is that does not love it: namely, the Pry family, Pauline and Paul.

THE NYMPH AND THE SHEPHERD
or
SHE WENT THAT–A–WAY

Few things are less endearing than a personal comparison,

But I know a lady who is very like the elusive mother of Mr. Milne's James James Morrison Morrison.

She would be a perfect wife could she but be restrained by a leash
    or a fetter,
Because she has the roving tendencies of an Irish setter.
Her husband assists her from the cab and stops to pay the fare,
And when he turns around she isn't there,
She is a hundred yards off, blithe as a flock of linnets,
And in a fair way to do the mile under four minutes.
He assists her from the train and by the time he has caught a por-
    ter she is at the top of the moving stairway,
And again to do the mile under four minutes she is in a fair way.
She shoots ahead of him in London crowds and leaves him behind
    fumbling with lire in Pisa,
Despite the fact that he is in sole possession of all the travelers'
    checks and their joint passport and visa.
If in the Louvre she exclaims, "Oh, look at the Mona Lisa!" and
    he pauses to look at the Mona Lisa,
By the time he has looked she is three corners and forty master-
    pieces away, and himself alone with the same old money and
    passport and visa.
Sometimes he is touched and flattered by her faith in him, but
    mostly he feels like Queen Victoria's chair,
Which Queen Victoria never looked behind at before she sat down,
    because she just knew it would be there.

THE EMANCIPATION OF MR. POPLIN
or
SKOAL TO THE SKIMMERLESS

To tragedy I have no addiction;
What I always say is there's enough trouble in real life without
    reading about it in fiction.
However, I don't mind tears and smiles in a judicious blending,
And I enjoy a stormy beginning if it leads to a halcyon ending.
That is why I like the story of Byron Poplin, who prided himself
    on never having had an allergy, because he considered aller-
    gies a form of hypochondria,

[479]

And then he fell in love with a beautiful hat-check girl named
Andrea.
He would check and recheck his hat to the tune of six or seven
quarters an evening in his eagerness to survey her allures,
But all she ever said was, "This yours?"
He followed her here and there and all he got was there a No and
here a No,
And he was as frustrated as Cyrano.
She grew more gelid as he grew more torrid,
And he developed a rash on his forehead.
There was melancholy music in his heart,
But his forehead looked like a raspberry tart.
He attributed the rash to unrequited love and so he felt like the
hero halfway through an operetta by Romberg,
But a dermatologist told him it was merely the result of an allergy
to the lining band of his Homburg.
Mr. Poplin is now anathema to cloakroom attendants because he
goes around hatless as well as cloakless, but he is both allergy-
and Andrea-free,
And by not buying his hat six or seven times a night he has been
able to pay the dermatologist's modest fee;
Indeed, he eventually saved enough quarters to buy a convertible,
in which he drives bareheaded and happy as an earl,
So let us leave him without further ado and also without a hey-
nonny-nonny and a hat-check girl.

THE BUSES HEADED FOR SCRANTON

The buses headed for Scranton travel in pairs.
The lead bus is the bolder,
With the taut appearance of one who greatly dares;
The driver glances constantly over his shoulder.

The buses headed for Scranton are sturdy craft,
Heavy-chested and chunky;

They have ample vision sideways and fore and aft;
The passengers brave, the pilots artful and spunky.

Children creep hand in hand up gloomy stairs;
The buses headed for Scranton travel in pairs.

They tell of a bus that headed for Scranton alone;
It dwindled into the West.
It was later found near a gasoline pump — moss-grown,
Deserted, abandoned, like the *Mary Celeste*.

Valises snuggled trimly upon the racks,
Lunches in tidy packets,
Twelve *Daily Newses* in neat, pathetic stacks,
Thermoses, Chiclets, and books with paper jackets.

Some say the travelers saw the Wendigo,
Or were eaten by bears.
I know not the horrid answer, I only know
That the buses headed for Scranton travel in pairs.

FEE FI HO HUM,
NO WONDER BABY SUCKS HER THUMB

I don't know whether you know what's new in juvenile literature
    or not,
But I'll tell you what's new in juvenile literature, there's a new
    plot.
I grew up on the old plot, which I considered highly satisfactory,
And the hope of having stories containing it read to me restrained
    me occasionally from being mendacious or refractory.
There were always two older sons and a youngest son, or two older
    daughters and a youngest daughter,
And the older pair were always arrogant, selfish rascals, and the
    youngest was always a numskull of the first water,
And the older ones would never share their bread and cheese with

[481]

little old men and women, and wouldn't help them home with their loads,

And ended up with their fingers caught in cleft logs, or their conversation issuing in the form of toads,

And the young numskulls never cared what happened to their siblings, because they had no family loyalty,

They just turned over all their bread and cheese to elderly eccentrics and ended up married to royalty, which I suppose explains what eventually happened to royalty.

That was admittedly not a plot to strain the childish understanding,

But it was veritably Proustian compared to the new plot that the third generation is demanding.

Whence these haggard looks?

I am trapped between one lovable grandchild and her two detestable favorite books.

The first is about a little boy who lost his cap and looked everywhere for it, behind the armchair and inside the refrigerator and under the bed,

And where do you think he found it? On his head!

The second is about a little girl who lost one shoe on the train, and until she found it she would give the porter and the other passengers no peace,

And finally where do you think she found it? In her valise!

A forthcoming book utilizing this new plot will tell the story of a child who lost her grandfather while he was reading to her, and you'll never guess where she discovered *him*.

Spang in the middle of Hans Christian Andersen and the Brothers Grimm.

AN ENTHUSIAST IS A DEVOTEE IS A ROOTER
or
MR. HEMINGWAY, MEET MR. STENGEL

Into the Grand Canyon of the Colorado
Drop, my boon companion, the word "aficionado."

Brand me as provincial, hoot me for a jingo,
Hint that I'm an Oedipus to love my mother lingo,
On my reputation cast a nasty shadow,
Adamant you'll find me anent "aficionado."

Never may I languish prey to xenophobia.
Sydney Smith admire I, and Luca della Robbia,
And should Fate transport me into regions foreign
I could wear a chlamys, I could wear a sporran;
Yet, gazing at the Parthenon, strolling through the Prado,
Art lover I might be, but no aficionado.

Monosyllabic Master, whither are we heading
Since you thrust upon us this verbal featherbedding?
You who freed the language of fetters euphemistic,
You who taught us terseness, muscular and fistic,
You whose prose is soldierly, Spartan and Mohican —
Why employ ten letters to do the job that three can?

This reproachful tribute to a first-class writing man
Comes from no aficionado,
Just
A loyal
Fan.

YOUR LEAD, PARTNER, I HOPE WE'VE READ THE SAME BOOK

When I was just a youngster,
Hardly bigger than a midge,
I used to join my family
In a game of auction bridge.
We were patient with reneging,
For the light was gas or oil,
And our arguments were settled
By a reference to Hoyle.

Auction bridge was clover;
Then the experts took it over.
You could no longer bid by the seat of your pants,
The experts substituted skill for chance.

The experts captured auction
With their lessons and their books,
And the casual week-end player
Got a lot of nasty looks.
The experts captured auction
And dissected it, and then
Somebody thought up contract,
And we played for fun again.
It was pleasant, lose or win,
But the experts muscled in,
And you couldn't deal cards in your own abode
Without having memorized the latest code.

We turned to simpler pastimes
With our neighbors and our kin;
Oklahoma or canasta,
Or a modest hand of gin.
We were quietly diverted
Before and after meals,
Till the experts scented suckers
And came yapping at our heels.
Behold a conquered province;
I'm a worm, and they are robins.
On the grandchildren's table what books are displayed?
Better Slapjack, and *How to Win at Old Maid.*

In a frantic final effort
To frivol expert-free,
I've invented Amaturo
For just my friends and me.
The deck has seven morkels

Of eleven guzzards each,
The game runs counterclockwise,
With an extra kleg for dreech,
And if you're caught with a gruice,
The score reverts to deuce.
I'll bet that before my cuff links are on the bureau
Some expert will have written *A Guide to Amaturo.*

HO, VARLET! MY TWO CENTS' WORTH
OF PENNY POSTCARD!

One thing about the past,
It is likely to last.
Some of it is horrid and some sublime,
And there is more of it all the time.
I happen to be one who dotes
On ruins and moats;
I like to think on the days when knights were bold and ladies demure,
And I regret that my strength is only as the strength of nine because my heart is not one hundred per cent pure.
However, I also like to think on periods other than the Arthurian,
I like to think on the period when most types of invertebrate marine life flourished and coral-reef building began — namely, the Silurian.
I believe that Cro-Magnon caves and huts on stilts in lakes would make nifty abodes,
And I am given to backward glances o'er traveled roads.
Because I am one in whom Waverley romanticism prevails,
I guess that is why I am fascinated by the United States mails.
The attitude of the Post Office Department is much to my taste;
It holds that posthaste makes post waste.
In these drab days when trains and airplanes fill the grade crossings and skies by the million,

The mails are still carried by dusty couriers on fat palfreys, riding
    pillion.
So as a dreamy-eyed antiquarian I hereby, dear Post Office Depart-
    ment, express my appreciation to you:
Thanks to whom we can diurnally eat archaic and have it, too.

IT WOULD HAVE BEEN QUICKER TO WALK
or
DON'T TELL ME WE'RE THERE ALREADY

Let us call her Mrs. Mipping, but her name is legion,
And she is to be found in any taxi helping to congest any con-
    gested region.
Human experience largely consists of surprises superseding sur-
    mises,
And most surprises are unpredictable, which is why they come as
    surprises,
There is one surprise, however, that is as predictable as a state-
    ment by a Republican or Democratic national chairman or a
    picture window in a pre-fab,
And that is the surprise of Mrs. Mipping when she gets to where
    she was going in a cab.
In fact, she gets two surprises at a clip:
The first, that she has reached her destination, and the second,
    that she is expected to pay for the trip.
If she is heading down to 5th Avenue and 52nd Street she doesn't
    start to assemble her packages at 57th or 55th or even 53rd,
But when the cab pulls up at her corner she flutters like a bewil-
    dered bird,
And she proceeds to gather up her impedimenta
While the faces of the several dozen drivers blocked behind her
    turn magenta,
And only then does she realize that a figure has been registered on
    the meter,

And she is thunderstruck as by an explosion of gunpowder, which
　　is largely composed of sulphur, charcoal and saltpeter.
Down go the packages on the seat again,
And she fumbles in her bag for her purse and fumbles in her purse
　　for change and finally hands the driver a ten.
By the time the transaction is completed it is growing dark,
And traffic is backed up all the way to Central Park.
I believe that the Traffic Commissioner could soon iron out the
　　situation as smooth as silk
Simply by opening charge accounts with the taxi companies for
　　Mrs. Mipping and her addlepated ilk.

COME ON IN, THE SENILITY IS FINE

People live forever in Jacksonville and St. Petersburg and Tampa,
But you don't have to live forever to become a grampa.
The entrance requirements for grampahood are comparatively
　　mild,
You only have to live until your child has a child.
From that point on you start looking both ways over your shoulder,
Because sometimes you feel thirty years younger and sometimes
　　thirty years older.
Now you begin to realize who it was that reached the height of im-
　　becility,
It was whoever said that grandparents have all the fun and none of
　　the responsibility.
This is the most enticing spiderweb of a tarradiddle ever spun,
Because everybody would love to have a baby around who was no
　　responsibility and lots of fun,
But I can think of no one but a mooncalf or a gaby
Who would trust their own child to raise a baby.
So you have to personally superintend your grandchild from dia-
　　pers to pants and from bottle to spoon
Because you know that your own child hasn't sense enough to
　　come in out of a typhoon.

You don't have to live forever to become a grampa, but if you do
    want to live forever,
Don't try to be clever;
If you wish to reach the end of the trail with an uncut throat,
Don't go around saying Quote I don't mind being a grampa but I
    hate being married to a gramma Unquote.

EXIT, PURSUED BY A BEAR

Chipmunk chewing the Chippendale,
Mice on the Meissen shelf,
Pigeon stains on the Aubusson,
Spider lace on the Delf.

Squirrel climbing the Sheraton,
Skunk on the Duncan Phyfe,
Silverfish in the Gobelins
And the calfbound volumes of *Life.*

Pocks on the pink Picasso,
Dust on the four Cézannes,
Kit on the keys of the Steinway,
Cat on the Louis Quinze.

Rings on the Adam mantel
From a thousand bygone thirsts,
Mold on the Henry Millers
And the Ronald Firbank firsts.

The lion and the lizard
No heavenly harmonies hear
From the high-fidelity speaker
Concealed behind the Vermeer.

Jamshid squats in a cavern
Screened by a waterfall,

Catered by Heinz and Campbell,
And awaits the fireball.

ALL'S BRILLIG IN TIN PAN ALLEY

I. I SAW EUTERPE KISSING SANTA CLAUS

Thomas Lovell Beddoes inquired, "If there were dreams to sell, what would you buy?"
He never got a reply,
But to whom was he talking?
Probably to people who had never even seen a dream walking.
As an Inquiring Reporter,
Thomas Lovell Beddoes should have posed his question in another quarter.
Had he sought his answers just below where Broadway bisects the lower Fifties,
He would have come up with some nifties.
In the Brill Building lobby
Dream buying is a profitable hobby.
It is there that the imaginative tune carpenter or smith
Can purchase a shadow to walk down the avenue with.
There lurks the phrase that neither grammar nor plausibility apply to;
There he may find tulips to tiptoe through and blackbirds to say bye-bye to;
There amid the lyrical crowds
He may lay in a supply of sunshine with which to paint the clouds.
(Or, if it is not immediately available at the Brill,
Anyone can direct him to the Old Master Painter on a faraway hill.)
There prowls the dream prospector in search of the ultimate strike:
A melody that a pretty girl is like.
It was there the other day that I dreamed I saw Stephen Foster;
He couldn't have looked loster.

[489]

May I remark, at the risk of being called an egghead or New
    Dealer,
That the characters in many of our popular songs are fair game
    for the nearest mental healer?
The evidence is voluminous,
And the fact that these people are invariably boys and girls rather
    than men and women is not the least ominous.
My mostest favorite couple is a brace of young lunatics who, hand
    in hand,
Are wandering at large in what they are pleased to designate a
    Winter Wonder*land*.
(In the Brill Building this kind of nomenclature
Is second nature.)
In the middle of a meadow these two mooncalves not only con-
    ceive the notion of building a snowman,
They proceed to call him Parson Brown, and when he asks them if
    they are married they answer, No, man.
Realizing that this abrupt answer may have wounded the sensibil-
    ities of Parson Brown,
Why, they hasten to assure him that he can unite them when he
    is in town.
By this time the bluebird — and don't ask me what bluebird —
    has been replaced by a new bird, and they romp off through
    the snowbanks,
Depositing their happiness, I imagine, in no banks.
Well, I'll go my way, let them go theirs,
Parson Brown has promised me an introduction to the Man Up-
    stairs.

THE LITERARY SCENE

I

The Marquis de Sade
Wasn't always mad.

[490]

What addled his brain
Was Mickey Spillane.

II

Some words, like ugly courtiers,
Should lag behind the portieres.
Here's two such hippopotami:
Ambivalence, dichotomy.
I deprecate their prevalence,
Dichotomy, ambivalence.
Why do the learned quarterlies
Such couthless cant immortalize?

III

How many miles to Babylon?
Love-in-a-mist and Bovril.
Are there more Sitwells than one?
Oh yes, there are Sacheverell.

ANYBODY ELSE HATE NICKYNAMES?

These are the times when all our feminine notables are beautified
And, unfortunately, the times when all our masculine notables are
    cutified.
This is the day of public diminutives,
Of Virginny instead of Virginiatives.
You don't remember Addison Sims of Seattle, you remember Ad-
    die,
Who today drives a Caddie.
Today we are much togetherer than we were,
And Jerry is hurt unless you call him Jer.
Honest Jack disappears, and Jackies turn up like bad pennies,
And Lennies and Kennies.
O *tempora!* O *mores!* Or rather, O tempy, O mory!
O Binnorie, O Binnorie!

O idols with mouths of babes and feet of straw!
O shades of Jackie L. Sullivan and Jackie J. McGraw!
This infantilism has almost knocked me flat,
But I'm still fighting like a one-eyed Kilkenneth cat.

CAESAR KNIFED AGAIN
or
CULTURE BIZ GETS HEP, BOFFS PROFS

To win the battle of life you have to plan strategical as well as tactical,
So I am glad that our colleges are finally getting practical.
If they're going to teach know-how
It's up to them to show how,
And one way to show it
Is to get rid of dead languages taught by professors who are also dead but don't know enough to know it.
It's high time to rescue our kids from poetry and prunes and prisms;
Once they start in on ideas and ideals they'll end up spouting ideologies and isms.
Get them interested in hotel management and phys. ed. and business administration instead of the so-called finer arts
And you'll cut off the flow of eggheads and do-gooders and bleeding hearts.
Every campus gets what it deserves and deserves what it gets,
So what do you want on yours — a lot of pinko longhairs, or red-blooded athaletes and drum majorettes?
Another thing, now every autumn it's like the coach had to open up a *new* factory,
But get rid of the classics and he can play his stars year after year until they're ready for the glue factory,
Because they can never graduate, but no crowd of self-appointed reformers can raise a nasty aroma,

Because the reason they can never graduate is there won't be any-
    body left who can write the Latin for their diploma.
So now let's all go to the Victory Prom
And join in singing Alma Mom.

DO YOU PLAN TO SPEAK BANTU?
or
ABBREVIATION IS THE THIEF OF SANITY

The merchant, as crafty a man is he
As Haughton or Stagg or Zuppke;
He sells his wares by the broad turnpike,
Or, as some would have it, tpke.

The merchant offers us merchandise
Frozen or tinned or sudsy,
And the way that he spells his merchandise,
I have to pronounce it mdse.

'Twixt the wholesale price and the retail price
The merchant doth daily hustle,
His mdse he sells at the retail price,
But he buys his mdse whsle.

Let us purchase some whsle mdse, love,
And a shop will we set up
Where the turnpike runs through the township, love,
Where the tpke runs through the twp.

And you shall be as precious, love,
As a mermaidsk from Murmansk,
And I will tend the customers, love,
In a suit with two pr. pantsk.

I CAN HARDLY WAIT FOR THE SANDMAN

There are several differences between me and Samuel Taylor Coleridge, whose bust I stand admiringly beneath;
He found solace in opium, I found it in Codman's Bayberry Chewing Gum, at least until it started loosening my teeth.
Another difference between me and Samuel Taylor Coleridge is
more massive in design:
People used to interrupt him while he was dreaming his dreams,
but they interrupt me while I am recounting mine.
Now, if anybody buttonholes you to tell you about how they dreamt
they were falling, or flying, or just about to die and they ac-
tually would have died if they hadn't woken up abruptly,
Well, they deserve to be treated interruptly,
But when somebody with a really interesting dream takes the floor,
I don't think people ought to break away and start listening to the
neighborhood bore.
Therefore I feel I need offer no apology
For having gathered a few of my more representative dreams into
a modest anthology.
Once I dreamt I was in this sort of, you know, desert with cactuses
only they were more like caterpillars and there were skulls
and all the rest,
And right in the middle of this desert was a lifeboat with the name
Mary Celeste,
And if I hadn't woken up because the heat was so blistery,
Why, I bet I would have solved this mystery of nautical history.
Another time I dreamt I was climbing this mountain although ac-
tually it was more like a beach,
And all of a sudden this sort of a merry-go-round I forgot to tell
you about turned into a shack with a sign saying, LEDA'S
PLACE, SWANBURGERS 10¢ EACH.
I hope you will agree that of dreams I am a connoisseur,
And next time I will tell you about either how I dreamt I went
down the rabbit hole or through the looking glass, whichever
you prefer.

IF FUN IS FUN, ISN'T THAT ENOUGH?

Child, the temptation please resist
To deify the humorist.
Simply because we're stuck with solons
Whose minds resemble lazy colons,
Do not assume our current jesters
Are therefore Solomons and Nestors.
Because the editorial column
Is ponderously trite and solemn
Don't think the wisdom of the ages
Awaits you in the comic pages.
There is no proof that Plato's brain
Weighed less than that of Swift or Twain.
If funny men are sometimes right
It's second guessing, not second sight;
They apply their caustic common sense
After, and not before, events.
Since human nature's a *fait accompli*
They puncture it regularly and promptly.
Some are sophisticates, some earthy,
And none are totally trustworthy;
They'll sell their birthright every time
To make a point or turn a rhyme.
This motto, child, is my bequest:
There's many a false word spoken in jest.

MR. BURGESS, MEET MR. BARMECIDE

Sometimes I play a game that is of interest only to me:
I try to think of the character in fiction who I would rather not be.
Sometimes, while my ideas I seek to adjust,
I would rather not be Lear, or Tess, or the hero of *A Handful of Dust*,

[495]

But eventually one incontrovertible conclusion emerges,

I would most of all rather not be Yowler the Bobcat in the Nature
  stories of Thornton W. Burgess.

What with one generation and another, I have long been immersed
  in Nature stories up to my ears,

And so far as I know, unless someone pilfered an installment to
  wipe out an ashtray with, Yowler hasn't had a bite to eat in
  twenty years.

Just as he has Johnny Chuck set up neat as you please,

Why, Johnny Chuck is tipped off by a Merry Little Breeze.

Just as he has a clean shot at Jumper the Hare, who would do his
  system more good than a bucket of viosterol,

The same Merry Little Breeze tickles Jumper's sensitive nostril.

Currently, Yowler has his eye on the mouth-watering twins of Mrs.
  Lightfoot, an addlepated deer,

But he might just as well dehydrate his mouth and go home; that
  Merry Little Breeze is frolicking near.

Now the author pauses to draw a character sketch of this frustrated
  carnivorous rover;

And writes, "Fortunately for him he had long ago learned to be patient," which to my mind is stating the case under rather than
  over.

Patient, indeed!

I cry with Cassius, "Upon what meat doth this our Yowler feed?"

NEVER MIND THE OVERCOAT,
BUTTON UP THAT LIP

Persons who have something to say like to talk about the arts and
  politics and economics,

And even the cultural aspects of the comics.

Among persons who have nothing to say the conversational content worsens;

They talk about other persons,

Sometimes they talk about persons they know personally, and rear-
  range their lives for them,
And sometimes they talk about persons they know through the tab-
  loids, and rearrange their husbands and wives for them.
I have better things to talk about than fortune hunters who harry
  debs;
The causerie in my coterie is of how come Sir Arthur rewrote "The
  Red-headed League" under the title of "The Adventure of the
  Three Garridebs."
Gossip never darkens my doors
And I wouldn't trade one Gaboriau for a hatful of Gabors.
Do not praise me because to curious ears I will not pander,
I myself am not responsible for my abstention from libel and slan-
  der.
For this laudable trait there is a coony little old lady whom I am
  under obligation to;
She taught me that if you hear a juicy tidbit and don't repeat it
  within twenty-four hours, why, after that it is juiceless and
  there is no temptation to.
If you heed this precept you will never find yourself in a gossiper's
  role;
I know, because in 1915 when I discovered that Marie Jeanne
  Bécu Du Barry wasn't married to Louis XV I sat on the item
  for twenty-four hours and from that day till this I haven't
  breathed it to a living soul.

MY MY

I. MY DREAM

Here is a dream.
It is my dream —
My own dream —
I dreamt it.
I dreamt that my hair was kempt,
Then I dreamt that my true love unkempt it.

2. MY CONSCIENCE

I could of
If I would of,
But I shouldn't,
So I douldn't.

I CAN'T HAVE A MARTINI, DEAR,
BUT YOU TAKE ONE
or
ARE YOU GOING TO SIT THERE
GUZZLING ALL NIGHT?

Come, spread foam rubber on the floor,
And sawdust and excelsior;
Soundproof the ceiling and the wall,
Unwind the clock within the hall,
Muffle in cotton wool the knell
Of doorbell and of decibel.
Ye milkman and ye garbage man,
Clink not the bottle, clash not the can;
Ye census taker, pass on by,
And Fuller Brush man, draw not nigh;
Street cleaner, do not splash or sprinkle;
Good Humor man, forbear to tinkle;
Ye Communists, overt or crypto-,
Slink past this shuttered house on tiptoe,
And cat, before you seek admittance,
Put sneakers on yourself and kittens;
Let even congressmen fall quiet,
For Chloë is on her latest diet,
And when Chloë is straightening out her curves
She's a sensitive bundle of quivering nerves.
Me you will find it useless to quiz
On what her latest diet is,
So rapidly our Chloë passes

From bananas to wheat germ and molasses.
First she will eat but chops and cheese,
Next, only things that grow on trees,
Now buttermilk, now milk that's malted,
And saccharin, and salt de-salted,
Salads with mineral oil and lemon in,
Repugnant even to palates feminine,
Lean fish, and fowl as gaunt as avarice,
And haggard haggis and curds cadaverous.
Today may bring gluten bread and carrots,
Tomorrow the eggs of penguins or parrots,
Because Chloë's dietetic needs
Shift with each article she reads.
But whatever her diet, from whence or whither,
When Chloë's on it, there's no living with her.

I ALWAYS SAY THERE'S NO PLACE LIKE NEW YORK IN THE SUMMER
or
THAT COTTAGE SMALL BY A WATERFALL WAS SNAPPED UP LAST FEBRUARY

Estivation means passing the summer in a torpid condition, which
is why I love to estivate,

But I find that planning my estivation is as chaotic as the night-
mares caused by that fried lobster with garlic sauce which I
when restive and indigestive ate.

When icicles hang by the wall and people smear Chap Stick on
their faces

I can't seem to take it in that the hounds of Spring are actually on
Winter's traces.

The subfreezing months are what my wits are frozen and subhu-
man in;

Sing cuccu never so lhude, cuccu cannot convince me that Sumer
is icumen in.

[499]

Consequently, on my Sumer plans I do not embark
Until the first crocus has ventured into Central Park.
But come the first crocus,
You can't locate a desirable Sumer location even with the aid of
abracadabra, open sesame, hanky panky and hocus pocus.
By the time you start pleading with rural realtors estival,
Why, they have had themselves a financial festival.
Be it seaside or lakeside, they have rented every habitable tent and
bungalow,
Presumably to foresighted tenants who must have stood in line
since the days of Jean Ingelow or even Michelangelo.
The only properties left are such as were despised by Thoreau be-
fore he departed for Walden,
With President Pierce plumbing and the kind of lighting under
which Priscilla almost got Miles Standish mixed up with John
Alden.
This coming Sumer I must remind myself to remember
That the time to arrange for the Sumer after this is before this
coming September.
Meanwhile I guess I'll just sit in the city sipping gin and tonics,
Nibbling those tasty garden-fresh vegetables raised in a twelfth-
floor dining alcove by hydroponics.

UP FROM THE EGG:
THE CONFESSIONS OF A NUTHATCH AVOIDER

Bird watchers top my honors list.
I aimed to be one, but I missed.
Since I'm both myopic and astigmatic,
My aim turned out to be erratic,
And I, bespectacled and binocular,
Exposed myself to comment jocular.
We don't need too much birdlore, do we,
To tell a flamingo from a towhee;
Yet I cannot, and never will,

[500]

Unless the silly birds stand still.
And there's no enlightenment so obscure
As ornithological literature.
Is yon strange creature a common chickadee,
Or a migrant *alouette* from Picardy?
You rush to consult your Nature guide
And inspect the gallery inside,
But a bird in the open never looks
Like its picture in the birdie books —
Or if it once did, it has changed its plumage,
And plunges you back into ignorant gloomage.
That is why I sit here growing old by inches,
Watching the clock instead of finches,
But I sometimes visualize in my gin
The Audubon that I audubin.

I KNOW EXACTLY WHO DROPPED THE OVERALLS IN MRS. MURPHY'S CHOWDER

I know a man named Mr. Nagle.
He is what the Scots call a wallydraigle.
A wallydraigle is a weak underdeveloped creature, sometimes the
    last-born of a litter,
And I can think of no description fitter.
You'd never know Mr. Nagle was there
If he weren't in your hair.
His collar is never quite in touch with his neck,
And he drops in on Sunday afternoon to ask if you can cash a small
    check.
He makes a beeline for that antique gilt chair with the wobbly leg,
And leans back in it creakily while feeding pretzels and popcorn
    to the dog which you have just finished training not to beg.
His anecdotes are proof that he believes it better to travel hopefully
    than to arrive,

And when he tosses his chewing-gum wrappers at the wastebasket,
    he hits it three times out of five.
The economics of housewifery are beyond his scope;
After he has washed his hands, you find he has used three fresh
    towels and two new cakes of soap.
Yes, Mr. Nagle is the housewife's pet.
He can mess up half a dozen clean ash trays with one regular-size
    cigarette.
Sometimes he goes to the opposite pole,
He puts dead matches back in the matchbox, and cracks nuts and
    puts the shells back in the bowl.
No matter how deeply you are planted in a peaceful day at home,
    Mr. Nagle can uproot you;
Scots wha' hae wi' wallydraigles bled, I salute you.

OLD IS FOR BOOKS

A poet named Robert Browning eloped with a poetess named Eliz-
    abeth Barrett,
And since he had an independent income they lived in an Italian
    villa instead of a London garret.
He created quite a furor
With his elusive caesura.
He also created a youthful sage,
A certain Rabbi Ben Ezra who urged people to hurry up and age.
This fledgling said, Grow old along with me,
The best is yet to be.
I term him fledgling because such a statement, certes,
Could emanate only from a youngster in his thirties.
I have a friend named Ben Azzara who is far from a fledgling,
Indeed he is more like from the bottom of the sea of life a barna-
    cled dredgling.
He tells me that as the years have slipped by
He has become utterly dependent on his wife because he has for-
    gotten how to tie his tie.

He says he sleeps after luncheon instead of at night.
And he hates to face his shaving mirror because although his re-
maining hair is brown his mustache comes out red and his
beard comes out white.
Furthermore, he says that last week he was stranded for thirty-six
hours in his club
Because he couldn't get out of the tub.
He says he was miserable, but when he reflected that the same
thing probably eventually happened to Rabbi Ben Ezra
It relieved his mizra.

PERIOD PERIOD

PERIOD I

Our fathers claimed, by obvious madness moved,
Man's innocent until his guilt is proved.
They would have known, had they not been confused,
He's innocent until he is accused.

PERIOD II

The catch phrase "Nothing human to me is alien"
Was coined by some South European rapscallion.
This dangerous fallacy I shall now illumine:
To committees, nothing alien is human.

NO WOE IS GOSSAMER TO MR. BESSEMER

Perhaps Mr. Bessemer is not a pessimist but, last and first,
He expects the worst.
It could be aptly put
That Mr. Bessemer got out of the cradle on the wrong foot.
He suspects that any dish prepared outside the home and many
prepared inside the home will break him out in purple spots
and red spots,
And that the Federal Communications Commission anticipates

where he is going to place his radio and TV and rushes ahead
to fill his air with dead spots;
He is certain that the train he must catch will leave early, and that,
once caught, it will arrive late,
And, as a Michigan alumnus, that the Big Ten title will go to
Ohio State.
But it is on the subject of the weather
That his forebodings really get together.
Mr. Bessemer is the holidaymakers' bane;
His ears are filled with ancestral voices prophesying rain.
Be the sunset garish as a festival in Spain,
Mr. Bessemer predicts rain;
Be the sunrise cheery as Mr. Wodehouse's fiction,
Rain is his prediction;
While if on the eve of a three-day week end the skies be runny,
He conjures up a northeaster; in fact, some people call him the
North Easter bunny.
Yes, Mr. Bessemer has predicted rain under all circumstances ex-
cept one,
And that was during a drought in Texas, and a big cloud came up,
and he predicted sun.

I'LL EAT MY SPLIT-LEVEL TURKEY
IN THE BREEZEWAY

A lady I know disapproves of the vulgarization of Christmas; she
believes that Christmas should be governed purely by spirit-
ual and romantic laws;
She says all she wants for Christmas is no more suggestive songs
about Santa Claus.
Myself, I am more greedy if less cuddle-y,
And being of '02 vintage I am perforce greedy fuddy-duddily,
So my own Christmas could be made glad
Less by the donation of anything new than just by the return of a
few things I once had.

[504]

Some people strive for gracious living;

I have recurrent dreams of spacious living.

Not that I believe retrogression to be the be-all and the end-all,

Not that I wish to spend the holidays sitting in a Turkish corner
smoking Sweet Caps and reading *Le Rouge et le Noir* by
Stendhal,

Nor do I long for a castle with machicolations,

But I would like a house with a porte-cochere so the guests
wouldn't get wet if it rained the evening of my party for my
rich relations.

Also, instead of an alcove I'd like a dining room that there wasn't
any doubt of,

And a bathtub that you didn't have to send $7.98 to Wisconsin
for a device that enables you to hoist yourself out of,

And if there is one thought at which every cockle of my heart perks
up and warms,

It is that of an attic in which to pile old toys and magazines and
fancy dress costumes and suitcases with the handle off and
dressmaker's forms.

I'd like a house full of closets full of shelves,

And above all, a house with lots of rooms all with doors that shut
so that every member of the family could get off alone by
themselves.

Please find me such a relic, dear Santa Claus, and when you've
done it,

Please find me an old-fashioned cook and four old-fashioned maids
at $8.00 a week and a genial wizard of a handyman to run it.

THE SELF–EFFACEMENT OF ELECTRA THORNE

Everybody knows who is the greatest actress ever born;

Why, if you rolled the Misses Hayes and Cornell into one and
tripled them, you would only begin to approximate Electra
Thorne.

Some call Electra Thorne ill-tempered because when her dear old

[505]

mother let her go on with her slip showing she kicked her
dear old mother in the breeks,
But gosh, everybody around the theater had been wanting to do
that for weeks.
It seems unfair to call her prone to temperamental rage
Simply because she insisted on the firing of an elderly bit player
because he reminded her of her father, whose financial fail-
ure forced her out of Sarah Lawrence onto the stage.
As for egocentricity, good heavens!
What's egocentric about wanting the marquee to read

ELECTRA THORNE
IN
OPHELIA AND HAMLET
WITH
MAURICE EVANS
?

Yet on their honeymoon there was some trepidation in the mind
of Hoover Grimalkin, her groom;
He was wondering how to register for the room.
He was a writer who had won three Pulitzer Prizes, two Critics'
Awards and an Oscar,
And he was at work on the libretto of a bebop version of *Tosca*.
His bride had assured him that she did not wish her career to in-
trude upon their private life,
He was the artist in the family, she said, and her only desire was
to be a common, ordinary, everyday, just plain wife.
But Mr. Grimalkin had not been totally unobservant during his
wooing;
He had a distinct feeling: no billing, no cooing.
So, thinking quickly, he asked Electra to register, he said his hand-
writing was a disgrace.
And she registered as "Mrs. Hoover Grimalkin and husband," and
now he walks her poodle every day in Sutton Place.

THE SNARK WAS A BOOJUM WAS A PRAWN

A giant new prawn has been dredged up near Santiago, Chile . . . it is succulent and mysterious. . . . The new prawn has not been named, a fact that is causing no concern in Chile. — TIMES

Could some descending escalator
Deposit me below the equator,
I'd hunt me a quiet Chilean haunt,
Some Santiago restaurant;
The fact I speak no *Español*
Would handicap me not at all,
Since any language would be aimless
In ordering a tidbit nameless;
I'd simply tie my napkin on
And gesture like a giant prawn,
Then, served the dish for which I yearned,
Proceed to munch it, unconcerned.
Happy crustacean, anonymous prawn,
From distant Latin waters drawn,
Hadst thou in Yankee seas appeared,
Account executives would have cheered,
Vice-presidents in paroxysms
Accorded thee multiple baptisms;
Yea, shouldst thou hit our markets now,
Soon, prawn, wouldst thou be named — and how!
I see the bright ideas drawn:
Prawno, Prawnex, and Vitaprawn;
And, should upper-bracket dreamers wake,
Squab o' Neptune, and Plankton Steak.
Small wonder thou headest for Santiago,
Where gourmets ignore such frantic farrago;
That's exactly where I myself would have went if I'd
Been mysterious, succulent, unidentified.

THERE'LL ALWAYS BE A WAR
BETWEEN THE SEXES
or
A WOMAN CAN BE SOMETIMES PLEASED,
BUT NEVER SATISFIED

I used to know a breadwinner named Mr. Purefoy who was far
    from the top of the heap,

Indeed he could only be called a breadwinner because he had once
    won half a loaf of whole wheat in the Irish Sweep.

His ambition was feverish,

His industry was eager-beaverish,

His wife was a thrifty helpmeet who got full value for every dis-
    bursement,

Yet their financial status showed no betterment, just perpetual
    worsement.

The trouble with these two was that they dissipated their energies,

They didn't play the percenages.

If he got angry at a slovenly, insolent waiter when they were din-
    ing in town

She would either bury her face in the menu or try to calm him
    down.

If she got angry at the woman in front of her at the movies and
    loudly suggested that she push her hat a little lower,

He pretended he didn't know her.

He defended his unappreciative employer against her loyal wifely
    ire,

And when he got burned up about the bills from the friendly ex-
    orbitant little grocer around the corner she tried to put out
    the fire.

One day they had a thought sublime,

They thought, Let's both get mad at the same person or situation
    at the same time.

I don't know about Mars, but Earth has not a denizen,

Who can withstand the wrath of a husband and wife being wrath-
    ful in unison.

To be said, little remains;
Only that after they merged their irascibility, it required the full
    time of three Certified Public Accountants and one Certified
    Private Accountant to keep track of their capital gains.

PREFACE TO THE PAST

Time all of a sudden tightens the tether,
And the outspread years are drawn together.
How confusing the beams from memory's lamp are;
One day a bachelor, the next a grampa.
What is the secret of the trick?
How did I get so old so quick?
Perhaps I can find by consulting the files
How step after step added up to miles.
I was sauntering along, my business minding,
When suddenly struck by affection blinding,
Which led to my being a parent nervous
Before they invented the diaper service.
I found myself in a novel pose,
Counting infant fingers and toes.
I tried to be as wise as Diogenes
In the rearing of my two little progenies,
But just as I hit upon wisdom's essence
They changed from infants to adolescents.
I stood my ground, being fairly sure
That one of these days they must mature,
So when I was properly humbled and harried,
They did mature, and immediately married.
Now I'm counting, the cycle being complete,
The toes on my children's children's feet.
Here lies my past, good-by I have kissed it;
Thank you, kids, I wouldn't have missed it.

THE STRANGE CASE OF THE
LUCRATIVE COMPROMISE

Some people are in favor of compromising, while other people to
compromise are loath.

I cannot plump for either side, I think there is something to be
said for both.

But enough of discussion, let us proceed to example,

Of which the experience of Porteous Burnham should be ample.

The infant Burnham was a prodigious phenomenon, a phenomenon truly prodigious,

His parents and teachers regarded him with awe verging on the
religious.

His genius was twofold, it appeared to have no ceiling,

And it was directed toward the science of lexicography and the
science of healing.

Anatomy and etymology were Pablum to the infant Burnham;

At the age of five he knew that people don't sit down on their
sternum,

Although he would occasionally say so in jest,

Later explaining that the word derived from the Greek *sternon,*
meaning chest.

At the age of twenty-one he was an M.D. and a D.Litt., but his
career hung in the balance,

Because he couldn't choose between his talents,

Until one day he was approached by an advertising agency that had
heard of his dual gift,

And to work out a compromise they made shift,

And now he is the one who thinks up those frightening pseudo-
scientific names for all the strange new ailments the con-
sumer gets —

That is, if he uses the wrong sponsor's toothpaste or cigarettes;

And he makes a hundred thousand dollars a year, U.S. not Mexican,

Because the compromise landed him in a luxurious penthouse on
Park Avenue, which is midway between Medicine and Lexicon.

THE STRANGE CASE OF MR. WOOD'S
FRUSTRATION
or
A TEAM THAT WON'T BE BEATEN
BETTER STAY OFF THE FIELD

Once there was a man named Mr. Culpepper Wood,
And for him the best was none too good.
Unfortunately, he never got to get the best;
While somebody else was walking off with it, he was still looking
    for it with the rest.
When he got his name on the cup,
It was always as runner-up.
Nobody than he was kithier and kinnier,
But he came from one of the second families of Virginia.
His character was without a smirch,
But it never got him further than the Second Presbyterian Church.
He was of high financial rank,
But his account landed in the Second National Bank.
He finally realized he hadn't made the grade
When he was knocked down by a repossessed scooter and the Boy
    Scouts administered Second Aid.
It was then that he allowed that he reckoned
That he was tired of being second.
He took an advanced course in baby talk at a progressive uni-
    versity,
After which he spent three days in the desert without even a mi-
    rage to sip, and cried triumphantly, "Now me firsty."

TABLE TALK

YORKSHIRE PUDDING

Let us call Yorkshire pudding
A fortunate blunder;

[511]

It's a sort of popover
That tripped and popped under.

THE SWEETBREAD

That sweetbread gazing up at me
Is not what it purports to be.
Says Webster in one paragraph,
It is the pancreas of a calf.
Since it is neither sweet nor bread,
I think I'll take a bun instead.

THE PIZZA

Look at itsy-bitsy Mitzi!
See her figure slim and ritzy!
She eatsa
Pizza!
Greedy Mitzi!
She no longer itsy-bitsy!

THE SHAD

I'm sure that Europe never had
A fish as tasty as the shad.
Some people greet the shad with groans,
Complaining of its countless bones;
I claim the bones teach table poise
And separate the men from boys.
The shad must be dissected subtle-y;
Besides, the roe is boneless, utterly.

TO EE IS HUMAN

Once there were two men named Mr. Webster and Mr. Merriam,
And they had many differences but in the face of a common
danger they decided to bury 'em.

Some people, vouchsafed Mr. Webster, can't see the wood for the
   trees,
But I can't see the language for the rising tide of double e's.
I know, vouched Mr. Merriam even more safely, that jargon will
   someday overwhelm our mother tongue, but I can remember
   before it had begun to,
And the suffix *er* denoted who did it and suffix *ee* denoted who
   it was done to.
In my day, barked Mr. Webster, an employer employed an em-
   ployee, and a trustee was one who was trusted.
Which, bowwowed Mr. Merriam, although beside the point, is
   why many trusters went busted.
Who, rapped Mr. Webster, escapes an escapee?
That, knock-knocked Mr. Merriam, is what puzzles me.
Has the moment come, rapiered Mr. Webster, to abjectly sur-
   render to journalese?
On that, riposted Mr. Merriam, you may bet not only your shirt
   but also your jacket and trousers, I mean trousees.
Well, epitaphed Mr. Webster, none so blind as those who will
   not see;
In the future please address me not as Mr. Webster but as
   Mr. Webstee.

THAT'S FUNNY, WASN'T IT? NO, IT WON'T BE

Stranger, ignore yon loud bassoon
And harken, ere thou departest,
To the plaintive notes of a minor tune,
The wail of the comic artist.
The shadows lengthen across his career,
Each day is a new conundrum,
As the wingèd horses of yesteryear
Are progressively shot from under him.

His predecessors had ready themes,
Dependable sturdy stanchions,

And never foresaw in their direst dreams
The birth of a social conscience.
A permanent company they employed
Of dramatis personae;
There were Abie and Ike, and Pat and Mike,
And Rastus, Ole, and Tony.

But the humor that once raised mirthful whoops
Grew more and more precarious;
The facetious baiting of minor groups
Seemed less and less hilarious.
So the artist discarded the racial joke
And packed it away in camphor,
And assembled a group of risible folk
That nobody gives a damn for.

There's the couple marooned on the desert isle
With a caption faintly risqué,
And the portly sultan with lecherous smile
And entourage odalisqué,
The fakir complete with his bag of tricks,
The witch doctor, his cousin-german,
The felon reviewing his awkward fix,
And the khan on the flying Kirman.

So far, so good, but the world is filled
With sensitive True Believers,
There may come a complaint from the Sultans' Guild
Or the Magic Carpet Weavers.
How long can the ink-stained wretch rely
On his file of new sidesplitters
In the face of a logical outraged cry
From the Union of Counterfeiters?

Stranger, the wedding feast is done,
But linger, ere thou departest,

To murmur a prayer, just a little one,
For the soul of the comic artist.
May he sit secure on a laughing star
And cartoon on heavenly ceilings
The saints, who so superior are
That nothing can hurt their feelings.

WHAT'S IN A NAME? HERE'S WHAT'S IN A NAME
or
I WONDER WHAT BECAME OF JOHN AND MARY

In movies I prefer something unpretentious, like "Marty,"
But who wants an unpretentious party?
I always say a nice, pretentious party will do more for your ego
    than doctors or medicine;
I wish you could have been at the one I tossed recently to celebrate
    the payment of my bill from Con Edison.
There was Cary Middlecoff, Carey Latimer, Cary Grant, Gary
    Cooper, Gary Crosby, and, I think but I'm not quite sure,
Garry Moore.
Also Rocky Marciano, Rocky Graziano, Rocky Castellani, Rock
    Hudson, and, showing great endurance,
A man from Prudential Insurance.
I don't want to talk your ear off,
But I mustn't forget Kim Stanley, Kim Hunter, Kim Novak, and
    Akim Tamiroff;
An added entry
Was Speed Lamkin and Race Gentry;
And guess who crowded together hotly discussing Schopenhauer
    and Nietzsche —
Donna Atwood, Donna Reed, and Don Ameche!
And who up for the conga should line
But Julie Andrews, Julie Wilson, Julie Harris, Julie Haydon, Julie
    Adams, and Jule Styne!

It was such a pretentious party that all my vapors did disappear.
I also had Katie and Audrey just to prove that it can Hepburn
here.

TRY IT SUNS. AND HOLS.; IT'S CLOSED THEN

I know a little restaurant
Behind a brownstone stoop
Where *potage du jour* is French
For a can of onion soup.

You order a Martini without an olive in it;
They bring you a Martini, it has an olive in it.
Throw the olive on the floor,
That's what the floor is for.

The tables teem with ladies
Tuned up by Mistress Arden,
And Muzak fills the air
With "In a Persian Garden."

You order legs of frog, and please omit the garlic;
They bring you legs of frog, all redolent of garlic.
Throw the frogs' legs on the floor,
That's what the floor is for.

The Daiquiris are flowing
Before the meal and after;
The smoke from fifty filter tips
Is shaken by the Schraffter.

You ask them for an ash tray, a receptacle for ashes;
They do not bring an ash tray, instead they bring a menu.
Throw the ashes on the floor,
That's what the floor is for.

I know a little restaurant
Where client and agent grapple,
Where *ananas au kirsch*
Is French for canned pineapple.

You ask them for the check, for *l'addition,* for the bill;
They do not bring the check, they bring another menu.
Throw the menu on the floor,
Walk quickly through the door,
That's what the door is for.

POSIES FROM A SECOND CHILDHOOD
or
HARK HOW GAFFER DO CHAFFER

DADDY'S HOME, SEE YOU TOMORROW

I always found my daughters' beaux
Invisible as the emperor's clothes,
And I could hear of them no more
Than the slamming of an auto door.
My chicks would then slip up to roost;
They were, I finally deduced,
Concealing tactfully, pro tem,
Not beaux from me but me from them.

THE ABSENTEES

The healthy human child will keep
Away from home, except to sleep.
Were it not for the common cold,
Our young we never would behold.

A BOY'S WILL IS THE WIND'S WILL?

Mr. Longfellow spoke only part of the truth,
Though a fatherly poet of pre-eminent rank;
A girl's will is the twister's will.
It can drive a parent through a two-inch plank.

[517]

HOW TO HARRY A HUSBAND

or
IS THAT ACCESSORY REALLY NECESSARY?

Husband stands at door of flat,
Coat in elbow, hand on hat,
In his pocket, from broker shady,
Two good seats for *My Fair Lady.*
Patiently he stands there humming,
Coming, darling? Darling, coming?

But she's a freak and she's a hag,
She's got the wrong, she murmurs, bag,
She's got, she adds in wild distress,
To change the bag or change the dress.
She'd as soon appear with stockings ragged
As be seen incongruously bebaggèd.

Husband rings the bell for lift,
Hears it chunk and upward drift,
Well knows taxis in the rain
Rarer than the whooping crane.
Impatiently he stands there snarling,
Darling, coming? Coming, darling?

Another bag at last she chooses
And everything in the first bag loses.
She fumbles with many a dainty curse
For lipstick, glasses, keys, and purse.*
He grunts, as dies preprandial liquor,
To change from the skin out would have been quicker.

They disrupt the middle of the show,
Their seats are middle of the row,
They crawl and climb like tandem tractors
Between the audience and the actors,

Whose delicious rapport might have lagged
Had she been incongruously bebagged.

    * Then —
  She turns it inside out and scratches
  For handkerchief, cigarettes, and matches,
  Tweezers, compact, and aspirin,
  And Band-Aids redolent of My Sin,
  Driver's license and Charga-Plate,
  A sweepstake ticket one year late,
  A colored chart of a five-day diet,
  A Penguin commended by Gilbert Highet,
  A tearful appeal from a charitymonger,
  And a catalogue from Lewis & Conger.
  This is she whose eyes start from their sockets
  At the contents of her small son's pockets.

RAPUNZEL, RAPUNZEL, LET'S LET DOWN OUR HAIR

Once there was a fair young damsel and she early went, from an inferiority complex, out of her wits,

Because her friends at Wolfcroft were Miss Diana Fitz-James, Miss Perdita Fitz-Clarence, and the Honorable Miss Mavis Fitz-Something-or-other, and she herself was only Miss Rapunzel Fitts.

Rapunzel went around singing that mares and does won't eat ivy, but little lambs 'll,

So she was really more a dumsel than a damsel.

She had another song for festive occasions, when none was so festive as she;

She sang "Marilyn Monrollalong o'er the Debussy."

She was a joy to behold, but her mind worked clumsily,

Or, shall we say, dumsily.

After three semesters of *Hamlet* she still couldn't tell handsaws from hawks,

And she thought the Gunpowder Plot involved poisoning the Parliament with toadstools because she had learned on a nature-walk that fungus was made before Fawkes.

In a Scandinavian fjord where she visited her friend Miss Fjitz-
    ffjoulkes on a rocky islet
She responded, when asked if her brother in the Air Force was a
    pilot yet, No, he's a yet pilot.
The last I heard of her, she had married a realtor, name of Babbitt,
And she was at a dinner with her mind on green peas, sitting be-
    side another realtor who said, I'm from Cedar Rapids, and
    she thought he said, I'm Peter Rabbit.
This episode was on Rapunzel's memory permanently etched,
And she has grown old wondering whether he really was Peter
    Rabbit, or whether he was just a little bit tetched.

WHAT, NO SHEEP?

WHAT, NO SHEEP? These are a few of the 600 products sold in the
"sleep shop" of a New York department store.
        — From an advertisement of the
        Consolidated Edison Company in the TIMES

I don't need no sleepin' medicine —
I seen a ad by ole Con Edison.
Now when I lay me on my mattress
You kin hear me snore from hell to Hatteras,
With muh Sleep Record,
Muh Vaporizer,
Muh Electric Slippers,
Muh Yawn Plaque,
Muh Slumber Buzzer,
Muh miniature Electric Organ,
An' muh wonderful Electric Blanket.

My old woman couldn't eat her hominy —
Too wore out from the durned insominy.
She give insominy quite a larrupin',
Sleeps like a hibernatin' tarrapin,
With her Eye Shade,

Her Clock-Radio,
Her Sinus Mask,
Her Massagin' Pillow,
Her Snore Ball,
Her miniature Electric Organ,
An' her wonderful Electric Blanket.

Evenin's when the sunlight westers
I pity muh pioneer an-cestors.
They rode the wilderness wide and high,
But how did they ever go sleepy-bye
Without their Eye Shade,
Their Clock-Radio,
Their Sleep Record,
Their Vaporizer,
Their Sinus Mask,
Their Electric Slippers,
Their Yawn Plaque,
Their Slumber Buzzer,
Their Massagin' Pillow,
Their Snore Ball,
Their miniature Electric Organ,
An' their wonderful Electric Blanket?

WHAT THE WELL–READ PATIENT
IS TALKING ABOUT
or
LOOK, MA, WHAT I GOT!

The more I leaf through the dictionary in my physician's waiting
    room the more my ego grows;
I feel rather like the man who was delighted to find that all his
    life he had been speaking prose,
Because I discover that my modest minor ailments,

Why, when expressed in scientific terminology, they are major physical derailments.

What I thought were merely little old mumps and measles turn out to have been parotitis and rubella,

And chicken pox, that's for the birds, have I told you about my impressive varicella?

I apologize for my past solecisms, which were heinous,

Never again shall I mention flat feet or bunions when referring to the hallux valgus on my pes planus.

It projects me into a state of hypnosis

To reflect that a watched pot never boils, it furunculosis.

Once my internal rumblings at parties caused me to wish I could shrink to nothing, or at least to a pigmy,

But now I proudly inquire, Can everybody hear my borborygmi?

My one ambition is to become as rich as Croesus.

So that instead of this bourgeois backache I can afford some spondylolisthesis,

Although then I suppose I would look back on my impecunious days with acute nostalgia

Because my headaches would also have progressed from rags to riches, or from Horatio Alger to cephalalgia.

I have certainly increased my learning by more than a smidgin,

Now I know that that specifically projecting Hollywood starlet is not a squab, she's a steatopigeon.

Indeed, I know so much that it would be truly tragic were I to be afflicted with aphasia,

And if you can't swallow that statement it is my diagnosis that you are suffering from achalasia.

CROSSING THE BORDER

Senescence begins
And middle age ends
The day your descendants
Outnumber your friends.